The Age of Migration

Also by Stephen Castles

Immigrant Workers and Class Structure in Western Europe (with Godula Kosack)
The Education of the Future (with Wiebke Wüstenberg)
Here for Good: Western Europe's New Ethnic Minorities
Citizenship and Migration: Globalization and the Politics of Belonging
   (with Alastair Davidson)
Ethnicity and Globalization: From Migrant Worker to Transnational Citizen
Migration, Citizenship and the European Welfare State: A European Dilemma
   (with Carl-Ulrik Schierup and Peo Hansen)
Migration and Development: Perspectives from the South
   (edited with Raul Delgado Wise)

Also by Mark J. Miller

Foreign Workers in Europe: An Emerging Political Force
Administering Foreign Worker Program: Lesson from Europe (with Philip L. Martin)
The Unavoidable Issue: United States Immigration Policy in the 1980s
   (with Demetrios G. Papademetriou)
The War on Terror in Comparative Perspective (with Boyka Stefanova)

About the Authors

Stephen Castles is Professor of Migration and Refugee Studies at the International Migration Studies Institute, University of Oxford, United Kingdom.

Mark J. Miller is Emma Smith Morris Professor of Political Science and International Relations at the University of Delaware.

The Age of Migration

International Population Movements
in the Modern World

Fourth Edition

Stephen Castles

Mark J. Miller

THE GUILFORD PRESS
New York   London

Published in the United States of America by
The Guilford Press
A Division of Guilford Publications, Inc.
72 Spring Street, New York, NY 10012
www.guilford.com

Published in North America under license from Palgrave Macmillan

Last digit is print number: 9   8   7   6   5   4   3   2

Library of Congress Cataloging-in-Publication Data

Castles, Stephen.
    The age of migration : international population movements in the modern world / Stephen Castles, Mark J. Miller. - 4th ed.
      p. cm.
    Includes bibliographical references and index.
    ISBN 978-1-60623-070-1 (hardcover : alk. paper) - ISBN 978-1-60623-069-5 (pbk : alk. paper)
    1. Emigration and immigration.   I. Miller, Mark J.   II. Title.
    JV6032.C37 2009
    325-dc22

                                        2008040916

Contents

List of Tables, Boxes and Maps

Tables

Boxes

Maps

Preface to the Fourth Edition

The Age of Migration was originally published in 1993, with the aim of providing an accessible introduction to the study of global migrations and their consequences for society. It was designed to combine theoretical knowledge with up-to-date information on migration flows and their implications for states as well as people everywhere. International migration has become a major theme of public debate, and *The Age of Migration* is widely used by policy-makers, scholars and journalists. It is recommended as a textbook in politics and social science courses all over the world.

As with previous editions, the Fourth Edition is essentially a new book. It has been thoroughly revised and updated. A new Chapter 3 has been added to address the relationship between migration and the development of the countries of origin. A new Chapter 9 is devoted to expanded analysis of migration and security, a theme formerly covered in Chapter 5. Another key change is the creation of a website for the Fourth Edition. This is designed as a resource for students and other users. It contains Internet links and additional information and examples to complement the text of the book (for more detail see p. xvii and the Guide to Further Reading at the end of most chapters).

The Fourth Edition examines recent events and emerging trends. Labour migration to new industrial economies is growing fast, while violent conflicts are leading to vast movements of displaced people, especially in less developed regions. Improvements in transport and communication facilitate temporary, circular and repeated movements. New types of mobility are emerging as increasing numbers of people move for education, marriage, retirement or in search of new lifestyles.

The new edition examines the migration effects of the 2004 and 2007 enlargements of the European Union, and the role of migrant labour in the 'new economy' of the highly developed countries. Demographic changes in immigration countries are raising awareness of future demand for migrant labour, while, at the same time, public concern about ethnic diversity is leading to measures to increase social cohesion, for instance through 'integration contracts' and citizenship tests. We compare the rioting in France from 2005 to 2007 with mass demonstrations in support of legalization of undocumented workers in the USA in 2006. We also provide a survey of noncitizen political participation around the world.

Much has changed in the world since publication of the first edition, yet the book's central argument remains the same. International population movements are reforging states and societies around the world in ways that affect bilateral and regional relations, security, national identity and sovereignty. People have always migrated in search of new opportunities or to escape conflict and persecution. But international migration is reaching new heights today. As a key dynamic within globalization, migration is an essential part of economic and social change, and is contributing to a fundamental transformation of the international political order. However, what sovereign states do in the realm of migration policies continues to matter a great deal. The notion of open borders remains elusive even within regional integration frameworks, except for European citizens circulating within the European Union.

At the beginning of the new millennium, a single event appeared to have reshaped public perceptions of international migration: the terrorist attacks of 11 September, 2001. However, we argue that this event has not brought about fundamental changes in the complex processes which define the contemporary age of migration. Indeed, 11 September testified to an imperative to understand how international population mobility has transformed the security dilemmas of the world's most powerful states. Governments around the world struggle to adjust to altered circumstances. Outmoded security concepts bear mute testimony to the importance of understanding the epochal transformations that characterize this period of globalization and increasing population mobility. There is a strong tendency towards intergovernmental collaboration to improve control of migration, but little willingness to cooperate to improve the rights of migrants.

The authors thank the following for help in preparing and editing the manuscripts of the various editions: Gloria Parisi, Debjani Bagchi, Aaron C. Miller, James O. Miller, Stefano Nemeth and Mary McGlynn in Delaware; Colleen Mitchell, Kim McCall and Lyndal Manton in Wollongong; and Margaret Hauser and Briony Truscott in Oxford. Simona Vezzoli of the International Migration Institute (IMI, Oxford) carried out the complicated task of preparing the Bibliography of the Fourth Edition. The maps in the earlier editions were drawn by David Martin of Cadmart Drafting, Wollongong, while Hein de Haas of the IMI prepared new regional maps for the Fourth Edition.

University of Delaware students who contributed to the Fourth Edition include Laura Andersen, Christopher Counihan, Kate Gibson, Robyn Mello, Piotr Plewa, Juris Pupcenoks, Cédric Sage and Juliette Tolay. Mark Miller also thanks the clerical staff of the Department of Political Science and International Relations at the University of Delaware and that of the Center for Migration Studies in Staten Island, New York, for their unflagging assistance.

Research assistance was provided by University of Oxford students Annemarie Hulbert and Noorain Khan. Stephen Castles would also like to thank his colleagues at Oxford University's International Migration Institute, especially Oliver Bakewell and Hein de Haas, for the many discussions on migration issues that have contributed to the Fourth Edition. He also thanks colleagues at the James Martin 21st Century School (especially the Director, Ian Goldin), the Refugee Studies Centre, and the Centre on Migration, Policy and Society for ideas and support.

We would like to thank our publisher, Steven Kennedy, above all for his patience, but also for his editorial and substantive advice. Stephen Wenham of Palgrave has also given a great deal of support on the Fourth Edition. The authors would like to thank Sue Clements for her thorough and speedy copy-editing.

We are indebted to John Solomos, Fred Halliday, Ellie Vasta, Martin Ruhs and Jock Collins for their constructive comments. The authors wish to acknowledge the many valuable criticisms of earlier editions from reviewers and colleagues, although it is not possible to respond to all of them.

STEPHEN CASTLES
MARK J. MILLER

List of Abbreviations

A8	The new Central and Eastern European member states (the A10 minus Cyprus and Malta)
A10	The ten new member states which gained accession to the EU on 1 May 2004: Czech Republic, Cyprus, Estonia, Hungary, Latvia, Lithuania, Malta, Poland, Slovakia and Slovenia
AAE	Amicale des Algériens en Europe
ABS	Australian Bureau of Statistics
AFL-CIO	American Federation of Labor-Congress of Industrial Organizations
ALP	Australian Labor Party
ANC	African National Congress
AOM	Age of Migration
APEC	Asia-Pacific Economic Cooperation
AU	African Union
BfA	Bundesanstalt für Arbeit (Federal Labour Office) (Germany)
BMET	Bureau of Manpower, Employment and Training (Bangladesh)
CDU	Christian Democratic Union (Germany)
CGT	Confédération Générale du Travail (France)
CIA	Central Intelligence Agency (USA)
CRE	Commission for Racial Equality (UK)
CSIMCED	Commission for the Study of International Migration and Cooperative Economic Development
DHS	Department of Homeland Security (USA)
DIAC	Department of Immigration and Citizenship (Australia)
DIMA	Department of Immigration and Multicultural Affairs (Australia) (now DIAC)
DRC	Democratic Republic of the Congo
EC	European Community
ECOWAS	Economic Community of West African States
ECSC	European Coal and Steel Community
ESB	English-speaking background
EU	European Union
EU15	The 15 member states of the EU up to April 2004
EU25	The 25 member states of the EU from May 2004 to December 2006
EU27	The 27 member states of the EU since January 2007

EVW	European Voluntary Worker
FAS	Fonds d'Action Sociale (Social Action Fund, France)
FDI	foreign direct investment
FN	Front National (National Front, France)
FRG	Federal Republic of Germany
FRY	Federal Republic of Yugoslavia
GATS	General Agreement on Trade in Services
GATT	General Agreement on Tariffs and Trade
GCC	Gulf Cooperation Council
GCIM	Global Commission on International Migration
GDP	Gross Domestic Product
GDR	German Democratic Republic
HCI	Haut Conseil à l'Integration (High Council for Integration, France)
HLMs	*habitations à loyers modestes* (public housing societies, France)
HTA	hometown association
ICRC	International Committee of the Red Cross
IDP	internally displaced person
IIRIRA	Illegal Immigration Reform and Immigrant Responsibility Act (USA)
ILO	International Labour Organization
IMF	International Monetary Fund
IMI	International Migration Institute (University of Oxford)
INS	Immigration and Naturalization Service (USA) (now DHS)
IOM	International Organization for Migration
IRC	International Rescue Committee
IRCA	Immigration Reform and Control Act 1986 (USA)
IT	information technology
KDP	Kurdish Democratic Party
MENA	Middle East and North Africa
MERCOSUR	Latin American Southern Common Market
MSF	Médecins Sans Frontières
NAFTA	North American Free Trade Agreement
NESB	non-English-speaking background
NGO	non-governmental organization
NIC	newly-industrializing country
NRC	National Research Council (USA)
OAU	Organization for African Unity (now AU)
OCW	overseas contract worker
ODA	overseas development assistance
OECD	Organization for Economic Cooperation and Development
ONI	Office National d'Immigration (National Immigration Office) (France)

ONS	Office of National Statistics (UK)
OPEC	Organization of Petroleum Exporting Countries
OWWA	Overseas Workers' Welfare Administration (Philippines)
PKK	Kurdish Workers Party
POEA	Philippine Overseas Employment Administration
PUK	Patriotic Union of Kurdistan
RSA	Republic of South Africa
SADC	South African Development Community
SCIRP	Select Commission on Immigration and Refugee Policy (USA)
SEA	Single European Act
SGI	Société Générale d'Immigration (France)
TEU	Treaty on European Union
TFW	temporary foreign worker
TPV	Temporary Protection Visa
UAE	United Arab Emirates
UN	United Nations
UNDESA	United Nations Department of Economic and Social Affairs
UNDP	United Nations Development Programme
UNHCR	United Nations High Commissioner for Refugees
UNICEF	United Nations Children's Fund (formerly United Nations International Children's Emergency Fund)
UNPD	United Nations Population Division
UNWRA	United Nations Works and Relief Agency for Palestine Refugees in the Near East
WASP	White Anglo-Saxon Protestant
WFP	World Food Programme
WRS	Worker Registration Scheme (for A8 workers in the UK from 1 May 2004)
WTO	World Trade Organization

The Age of Migration Website

A special website—www.age-of-migration.com—has been set up for the Fourth Edition of *The Age of Migration*. This is freely accessible and is designed as a resource for students and other users. It contains web links and additional case studies to expand the analysis of the book. It also includes a web-only chapter: The Migratory Process: A Comparison of Australia and Germany. This is an updated and revised version of Chapter 9 from the Third Edition. The website will also contain regular updates to cover important developments that affect the text.

The Guide to Further Reading at the end of most chapters draws attention to the specific case material relevant to that chapter on *AOM*4 website. This material is numbered for ease of navigation; that is, case material for Chapter 4 is called Case 4.1, Case 4.2 and so on.

Note on Migration Statistics

When studying migration and minorities it is vital to use statistical data, but it is also important to be aware of the limitations of such data. Statistics are collected in different ways, using different methods and different definitions by authorities of various countries. These can even vary between different agencies within a single country.

A key point is the difference between *flow* and *stock* figures. The *flow* of migrants is the number of migrants who enter a country (*inflow, entries* or *immigration*) in a given period (usually a year), or who leave the country (*emigration, departures* or *outflow*). The balance between these figures is known as *net migration*. The *stock* of migrants is the number present in a country on a specific date. Flow figures are useful for understanding trends in mobility, while stock figures help us to examine the long-term impact of migration on a given population.

Until recently, figures on immigrants in 'classical immigration countries' (the USA, Canada, Australia and New Zealand) were mainly based on the criterion of a person being *foreign-born* (or *overseas-born*), while data for European immigration countries were based on the criterion of a person being a *foreign national* (or *foreign resident, foreigner* or *alien*). The foreign-born include persons who have become *naturalized,* that is, who have taken on the nationality (or citizenship) of the receiving country (which applies to most immigrants in classical immigration countries). The category excludes children born to immigrants in the receiving country (the *second generation*) if they are citizens of that country. The term *foreign nationals* excludes those who have taken on the nationality of the receiving country, but includes children born to immigrants who retain their parents' nationality (which can be a large proportion of the second and even third generations in countries which do not confer citizenship by right of birth) (see OECD, 2006: 260–261).

The two ways of looking at the concept of immigrants reflect the perceptions and laws of different types of immigration countries. However, with longer settlement and recognition of the need to improve integration of long-term immigrants and their descendants, laws on nationality and ideas on its significance are changing. Many countries now provide figures for *both* the foreign-born and foreign nationals. These figures cannot be aggregated and are useful in different contexts, so we will use both types in the book, as appropriate. In addition, some countries now provide data on children born to immigrant parents, or on ethnicity, or on race, or on combinations of these. When using statistics it is therefore very important to be aware of the definition of terms (which should always be given clearly in presenting data), the significance of different concepts and the purpose of the specific statistics (for detailed discussion see OECD, 2006, Statistical Annexe).

Chapter 1

Introduction

On the surface, two series of major events in France in 2005 and in the USA in 2006 appeared unrelated. The rioting that convulsed much of France seemed quite unlike the generally peaceful mass rallies in support of migrant rights in the USA. In the French riots, bands of youths burned cars and battled police following the deaths of two boys who were being chased by the police. In the USA, the breathtaking scale of the demonstrations surpassed the wildest dreams of organizers.

Yet, the bulk of the participants in both series of events were young persons of migrant background, both citizens and non-citizens. The French protests expressed anger against the police, and against the discrimination and high unemployment experienced by young adults of African and North African background. The US protests reflected concerns about the progress of legislation, which was seen as hostile to immigrants, in the House of Representatives. At the same time, the demonstrators supported a bill before the US Senate that would have authorized a legalization of undocumented migrants – a bill that eventually failed to be enacted into law.

Both the French riots and the US demonstrations showed how international migration has reforged societies in recent decades. As in most highly developed states, youth cohorts in France and the United States differ strikingly from older generations. Due to international migration, younger generations are much more diverse. Quite literally, international migration has changed the face of societies. The commonality of the two situations lies in the rapidly increasing ethnic and cultural diversity of immigrant-receiving societies, and the dilemmas that arise for states and communities in finding ways to respond to these changes. Most of the youths involved in the rioting in France were migrants or the children or grandchildren of migrants. In the USA, the massive participation of young persons of Latin American background, both legally and illegally resident, stood out. In both instances, young people were protesting against their perception of being excluded from the societies in which they had grown up (and often been born). By contrast, some politicians and elements of the media claimed that immigrants were failing to integrate, were deliberately maintaining distinct cultures and religions, and had become a threat to security and social cohesion.

Similar events were to be found in many places. In the Netherlands in 2004, the murder of the film maker Theo Van Gogh, who had made a film critical of Muslims and Islam, by a Dutch Muslim of Moroccan background

1

produced a similar drama. The backlash against multicultural policies in the Netherlands led to changes in Dutch naturalization requirements, including an 'integration test' based on Dutch language knowledge and 'Dutch values'.

In Australia in late 2005, groups of white 'surfer' youths attacked young people 'of Middle Eastern appearance', claiming that they had harassed local girls at Cronulla, a beachside suburb of Sydney. In the following days, hundreds of Lebanese-origin youths came to Cronulla to retaliate. Right-wing radio talk show hosts called on white youth to mobilize, and the result was civil disturbances on a level unseen for years. The political fall-out seemed likely to further isolate Australia's Lebanese Muslims – a community with high rates of unemployment and considerable experience of racial discrimination (Collins et al., 2001). The Cronulla events strengthened the conservative Howard Government's resolve to modify Australia's policies of multiculturalism.

Newer immigration countries were not immune to unexpected challenges. In Dubai in March 2006 foreign workers building the world's tallest building demonstrated against low wages, squalid dormitories, and dangerous conditions. Their main grievance was that employers often simply refused to pay wages. Dubai is one of the oil-rich United Arab Emirates, where the migrant workforce – mainly from India, Pakistan and Bangladesh – far outnumbers the local population. Lack of worker rights, prohibition of unions and fear of deportation have forced migrant workers to accept exploitative conditions. Women migrants, who often work as domestic helpers, are especially vulnerable. The Dubai Government was forced to set up an inquiry and to insist that employers meet their obligations (DeParle, 2007).

The challenges of global migration

Momentous events around the world increasingly involve international migration. That is why we have called this book *The Age of Migration*. This does not imply that migration is something new – indeed, human beings have always moved in search of new opportunities, or to escape poverty, conflict or environmental degradation. However, migration took on a new character with the beginnings of European expansion from the sixteenth century (see Chapter 4). A high point was the mass migrations from Europe to North America from the mid-nineteenth century until World War I. Some scholars call this the 'age of mass migration' (Hatton and Williamson, 1998) and argue that these international movements were bigger than today's. However, the 1850–1914 period was mainly one of transatlantic migration, while the movements that started after 1945 and expanded sharply from the 1980s involve all regions of the world. Mobility has become much easier as a result of recent political and cultural changes, as well as the development of new transport and communication technologies. International migration, in turn, is a central dynamic within globalization.

A hallmark of states in the modern era has been the principle of sovereignty, the idea that the government of a nation-state constitutes the final and absolute authority in a society, and that no outside power has the right to intervene in the exercise of this authority. The nation-state system is traced back by historians to the 1648 treaties of Westphalia, which ended the devastating Thirty Years War in Europe. The 'Westphalian system' evolved from its European origins to become a global system of governments, first through European colonization of other continents, and then through decolonization and the formation of nation-states on the Western model throughout the world.

A defining feature of the age of migration is the challenge posed by international migration to the sovereignty of states, specifically to their ability to regulate movements of people across their borders. The extensiveness of irregular (also called undocumented or illegal) migration around the world has probably never been greater than it is today. Paradoxically, efforts by governments to regulate migration also are at an all-time high and involve intensive bilateral, regional and international diplomacy. A second challenge is posed by 'transnationalism': as migration becomes easier and people become more mobile, many of them have important and durable relationships of a political, economic, social or cultural nature in two or more societies at once. This is seen as undermining the undivided loyalty seen as crucial to sovereign nation-states.

While movements of people across borders have shaped states and societies since time immemorial, what is distinctive in recent years is their global scope, their centrality to domestic and international politics and their enormous economic and social consequences. Migration processes may become so entrenched and resistant to governmental control that new political forms may emerge. This would not necessarily entail the disappearance of national states; indeed, that prospect appears remote. However, novel forms of interdependence, transnational societies and bilateral and regional cooperation are rapidly transforming the lives of millions of people and inextricably weaving together the fate of states and societies.

For the most part the growth of transnational society and politics is a beneficial process, because it can help overcome the violence and destructiveness that characterized the era of nationalism. But it is neither inevitably nor inherently so. Indeed, international migration is sometimes linked to conflict. Major determinants of historical change are rarely profoundly changed by any single event. Rather, singular events like 9/11 (the 2001 terrorist attacks on the World Trade Centre in New York and the Pentagon in Washington DC) reflect the major dynamics and determinants of their time. It is scarcely coincidental that migration figured so centrally in the chain of events leading up to the terrorist attacks.

The US response to such events, the 'war on terror' announced by President Bush in 2001, and the attacks on Afghanistan and Iraq, have exacerbated the ideological rifts that provide a basis for violent fundamentalism. The attacks by Islamic radicals on trains, buses and airports in Spain in 2004 and in the UK in 2005 and 2007 were a further upward twist in the spiral of violence. Some of the militants involved were immigrants or the offspring of post-World War II migrants. Initially, the attacks were thought to be 'home grown', indicating that Al-Qaida had succeeded in serving as a model for emulation in the West. However, as investigations progressed, several of the Islamic militants involved were found to have had links with Al-Qaida in Pakistan or Afghanistan. Through such events, perceptions of threat to the security of states have come to be linked to international migration and to the problems of living together in one society for culturally and socially diverse ethnic groups.

These developments in turn are related to fundamental economic, social and political transformations that shape today's world. Millions of people are seeking work, a new home or simply a safe place to live outside their countries of birth. For many less developed countries, emigration is one aspect of the social crisis which accompanies integration into the world market and modernization. Population growth and the 'green revolution' in rural areas lead to massive surplus populations. People move to burgeoning cities, where employment opportunities are inadequate and social conditions miserable. Massive urbanization outstrips the creation of jobs in the early stages of industrialization. Some of the previous rural–urban migrants embark on a second migration, seeking to improve their lives by moving to newly industrializing countries in the South or to highly developed countries in the North.

The movements take many forms: people migrate as manual workers, highly qualified specialists, entrepreneurs, refugees or as family members of previous migrants. Class plays an important role: destination countries compete to attract the highly skilled through privileged rules on entry and residence, while manual workers and refugees often experience exclusion and discrimination. New forms of mobility are emerging: retirement migration, mobility in search of better (or just different) lifestyles, repeated or circular movement. The barrier between migration and tourism is becoming blurred, as some people travel as tourists to check out potential migration destinations. Whether the initial intention is temporary or permanent movement, many migrants become settlers. Migratory networks develop, linking areas of origin and destination, and helping to bring about major changes in both. Migrations can change demographic, economic and social structures, and bring a new cultural diversity, which often brings into question national identity.

This book is about contemporary international migrations, and the way they are changing societies. The perspective is international: large-scale movements of people arise from the accelerating process of global integration. Migrations are not an isolated phenomenon: movements of commodities and capital almost always give rise to movements of people. Global cultural interchange, facilitated by improved transport and the proliferation of print and electronic media, also leads to migration. International migration ranks as one of the most important factors in global change.

There are several reasons to expect the age of migration to endure: growing inequalities in wealth between the North and South are likely to impel increasing numbers of people to move in search of better living standards; political, environmental and demographic pressures may force many people to seek refuge outside their own countries; political or ethnic conflict in a number of regions could lead to future mass flights; and the creation of new free trade areas will cause movements of labour, whether or not this is intended by the governments concerned. But migration is not just a reaction to difficult conditions at home: it is also motivated by the search for better opportunities and lifestyles elsewhere. It is not just the poor who move: movements between rich countries are increasing too. Economic development of poorer countries can actually lead to greater migration because it gives people the resources to move. Some migrants experience abuse or exploitation, but most benefit and are able to improve their lives through mobility. Conditions may be tough for migrants but are often preferable to poverty, insecurity and lack of opportunities at home – otherwise migration would not continue.

No one knows exactly how many international migrants there are. The United Nations Population Division (UNPD) estimate for mid-year 2005 stood at nearly 191 million (UNDESA, 2005). By 2007, the figure approached 200 million or approximately 3 per cent of the world's population of 6.5 billion people.

Migrants as a percentage of the world's population have remained fairly stable in recent years, between 2 and 3 per cent. However, absolute numbers

Table 1.1 *Number of international migrants by region: 1960–2005, millions*

Region	1960	1970	1980	1990	2000	2005
World	76	81	99	155	177	191
More developed regions	32	38	48	82	105	115
Less developed regions	43	43	52	73	72	75
Africa	9	10	14	16	17	17
Asia	29	28	32	50	50	53
Europe	14	19	22	49	58	64
Latin America and Caribbean	6	6	6	7	6	7
North America	13	13	18	28	40	45
Oceania	2	3	4	5	5	5

Note: the UN defines migrants as persons who have lived outside their country of birth for 12 months or over.

Source: (UNDESA, 2005).

Map 1.1 *Global migratory movements from 1973*

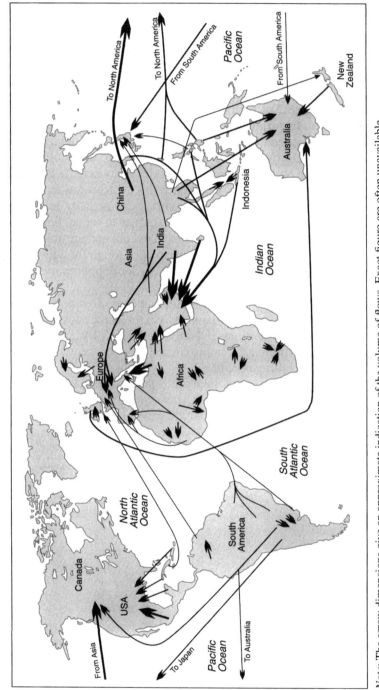

Note: The arrow dimensions give an approximate indication of the volume of flows. Exact figure are often unavailable.

have doubled over the past quarter-century. Previous epochs have also been characterized by massive migrations. Between 1846 and 1939, some 59 million people left Europe, mainly for major areas of settlement in North and South America, Australia, New Zealand and South Africa (Stalker, 2000: 9). Comparison of data on pre- World War I international migration with statistics on contemporary population movements suggests remarkable continuity in volume between the two periods (Zlotnik, 1999). However, credible statistics about international migration are lacking in some areas of the world. A great unknown involves the scope of illegal migration. Reliable estimates are lacking in most places. In the USA, however, an estimated 12 million were thought to reside illegally amidst a population of 300 million in 2006 (Passel, 2006).

Many of those who move are in fact 'forced migrants': people who have been forced to flee their homes and seek refuge elsewhere. The reasons for flight can include political or ethnic violence or persecution, development projects like large dams, or natural disasters like the 2004 Asian Tsunami. In 2006 there were about 10 million officially recognized refugees in the world – a considerable decline from the peak figures of the early 1990s. But this decline was partly due to states' unwillingness to admit refugees. The number of internally displaced persons (IDPs) – forced migrants who remained in their country of origin because they found it impossible to cross an international border to seek refuge – grew to about 26 million.

In fact, the vast majority of human beings remain in their countries of birth. Migration is the exception, not the rule. Yet the impact of international migration is frequently much greater than is suggested by figures such as the UN estimates. People tend to move not individually, but in groups. Their departure may have considerable consequences for their area of origin. Remittances (money sent home) by migrants may improve living standards and encourage economic development. In the country of immigration, settlement is closely linked to employment opportunities and is almost always concentrated in industrial and urban areas, where the impact on receiving communities is considerable. Migration thus affects not only the migrants themselves but the sending and receiving societies as a whole. There can be few people in either industrial or less developed countries today who do not have personal experience of migration and its effects.

Contemporary migrations: general trends

International migration is part of a transnational revolution that is reshaping societies and politics around the globe. The old dichotomy between migrant-sending and migrant-receiving states is being eroded. Most countries experience both emigration and immigration (although one or the other often predominates) while some countries have taken on an

Box 1.1 The US–Mexico 'immigration honeymoon'

The elections of George W. Bush, Jr. and Vincente Fox in 2000 appeared to augur well for major changes in US–Mexico relations. Both presidents wanted to improve relations, especially through closer cooperation on migration issues. President Bush had supported expanded admission of Mexican temporary workers while governor of Texas. The Mexican president backed a legalization programme for illegally resident Mexicans in the USA – then estimated to number 4–5 million. President Bush's first foreign visit was to President Fox's ranch and the US–Mexico migration initiative topped the agenda. The presidents announced the formation of a high-level bilateral group of officials who were to meet regularly to determine the content of the initiative.

At one point, Mexican Foreign Minister Jorge Casteñeda spoke of Mexico wanting 'the whole enchilada', presumably a legalization program for illegally resident Mexicans in the US, increased admissions of Mexican temporary workers, measures to decrease the mounting toll of deaths at the US–Mexico border and expanded legal admission of family members of Mexicans residing legally in the US.

In early September of 2001, President Fox made a triumphal tour of the USA to tout the initiative, which culminated in an address to a joint session of the US Congress. However, he returned home empty-handed, as it became clear that there was significant Congressional opposition to the initiative. After the terrorist attacks on 9/11, the initiative was put on the back burner. Many US officials were rankled by the Mexican government's response to 9/11. Mexican–US disagreements over Iraq further exacerbated strained relations. The first term of George W. Bush ended with little or no discernible progress on the initiative.

→

important role as transit zones for migrants. The differing ways in which such trends have affected the worlds' regions is a major theme throughout this book. Areas such as the USA, Canada, Australia, New Zealand or Argentina are considered 'classical countries of immigration'. Their current people are the result of histories of large-scale immigration – often to the detriment of indigenous populations. Today, migration continues in new forms. Virtually all of Northern and Western Europe became areas of labour immigration and subsequent settlement after 1945. Since the 1980s, Southern European states like Greece, Italy and Spain, which for a long time were zones of emigration, have become immigration areas. Today Central and Eastern European states, particularly Hungary, Poland and the Czech Republic, are becoming immigration lands.

The Middle East and North Africa (MENA), the vast area stretching from Morocco to Pakistan, is affected by complex population movements. Some countries, like Turkey, Jordan and Morocco, are major sources of migrant labour. The Gulf Oil states experience mass temporary inflows

→

The re-election of President Bush gave the initiative a new lease on life. Comprehensive immigration reform became a priority for the second term. In 2006, both houses of Congress adopted immigration bills. However, the House of Representatives bill eschewed legalization and called for additional barriers along the US–Mexico border and other restrictive measures. Meanwhile, the Senate adopted a bill that would have opened a path to legal status for millions of illegally resident aliens; but the two bills could not be reconciled by a conference committee as differences were too large to bridge.

The mid-term elections of 2006 gave the Democrats control of both houses of the new Congress. President Bush announced his support for immigration legislation similar to the Senate bill and sharply criticized (largely Republican) opponents of any form of legalization. In the spring of 2007, a group of Senators announced a bipartisan 'compromise' bill. Major provisions included an 'earned legalization', which President Bush claimed would not constitute an amnesty like the legalization undertaken in 1986. Instead, applicants would be required to work as temporary foreign workers for six years in order to qualify for adjustment to permanent resident alien status. The bill also included a provision for admission of 400,000 guestworkers annually. However, amendments quickly scaled back the guestworkers to 200,000 per year. Then backers of the Senate bill lost a key vote and opponents claimed victory.

Newly elected Mexican President Calderon sought to de-emphasize the centrality of migration in US–Mexican relations. President Bush's badly sagging popularity diminished prospects for the comprehensive immigration reform that would constitute a principal legacy of his presidency. For all the expectations raised in 2001, little of substance had changed in the US–Mexico migration relationship by 2008.

of workers. Political turmoil in the region has led to mass flows of refugees. In recent years, Afghanistan has been a major source of refugees, while Iran and Pakistan have been the main receiving countries. In Africa, colonialism and white settlement led to the establishment of migrant labour systems for plantations and mines. Decolonization since the 1950s has sustained old migratory patterns – such as the flow of mineworkers to South Africa – and started new ones, such as movements to Kenya, Gabon, and Nigeria. Africa has more refugees and IDPs relative to population size than any other region of the world. Asia and Latin America have complicated migratory patterns within the region, as well as increasing flows to the rest of the world. Two examples of recent developments are discussed in Boxes 1.1 and 1.2 to give an idea of the complex ramifications of migratory movements for both North and South.

Throughout the world, long-standing migratory patterns are persisting in new forms, while new flows are developing in response to economic,

Box 1.2 Ethnic cleansing and conflict in Central Africa

The end of the Cold War brought with it an upsurge in violence related to formerly suppressed ethnic tensions in many parts of Eastern Europe, Central Asia and Sub-Saharan Africa. Ethnic cleansing – violence directed against civilian populations to drive them from a given territory or exterminate them – was seen as especially serious in former Yugoslavia and Rwanda. The West intervened in Bosnia and Kosovo, but was unwilling to do so in Rwanda.

Colonialism, with its European-imposed boundaries and its divide and rule strategies, created conditions which precipitated ethnic tensions in many African states after decolonization. In densely populated Rwanda, the colonial powers (first Germany, then Belgium after World War I) favoured the Tutsi minority and subordinated the Hutu majority. At independence, the Tutsi 'elite' was given power but lost it in light of sheer numerical inferiority. This created a Tutsi diaspora, mainly in neighbouring Zaire, Uganda, and Burundi.

Exiles launched a campaign from Ugandan territory with the support of the Ugandan government to overthrow the Hutu-dominated Rwandan government. Negotiations followed which resulted in the Arusha Peace Agreement of August 1993. In 1994, however, the Rwandan President was killed when his aircraft was hit with a rocket, and a campaign of violence by the *Interahamwe* Hutu militia immediately took place against Tutsi and moderate-Hutu populations. The international community responded too little and too late. Hundreds of thousands of Rwandans were killed with machetes and other arms in just three months. All the while, Tutsi-dominated rebel forces advanced relentlessly and seized control, but sporadic violence continued within and over Rwandan borders. In 2004, the Rwandan government put the final death toll resulting from the genocide at 937,000 (UN, 2004).

One of the most distressing effects of ethnic conflict – which inevitably becomes a cause of persistent instability – is the mass number of forced migrants that result. According to the United Nations Assistance Mission in Rwanda (UNAMIR), Rwanda had 1.8 million IDPs and approximately 1.75 million refugees in Zaire, Uganda, and Burundi by the end of 1994.

Although the Rwandan genocide received neither the international intervention it needed nor the media attention it deserved, conflict throughout the rest of the region has received even less. Burundi, Rwanda's neighbour and

→

political and cultural change, and violent conflicts. Yet, despite the diversity, it is possible to identify certain general tendencies:

1. The *globalization of migration*: the tendency for more and more countries to be crucially affected by migratory movements at the same time. Moreover, immigration countries tend to receive migrants from a larger number of source countries, so that most countries of immigration have entrants from a broad spectrum of economic, social and cultural backgrounds.

⟶

one of Africa's most densely populated countries, has experienced a very similar Hutu–Tutsi conflict since 1993 which has cost in excess of 300,000 lives from the combination of killing, malnutrition, and disease. The number of Burundian IDPs peaked in 1999 at 900,000 (12 per cent of the population), and most recent estimates pinpoint at least 400,000 refugees and 117,000 IDPs still in need of return (Delrue, 2006). However, the current reconciliation process in Burundi offers hope of change.

The largest conflicts took place in the Democratic Republic of Congo (DRC, formerly Zaire), Africa's third largest country. In 1997, the Zairian government began to arm Rwandan Hutu refugees as part of a broader effort to quell the anti-government insurgency in the Eastern part of the country. The government soon collapsed and the Ugandan and Rwandan-backed insurgency gained momentum. Violence in DRC involved combatants from seven other nations – Angola, Burundi, Zimbabwe, Namibia, Uganda, Rwanda, and Eritrea. The DRC has abundant and diverse natural resources, and the government, multinational corporations, foreign governments, and many rebel militias all wanted control of these.

The DRC civil war – which officially ended in 2002 – and its aftermath have resulted in the largest death toll since World War II, with 2006 estimates of 4 million dead and an additional 1,200 deaths per day (UNICEF, 2007). A survey by the International Rescue Committee (IRC) concluded that 98 per cent of deaths were a result of preventable and curable diseases. There were still believed to be 1.7 million IDPs in DRC and 450 800 refugees throughout the region in 2006 (USCRI, 2006). Democratic elections were held in July 2006 to elect a new president in DRC, and Joseph Kabila was declared the winner. Despite the election and the presence of the 18,357 soldiers-strong UN peacekeeping mission, violence continued in 2007 (MONUC, 2007).

The Central African crisis has been as emblematic of world affairs in the post-Cold War period as the North American Free Trade Agreement (NAFTA) or the global 'War on Terror'. Ethnic violence has led to millions of deaths and mass movements of people. Emigrant-led insurgencies have toppled two Central African governments and threatened several others. Uncontrollable refugee flows have destabilized an entire region, and UN forces have been forced to install near-permanent missions in an attempt to quell future violence.

2. The *acceleration of migration*: international movements of people are growing in volume in all major regions at the present time. This quantitative growth increases both the urgency and the difficulties of government policies. However, as indicated by the decrease in the global refugee total since 1993, international migration is not an inexorable process. Governmental policies can prevent or reduce international migration and repatriation is a possibility.

3. The *differentiation of migration*: most countries do not simply have one type of immigration, such as labour migration, refugees or permanent

settlement, but a whole range of types at once. Typically, migratory chains which start with one type of movement often continue with other forms, despite (or often just because of) government efforts to stop or control the movement. This differentiation presents a major obstacle to national and international policy measures.

4. The *feminization of migration*: women play a significant role in all regions and in most types of migration. In the past most labour migrations and many refugee movements were male-dominated, and women were often dealt with under the category of family reunion. Since the 1960s, women have played a major role in labour migration. Today women workers form the majority in movements as diverse as those of Cape Verdians to Italy, Filipinos to the Middle East and Thais to Japan. Some refugee movements contain a significant majority of women, as do certain networks of trafficked persons. Gender variables have always been significant in global migration history, but awareness of the specificity of women in contemporary migrations has grown.

5. The *growing politicization of migration*: domestic politics, bilateral and regional relationships and national security policies of states around the world are increasingly affected by international migration. There is increasing realization that migration policy issues require enhanced global governance, and cooperation between receiving, transit and sending countries.

6. The *proliferation of migration transition*: this occurs when traditional lands of emigration become lands of transit migration and immigration as well. This is often the prelude to becoming predominantly immigration lands. States as diverse as Poland, Spain, Morocco, Mexico, the Dominican Republic, Turkey and South Korea are experiencing various stages of a migration transition.

International migration in global governance

Globalization has challenged the authority of national governments from above and below. The growth of transnational society has given rise to novel issues and problems and has blurred formerly distinctive spheres of authority and decision-making. As a result, authoritative decision-making for polities is increasingly conceptualized as global governance (Rosenau, 1997). The complexity and fragmentation of power and authority that have resulted from globalization typically require government (whether national, regional or local) to interact with other organizations and institutions, both public and private, foreign and domestic, to achieve desired goals. An important manifestation of global governance is the significant expansion of regional consultative processes focusing on international migration.

Until recently, international migration had not generally been seen by governments as a central political issue. Rather, migrants were divided up into categories, such as permanent settlers, foreign workers or refugees, and dealt with by a variety of special agencies, such as immigration departments, labour offices, aliens police, welfare authorities and education ministries. This situation began to change in the mid-1980s. The Paris-based Organization for Economic Cooperation and Development (OECD) convened the first international conference on international migration in 1986 (OECD, 1987). The OECD had found evidence of growing convergence in migration policy concerns and challenges faced by its member states. The USA opposed North/South dialogue and little of substance was accomplished. However, as the European Union (EU) countries removed their internal boundaries in the late 1980s, they became increasingly concerned about strengthening external boundaries in order to prevent an influx from the South and the East. The Clinton Administration ordered the Department of State and the CIA to include international migration in their assessments. By the 1990s, the mobilization of extreme-right groups in Europe over immigration helped bring these issues to the centre of the political stage.

The adoption of the 1990 Convention on the Rights of Migrant Workers and Their Families by the UN General Assembly brought into sharp relief global tensions and differences surrounding international migration. Immigration countries refused to sign the convention, and it did not come into force until 2003. By 2006 it had been signed by just 34 of the UN's 192 states – virtually all of them countries of emigration (UNDESA, 2006a). North/South differences were also apparent at the 1994 UN Cairo Population Conference. The world's most powerful states rebuffed a call for an intergovernmental meeting about international migration by the governments of lands of emigration.

Globalization has led to the strengthening of global institutions: the World Trade Organization for trade, the International Monetary Fund for finance, the World Bank for economic development, and so on. But the will to cooperate has not been as strong in the migration field. There are international bodies with specific tasks – such as the United Nations High Commissioner for Refugees (UNHCR) and the International Labour Office (ILO) for migrant workers – but no institution with overall responsibility for global cooperation and for monitoring migrant rights. The International Migration Organization does have wider terms of reference, but it is a non-UN body and lacks the capacity to bring about significant change. The key issue is the unwillingness of rich labour-importing countries to enforce migrant rights and to make concessions that might improve outcomes for countries of origin, because that would increase the costs of migrant labour.

However, there are signs of change. In 2003, following consultation with UN Secretary General Kofi Anan, a Global Commission on International Migration (GCIM), consisting of prominent people advised by migration experts, was set up. Its report (GCIM, 2005) emphasized the potential benefits of migration for development (see Chapter 3). In 2003 the UN General Assembly also decided to hold a High-Level Dialogue on International Migration and Development in 2006. The Secretary General's report on this meeting recommended a forum for UN member states to discuss migration and development issues further. However, the forum was to be purely advisory and was not intended to facilitate negotiations. The first Global Forum on Migration and Development was hosted by the Belgian government in July 2007, with a second in Manila in October 2008.

Ethnic diversity, racism and multiculturalism

Regulation of international migration is one of the two central issues arising from the population movements of the current epoch. The other is the effect of growing ethnic diversity on the societies of immigration countries. Settlers are often distinct from the receiving populations: they may come from different types of societies (for example, agrarian-rural rather than urban-industrial) with different traditions, religions and political institutions. They often speak a different language and follow different cultural practices. They may be visibly different, through physical appearance (skin colour, features and hair type) or style of dress. Some migrant groups become concentrated in certain types of work (often of low social status) and live segregated lives in low-income residential areas. The position of immigrants is often marked by a specific legal status: that of the foreigner or non-citizen. The differences are frequently summed up in the concepts of 'ethnicity' or 'race'. In many cases, immigration complicates existing conflicts or divisions in societies with long-standing ethnic minorities.

The social meaning of ethnic diversity depends to a large extent on the significance attached to it by the populations and states of the receiving countries. The classic immigration countries have generally seen immigrants as permanent settlers who were to be assimilated or integrated. However, not all potential immigrants have been seen as suitable: the USA, Canada and Australia all had policies to keep out non-Europeans and even some categories of Europeans until the 1960s. Countries which emphasized temporary labour recruitment – Western European countries in the 1960s and early 1970s, more recently the Gulf oil states and some of the fast-growing Asian economies – have tried to prevent family reunion and permanent settlement. Despite the emergence of permanent settler populations, such countries have declared themselves not to be countries of immigration, and have denied citizenship and other rights to settlers. Between these two extremes is a wealth of variations, which will be discussed in later chapters.

Culturally distinct settler groups almost always maintain their languages and some elements of their homeland cultures, at least for a few generations. Where governments have recognized permanent settlement, there has been a tendency to move from policies of individual assimilation to acceptance of some degree of long-term cultural difference. The result has been the granting of minority cultural and political rights, as embodied in the policies of multiculturalism introduced in Canada, Australia and Sweden since the 1970s. However, as previously noted, the post-9/11 era has witnessed a retreat from multiculturalism in many democracies that espoused it in the 1970s or 1980s. Governments which reject the idea of permanent settlement also oppose pluralism, which they see as a threat to national unity and identity. In such cases, immigrants tend to turn into marginalized ethnic minorities. In other cases (France, for example), governments may accept the reality of settlement, but demand individual cultural assimilation as the price for granting of rights and citizenship.

Whatever the policies of the governments, immigration may lead to strong reactions from some sections of the population. Immigration often takes place at the same time as economic restructuring and far-reaching social change. People whose conditions of life are already changing in an unpredictable way often see the newcomers as the cause of insecurity. One of the dominant images in the highly developed countries today is that of masses of people flowing in from the poor South and the turbulent East, taking away jobs, pushing up housing prices and overloading social services. Similarly, in immigration countries of the South, such as Malaysia and South Africa, immigrants are blamed for crime, disease and unemployment. Extreme-right parties have grown and flourished through anti-immigrant campaigns. Racism is a threat, not only to immigrants themselves, but also to democratic institutions and social order. Analysis of the causes and effects of racism must therefore take a central place in any discussion of international migration and its effects on society.

International migration does not always create diversity. Some migrants, such as Britons in Australia or Austrians in Germany, are virtually indistinguishable from the receiving population. Other groups, like Western Europeans in North America, are quickly assimilated. 'Professional transients' – that is, highly skilled personnel who move temporarily within specialized labour markets – are rarely seen as presenting an integration problem. But these are the exceptions; in most instances, international migration increases diversity within a society. This presents a number of problems for the state. The most obvious concerns social policy: social services and education may have to be planned and delivered in new ways to correspond to different life situations and cultural practices.

More serious is the challenge to national identity. The nation-state, as it has developed since the eighteenth century, is premised on the idea of cultural as well as political unity. In many countries, ethnic homogeneity, defined in terms of common language, culture, traditions and history, has been seen as the basis of the nation-state. This unity has often been fictitious – a construction of the ruling elite – but it has provided powerful national myths. Immigration and ethnic diversity threaten such ideas of the nation, because they create a people without common ethnic origins. The classical countries of immigration have been able to cope with this situation most easily, since absorption of immigrants has been part of their myth of nation-building. But countries which place common culture at the heart of their nation-building process have found it difficult to resolve the contradiction. Movements against immigration have also become movements against multiculturalism, which have led to a retreat from multicultural policies in many places.

One of the central ways in which the link between the people and the state is expressed is through the rules governing citizenship and naturalization. States which readily grant citizenship to immigrants, without requiring common ethnicity or cultural assimilation, seem most able to cope with ethnic diversity. On the other hand, states which link citizenship to cultural belonging tend to have exclusionary policies which marginalize and disadvantage immigrants. It is one of the central themes of this book that continuing international population movements will increase the ethnic diversity of more and more countries. This has already called into question prevailing notions of the nation-state and citizenship. Debates over new approaches to diversity will shape the politics of many countries in coming decades.

Aims and structure of the book

The Age of Migration sets out to provide an understanding of the emerging global dynamics of migration and of the consequences for migrants and non-migrants everywhere. That is a task too big for a single book: although we do look at issues concerning origin and transit countries in many places (especially Chapters 3, 6 and 7), our main emphasis is on the challenges for receiving societies. Our accounts of the various migratory movements must inevitably be concise, but a global view of international migration is the precondition for understanding each specific flow. The central aim of this book is therefore to provide an introduction to the subject of international migration and the emergence of increasingly diverse societies, which will help readers to put more detailed accounts of specific migratory processes in context.

Our first specific objective is to describe and explain contemporary international migration. We set out to show its enormous complexity, and to communicate both the variations and the common factors in international population movements as they affect more and more parts of the world.

The second objective is to explain how migrant settlement is bringing about increased ethnic diversity in many societies, and how this is related to broader social, cultural and political developments. Understanding these changes is the precondition for political action to deal with problems and conflicts linked to migration and ethnic diversity.

The third objective is to link the two discourses, by examining the complex interactions between migration and growing ethnic diversity. There are large bodies of empirical and theoretical work on both themes. However, the two are often inadequately linked. In real life, immigration and ethnic relations are closely interrelated in a variety of ways. The linkages can best be understood by analysing the migratory process in its totality.

The Age of Migration is structured as follows. A first group of chapters provides the theoretical and historical background necessary to understand contemporary global trends. Chapter 2 examines the theories and concepts used to explain migration and formation of ethnic minorities, and emphasizes the need to study the migratory process as a whole. Chapter 3 is newly written for this edition, and focuses on the relationships between globalization, migration and development. Chapter 4 describes the history of international migration from early modern times until 1945.

A second group of chapters provides descriptive accounts and data on contemporary migrations within and between world regions. Chapter 5 is concerned with migration to highly developed countries. It examines the patterns of labour migration which developed during the post-1945 boom, and goes on to discuss changes in migratory patterns after the 'oil crisis' of 1973. The increasing volume and complexity of migrations since the late 1980s are described, including the effects of the 2004 and 2007 enlargements of the EU. Chapter 6 examines the migratory patterns that affect the Asia Pacific Region, while Chapter 7 deals with the Middle East and North Africa, Sub-Saharan Africa and Latin America. These areas are major sources of migrants to highly developed countries. However, intraregional movements are often larger than longer-distance migrations, particularly where the emergence of new industrial countries is leading to economic and demographic imbalances. These chapters confirm the analysis of Chapter 3 on the key role of migration in contemporary processes of economic development and social transformation.

We then turn to the international politics of migration. Chapter 8 assesses the capacity of industrial states to regulate international migration. It examines irregular migration, human trafficking and the policies designed to curb them. It also compares the significance of regional integration frameworks (the EU and NAFTA) for control of migration. Chapter 9 examines migration and security. Such questions are not new but the 9/11 events in the USA and subsequent attacks in Europe have dramatically heightened concerns over migrant and migrant-background populations being mobilized into violence-prone extremist movements.

The next three chapters analyse the effects of immigration on highly developed countries. Chapter 10 considers the economic position of migrant workers and the impacts of immigration on the economy. It goes on to discuss the key role of migration in the development of a 'new economy' based on employment practices such as sub-contracting, temporary employment and informal-sector work. Chapter 11 examines the position of immigrants within the societies of highly developed immigration countries, looking at such factors as legal status, social policy, formation of ethnic communities, racism, citizenship and national identity. Chapter 12 examines some of the political effects of ethnic diversity, looking both at the involvement of immigrants and minorities in politics and at the way mainstream politics are changing in reaction to migrant settlement.

Chapter 13 sums up the arguments of the book and reviews trends in global migration in the early twenty-first century. International mobility of people seems certain to grow, leading to greater ethnic diversity in receiving countries, and new forms of transnational connectivity. We discuss the dilemmas faced by governments and people in attempting to find appropriate responses to the challenges of an increasingly mobile world, and point to some of the major obstacles blocking the way to better international cooperation.

Guide to further reading

There are too many books on international migration to list here. Many important works are referred to in the Further Reading for other chapters. A wide range of relevant literature is listed in the Bibliography.

Important information on all aspects of international migration is provided by several specialized journals, of which only a selection can be mentioned here. *International Migration Review* (New York: Center for Migration Studies) was established in 1964 and provides excellent comparative information. *International Migration* (Geneva: IOM) is also a valuable comparative source. *Social Identities* started publication in 1995 and is concerned with the 'study of race, nation and culture'. A journal concerned with transnational issues is *Global Networks* (Oxford: Blackwells). Journals with a European focus include the *Journal of Ethnic and Migration Studies* (Brighton: Sussex Centre for Migration Research, University of Sussex), and the *Revue Européenne des Migrations Internationales* (Paris, in French and English). Britain has several journals including *Race and Class* (London: Institute for Race Relations) and *Ethnic and Racial Studies* (New York and London: Routledge). In Australia there is the *Journal of Intercultural Studies* (Melbourne: Monash University). The *Asian and Pacific Migration Journal* (Quezon City, Philippines: Scalabrini Migration Center) provides information and analyses movements in the world's most populous region. *Frontera Norte* (Mexico: El Colegio de la Frontera Norte) and *Migración y Desarrollo* (University of Zacatecas) include articles in Spanish and English.

Some publications with a 'magazine' format provide up-to-date information and shorter commentaries, such as *Asian Migrant* (Quezon City, Philippines: Scalabrini Migration Center) and *Hommes et Migrations* (Paris).

Several international organizations provide comparative information on migrations. The most useful is the OECD's annual International Migration Outlook, which between 1991 and 2004 was entitled Trends in International Migration. Earlier annual reports on international migration to OECD member states from 1973 to 1990 were known as SOPEMI reports

(SOPEMI being the French language acronym for Continuous Reporting System on Migration). The IOM published its *World Migration Report* for the first time in 2000, and the latest appeared in 2008.

There are many Internet sites concerned with issues of migration and ethnic diversity. A few of the most significant are listed here. They are also provided as hyperlinks on the AOM4 Website. Since they are hyperlinked with many others, this list should provide a starting point for further exploration:

Asia Pacific Migration Research Network (APMRN):
    http://apmrn.anu.edu.au/
Centre for Migration Studies, New York: http://www.cmsny.org/
Centre on Migration, Policy and Society, University of Oxford:
    http://www.compas.ox.ac.uk/
European Council on Refugees and Exiles: http://www.ecre.org/
European Research Centre on Migration and Ethnic Relations
    (ERCOMER): http://www.ercomer.org/
Federation of Centers for Migration Studies, G. B. Scalabrini:
    http://www.scalabrini.org/fcms/
Forced Migration Online: http://www.forcedmigration.org/
Immigration History Research Center, Minnesota:
    http://www1.umn.edu/ihrc/
Institute for Migration and Ethnic Studies (IMES), Amsterdam:
    http://www2.fmg.uva.nl/imes/
Institute for Migration Research and Intercultural Studies (IMIS),
    Osnabrück: http://www.imis.uni-osnabrueck.de/e_index.htm
International Centre for Migration and Health: http://www.icmh.ch/
International Metropolis Project: http://www.international.metropolis.net/
International Migration Institute, University of Oxford:
    http://www.imi.ox.ac.uk/
International Organization for Migration: http://www.iom.int/
Inter-University Committee on International Migration:
    http://web.mit.edu/cis/www/migration/
Migration Information Source:
    http://www.migrationinformation.org/index.cfm/
Migration News: http://migration.ucdavis.edu/
Refugee Studies Centre, University of Oxford: http://www.rsc.ox.ac.uk/
Southern African Migration Project: http://www.queensu.ca/samp/
Swiss Forum for Migration and Population Studies:
    http://www.migration-population.ch/Home.506.0.html
United Nations High Commission for Refugees (UNHCR):
    http://www.unhcr.org/cgi-bin/texis/vtx/home
US Committee for Refugees and Immigrants (USCRI):
    http://www.refugees.org/

Chapter 2

Theories of Migration

International migration is hardly ever a simple individual action in which a person decides to move in search of better life-chances, pulls up his or her roots in the place of origin and quickly becomes assimilated in the new country. Much more often migration and settlement are a long-drawn-out process that will be played out for the rest of the migrant's life, and affect subsequent generations too. Migration can even transcend death: members of some migrant groups have been known to arrange for their bodies to be taken back for burial in their native soil (see Tribalat, 1995: 109–111). Migration is a collective action, arising out of social change and affecting the whole society in both sending and receiving areas. Moreover, the experience of migration and of living in another country often leads to modification of the original plans, so that migrants' intentions at the time of departure are poor predictors of actual behaviour. Similarly, no government has ever set out to build an ethnically diverse society through immigration, yet labour recruitment policies often lead to the formation of ethnic minorities, with far-reaching consequences for social relations, public policies, national identity and international relations.

The study of international migration has often fallen into two rather separate bodies of social scientific investigation: first, research on the *determinants, processes and patterns of migration*, and, second, research on *the ways in which migrants become incorporated into receiving societies* (compare Massey et al., 1998: 3). We argue that this distinction is artificial, and detrimental to a full understanding of the migratory process. We use the term 'migration studies' in the widest sense, to embrace both bodies of investigation. In addition, we believe the second area should be understood more broadly as *the ways in which migration brings about change in both sending and receiving societies.*

This chapter provides a theoretical framework for understanding the more descriptive accounts of migration, settlement and minority formation in later chapters. However, the reader may prefer to read those first and come back to the theory later. In various places, our account draws attention to the links between internal and international migration. In many countries – especially those with very big populations like China, India, Brazil or Nigeria – internal migration is far larger than international. The two are often closely linked, and internal rural–urban migration may be a prelude to cross-border movement (Skeldon, 1997). However, this book does not deal systematically with internal migration.

Explaining the migratory process

The concept of the *migratory process* sums up the complex sets of factors and interactions which lead to international migration and influence its course. Migration is a process which affects every dimension of social existence, and which develops its own complex dynamics. The great majority of people in the world (97 per cent in 2000) (UNDESA, 2005) are not international migrants, yet their communities and way of life are changed by migration. The changes are generally much bigger for the migrants themselves, and they can be seen at every stage of the migratory process, whether in countries of origin, transit or destination.

Research on migration is therefore intrinsically interdisciplinary: sociology, political science, history, economics, geography, demography, psychology, cultural studies and law are all relevant (Brettell and Hollifield, 2007). These disciplines look at different aspects of population mobility, and a full understanding requires contributions from all of them. Within each social scientific discipline there is a variety of approaches, based on differences in theory and methods. For instance, researchers who base their work on quantitative analysis of large data-sets (such as censuses or representative surveys) will ask different questions and get different results from those who do qualitative studies of small groups. Those who examine the role of migrant labour within the world economy using historical and institutional approaches will again get different findings.

Each of these methods has its place, as long as it lays no claim to be the only correct one. As interest in migration research has grown in recent years, theoretical approaches have proliferated and interacted, leading to more complex understanding of migration and its links with broader processes of change. Of special importance has been the application of theories of globalization and transnationalism to migration. A detailed survey of migration theory is not possible here (see Massey et al., 1993, 1994, 1998; Portes and DeWind, 2004; Brettell and Hollifield, 2007), but we will outline some main issues and provide pointers for further reading.

Economic theories of migration

Neoclassical theory remains the dominant paradigm in economics, and has had an important role in migration studies. However, some of its key assumptions and findings have been questioned through alternative approaches. The neoclassical perspective has its antecedents in the earliest systematic theory on migration: that of the nineteenth-century geographer Ravenstein, who formulated statistical laws of migration (Ravenstein, 1885, 1889). These were general statements unconnected with any actual migratory movement (Cohen, 1987: 34–35; Zolberg, Suhrke and Aguao, 1989: 403–405). Such 'general theories' emphasize tendencies of people to move from densely to sparsely populated areas or from low- to high-income areas, or link migrations to fluctuations in the business cycle. These approaches are often known as 'push-pull' theories, because they perceive the causes of migration to lie in a combination of 'push factors', impelling people to leave the areas of origin, and 'pull factors', attracting them to certain receiving countries. 'Push factors' include demographic growth, low living standards, lack of economic opportunities and political repression, while 'pull factors' include demand for labour, availability of land, good economic opportunities and political freedoms.

Today this model is mainly found in economics, but is also used by some sociologists, demographers and geographers. It is individualistic and ahistorical. It emphasizes the individual decision to migrate, based on rational comparison of the relative costs and benefits of remaining at home or moving. Neoclassical theory assumes that potential migrants have perfect knowledge of wage levels and employment opportunities in destination regions, and that their migration decisions are overwhelmingly based on these economic factors. Constraining factors, such as government restrictions, are mainly dealt with as distortions of the rational market. The central concept is 'human capital': people decide to invest in migration, in the same way as they might invest in education or vocational training, and will migrate if the expected rate of return from higher wages in the destination country is greater than the costs incurred through migrating (Chiswick, 2000). Borjas puts forward the model of an 'immigration market':

> Neo-classical theory assumes that individuals maximize utility: individuals 'search' for the country of residence that maximizes their well-being ... The search is constrained by the individual's financial resources, by the immigration regulations imposed by competing host countries and by the emigration regulations of the source country. In the immigration market the various pieces of information are exchanged and the various options are compared. In a sense, competing host countries make 'migration offers' from which individuals compare and choose. The information gathered in this marketplace leads many individuals to conclude that it is 'profitable' to remain in their birthplace ... Conversely, other individuals conclude that they are better off in some other country. The immigration market nonrandomly sorts these individuals across host countries. (Borjas, 1989: 461)

Borjas claims that 'this approach leads to a clear – and empirically testable – categorization of the types of immigrant flows that arise in a world where individuals search for the "best" country' (Borjas, 1989: 461). The mere existence of economic disparities between various areas should be sufficient to generate migrant flows. In the long run, such flows should help to equalize wages and conditions in underdeveloped and developed regions, leading towards economic equilibrium. Borjas has argued that this may lead to negative effects for immigration countries, notably the decline of average skill levels and lower wages for lower-skilled local workers (Borjas, 1990; Borjas, 2001). However, this finding is contested within neoclassical research: Chiswick claims that migrants are positively self-selected: the more highly skilled are more likely to move because they obtain a higher return on their human capital investment in mobility. This has negative effects for countries of origin, by causing a 'brain drain' (Chiswick, 2000).

However, studies of specific migration experiences cast doubt on neoclassical theory. It is rarely the poorest people from the least developed countries who move to the richest countries; more frequently the migrants are people of intermediate social status from areas which are undergoing economic and social change. Similarly, the push-pull model predicts movements from densely populated areas to more sparsely peopled regions, yet countries of immigration like the Netherlands and Germany are among the world's more densely populated. Finally, the push-pull model cannot explain why a certain group of migrants goes to one country rather than another: for example, why have most Algerians migrated to France and not Germany, while the opposite applies to Turks?

Neoclassical migration theories have therefore been criticized as incapable of explaining actual movements or predicting future ones (see Sassen, 1988; Boyd, 1989; Portes and Rumbaut, 2006: 16–17). It seems absurd to treat migrants as individual market-players who have full information on their options and freedom to make rational choices. Instead migrants have limited and often contradictory information, and are subject to a range of constraints (especially lack of power in the face of employers and governments). Migrants compensate by developing cultural and social capital (see below). Moreover, historians, anthropologists, sociologists and geographers have shown that migrants' behaviour is strongly influenced by historical experiences as well as by family and community dynamics (Portes and Böröcz, 1989).

It is essential to introduce a wider range of factors into economic research. One attempt to do this is *dual (or segmented) labour market theory*, which shows the importance of institutional factors as well as race and gender in bringing about labour market segmentation. Piore (1979) argues that international migration is caused by structural demand within advanced economies for both highly skilled workers and lower-skilled manual workers to carry out production tasks (e.g. assembly line work or garment manufacture) and to staff service enterprises (catering, cleaning, aged care, etc.). A division into primary and secondary labour markets emerges (Piore, 1979), while the most dynamic 'global cities' are marked by economic polarization – a growing gulf between the highly paid core workers in finance, management and research, and the poorly paid workers who service their needs (Sassen, 1991). The workers in the primary labour market are positively selected on the basis of human capital, but also often through membership of the majority ethnic group, male gender and, in the case of migrants, regular legal status. Conversely, those in the secondary labour market are disadvantaged by lack of education and vocational training, as well as by gender, race, minority status and irregular legal status.

Other authors have argued that divisions on the basis of race, ethnicity and gender lead not just to dualism but to more complex segmentation of the labour market, based for instance on enclave economies (Portes and Bach, 1985) or niches for ethnic entrepreneurs (Light and Bonacich, 1988; Waldinger et al., 1990). Segmented labour market theory helps explain the important role of employers and governments in international migration and the persistence of migration even when international wage differentials decline (Massey et al., 1998: 28–34).

The *new economics of labour migration* approach emerged in the 1980s (Taylor, 1987; Stark, 1991). It argued that migration decisions are not made by isolated individuals, but by families, households or even communities. Such groups may decide that one or more of their members should migrate, not just to get higher wages, but also to diversify income sources and to provide resources for investment in existing activities, such as the family farm. Migration cannot be adequately explained just by income differences between two countries – such factors as the chances of secure employment, availability of investment capital, and the need to manage risk over long periods need to be considered. For instance, as Massey et al. (1987) point out, Mexican farmers may migrate to the USA because, even though they have sufficient land, they lack the capital to make it productive. Similarly, the role of remittances cannot be understood simply by studying the behaviour of migrants themselves. Rather it is necessary to examine the long-term effects of remittances on investment, work and social relationships right across the community (Taylor, 1999).

The unit of analysis for the new economics of labour migration is therefore not the individual but the social group, and researchers use methods derived from sociology and anthropology, such as the household survey and the qualitative interview, to understand migration decisions. Nonetheless, the primacy of economic factors remains apparent through the focus on capital and credit markets in sending regions, as well as on migration as a way of compensating for lack of insurance systems to protect against crop failure and unemployment or to provide for retirement (Massey et al., 1998: 21–28).

These differing economic approaches lead to equally varied ideas for migration policy. Neoclassical economists sometimes advocate 'open borders' and 'freedom of migration', believing that this will in the long run lead to a global equalization of wage levels. In his early work, Borjas suggested that the US government should 'deregulate the immigration market' by selling visas to the highest bidder (Borjas, 1990: 225–228). However, critics have pointed out that wage levels – especially for low-skilled work – might fall to levels as low as those in the poorest countries of origin, causing social turmoil in more developed countries. In more recent work, Borjas argues for a stronger role for immigration policy: the

USA should limit numbers to about 500,000 a year and introduce a points system that favours skilled workers (Borjas, 2001: chapter 11).

The new economics approach is similar to neoclassical theory in that it focuses on the supply side of migration: that is, the factors that impel people to cross borders in search of work. However, neoclassical theory concentrates on individual wage maximization, while the new economics focuses on collective decisions concerned with a much wider range of factors. Policies concerned merely with controlling entry are unlikely to succeed, but governments could influence migration decisions by policies that help shape insurance and credit markets as well as investment opportunities in countries of origin (Massey et al., 1998: 27). That would entail much stronger links between policies on migration, international trade and development than exist at present.

By contrast, segmented labour market theory focuses on the demand-side, emphasizing that migration is driven by structural factors in modern capitalist economies. Strong employer demand for low-skilled labour that is easy to control and exploit (such as undocumented workers) is likely to undermine border restriction policies, creating a black market for migrant labour, and opportunities for people smugglers and recruitment agents. Governments could counteract undocumented migration only through measures to fundamentally change labour markets and to remove incentives for employing workers of this kind. This in turn could render unviable important sectors of business, such as agriculture, food processing and labour-intensive services.

In their important survey of migration theory, Massey et al. (1998: 50–59) argue that the various economic theories operate at different levels of analysis and focus on different aspects of migration, but that they all provide important insights into migration. However, the differences in the economic approaches and their policy implications also point to another conclusion: that migration cannot be understood simply through economic analysis, and that a much broader enquiry is needed. Examination of historical and contemporary migrations (see Chapters 4–7) shows that states (particularly of receiving countries) play a major role in initiating, shaping and controlling movements. The most common reason to permit entry is the demand for workers, but demographic or humanitarian considerations may also be important. Immigration as part of nation-building has played a major role in new world countries such as the USA, Canada, Argentina, Brazil and Australia. Policies on refugees and asylum seekers are also major determinants of contemporary population movements.

Thus it seems crucial to reconceptualize migration as a complex process in which economic, political, social and cultural factors all work together. Concentration on push or pull factors is simplistic and misleading. Migration decisions are influenced by a wide range of conditions in both sending and receiving areas. These conditions are not static, but in a process of constant change, linked both to global factors and to the way these interact with local historical and cultural patterns. It is important, Zolberg et al. suggest, to analyse labour migration 'as a movement of workers propelled by the dynamics of the transnational capitalist economy, which simultaneously determines both the "push" and the "pull" ' (Zolberg, Suhrke and Aguao, 1989: 407). Migrations are collective phenomena, which should be examined as subsystems of an increasingly global economic and political system.

The historical–structural approach and world systems theory

An alternative explanation of international migration was provided in the 1970s and 1980s by what came to be called the *historical–institutional approach*. In the context of an unequal distribution of economic and political power in the world economy, migration was seen mainly as a way of mobilizing cheap labour for capital. It perpetuated uneven development, exploiting the resources of poor countries to make the rich even richer (Castles and Kosack, 1973; Cohen, 1987; Sassen, 1988). While economic theories tended to focus on voluntary migrations of individuals, like that from Europe to the USA before 1914, historical–structural accounts looked at mass recruitment of labour, whether for the factories of Germany, for the agribusiness of California or for infrastructure projects like Australia's Snowy Mountain Hydroelectric Scheme. The availability of labour was both a legacy of colonialism and the result of war and regional inequalities within Europe.

The intellectual roots of such analyses lay in Marxist political economy – especially in *dependency theory*, which was influential in Latin America in the 1960s: the underdevelopment of Third World countries was a result of the exploitation of their resources (including labour) through colonialism, while in the postcolonial period dependency was being exacerbated by unfair terms of trade with powerful developed economies (Frank, 1969; Baeck, 1993). In the 1970s and 1980s a more comprehensive *world systems theory* developed (Amin, 1974; Wallerstein, 1984). It focused on the way less developed 'peripheral' regions were incorporated into a world economy controlled by 'core' capitalist nations. The penetration of multinational corporations into less developed economies accelerated rural change, leading to poverty, displacement of workers, rapid urbanization and the growth of informal economies.

Dependency and world systems theory were at first mainly concerned with internal migration (Massey et al., 1998: 35), but from the mid-1970s, as the key role of migrant workers in northern economies became more obvious, world systems theorists began to analyse international labour migration as one of the ways in which relations of domination were forged between the core economies of capitalism and its underdeveloped periphery. Migration reinforced the effects of military hegemony and control of world trade and investment in keeping the Third World dependent on the

First. Such theories can be seen as precursors of the globalization theories that emerged in the 1990s (see Chapter 3).

However, historical–structural approaches were criticized by some migration scholars in the 1980s: if the logic of capital and the interests of Western states were so dominant, how could the frequent breakdown of migration policies be explained, such as the unplanned shift from labour migration to permanent settlement in certain countries? Both neoclassical and historical–structural perspectives seemed too one-sided to analyse adequately the great complexity of contemporary migrations. The neoclassical approach neglected historical causes of movements, and downplayed the role of the state, while the historical–functional approach emphasized economic and social structure, and often saw the interests of capital as all-determining, while paying inadequate attention to human agency (the motivations and actions of the individuals and groups involved).

Migration systems and networks: the trend to an interdisciplinary approach

Out of such critiques emerged a number of new approaches. *Migration systems theory* has its roots in geography, while *migration networks theory* originates in sociology and anthropology. However, both seek to provide a basis for dialogue across social science disciplines. With the rapid growth of migration research since the 1990s, such initiatives are helping to pave the way for more comprehensive conceptual frameworks for understanding migration.

A *migration system* is constituted by two or more countries which exchange migrants with each other. A main focus is on regional migration systems, such as the South Pacific, West Africa or the Southern Cone of Latin America (Kritz et al., 1992). However, distant regions may be interlinked, such as the migration system embracing the Caribbean, Western Europe and North America; or that linking North and West Africa with France. A specific country can be part of several migration systems. The migration systems approach means examining both ends of the flow and studying all the linkages between the places concerned. These linkages can be categorized as 'state-to-state relations and comparisons, mass culture connections and family and social networks' (Fawcett and Arnold, 1987: 456–457).

Migration systems theory suggests that migratory movements generally arise from the existence of prior links between sending and receiving countries based on colonization, political influence, trade, investment or cultural ties. Thus migration from Mexico originated in the southwestward expansion of the USA in the nineteenth century and the recruitment of Mexican workers by US employers in the twentieth century (Portes and Rumbaut, 2006: 354–355). The migration from the Dominican Republic to the USA was initiated by the US military occupation of the 1960s. Similarly, both the Korean and the Vietnamese migrations to America were the long-term consequence of US military involvement (Sassen, 1988: 6–9). The migrations from India, Pakistan and Bangladesh to Britain are linked to the British colonial presence on the Indian subcontinent. Similarly, Caribbean migrants have tended to move to their respective former colonial power: from Jamaica to Britain, Martinique to France and Surinam to the Netherlands. The Algerian migration to France (and not to Germany) is explained by the French colonial presence in Algeria, while Turkish migration to Germany was the result of labour recruitment by Germany in the 1960s and early 1970s.

The basic principle of the migration systems approach is that any migratory movement can be seen as the result of interacting macro- and micro-structures. Macro-structures refer to large-scale institutional factors, while micro-structures embrace the networks, practices and beliefs of the migrants themselves. These two levels are linked by a number of intermediate mechanisms, referred to as 'meso-structures'.

The *macro-structures* include the political economy of the world market, interstate relationships, and the laws, structures and practices established by the states of sending and receiving countries to control migration settlement – the key topics of historical–institutional approaches. The evolution of production, distribution and exchange within an increasingly integrated world economy over the last five centuries has clearly been a major determinant of migrations. The role of international relations and of states in organizing or facilitating movements is also significant (Dohse, 1981; Böhning, 1984; Cohen, 1987; Mitchell, 1989; Hollifield, 2000, 2004a).

The *micro-structures* are the informal *social networks* developed by the migrants themselves, in order to cope with migration and settlement. Earlier scholars used the concept of 'chain migration' in this context (Price, 1963: 108–110). Research on Mexican migrants in the 1970s showed that 90 per cent of those surveyed had obtained legal residence in the USA through family and employer connections (Portes and Bach, 1985). Today many authors emphasize the role of *cultural capital* (information, knowledge of other countries, capabilities for organizing travel, finding work and adapting to a new environment) in starting and sustaining migratory movements. Informal networks provide vital resources for individuals and groups, and may be analysed as *social capital* (Bourdieu and Wacquant, 1992: 119), which includes personal relationships, family and household patterns, friendship and community ties, and mutual help in economic and social matters. Informal networks bind 'migrants and non-migrants together in a complex web of social roles and interpersonal relationships' (Boyd, 1989: 639).

The family and community are crucial in migration networks (here we see a similarity with the new economics of labour migration). Research on Asian migration has shown that migration decisions are usually made not by individuals but by families. In situations of rapid change, a family may decide to send one or more members to work in another region or country, in order to maximize income and survival chances. In many cases, migration decisions are made by elders (especially men), and younger people and women are expected to obey patriarchal authority. The family may decide to send young women to the city or overseas, because the labour of the young men is less dispensable on the farm. Young women are also often seen as more reliable in sending remittances. Such motivations correspond with increasing international demand for female labour, contributing to a growing feminization of migration (here we see a connection with segmented labour market theory.

Family linkages often provide the financial, cultural and social capitals which make migration possible. Typically migratory chains are started by an external factor, such as recruitment or military service, or by an initial movement of young (usually male) pioneers. Once a movement is established, the migrants mainly follow 'beaten paths' (Stahl, 1993), and are helped by relatives and friends already in the area of immigration. Networks based on family or on common origin help provide shelter, work, assistance in coping with bureaucratic procedures and support in personal difficulties. These social networks make the migratory process safer and more manageable for the migrants and their families. Migratory movements, once started, become self-sustaining social processes. Massey et al. suggest the term *cumulative causation* to refer to this tendency: 'Causation is cumulative in the sense that each act of migration alters the social context within which subsequent migration decisions are made, typically in ways that make additional movement more likely' (Massey et al., 1998: 45–46).

Migration networks also facilitate processes of settlement and community formation in the immigration area. Migrant groups develop their own social and economic infrastructure: places of worship, associations, shops, cafés, professionals (such as lawyers and doctors), and other services. This is linked to family reunion: as length of stay increases, the original migrants (whether workers or refugees) begin to bring in their spouses and children, or found new families. People start to see their life perspectives in the new country. This process is especially linked to the situation of migrants' children: once they go to school in the new country, learn the language, form peer group relationships and develop bicultural or transcultural identities, it becomes more and more difficult for the parents to return to their homelands. Such social processes embrace non-migrants too: employers seek to retain capable workers, and therefore support long-term stay. As local communities become more culturally diverse, immigrants take on roles in local social, cultural and political groupings.

The intermediate *meso-structures* have attracted increasing attention in recent years. Certain individuals, groups or institutions take on the role of mediating between migrants and political or economic institutions. A 'migration industry' emerges, consisting of recruitment organizations, lawyers, agents, smugglers and other intermediaries (Harris, 1996: 132–136). Such people can be both helpers and exploiters of migrants. In situations of illegal migration or of oversupply of potential migrants, the exploitative role may predominate: many migrants have been swindled out of their savings and have found themselves marooned without work or resources in a strange country. The emergence of a migration industry with a strong interest in the continuation of migration has often confounded government efforts to control or stop movements (Castles, 2004a). As King has pointed out, this 'privatisation of migration' is entirely consistent with dominant trends to liberalization and deregulation in the global economy (King, 2002: 95).

Macro-, meso- and micro-structures are intertwined in the migratory process, and there are no clear dividing lines between them. No single cause is ever sufficient to explain why people decide to leave their country and settle in another. It is essential to try to understand all aspects of the migratory process, by asking questions such as the following:

1. What economic, social, demographic, environmental or political factors have changed so much that people feel a need to leave their area of origin?
2. What factors provide opportunities for migrants in the destination area?
3. How do social networks and other links develop between the two areas, providing prospective migrants with information, means of travel and the possibility of entry?
4. What legal, political, economic and social structures and practices exist or emerge to regulate migration and settlement?
5. How do migrants turn into settlers, and why does this lead to discrimination, conflict and racism in some cases, but to pluralist or multicultural societies in others?
6. What is the effect of settlement on the social structure, culture and national identity of the receiving societies?
7. How do emigration and return migration change the sending area?
8. To what extent do migrations lead to new linkages between sending and receiving societies?

Transnational theory

This last question has attracted much attention in recent years, leading to the emergence of a new body of theory on *transnationalism* and *transnational communities*. One aspect of globalization is rapid improvement in technologies of transport and communication, making it increasingly easy for migrants to maintain close links with their areas of origin. This facilitates the growth of circular or temporary mobility, in which people migrate repeatedly between two or more places where they have economic, social or cultural linkages. Debates on transnationalism were stimulated by the work of Basch et al. (1994), who argued that 'deterritorialized nation-states' were emerging, with important consequences for national identity and international politics. This approach builds on theories of migration networks, but argues that their importance goes way beyond the micro-level. Portes defines transnational activities as

> those that take place on a recurrent basis across national borders and that require a regular and significant commitment of time by participants. Such activities may be conducted by relatively powerful actors, such as representatives of national governments and multinational corporations, or may be initiated by more modest individuals, such as immigrants and their home country kin and relations. These activities are not limited to economic enterprises, but include political, cultural and religious initiatives as well. (Portes, 1999: 464)

The notion of a transnational community puts the emphasis on human agency. In the context of globalization, transnationalism can extend previous face-to-face communities based on kinship, neighbourhoods or workplaces into far-flung virtual communities, which communicate at a distance. Portes and his collaborators emphasize the significance of transnational business communities (whether of large-scale enterprises or of small ethnic entrepreneurs), but also note the importance of political and cultural communities. They distinguish between *transnationalism from above* – activities 'conducted by powerful institutional actors, such as multinational corporations and states' – and *transnationalism from below* – activities 'that are the result of grass-roots initiatives by immigrants and their home country counterparts' (Portes et al., 1999: 221).

A much older term for transnational communities is *diaspora*. This concept goes back to ancient Greece: it meant 'scattering' and referred to city-state colonization practices. Diaspora is often used for peoples displaced or dispersed by force (e.g. the Jews; African slaves in the New World). It was also applied to certain trading groups such as Greeks in Western Asia and Africa, or the Arab traders who brought Islam to South-East Asia, as well as to labour migrants (Indians in the British Empire; Italians since the 1860s) (Cohen, 1997; Van Hear, 1998). The term diaspora often has strong emotional connotations, while the notion of a transnational community is more neutral.

Today, many researchers argue that globalization leads to rapid proliferation of transnational communities (Vertovec, 1999: 447). They may become an increasingly important way to organize activities, relationships and identity for the growing number of people with affiliations in two or more countries. Glick-Schiller (1999: 203) suggests the use of the term *transmigrant* to identify people who participate in transnational communities based on migration. Vertovec (2004: 971) argues that transnational practices among migrants 'involve fundamental modes of transformation discernible in at least three basic domains': the socio-cultural, the political and the economic. Levitt and Glick-Schiller

(2004: 1003) state that 'the lives of increasing numbers of individuals can no longer be understood by looking only at what goes on within national boundaries'. This makes it necessary to revisit basic assumptions about social institutions such as the family, citizenship and nation-states, and, indeed, calls for 'a reformulation of the concept of society'.

By contrast, Guarnizo et al. (2003: 1212) state that the growing use of the term transnational has been accompanied by 'mounting theoretical ambiguity and analytical confusion'. They argue that such concepts as 'transmigrant' do not permit precise definitions, and that the ethnographic methods prevailing in transnational research do not make it possible to establish the true extent of transnational consciousness and behaviour. Guarnizo et al. examine the scale, relative intensity and social determinants of transnational political engagement through a survey of three Latin American immigrant groups (Colombians, Dominicans and Salvadorians) in four US metropolitan areas. They conclude that the number of immigrants regularly involved in cross-border activism is relatively small. Transnational engagement is significantly different by gender and is associated with age, human capital and social capital. Transnational political activities are not the refuge of marginalized or poorly educated migrants, but often include people with relatively high social status. Nor do such activities decline with length of residence in the USA.

Significantly, Guarnizo et al. find that transnational political activity is far from being 'deterritorialized' or undermining the nation-state. Rather it relates to specific territorial areas both in the USA and in homelands, is strongly linked to existing political systems, and often coincides with power relations based on the patriarchal structures typical of Latin American politics. Thus they find no contradiction between transnational activism and integration of immigrants into the political institutions of the USA (Guarnizo et al., 2003: 1239). This is important, because politicians and academics often argue that transnational links can undermine integration in the receiving country (see Chapter 11).

The rapid growth of transnational theory has raised more questions than can be answered with the research findings at our disposal. The degree to which migrants do actually engage in transnational behaviour has not been adequately established. Nor do we know how salient such behaviour is for receiving and sending societies, and for the relationships between them. (For a discussion of the role of diasporas or transnational communities in development of their homelands, see Chapter 3.) Transnationalism is an important field for further research, but inflationary use of such terms as 'transnational communities' and 'transmigrants' should be avoided. The majority of migrants probably do not fit the transnational pattern. Temporary labour migrants who sojourn abroad for a few years, send back remittances, communicate with their family at home and visit them occasionally are not necessarily 'transmigrants'. Nor are permanent migrants who leave forever, and simply retain loose contact with their homeland. The key defining feature is that transnational activities are a central part of a person's life.

Where this can be shown empirically to apply to a group of migrants, one can appropriately speak of a transnational community.

From migration to settlement

Although each migratory movement has its specific historical patterns, it is possible to generalize on the social dynamics of the migratory process. It is necessary, however, to differentiate between economically motivated migration and forced migration. Most economic migrations start with young, economically active people. They are often 'target-earners', who want to save enough in a higher-wage economy to improve conditions at home, by buying land, building a house, setting up a business, or paying for education or dowries. After a period in the receiving country, some of these 'primary migrants' return home, but others prolong their stay, or return and then remigrate. As time goes on, many erstwhile temporary migrants send for spouses, or find partners in the new country. With the birth of children, settlement takes on a more permanent character.

It is this powerful internal dynamic of the migratory process that often confounds expectations of the participants and undermines the objectives of policy-makers in both sending and receiving countries (Böhning, 1984; Castles, 2004a). In many migrations, there is no initial intention of family reunion and permanent settlement. However, when governments try to stop flows – for instance, because of a decline in the demand for labour – they may find that the movement has become self-sustaining. What started off as a temporary labour flow is transformed into family reunion, undocumented migration or even asylum-seeker flows. This is a result of the maturing of the migratory movement and of the migrants themselves as they pass through the life cycle. It may also be because dependency on migrant workers in certain sectors has become a structural feature of the economy.

The failure of policy-makers and analysts to see international migration as a dynamic social process is at the root of many political and social problems. The source of this failure is often a one-sided focus on economic models of migration, which claim that migration is an individual response to market factors. This has led to the belief that migration can be turned on and off like a tap, by changing policy settings which influence the costs and benefits of mobility for migrants. But migration may continue due to social factors, even when the economic factors which initiated the movement have been completely transformed.

Such developments are illustrated by the Western European experience of settlement following the 'guestworker'-type migration from 1945 to 1973. Similar outcomes arose from movements from former colonies to the UK, France and the Netherlands, and migration from Europe, Latin America and Asia to the USA, Australia and Canada (see Chapter 5). One lesson of the last half-century is that it is extremely difficult for countries with democratic rights and strong legal systems to prevent migration turning into settlement. The situation is somewhat different in labour-recruiting countries which lack effective human rights guarantees, such as the Gulf states or some East and South-East Asian countries, where restrictions by the receiving governments may hinder family reunion and permanent settlement (Chapters 6 and 7).

The dynamics are different in the case of refugees and asylum seekers. They leave their countries because persecution, human rights abuse and generalized violence make life there unsustainable. Most forced migrants remain in the neighbouring countries of first asylum – which are usually poor and often politically unstable themselves. Onward migration to countries which offer better economic and social opportunities is only possible for a small minority. However, there is selectivity: it is mainly those with financial resources, human capital (especially education) and social networks in destination countries who are able to migrate onwards (Zolberg and Benda, 2001). Onward migration is motivated both by the imperative of flight from violence, and by the hope of building a better life elsewhere. Attempts by policy-makers to make clear distinctions between economic and forced migrants are hampered by these 'mixed motivations'.

This has led to the notion of the *migration-asylum nexus*. Labour migrants, permanent settlers and refugees move under different conditions and legal regimes. Yet all these population movements are symptomatic of modernization and globalization. Colonialism, industrialization and integration into the world economy destroy traditional forms of production and social relations, and lead to the reshaping of nations and states. Underdevelopment, impoverishment, poor governance, endemic conflict and human rights abuse are closely linked. These conditions lead both to economically motivated migration and to politically motivated flight. Many migratory movements involve both economic migrants and refugees, leading the UNHCR to speak of 'mixed flows'.

The formation of ethnic minorities

The long-term effects of immigration on society emerge in the later stages of the migratory process when migrants settle permanently. Outcomes can be very different, depending on the actions of the receiving state and society. At one extreme, openness to settlement, granting of citizenship and gradual acceptance of cultural diversity may allow the formation of *ethnic communities*, which are seen as part of a multicultural society. At the other extreme, denial of the reality of settlement, refusal of citizenship and rights to settlers, and rejection of cultural diversity may lead to formation of *ethnic minorities*, whose presence is widely regarded as undesirable and divisive. Most countries of immigration have tended to lie somewhere between these two extremes.

Critics of immigration portray ethnic minorities as a threat to economic well-being, public order and national identity. Yet these ethnic minorities may in fact be the creation of the very people who fear them. Ethnic minorities may be defined as groups which

(a) have been assigned a subordinate position in society by dominant groups on the basis of socially constructed markers of phenotype (that is, physical appearance or 'race'), origins or culture;

(b) have some degree of collective consciousness (or feeling of being a community) based on a belief in shared language, traditions, religion, history and experiences.

An ethnic minority is therefore a product of both 'other-definition' and of 'self-definition'. *Other-definition* means ascription of undesirable characteristics and assignment to inferior social positions by dominant groups. *Self-definition* refers to the consciousness of group members of belonging together on the basis of shared cultural and social characteristics. The relative strength of these processes varies. Some minorities are mainly constructed through processes of exclusion (which may be referred to as *racism* or *xenophobia*) by the majority. Others are mainly constituted on the basis of cultural and historical consciousness (or *ethnic identity*) among their members. The concept of the ethnic minority always implies some degree of marginalization or exclusion, leading to situations of actual or potential conflict. Ethnicity is rarely a theme of political significance when it is simply a matter of different group cultural practices.

Ethnicity

In popular usage, ethnicity is usually seen as an attribute of minority groups, but most social scientists argue that everybody has ethnicity, defined as a sense of group belonging, based on ideas of common origins, history, culture, experience and values (see Fishman, 1985: 4; Smith, 1986: 27). These ideas change only slowly, which gives ethnicity durability over generations and even centuries. But that does not mean that ethnic consciousness and culture within a group are homogeneous and static. Cohen and Bains argue that ethnicity, unlike race, 'refers to a real process of historical individuation – namely the linguistic and cultural practices through which a sense of collective identity or "roots" is produced and transmitted from generation to generation, *and is changed in the process'* (Cohen and Bains, 1988: 24–25, emphasis in original).

Scholars differ in their explanations of the origins of ethnicity; one can distinguish primordialist, situational or instrumental approaches. Geertz, for example, sees ethnicity as a *primordial attachment*, which results 'from being born into a particular religious community, speaking a particular language, or even a dialect of a language and following particular social practices. These congruities of blood, speech, custom and so on, are seen to have an ineffable, and at times, overpowering coerciveness in and of themselves' (Geertz, 1963, quoted from Rex, 1986: 26–27). In this approach, ethnicity is not a matter of choice; it is presocial, almost instinctual, something one is born into.

By contrast, many anthropologists use a concept of *situational ethnicity*. Members of a specific group decide to 'invoke' ethnicity as a criterion for self-identification, in a situation where such identification is useful. This explains the variability of ethnic boundaries and changes in salience at different times. The markers chosen for the boundaries are also variable, generally emphasizing cultural characteristics, such as language, shared history, customs and religion, but sometimes including physical characteristics (Wallman, 1986: 229). In this view there is no essential difference between the drawing of boundaries on the basis of cultural difference or of phenotypical difference. The visible markers of a phenotype (skin colour, features, hair colour, and so on) correspond to what is popularly understood as 'race'. However, we avoid using the term 'race' where possible, since there is increasing agreement among scientists that classification of humans into 'races' is unsound, since genetic variance within any one population is greater than differences between groups. 'Race' is thus a social construction produced by the process referred to as racism (Miles, 1989).

Similarly, some sociologists see ethnic identification or mobilization as rational or *instrumental* behaviour, designed to maximize the power of a group in a situation of market competition. Such theories have their roots in Max Weber's concept of 'social closure', whereby a status group establishes rules and practices to exclude others, in order to gain a competitive advantage (Weber, 1968: 342). For Weber (as for Marx), organization according to 'affective criteria' (such as religion, ethnic identification or communal consciousness) was in the long run likely to be superseded by organization according to economic interests (class) or bureaucratic rationality. Nonetheless, the instrumental use of these affiliations could be rational if it led to successful mobilization.

Other sociologists reject the concept of ethnicity altogether, seeing it as 'myth' or 'nostalgia', which cannot survive against the rational forces of economic and social integration in large-scale industrial societies (Steinberg, 1981). Yet it is hard to ignore the growing significance of ethnic mobilization, so that many attempts have been made to show the links between ethnicity and power. Studies of the 'ethnic revival' by the US sociologists Glazer and Moynihan (1975) and Bell (1975) emphasize the instrumental role of ethnic identification: phenotypical and cultural characteristics are used to strengthen group solidarity, in order to struggle more effectively for market advantages, or for increased allocation of resources by the state. This does not imply that markers, such as skin colour, language, religion, shared history and customs, are not real, but rather that the decision to use them to define an ethnic group is a fairly arbitrary 'strategic choice'.

Whether ethnicity is seen as 'primordial', 'situational' or 'instrumental', the key point is that ethnicity leads to identification with a specific group, but its visible markers – phenotype, language, culture, customs, religion, behaviour – may also be used as criteria for exclusion by other groups. Ethnicity only takes on social and political meaning when it is linked to processes of boundary-drawing between dominant groups and minorities. Becoming an ethnic minority is not an automatic result of immigration, but rather the consequence of specific mechanisms of marginalization, which affect different groups in different ways.

Racism

Racism towards certain groups is to be found in virtually all immigration countries. *Racism* may be defined as the process whereby social groups categorize other groups as different or inferior, on the basis of phenotypical or cultural markers. This process involves the use of economic, social or political power, and generally has the purpose of legitimating exploitation or exclusion of the group so defined.

Racism means making predictions about people's character, abilities or behaviour on the basis of socially constructed markers of difference. The power of the dominant group is sustained by developing structures (such as laws, policies and administrative practices) that exclude or discriminate against the dominated group. This aspect of racism is generally known as *institutional or structural racism*. Racist attitudes and discriminatory behaviour on the part of members of the dominant group are referred to as *informal racism*. Some social scientists now use the term *racialization* to refer to public discourses which imply that a range of social or political problems are a 'natural' consequence of certain ascribed physical or cultural characteristics of minority groups. Racialization can be used to apply to the social construction of a specific group as a problem, or in the wider sense of the 'racialization of politics' or the 'racialization of urban space' (Murji and Solomos, 2005).

In some countries, notably Germany and France, there is reluctance to speak of racism. Other terms such as 'hostility to foreigners', 'ethnocentrism' or 'xenophobia' are used. But the debate over the label seems sterile: it is more important to understand the phenomenon and its causes. Racism operates in different ways according to the specific history of a society. Often, supposed biological differences are not the main markers: culture, religion, language or other factors are taken as indicative of phenotypical differences. For instance, anti-Muslim racism (sometimes called Islamophobia) in Europe is based on cultural symbols which, however, are linked to phenotypical markers (such as Arab or African features).

The historical explanation for racism in Western Europe and in postcolonial settler societies (like the USA or Australia) lies in traditions, ideologies and cultural practices, which have developed through ethnic conflicts associated with nation-building and colonial expansion (compare Miles, 1989). In our view, the reasons for the recent increase in racism lie in fundamental economic and social changes which question the optimistic view of progress embodied in Western thought. Since the early 1970s, economic restructuring and increasing international cultural interchange have been experienced by many sections of the population as a direct threat to their livelihood, social conditions and identity. These shifts also question the dominance of previously privileged groups, leading to a reactive reassertion of nationalism and its symbols (Hage, 1998). As such changes have coincided with the arrival of new ethnic minorities, the tendency has been to perceive the newcomers as the cause of the threatening changes: an interpretation eagerly encouraged by the extreme right, but also by many mainstream politicians.

Since the events of 11 September 2001 and the proclamation of a 'global war on terror', racism has been oriented increasingly towards both 'racially-profiled' Muslim minorities within western countries and 'ethnoracially conceived countries' deemed to threaten western security. The result has been a broadening of 'racial Americanisation' on a world scale (Goldberg, 2005: 98–101) or the emergence of 'transnational racism' (Castles, 2005: 216–218). Moreover, the very changes which threaten disadvantaged sections of the population have also weakened the labour movement and working-class cultures, which might otherwise have provided some measure of protection. The decline of working-class parties and trade unions and the erosion of local communicative networks have created the social space for racism to become more virulent (Wieviorka, 1995; Vasta and Castles, 1996).

Ethnicity, class, gender and life cycle

Racial and ethnic divisions are only one aspect of social differentiation. Others include social class, gender and position in the life cycle. None of these distinctions is reducible to any other, yet they constantly cross-cut and interact, affecting life-chances, lifestyles, culture and social consciousness. Immigrant groups and ethnic minorities are just as heterogeneous as the rest of the population. The migrant is a gendered subject, embedded in a wide range of social relationships.

In the early stages of post-1945 international labour mobility, the vital nexus appeared to be that between migration and class. Migration was analysed in terms of the interests of various sectors of labour and capital (Castles and Kosack, 1973) or of the incorporation of different types of workers into segmented labour markets (Piore, 1979). Today, international migration continues to be closely linked to labour force dynamics and social class, which influence people's opportunities for migration and the conditions under which they can move and find work (see Chapter 10). However, there has been a growing awareness of the crucial links between class, ethnicity and gender.

Even in the early stages, the role of women in maintaining families and reproducing workers in the country of origin was crucial to the economic benefits of labour migration. Moreover, a large proportion of migrant workers were female. As Phizacklea (1983) pointed out, it was particularly easy to ascribe inferiority to women migrant workers, just because their primary roles in patriarchal societies were defined as wife and mother, dependent on a male breadwinner. They could therefore be paid lower wages and controlled more easily than men.

Today, migrant women still tend to be overrepresented in the least desirable occupations, such as repetitive factory work and lower-skilled positions in the personal and community services sectors. However, there has been some mobility into white-collar jobs in recent years, often linked to traditional caring roles. Minority women have experienced casualization of employment and increasing unemployment (which often does not appear in the statistics due to their status as 'dependents'). Complex patterns of division of labour on ethnic and gender lines have developed (see Chapter 10). One of these is the re-emergence of domestic work as an important employment area in developed countries (Anderson, 2000) as well as in new industrial economies (Wong, 1996).

However, gender can also become a focus for migrant women's resistance to discrimination (Vasta, 1993). Recent feminist studies such as (Phizacklea, 1998) propose a more transformatory interpretation of female migration: it can reinforce exploitation of women, but can also help those from patriarchal societies to gain more control over their own lives. This can make women reluctant to return to their countries of origin because this could involve losing new-won freedoms (King et al., 2006: 250–251). Transnational theory too has been criticized for ignoring the special experiences of female migrants (Pessar and Mahler, 2003), while the need for more analysis of the links between gender and ethnicity is receiving new attention in both Europe and North America (Lutz et al., 1995; Stasiulis and Yuval-Davis, 1995; Andall, 2003).

Anthias and Yuval-Davis (1989) analyse links between gender relations and the construction of the nation and the ethnic community. Women are not only the biological reproducers of an ethnic group, but also the 'cultural carriers' who have the key role in passing on the language and cultural symbols to the young (see also Vasta, 1990, 1992). Racism, sexism and class domination are three specific forms of 'social normalization and exclusion' which are intrinsic to capitalism and modernity, and which have developed in close relationship to each other (Balibar, 1991: 49). Racism and sexism both involve predicting social behaviour on the basis of allegedly fixed biological or cultural characteristics. According to Essed, racism and sexism 'narrowly intertwine and combine under certain conditions into one, hybrid phenomenon. Therefore it is useful to speak of *gendered racism* to refer to the racist oppression of Black women as structured by racist and ethnicist perceptions of gender roles' (Essed, 1991: 31, emphasis in original).

The role of gender in ethnic closure is evident in immigration rules which still often treat men as the principal immigrants while women and children are mere 'dependants'. Britain used gender-specific measures to limit the growth of the black population. In the 1970s, women from the Indian subcontinent coming to join husbands or fiancés were subjected to 'virginity tests' at Heathrow Airport. The authorities also sought to prevent Afro-Caribbean and Asian women from bringing in husbands, on the grounds that the 'natural place of residence' of the family was the abode of the husband (Klug, 1989: 27–29). Today, in many countries, women who enter as dependants do not have an entitlement to residence in their own right and may face deportation if they get divorced.

The stages of the life cycle – childhood, youth, maturity, middle age, old age – are also important determinants of economic and social positions, culture and consciousness (King et al., 2006). There is often a gulf between the experiences of the migrant generation and those of their children, who have grown up and gone to school in the new country. Such young people are aware of the contradiction between the ideologies of equal opportunity and the reality of discrimination and racism in their daily lives. This can lead to the emergence of counter-cultures and political radicalization. In turn, ethnic minority youth are perceived as a 'social time bomb' or a threat to public order, which has to be contained through social control institutions such as the police, schools and welfare bureaucracies (see Chapter 11).

Culture, identity and community

In the context of globalization, culture, identity and community often serve as a focus of resistance to centralizing and homogenizing forces (Castells, 1997). These have become central themes in debates on the new ethnic minorities. First, as already outlined, cultural difference serves as a marker for ethnic boundaries. Second, ethnic cultures play a central role in community formation: when ethnic groups cluster together, they establish their own neighbourhoods, marked by distinctive use of private and public spaces. Third, ethnic neighbourhoods are perceived by some members of the majority group as confirmation of their fears of a 'foreign takeover'. Ethnic communities symbolize a threat to the dominant culture and national identity. Fourth, dominant groups may see migrant cultures as static and regressive. Linguistic and cultural maintenance is taken as proof of backwardness and inability to come to terms with an advanced industrial society. Those who do not assimilate 'have only themselves to blame' for their marginalized position.

For ethnic minorities, culture plays a key role as a source of identity and as a focus for resistance to exclusion and discrimination. The culture of origin helps people maintain self-esteem in a situation where their capabilities and experience are undermined. But a static, primordial culture cannot fulfil this task, for it does not provide orientation in a hostile environment. The dynamic nature of culture lies in its capacity to link a group's history and traditions with the actual situation in the migratory process. Migrant or minority cultures are constantly recreated on the basis of the needs and experience of the group and its interaction with the actual social environment (Schierup and Ålund, 1987; Vasta et al., 1992). An apparent regression, for instance to religious fundamentalism, may be precisely the result of a form of modernization which has been experienced as discriminatory, exploitative and destructive of identity.

It is therefore necessary to understand the development of ethnic cultures, the stabilization of personal and group identities, and the formation of ethnic communities as facets of a single process. This process is not self-contained: it depends on constant interaction with the state and the various institutions and groups in the country of immigration, as well as with the society of the country of origin. Immigrants and their descendants do not have a static, closed and homogeneous ethnic identity, but rather dynamic *multiple identities*, influenced by a variety of cultural, social and other factors.

Culture is becoming increasingly politicized in all countries of immigration. As ideas of racial superiority lose their ideological strength, exclusionary practices against minorities increasingly focus on issues of cultural difference. At the same time, the politics of minority resistance crystallize more and more around cultural symbols – the political significance given to Islamic dress in France, Britain, the Netherlands and other immigration countries illustrates this trend. Yet such symbols are only partially based on imported forms of ethnicity. Their main power as definers of community and identity comes from the incorporation of new experiences of ethnic minority groups in the immigration country.

State and nation

Large-scale migrations and growing diversity may have important effects on political institutions and national identity. In the contemporary world, the approximately 200 nation-states are the predominant form of political organization. They derive their legitimacy from the claims of providing security and order and representing the aspirations of their people (or citizens). The latter implies two further claims: that there is an underlying cultural consensus which allows agreement on the values or interests of the people, and that there is a democratic process for the will of the citizens to be expressed. Such claims are often dubious, for most countries are marked by heterogeneity, based on ethnicity, class and other cleavages, while only a minority of countries consistently use democratic mechanisms to resolve value and interest conflicts. Nonetheless, the democratic nation-state has become a global norm (Habermas and Pensky, 2001; Shaw, 2000; Giddens, 2002).

Immigration of culturally diverse people presents nation-states with a dilemma: incorporation of the newcomers as citizens may undermine myths of cultural homogeneity; but failure to incorporate them may lead to divided societies, marked by severe inequality and conflict. Premodern states based their authority on the absolute power of a monarch over a specific territory. Within this area, all people were subjects of the monarch (rather than citizens). There was no concept of a national culture which transcended the gulf between aristocratic rulers and peasants. By contrast, the modern nation-state, as it developed in Western Europe and North America in the context of modernization, industrialization and colonialism, implies a close link between cultural belonging and political identity (Castles and Davidson, 2000).

A *state*, according to Seton-Watson (1977: 1), 'is a legal and political organization, with the power to require obedience and loyalty from its citizens'. The state regulates political, economic and social relations in a bounded territory. Most modern nation-states are formally defined by a constitution and laws, according to which all power derives from the people (or nation). It is therefore vital to define who belongs to the people. Membership is marked by the status of citizenship, which lays down rights and duties. Non-citizens are excluded from at least some of these. Citizenship is the essential link between state and nation, and obtaining citizenship is of central importance for newcomers to a country.

Seton-Watson describes a *nation* as 'a community of people, whose members are bound together by a sense of solidarity, a common culture, a national consciousness' (Seton-Watson, 1977: 1). Such subjective phenomena are difficult to measure, and it is not clear how a nation differs from an ethnic group, which is defined in a similar way (see above). Anderson provides an answer with his concept of the nation: 'it is an imagined political community – and imagined as both inherently limited and sovereign' (Anderson, 1983: 15). The implication is that an ethnic group that attains sovereignty over a bounded territory becomes a nation and establishes a nation-state. As Smith (1991: 14) puts it: 'A nation can ... be defined as a named human population sharing an historic territory, common myths and historical memories, a mass, public culture, a common economy and common legal rights and duties for all members.'

Anderson (1983) regards the *nation-state* as a modern phenomenon, whose birth date is that of the US Constitution of 1787. Gellner (1983) argues that nations could not exist in premodern societies, owing to the cultural gap between elites and peasants, while modern industrial societies require cultural homogeneity to function, and therefore generate the ideologies needed to create nations. However, both Seton-Watson (1977) and Smith (1986) argue that the nation is of much greater antiquity, going back to the ancient civilizations of East Asia, the Middle East and Europe. All these authors seem to agree that the nation is essentially a belief system, based on collective cultural ties and sentiments. These convey a sense of identity and belonging, which may be referred to as national consciousness.

Specific to the modern nation-state is the linking of national consciousness with the principle of democracy: every person classified as a member of the national community has an equal right to participate in the formulation of the political will. This linking of nationality and citizenship is deeply contradictory. In liberal theory, all citizens are meant to be free and equal persons who are treated as homogeneous within the political sphere. This requires a separation between a person's political rights and obligations and their membership of specific groups, based on ethnicity, religion, social class or regional location. The political sphere is one of universalism, which means abstraction from cultural particularity and difference. Difference is to be restricted to the 'non-public identity' (Rawls, 1985: 232–241).

This conflicts with the reality of nation-state formation, however, in which being a citizen depends on membership in a certain national community, usually based on the dominant ethnic group of the territory concerned. Thus a *citizen* is always also a member of a nation, a *national*. Nationalist ideologies demand that ethnic group, nation and state should be facets of the same community and have the same boundaries – every ethnic group should constitute itself as a nation and should have its own state, with all the appropriate trappings: flag, army, Olympic team and postage stamps. In fact, such congruence has rarely been achieved: nationalism has always been an ideology trying to achieve such a condition, rather than an actual state of affairs.

The historical construction of nation-states has involved the spatial extension of state power, and the territorial incorporation of hitherto distinct ethnic groups. These may or may not coalesce into a single nation over time. Attempts to consolidate the nation-state can mean exclusion, assimilation or even genocide for minority groups. It is possible to keep relatively small groups in situations of permanent subjugation and exclusion from the 'imagined community'. This has applied, for instance, to Jews and Gypsies in various European countries, to indigenous peoples in settler colonies and to the descendants of slaves and contract workers in some areas of European colonization. Political domination and cultural exclusion are much more difficult if the subjugated nation retains a territorial base, like the Scots, Welsh and Irish in the UK, or the Basques in Spain.

The experience of 'historical minorities' has helped to mould structures and attitudes which affect the conditions for new immigrant groups. The pervasive fear of 'ghettos' or 'ethnic enclaves' indicates that minorities seem most threatening when they concentrate in distinct areas. For nationalists, an ethnic group is a potential nation which does not (yet) control any territory, or have its own state. Most modern states have made conscious efforts to achieve cultural and political integration of minorities. Mechanisms include citizenship itself, centralized political institutions, the propagation of national languages, universal education systems and creation of national institutions like the army, or an established church (Schnapper, 1991, 1994). The problem is similar everywhere, whether the minorities are 'old' or 'new': how can a nation be defined, if not in terms of a shared (and single) ethnic identity? How are core values and behavioural norms to be laid down, if there is a plurality of cultures and traditions?

Citizenship

The states of immigration countries have had to devise policies and institutions to respond to the problems of increased ethnic diversity (see Aleinikoff and Klusmeyer, 2000, 2001). The central issues are: defining who is a citizen, how newcomers can become citizens and what citizenship means. In principle the nation-state only permits a single membership, but immigrants and their descendants have a relationship to more than one state. They may be citizens of two states, or they may be a citizen of one state but live in another. These situations may lead to 'transnational consciousness' or 'divided loyalties' and undermine the cultural homogeneity which is the nationalist ideal. Thus large-scale settlement inevitably leads to a debate on citizenship.

Citizenship designates the equality of rights of all citizens within a political community, as well as a corresponding set of institutions guaranteeing these rights (Bauböck, 1991: 28). However, formal equality rarely leads to equality in practice. Citizenship has always meant something different for men than for women, because the concept of the citizen has been premised on the male family-father, who represents his woman and children (Anthias and Yuval-Davis, 1989). The citizen has generally been defined in terms of the cultures, values and interests of the majority ethnic group. Finally, the citizen has usually been explicitly or implicitly conceived in class terms, so that gaining real participatory rights for members of the working class has been one of the central historical tasks of the labour movement. The history of citizenship has therefore been one of conflicts over the real content of the category in terms of civil, political and social rights (Marshall, 1964).

The first concern for immigrants, however, is not the exact content of citizenship, but how they can obtain it, in order to achieve a legal status formally equal to that of other residents. Access has varied considerably in different countries, depending on the prevailing concept of the nation. We can distinguish the following ideal types of citizenship:

1. The *imperial model*: definition of belonging to the nation in terms of being a subject of the same power or ruler. This notion pre-dates the French and American revolutions. It allowed the integration of the various peoples of multiethnic empires (the British, the Austro-Hungarian, the Ottoman, etc.). This model remained formally in operation in the UK until the Nationality Act of 1981, which created a modern type of citizenship for the first time. It also had some validity for the former Soviet Union. The concept almost always has an ideological character, in that it helps to veil the actual dominance of a particular ethnic group or nationality over the other subject peoples.

2. The *folk or ethnic model*: definition of belonging to the nation in terms of ethnicity (common descent, language and culture), which means exclusion of minorities from citizenship and from the community of

the nation. (Germany came close to this model until the introduction of new citizenship rules in 2000.)

3. The *republican model*: definition of the nation as a political community, based on a constitution, laws and citizenship, with the possibility of admitting newcomers to the community, providing they adhere to the political rules and are willing to adopt the national culture. This assimilationist approach dates back to the French and American revolutions. France is the most obvious current example.

4. The *multicultural model*: the nation is also defined as a political community, based on a constitution, laws and citizenship that can admit newcomers. However, in this model they may maintain their distinctive cultures and form ethnic communities, providing they conform to national laws. This pluralist or multicultural approach became dominant in the 1970s and 1980s in Australia, Canada and Sweden, and was also influential in other Western countries. However, there was a move away from multiculturalism in many places in the 1990s and the early twenty-first century.

All these ideal types have one factor in common: they are premised on citizens who belong to just one nation-state. Migrant settlement is seen as a process of transferring primary loyalty from the state of origin to the new state of residence. This process, which may be long-drawn-out and even span generations, is symbolically marked by naturalization and acquisition of citizenship of the new state. Transnational theory (see above) argues that this no longer applies for growing groups of migrants. Thus an additional ideal type of citizenship may be emerging:

5. The *transnational model*: social and cultural identities of transnational communities transcend national boundaries, leading to multiple and differentiated forms of belonging. Transnationalism could have important consequences for democratic institutions and political belonging in future. This corresponds with the fact that, through globalization, a great deal of political and economic power is shifting to transnational corporations and international agencies which are not currently open to democratic control (Castles and Davidson, 2000). The survival of democracy may depend on finding ways of including people with multiple identities in a range of political communities. It also means ensuring citizen participation in new locations of power, whether supranational or subnational, public or private.

The applicability of these models to specific countries will be discussed in more detail in Chapter 11. Such models are neither universally accepted nor static even within a single country (Bauböck and Rundell, 1998: 1273). Moreover, the distinction between citizens and non-citizens is becoming less clear-cut. Immigrants who have been legally resident in a country for many years can often obtain a special status, tantamount to 'quasi-citizenship'.

This may confer such rights as secure residence status; rights to work, seek employment and run a business; entitlements to social security benefits and health services; access to education and training; and limited political rights, such as the rights of association and of assembly. In some countries, long-term foreign residents have voting rights in local elections. Such arrangements create a new legal status, which is more than that of a foreigner, but less than that of a citizen. Hammar (1990: 15–23) has suggested the term *denizen* for people 'who are foreign citizens with a legal and permanent resident status'. This applies to millions of long-term foreign residents in Western Europe, many of whom were actually born in their countries of residence.

A further element in the emergence of quasi-citizenship is the development of international human rights standards, as laid down by bodies like the UN, the International Labour Organization (ILO) and the World Trade Organization (WTO). A whole range of civil and social rights are legally guaranteed for citizens and non-citizens alike in the states which adopt these international norms (Soysal, 1994). However, the legal protection provided by international conventions can be deficient when states do not ratify them or do not incorporate the norms into their national law, which is often the case with international measures to protect migrant rights (see Chapters 1 and 13).

The EU provides the furthest-going example for a new type of citizenship (see Chapter 8). The 1994 Maastricht Treaty established Citizenship of the European Union, which embraced the rights: to freedom of movement and residence in the territory of member states; to vote and to stand for office in local elections and European Parliament elections in the state of residence; to diplomatic protection by diplomats of any EU state in a third country; and to petition the European Parliament and to appeal to an ombudsman (Martiniello, 1994: 31). However, EU citizens living in another member state do not have the right to vote in elections for the national parliament of that state. People dependent on social security do not have a right to settle in another member country; and access to public employment is still generally restricted to nationals (Martiniello, 1994: 41). Europe is still divided between the 'Schengen Zone' (which allows free travel, but excludes some EU countries, while including some non-EU states) and the rest. So far, EU citizenship has done little for the majority of immigrants who come from outside the EU.

The process of European integration is continuing: the 1997 Treaty of Amsterdam (Article 63) established community competence in the areas of migration and asylum. The new policy came into force in the lead-up to the EU expansion of 1 May 2004, when 10 new member states (mainly in Central and Eastern Europe) were admitted. Two further states, Romania and Bulgaria, joined the Union on 1 January 2007. EU regulations lay down common standards for the treatment of asylum seekers and migrants, although exact rules and their implementation are still a matter of individual state sovereignty. Proposals made by the European Commission (EC) in

2005 for a common policy concerning economic migration were rejected by important member states (Castles, 2006b).

The long-term question is whether democratic states can successfully operate with a population differentiated into full citizens, quasi-citizens and foreigners. Migrations are likely to continue and there will be increasing numbers of people with affiliations to more than one society. Dual or multiple citizenship is becoming increasingly common. Nearly all immigration countries have changed their citizenship rules over the last 40–50 years – sometimes several times. Countries of emigration like Mexico, India and Turkey have also changed their rules on citizenship and nationality, in order to maintain links with their nationals abroad. More and more countries accept dual citizenship (at least to some extent) although such practices remain contested (Faist et al., 2004). A major focus of reform is the introduction of measures to integrate the second generation into the political community through birthright citizenship or easier naturalization (see Aleinikoff and Klusmeyer, 2000; Castles and Davidson, 2000: chapter 4). The consequence is that the meaning of citizenship is likely to change, and that the exclusive link to one nation-state will become more tenuous. This could lead to some form of 'transnational citizenship', as Bauböck (1994b) suggests. But that in turn raises the question of how states will regulate immigration if citizenship becomes more universalistic.

Conclusions

This chapter has reviewed some of the theoretical explanations of migration and ethnic minority formation. One central argument is that migration and settlement are closely related to other economic, political and cultural linkages being formed between different countries in an accelerating process of globalization. International migration – in all its different forms – must be seen as an integral part of contemporary world developments. It is likely to grow in volume in the years ahead, because of the strong pressures for continuing global integration.

A second argument is that the migratory process has certain internal dynamics based on the social networks which are at its core. These dynamics can lead to developments not initially intended either by the migrants themselves or by the states concerned. The most common outcome of a migratory movement, whatever its initial character, is settlement of a significant proportion of the migrants, and formation of ethnic communities or minorities in the new country. Thus the emergence of societies which are more ethnically and culturally diverse must be seen as an inevitable result of initial decisions to recruit foreign workers, or to permit immigration.

A third argument is that increasing numbers of international migrants do not simply move from one society to another, but maintain recurring and significant links in two or more places. They form transnational communities which live across borders. This trend is facilitated by globalization, both through improvements in transport and communications technology, and through diffusion of global cultural values. Transnational communities currently embrace only a minority of migrants, but may in the long run have enormous consequences for social identity and political institutions in both receiving countries and countries of origin.

The fourth argument concerns the nature of ethnic minorities and the process by which they are formed. Most minorities are formed by a combination of other-definition and self-definition. Other-definition refers to various forms of exclusion and discrimination (or racism). Self-definition has a dual character. It includes assertion and recreation of ethnic identity, centred upon premigration cultural symbols and practices. It also includes political mobilization against exclusion and discrimination, using cultural symbols and practices in an instrumental way. When settlement and ethnic minority formation take place at times of economic and social crisis, they can become highly politicized. Issues of culture, identity and community can take on great importance for the receiving society as a whole.

The fifth argument focuses on the significance of immigration for the nation-state. It seems likely that increasing ethnic diversity will contribute to changes in central political institutions, such as citizenship, and may affect the very nature of the nation-state.

These conclusions help to explain the growing political salience of issues connected with migration and ethnic minorities. The migratory movements of the last 60 years have led to irreversible changes in many countries. Continuing migrations will cause new transformations, both in the societies already affected and in further countries now entering the international migration arena. The more descriptive chapters later in the book will provide a basis for further discussion of these ideas.

Guide to further reading

Two recent works provide overviews of international migration theory: Massey et al. (1998) presents a systematic discussion and critique, while Brettell and Hollifield (2007) contains chapters addressing the contributions of some of the main social scientific disciplines. An important collection on migration theory and methodology is to be found in a special issue of *International Migration Review* (Portes and DeWind, 2004), while an earlier, but still valuable, compendium is to be found in a 1989 special issue of *International Migration Review* (1989, 23:3). Sassen (1988) gives an original perspective on the political economy of migration, while Borjas (1990 and 2001) presents the neoclassical view. Two recent studies on migration and settlement in Europe and the USA (Portes and Rumbaut, 2006) provide valuable theoretical background, while Boyle et al. (1998) is a good introductory text written by geographers. Kritz et al. (1992) is an excellent collection on migration systems theory.

Earlier works on gender and migration include Phizacklea (1983), Morokvasic (1984) and Lutz et al. (1995), while more recent perspectives are to be found in Andall (2003), Pessar and Mahler (2003) and Phizacklea (1998). Goldberg and Solomos (2002) is a comprehensive collection of essays on racial and ethnic studies. Rex and Mason (1986) provides detailed expositions of theoretical approaches. CCCS (1982), Mosse (1985), Cohen and Bains (1988), Miles (1989), Balibar and Wallerstein (1991), Essed (1991), Wieviorka (1991, 1992, 1995), Solomos (2003) and Murji and Solomos (2005) are good on racism. Anderson (1983), Gellner (1983) and Ignatieff (1994) provide stimulating analyses of nationalism, while Smith (1986, 1991) discusses the relationship between ethnicity and nation.

Analyses of the relationship between migration and citizenship are to be found in Bauböck (1991, 1994a, 1994b), Bauböck and Rundell (1998), Bauböck et al. (2006a, b), Aleinikoff and Klusmeyer (2000, 2001) and Castles and Davidson (2000). Gutmann (1994), Schnapper (1994), Soysal (1994) and Kymlicka (1995) present various perspectives on the same theme. DeWind et al. (1997) is a collection of articles on the changing character of immigrant incorporation in the USA. Good introductions to transnational communities include Basch et al. (1994), Cohen (1997), Portes et al. (1999), Vertovec (1999 and 2004) and Faist (2000). Van Hear (1998) discusses transnational theory from the perspective of refugee movements. Zolberg and Benda (2001) is useful for understanding the links between economic migration and refugee movements.

Chapter 3

Globalization, Development and Migration

A key question for academics and policy-makers today is *whether migration encourages development of the countries of origin or, conversely, hinders such development.* This concern is not new but the theme has become much more prominent in the last few years. This chapter examines the key issues in the debate on migration and development, and links it to broader social scientific research on globalization. A key argument in our analysis is that globalization leads to major social transformations in both South and North, which in turn provide the conditions for the current expansion and reconfiguration of global migration. This chapter serves as a conceptual bridge between the theory in Chapter 2, the examination of global migration history up to 1945 in Chapter 4, and the accounts of contemporary migrations in the various world regions in Chapters 5, 6 and 7.

The main concern in the migration-development debate is with *South–North migration* – that is, movement from Africa, Asia and Latin America to the developed countries of Europe, North America and Oceania – and increasingly also to new industrial economies in Southeast Asia, Latin America or the Persian Gulf. UN figures (see Table 1.1) show that the world total of migrants (defined as people living outside their country of birth for over a year) was about 100 million in 1980, of whom 48 million were in developed countries and 52 million in developing countries. By 2006, out of a global total of about 191 million migrants, 61 million had moved South–South (i.e. from one developing country to another), 53 million North–North, 14 million North–South and 62 million South–North (UNDESA, 2006b). In other words, most recent growth has been in South–North movements. This is an oversimplification, since former Soviet bloc countries and new industrial countries cannot be readily classified as North or South, but it is indicative of an important trend.

During the 1950s and 1960s development economists stressed that labour migration was an integral part of modernization. They were looking first and foremost at the *effects of development on migration*, but also at reciprocal *effects of migration on development*, namely that the reduction of labour surpluses (and hence unemployment) in areas of origin and the inflow of capital through *migrant remittances* (the money migrants send home to their families and communities) could improve productivity and incomes (Massey et al., 1998: 223).

The governments of countries like Morocco, Turkey and the Philippines shared this view. In the 1960s and 1970s, they encouraged their nationals to migrate to Western Europe or the USA – and later to Gulf oil countries. Such governments claimed that labour export would facilitate economic development at home. However, the long-term results of labour recruitment schemes were often disappointing, with little economic benefit for the country of origin – as shown in particular by a series of studies on Turkey (Paine, 1974; Abadan-Unat, 1988; Martin, 1991). The result was a predominantly pessimistic view that 'migration undermines the prospects for local economic development and yields a state of stagnation and dependency' (Massey et al., 1998: 272).

So why has there been a 'new surge of interest' (Newland, 2007) in migration and development? Why do international agencies and the governments of both migrant-sending and receiving countries believe that migration can make an important contribution to the development of poorer countries? And to what extent are such claims justified? These are the key questions to be addressed in this chapter. However, it important to examine the context for such debates: we therefore start by looking at contemporary processes of globalization and social transformation, and their consequences for population mobility.

Globalization

The theories of migration systems, migration networks and transnationalism discussed in Chapter 2 all stressed the need to understand migration as a part of much broader relationships between societies. They echoed the concern with global political economy found in world systems theory. From the late 1970s, however, a new paradigm emerged: *globalization* theory, which has become a widely accepted framework for debates about international migration.

The vast literature on the topic cannot be summarized here. Even to present a definition is difficult. One approach is to characterize globalization as 'the widening, deepening and speeding up of worldwide interconnectedness in all aspects of contemporary social life' (Held et al., 1999: 2). Thus a key indicator of globalization is a rapid increase in *cross-border flows* of all sorts, starting with finance and trade, but also including democracy and good governance, cultural and media products, environmental pollution and – most important in our context – people. A key organizing structure for these flows is the *transnational network*, which is to be found in multinational corporations, international organizations or – as already noted – in transnational communities. Key mechanisms of globalization are new information and communications technologies and cheap air travel (Castells, 1996). The concept of a scientific and technological revolution, led by computerization, is central to the idea that globalization is both new and inevitable.

Globalization is often portrayed primarily as an *economic process*, to describe activities that used to be centred on national economies but have now spilled beyond their boundaries:

> In its most general sense 'globalization' refers to the upsurge in direct investment and the liberalization and deregulation in cross-border flows of capital, technology and services, as well as the creation of a global production system – a new global economy. (Petras and Veltmayer, 2000: 2)

The key actors in this new economic world are the multinational corporations (MNCs) – large companies that operate in many countries – and the global financial and commodity markets. Globalization is 'driven by the logic of corporate profitability' (Bello and Malig, 2004: 85). Through electronic trading, the markets operate continuously across borders, and are seen as beyond the control of any state. Strong proponents of globalization regard the nation-state as obsolete – to be replaced by the power of markets and consumer choice (Ohmae, 1995). This view is linked to the neo-liberal principles of a 'small state', privatization of utilities and services, economic deregulation and the opening of markets (especially those of developing countries) to global competition. Opponents of globalization stress its negative consequences for national welfare systems, workers' rights and democracy (Martin and Schumann, 1997). Clearly globalization is not just about economics: it is also a *political process*, conceived in normative or ideological terms:

For the theorists of this process and its many advocates these flows, together with the resulting economic integration and social transformation, have created a new world order with its own institutions and configurations of power that have replaced the previous structures associated with the nation-state, and that have created new conditions in peoples' lives all over the world. (Petras and Veltmayer, 2000: 2)

Petras and Veltmayer, like other critics of globalization, argue that it is not a unique new world order, but rather the latest phase in the evolution of the capitalist world economy, which, since the fifteenth century, has penetrated into every corner of the globe. Indeed, the pace of economic integration is no greater than in the previous last great period of capitalist expansion from about 1870 to 1914 (Hirst and Thompson, 1996). The globalization paradigm emerged in the context of neoliberal strategies – led by the Reagan administration in the USA and the Thatcher government in the UK – designed to roll back the welfare states and the relatively high wage levels of the postwar boom period.

The opening of markets and removal of protection from organized labour led to massive social changes in the older industrial countries. Transfer of production to low-wage economies – like the *maquiladoras* of Mexico or the offshore production areas of South-East Asia – reshaped politics by weakening the left in industrial countries and by shoring up authoritarian regimes in the South (Froebel et al., 1980). Thus far from weakening the nation-state, globalization was really a new form of imperialism, designed to reinforce the power of core Northern states and their ruling classes (Weiss, 1997; Hardt and Negri, 2000; Petras and Veltmayer, 2000). This became even clearer in the early 2000s as US neoconservatives used their control of the world's most powerful military apparatus in an attempt to reassert global dominance (Bello and Malig, 2004; Bello, 2006).

Even a neoliberal world economy needs control mechanisms, but these are to be provided not by national governments, but by international institutions, especially the International Monetary Fund (IMF), the World Bank and the World Trade Organization (WTO). Their task is not to protect weak economies or vulnerable social groups, but rather to ensure that all economies and societies are opened up to the cold winds of competition – particularly through 'structural adjustment programmes'. These institutions have close links with the US Treasury, and their policies are strongly influenced by US and European interests. The result has been some spectacular policy failures, especially during the restructuring of the Russian economy and the Asian financial crisis in the 1990s: states which followed IMF recipes have often had extremely negative outcomes, while those – like Malaysia – which rejected IMF ideas have done better (Stiglitz, 2002).

One of the key arguments in favour of neoliberal globalization has been that it would lead to faster economic growth in poor countries, and thus, in the long run, to poverty reduction and convergence with richer countries (Milanovic, 2007: 34). There are many ways of measuring inequality, giving rise to controversy on its extent (for a detailed treatment see Held and Kaya, 2007). A study by Milanovic, a lead economist of the World Bank poverty research unit, summarizes the trends of the last 20–25 years:

> China and India pulled ahead. Latin America and Eastern Europe – the middle-income countries – declined, and Africa's position became even worse. The rich world (Western Europe, North America and Oceania) grew relatively fast. As for within-nation inequalities, they increased almost everywhere. *We are witnessing the Africanization of poverty*, since most the African nations are now extremely poor and many of them are actually poorer than they were in 1960. (Milanovic, 2007: 33, emphasis in original)

Milanovic finds that global inequality is 'probably the highest ever recorded' (2007: 39). Globalization therefore seems flawed as a paradigm to explain major global changes. It is more an ideology – summed up in the 'Washington consensus' on the importance of market liberalization, privatization and deregulation (Stiglitz, 2002: 67) – about how the world should be reshaped. Its basic premise is 'the leadership of civilization by economics' (Saul, 2006: xi). This has been linked to the idea that globalization is inevitable and that resistance is pointless and reactionary.

Some critics use the term 'globalism' rather than globalization (Cohen and Kennedy, 2000; Petras and Veltmayer, 2000; Saul, 2006) to emphasize this ideological character. By 2005, some analysts were arguing that globalism had collapsed, and that a fundamental change in the global order was beginning to emerge (e.g. Saul, 2006).

However, it seems important to distinguish between globalization as a *political project* and as an *economic process*. On the political level, the ideological dominance of globalization as a way of understanding the contemporary world seems to be over. Rising inequality, growing conflict and the failure to achieve fairer trade rules for poorer countries make it obvious that globalization has betrayed its promise. The emergence of new powers – notably China, India, Japan, Brazil and South Africa – challenges western domination of world politics. The world seems to be entering a period of reassertion of the importance of nation-states as social actors and economic regulators.

On the economic level, however, the dominance of an increasingly integrated capital world market shows no sign of receding. The never-closing real-time electronic bourses add new speculative products (derivatives, futures, hedge funds, private equity and so on) to the conventional commodity and financial markets. Privatization, deregulation and liberalization continue unabated. Local and national economies are pulled into the international production and trade circuits and are profoundly changed. New economic giants like China and India may challenge the old industrial powers, but they play by the same economic rules, and regard stability and system equilibrium as crucial to their own interests (Zhao, 2007).

Globalization remains a crucial context for understanding twenty-first-century migration. On the one hand, globalization drives migration and changes its directions and forms. On the other hand, migration is an intrinsic part of globalization and is itself a major force reshaping communities and societies. Globalization leads to pervasive processes of social transformation all around the world.

Social transformation

The idea of *transformation* implies a fundamental change in the way society is organized that goes beyond the continual processes of social change that are always at work (compare Polanyi, 1944). This arises when there are major shifts in dominant power relationships. The recent massive shifts in economic, political and military affairs represent such a fundamental change. Globalization has uneven effects. Indeed, it can be seen as a process of inclusion of particular regions and social groups in world capitalist market relations, and of exclusion of others (Castells, 1996). Penetration of southern economies by northern investments and multinational corporations leads to economic restructuring, through which some groups of producers are included in the new economy, while other groups find their workplaces destroyed and their qualifications devalued. Thus economic globalization means profound transformation of societies in all regions. The neglect of this connection on the part of the IMF and other international financial institutions has led to failures, which 'have set back the development agenda, by unnecessarily corroding the very fabric of society' (Stiglitz, 2002: 76–77).

The rapid growth in inequality between the 'advanced countries' and 'the rest of the world' is often referred to as *North–South inequality*. However, such general terms hide some important differences. First, many countries or areas do not fit this dichotomy: both the 'transitional economies' of former Soviet bloc countries and the 'new industrial economies' of Asia and Latin America have an intermediate position. Second, growing inequality is also to be found within the main regions, with new elites in the South gaining from their role in the transnational circuits of capital accumulation, while workers in former northern industrial centres lose their livelihoods. In Europe, this change is expressed in the decline of welfare states and the rise of racism against minorities (Schierup et al., 2006). Overall, therefore, globalization has led not only to a growing gulf between North and South, but also to increased inequality within each region.

Often social transformation starts in agriculture. The 'green revolution' of the 1980s involved the introduction of new strains of rice and other crops, which promised higher yields, but in return required big investments in fertilizers, insecticides and mechanization. The result was higher productivity (at least for a while – sometimes this declined as the soil became exhausted) but also concentration of ownership in the hands of richer farmers. The poorer farmers lost their livelihoods and often had to leave the land. The process continues today with the introduction of genetically modified seed-stock. The pressure on farmers in poor regions is increased by farm subsidies in rich countries – especially US cotton subsidies and the EU Common Agricultural Policy (Oxfam, 2002) – which depress world market prices. One result has been a large increase in suicides of farmers – the Indian Government has recorded 150,000 in the last 10 years (Swift, 2007).

The economic advances of emerging industrial powers such as China, India and Brazil are based on enormous growth in inequality between urban and rural incomes (Milanovic, 2007: 35–39). Displaced farmers migrate into burgeoning cities like Sao Paolo, Shanghai, Calcutta or Jakarta. The cities of the South are growing at a rate of about 70 million a year. In 2005, around 1 billion people were estimated to be living in slum areas, like the shanty-towns of southern Africa or the *favelas* of Brazil; this number is expected to double by 2030 (New Internationalist, 2006).

Urban employment growth cannot keep pace, and there are few jobs for the millions of newcomers. Many scrape a living through irregular and insecure work in the informal sector. Standards of housing, health and education are very low, while crime, violence and human rights violations are rife. Such conditions are powerful motivations to seek better livelihoods elsewhere, either in growth areas within the region or in the North. However, international migration is selective: only those with the financial capital to cover the high costs of mobility and the social capital to link up with opportunities abroad can make the move.

Clearly, the social transformations inherent in globalization do not just affect economic wellbeing – they also lead to increased violence and lack of human security in less developed countries. Growing numbers of people are forced to flee their homes as refugees or internally displaced persons (IDPs) (see Chapter 8). Situations of conflict, generalized violence and mass flight emerged in the South from the 1960s, in the context of struggles over decolonization and state formation (Zolberg et al., 1989). Local conflicts became proxy wars in the East–West confrontation, with the superpowers providing modern weapons to their protégés.

Such conflicts escalated from the 1980s onwards, due to failure to achieve sustainable economic growth and to build stable states in large areas of the South. International warfare was largely replaced by internal wars connected with ethnic divisions, problems of state formation and competition for economic assets. Ninety per cent of those killed in such conflicts are civilians. Mass population expulsion is often a strategic goal, so the 'new wars' have led to such an upsurge in forced migration (Kaldor, 1999). The great majority of those affected by violence are displaced within their own countries, or seek refuge in other – usually equally poor – countries in the region. Some, however, try to obtain asylum in the richer states of the North, where they hope to find more security and freedom – as well as better livelihoods. This is the reality of the observation of the Global Commission on International Migration (GCIM) that international migration is driven by 'development, demography and democracy' (GCIM, 2005: 12).

Globalization helps create the new technologies that facilitate mobility: air travel has become far cheaper and more readily available, and the electronic media spread images of first-world prosperity to the most remote villages. Globalization also creates the cultural capital needed for mobility: electronic communications facilitate the dissemination of knowledge of migration routes and work opportunities. Many of the world's excluded perceive that mobility brings the chance of prosperity, and are desperate to migrate. Globalization also creates the necessary social capital: informal networks facilitate migration even when official policies try to prevent it, while the 'migration industry' is one of the fastest-growing forms of international business. Migration networks help to reconnect South and North, at a time when many areas of the South have become economically irrelevant to the globalized economy (Duffield, 2001).

Clearly, migration is not just a result of social transformation but is in itself a form of social transformation, which has feedback effects on the societies involved. The flows and networks that constitute globalization take on specific forms at different spatial levels: the regional, the national and the local. These should not be understood in opposition to each other, but rather as elements of complex and dynamic relationships, in which global forces have varying impacts according to differing structural and cultural factors and responses at the other levels (see Held et al., 1999: 14–16). Historical experiences, cultural values, religious beliefs, institutions and social structures all channel and shape the effects of external forces, leading to forms of change and resistance that bring about very different outcomes in specific communities or societies.

For most people, the pre-eminent level for experiencing migration and its effects is the *local*. This applies especially where social transformations make it necessary for people to leave their community and move elsewhere: for instance through changes in agricultural practices or land tenure, through reconfiguration of production by multinational corporations, or through a development project (such as a dam, airport or factory) which physically displaces people. The departure of young active people, gender imbalances, and financial and social remittances all transform conditions in the local community. Similarly, the impact of immigration in host areas is felt in the way it affects economic restructuring and social relations in local communities.

Nor should the *national* dimension should be neglected. Despite globalist claims about the erosion of the nation-state, the number of nation-states in the UN has grown from 50 when the world body was established in 1945 to 192 at present. Nation-states remain important and will do so for the foreseeable future. They are the location for policies on cross-border movements, citizenship, public order, social welfare, health services and education. Nation-states retain considerable political significance and have important symbolic and cultural functions. However, it is no longer possible to ignore cross-border factors in decision-making and planning. One result of this is the growing importance of *regional* cooperation through bodies like the EU, NAFTA or the Economic Community of West African States (ECOWAS).

The inequality arising from globalization and social transformation is particularly evident with regard to migration. Differentiated migration regimes have been set up, to encourage the highly skilled to be mobile, while low-skilled workers and people fleeing persecution are excluded. As Bauman has argued, in the globalized world, 'mobility has become the most powerful and most coveted stratifying factor'. 'The riches are global, the misery is local' (Bauman, 1998: 9 and 74). Control of migration and differential treatment of various categories of migrants have become the basis for a new type of transnational class structure. Globalization has meant freedom of movement for capital and for the experts most vital to its profitability, while lower-skilled workers face highly restrictive legal regimes.

Migration and development

We can now return to the central question of this chapter: *does migration encourage development of the countries of origin, or hinder such development?* In the past, the key issue was whether the gains from *remittances* would outweigh the potential losses from departure of active workers – especially those with skills: the *brain drain* (Newland, 2003). It is often 'the best and brightest' who leave, whether as blue-collar workers or as college-educated professionals (Ellerman, 2003: 17). Emigration could lead to a shortage of the young, active workers needed for development. Indeed leaders of some countries have seen emigrants as 'deserters from the nation' (Khadria, 2008).

Now, ideas on the positive effects of migration on development are at the centre of policy initiatives. There has been a plethora of official conferences and reports on the theme (e.g. GCIM, 2005; World Bank, 2006; DFID, 2007). Migration and development was the topic of a High Level Dialogue of ministers and senior officials at the UN General Assembly in September 2006. This led to the establishment of a Global Forum on Migration and Development, which met in Brussels in 2007 and in Manila in 2008. In countries of origin like India migrants are being redefined as 'angels' or 'heroes of development' (Khadria, 2008). The main emphasis has been on the rapid growth of remittances to less developed countries (Ghosh, 2006; World Bank, 2006). However, attention has recently begun to shift to the potential role of migrant diasporas in contributing to the development of their homelands (IOM, 2005; Newland, 2007).

Kapur (2004) has pointed out that remittances have become a new 'development mantra': the money sent home by migrants is thought to promote local, regional and national development. Or, to put it less positively, the idea is that some of the world's most exploited workers should provide the capital for development, where official aid programmes have failed. It is useful to extend this notion of a 'new mantra' to include the whole range of benefits that migration is said to bring for development:

- Migrant remittances can have a major positive impact on the economic development of countries of origin
- Migrants also transfer home skills and attitudes – known as 'social remittances' – which support development
- 'Brain drain' is being replaced by 'brain circulation', which benefits both sending and receiving countries
- Temporary (or circular) labour migration can stimulate development
- Migrant diasporas can be a powerful force for development, through transfer of resources and ideas
- Economic development will reduce outmigration.

In the 1990s, Massey et al. (1998: 272) pointed to deficiencies in both theoretical understanding and data-gathering on the relationship between migration and development. Despite recent efforts, there are still many gaps. A World Bank Policy Research Working Paper found that the migration-development relationship is 'unsettled and unresolved' (Ellerman, 2003), while Newland (2007) states that 'the evidence base for the links between migration and development is still very weak'. All the factors listed above remain complex and controversial. We will discuss each in turn.

Economic remittances

Money sent home by migrants has become a crucial economic factor in many less developed countries. The United Nations Development Programme (UNDP) has estimated that 500 million people (8 per cent of the world's population) receive remittances. They flow directly to low-income households, and have a direct effect on poverty reduction (Newland, 2007). World Bank estimates for 2006 put the total of migrant transfers through official channels to developing countries at $199 billion – a growth of 107 per cent since 2001 (World Bank, 2007). However, unrecorded flows through informal channels may add 50 per cent or more to recorded flows:

> Including these unrecorded flows, the true size of remittances is larger than foreign direct investment flows and more than twice as large as official aid received by developing countries. Remittances are the largest source of external financing in many developing countries. (World Bank, 2007)

The main reason so many migrants send their money home through informal channels is the frequent high fees for transfer through banks or money transfer organizations (like Western Union or MoneyGram). Recently governments have realized the benefits of legal transfers, and have taken steps to reduce the costs and to make them more convenient. The GCIM suggested a range of measures (GCIM, 2005: 27–28). The British Government's Department for International Development (DFID) has set up a website called 'Send Money Home' (www.sendmoneyhome. org) to help people 'make an informed choice about the cheapest and most effective way to send their remittances' (DFID, 2007: 17).

Not all remittances are North–South flows: nearly half the migrants from developing countries work in other developing countries and South–South remittances are estimated at between 10 and 29 per cent of total remittance flows (Ratha and Shaw, 2007).

Table 3.1 gives information on the remittances received by certain developing countries. In dollar terms, India and China are the largest remittance receivers, although international migration is relatively small compared with their huge populations. Next come Mexico, Philippines and Morocco, where a large proportion of the population emigrate. However, as the data on remittances as a share of GDP show, many smaller countries have extremely high levels of economic dependence on migrant remittances. In Tonga, Moldova, Lesotho and Haiti, work opportunities at home

Table 3.1   *Top 10 remittance-receiving developing countries (2004) by billions of US dollars and by share of Gross Domestic Product (GDP)*

Country	Remittances: US$ billions	Country	Remittances as share of GDP: per cent
India	21.7	Tonga	31.1
China	21.3	Moldova	27.1
Mexico	18.1	Lesotho	25.8
Philippines	11.6	Haiti	24.8
Morocco	4.2	Bosnia and Herzogovina	22.5
Pakistan	3.9	Jordan	20.4
Brazil	3.6	Jamaica	17.4
Bangladesh	3.4	Serbia and Montenegro	17.2
Egypt	3.3	El Salvador	16.2
Vietnam	3.2	Honduras	15.5

Source: (World Bank, 2006).

are very limited, and emigration for work has become the norm for young labour-market entrants. Remittances can have major macroeconomic impacts in sending countries. Remittances to India in 2005 were equivalent to more than twice the Indian Government's expenditure on education or health. Investments from Indians abroad were also important for growth in equity and property markets (Chishti, 2007).

The flow of remittances may decline as migratory processes mature. For instance, during the 1990s, remittances to Turkey declined from a peak of US$5.4 billion in 1998 to US$1.7 billion in 2003. This was as a result of falling emigration and the permanent settlement of earlier migrants in Western Europe (Avci and Kirişci, 2008). However, remittances do not always decline. Some studies indicate that long-term transnational linkages develop, and that established migrants – even those who take on citizenship of the receiving country – may continue to support families in the homeland over long periods. Indeed, their ability to send money home may increase as their occupational situation improves (Guarnizo et al., 2003).

Remittances are the private property of migrants – the fruit of their hard labour and a reward for the high risks they often have to take. Migrants mainly send money home to their families to improve living standards, for instance through better nutrition and housing and the purchase of consumer goods, as well as to finance weddings, funerals and other ceremonies. Remittances benefit migrant households and contribute to poverty reduction. For instance, remittances make up 22 per cent of gross domestic product (GDP) in the Indian state of Kerala, which is the main source of Indian workers for the Gulf oil states (Chishti, 2007). However, remittances do not necessarily contribute to development, and may indeed, have negative effects, by increasing inequality between migrants and non-migrants, or by causing price inflation for land and other scarce resources (see Massey et al., 1998: 257–262).

This negative view is contested by other studies, which have found that migrant households' use of remittances to improve health and educational standards can improve the productivity of the labour force. Moreover, migrants and their families also invest directly in agriculture and rural industry, improving methods and incomes (De Haas, 2006a). At the same time, expenditure by migrant households creates demand and employment in the broader community. Even purchase of motor vehicles or lavish weddings can have economically beneficial 'multiplier effects'. The new economics of labour migration (see Chapter 2) emphasizes such effects, arguing that remittances can be a source of investment, income diversification and insurance in economies lacking formal institutions to fulfil these roles.

Refugees who succeed in finding jobs in relatively high-income countries also send home remittances. These can help perpetuate conflict by funding weapons and other resources for combatants, but can also be a valuable resource for reconstruction (and in the long-term for development) in postconflict situations (Nyberg-Sørensen et al., 2002).

Recent studies have highlighted the growth of 'collective remittances', through which migrant associations pool their members' resources to improve their home communities by building roads, or improving schools, churches or medical facilities. The hometown associations (HTAs) of Mexicans in the USA are well known, but such associations have also been reported for Africans in both Europe and the USA, and for Filipinos, Malaysians and Indonesians in Japan and other Asian countries. Long-term migrants are more likely to take leadership roles in HTAs, and to make collective remittances (Orozco and Rouse, 2007). The Mexican authorities have created incentives for collective remittances by adding $1 to each dollar sent home by HTAs. In some Mexican states (such as Zacatecas) the state government adds another dollar and the municipality yet another, creating a Tres por Uno (three for one) scheme (Ellerman, 2003: 22–23). Nonetheless, collective remittances are only a fraction of those sent back individually to families. Orozco and Rouse (2007) report that Mexican HTAs raised about $20 million for development projects in 2005, which was matched with $60 million from public funds. But this compared with total remittances to Mexico in 2006 of around $20 billion.

The general lesson that emerges from the many studies is that remittances do not automatically lead to sustainable economic and social development. Moreover, it is often forgotten that many migrants bring capital with them to destination countries, especially for educational fees. There is little data on this 'silent backwash flow' from the South to the North (Khadria, 2008). In 2006, a World Bank report called for a more cautious approach to remittances, saying that the benefits had been over-estimated, and that social and economic costs in developing countries had not been taken into account (Lapper, 2006). The claimed positive link between remittances and economic growth only applies if appropriate policies are put in place to improve governance and economic policies in countries of origin. Sound financial systems, stable currencies, a favourable investment climate and an honest administration are vital (GCIM, 2005). In other words: development initiatives are needed to mobilize productive remittances – not the other way round.

Social remittances

Although the term 'social remittances' is fairly recent, belief in the potential development impact of transfers of attitudes and behaviour from developed to less developed countries has a long tradition. A very positive assessment is to be found in a recent British Government policy document (DFID, 2007: 18).

Levitt defines social remittances as 'the ideas, behaviours, identities and social capital that flow from receiving- to sending-country communities' (Levitt, 1998: 926). Levitt's research examined the changes that came about in a Dominican village through the emigration of members of 65 per cent of the village's households, mainly to Boston. She showed the importance of social remittances for the formation of transnational communities, and argued that social remittances are a form of cultural diffusion that links global economic and political changes to local-level action and attitudes. However, Levitt warned that the impact of social remittances 'is both positive and negative. There is nothing to guarantee that what is learned in the host society is constructive or that it will have a positive effect on communities of origin' (Levitt, 1998: 944).

Recent case studies on the effects of emigration from five major sending countries confirm the ambivalent nature of social remittances (Castles and Delgado Wise, 2008). On the positive side, the Indian, Moroccan and Turkish studies all mention that migration has been a conduit for attitudes and skills conducive to change, and that this has had a positive impact on development. On the negative side, the very success of emigration may prove an impediment to development: if optimistic stories come back to the home community about the low risk and high benefits of moving to higher-wage economies, this can encourage more people to move. This may lead to a 'culture of emigration' in which spending a time working abroad becomes a normal 'rite of passage' for young people. The case studies of Mexico, Morocco and the Philippines refer to this phenomenon. Clearly, the absence of men and women in their most productive years can have negative effects on social change and economic growth.

Social remittances are transferred when migrants return on temporary visits or permanently, through visits by non-migrants to relatives abroad, and through phone calls, letters and videos (Levitt, 1998). Obviously, much depends on the circumstances of migrants abroad. Those who have experiences of exploitative work, poor housing and discrimination are not likely to transmit positive values back home. This applies especially to those who get drawn into criminal subcultures. Reports from Latin American countries indicate that children of migrants in the US sometimes become members of violent gangs. If deported, they may bring back a culture of drugs, violence and lawlessness to places where this has been hitherto absent.

Moreover, even positive social remittances will not automatically bring about reform. As with money remittances, there is a need for policy approaches that link transfer of new attitudes, behaviours and capabilities with development-friendly economic and social reforms in the country of origin. Certain kinds of social remittance flows can be purposefully stimulated (Levitt, 1998: 944), but this is only likely to work in the framework of comprehensive policy approaches designed to maximize the benefits of migration for development.

The idea that the transfer of the 'right' – that is, Western – attitudes and forms of behaviour from developed to less developed countries would bring about positive change goes back to the nineteenth-century idea of the 'civilizing mission' of Europe in the colonies. It was also central to the modernization theories of the 1950s and 1960s (Rostow, 1960), according to which: '[d]evelopment was a question of instilling the "right" orientations – values and norms – in the cultures of the non-Western world so as to enable its people to partake in the modern wealth-creating economic and political institutions of the advanced West' (Portes, 1997: 230). Such policies failed to stimulate development and to improve the living standards of the poor. Today, neoliberal globalization theory similarly argues that Western models of privatization and entrepreneurship are crucial to development, yet such approaches have so far led to greater inequality. A certain scepticism about the usefulness of importing Western attitudes and behaviours to the South seems justified.

Brain drain or brain circulation?

In the 1950s, the gradual growth of emigration of university-educated Indians (at first mainly to the UK) led to concern about the loss of human capital and to the coining of the term *brain drain*. The trickle became a flood after the 1965 amendments to the US Immigration and Nationality Act. By 1975 about 100,000 engineers, physicians, scientists, professors, teachers, and their dependents had migrated from India to the USA (Khadria, 2008). Australia and Canada also amended their discriminatory Europeans-only legislation and started encouraging skilled migration. With decolonization and improvements to education systems in Latin America, Asia and Africa, the flows of highly qualified personnel increased. By the late 1990s, a study found that 400,000 engineers and scientists from developing countries were working in research and development in the industrial countries, compared with about 1.2 million working in this sector at home (IOM, 2005: 173).

Today there is global competition to attract human capital, and many immigration countries have set up preferential entry systems that effectively create free movement for those with skills in management, engineering, information technology, education and medical practice. Much of the circulation of the highly skilled is between developed countries, but a significant share is from South to North. This may deprive poor countries of the personnel they need to provide essential services and to facilitate economic and social development (GCIM, 2005: 23–25).

This applies particularly to medical personnel. Eleven per cent of nurses and 18 per cent of doctors employed in OECD countries were foreign-born around 2000 (OECD, 2007: 162). The OECD study reports a very rapid increase in medical migration to rich countries since 2000 (OECD, 2007: 181–182). In 2005, there were 1.5 million foreign-born healthcare workers in the USA – 15 per cent of all staff in the sector (Clearfield and Batalova, 2007). A quarter per cent of all doctors in the USA and a third in the UK were foreign-trained (OECD, 2007: 181). The British National Health Service had more than 30,000 nurses of foreign origin in 2002, and is heavily dependent on trained staff from Africa and Asia (Alkire and Chen, 2006: 104–105). Migrant health workers provide a flexible labour force, crucial for instance in ensuring the continuity of services at night or the weekend (OECD, 2007: 164).

Countries of origin, by contrast, are deprived of vital human resources. Nurses born in the Philippines (110,000) and doctors born in India (56,000) were the largest sources for OECD countries around 2000. However the impact is often greater on smaller countries, especially in the Caribbean, the Pacific and Africa. Countries with expatriation rates over 50 per cent – which means that there are more doctors born in these countries working in OECD countries than at home – include Haiti, Fiji, Mozambique, Angola, Liberia, Sierra Leone and Tanzania. Expatriation rates of over 40 per cent affect Jamaica, Guinea Bissau, Senegal, Cape Verde, Congo, Benin and Tog, while Ghana, Kenya, Uganda and Malawi have lost over 30 per cent of their doctors. Haiti and Jamaica both have about 90 per cent of their nurses working in the OECD, while the Philippines, Mexico, Samoa and Mauritius all provide substantial numbers of nurses to richer countries (OECD, 2007: 176–177).

The loss is particularly serious for countries with very low densities of skilled medical personnel relative to population. This applies particularly to Francophone African countries like Senegal. The case of Malawi has attracted much attention: the country is struggling with the HIV-AIDS epidemic, but finds that many of its doctors and nurses are attracted away by better pay and conditions in the UK (GCIM, 2005: 24). The situation is less dramatic where training schools have sprung up to prepare medical personnel specifically for emigration, as in the Philippines and some Caribbean countries, but even here the loss is a concern, especially when – as in the Philippines – qualified doctors are being retrained as nurses, because it is easier to migrate in this role (Asis, 2008).

Some migrants are unable to get their qualifications recognized or fail to find employment commensurate with their skills. The image of surgeons working as waiters or engineers labouring on building sites reflects reality for some. Refugees, who cannot plan their migration or bring their certificates when they flee, are amongst the worst affected – in the UK a Council for Assisting Refugee Academics (CARA) has been set up to support them (www.academic-refugees.org). However, economic migrants are also affected: highly trained nurses from the South are to be found working as care-providers in US and European old people's homes. Migrants who cannot exercise their skills while abroad do not contribute to North–South transfer of technology when (and if) they return.

Movement of human capital from poor to rich countries takes place not only through the 'employment gate', but also through the 'academic gate', that is, the growing movement of people with bachelor's degrees from Southern universities who move to the North for graduate studies. Foreign graduate students pay high fees, and help support the tertiary education systems of developed countries (Khadria, 2008). In recent years, the USA, the UK, Canada, Australia and Germany have all changed their immigration rules to encourage such graduates to stay – especially those in electronics, engineering and science. Indian and Chinese PhDs form the scientific backbone of Silicon Valley and other high-tech production areas.

Loss of qualified personnel from less developed countries can lead to economic stagnation, waste of the public funds invested in higher education, and depletion of tax income. The draining of scarce human resources from poor countries to make up for personnel shortages and inadequate training provision in the North helps aggravate global inequality (IOM, 2005: 175). The brain drain has therefore become a major policy issue for governments of sending countries.

However, receiving-country governments and international agencies argue that highly skilled migration can bring gains for both receiving and sending countries. The aim is to replace the notion of *brain drain* with *brain gain* or *brain circulation* (Findlay, 2002; Lowell et al., 2002). Analysts point out that Taiwan experienced substantial loss of qualified persons in the 1960s and 1970s, but later on, when Taiwan's high-tech sector took off, the government was able to attract back experienced nationals from the USA. This was an important factor in Taiwan's rapid economic growth from the 1980s onwards (see Newland, 2007). Similarly, India started setting up Institutes of Technology from the 1950s on to support national development, but many of the graduates emigrated to the USA and other rich countries. However, large numbers of IT experts later returned to help establish India's own fast-growing IT sector (Khadria, 2008).

The brain circulation argument goes as follows. If highly skilled people cannot be employed at home, they are not damaging the economy by leaving. Qualified personnel emigrate not only because salaries are higher in the North, but also because working and living conditions in the South are poor, and opportunities for professional development are lacking. Indeed, training people to work abroad might be seen as a rational strategy, because in the short run it will increase remittance flows, and in the long run it may lead to return of experienced personnel and transfer of technology. In any case it is a human right to emigrate, and it is extremely difficult to prevent people leaving. Efforts to do so (for instance by claiming back education costs from those who leave) are likely to be counterproductive: they will encourage people to leave in an irregular way, and will deter experts from returning, even when they wish to. Similarly, attempts to get destination countries to pay compensation to source countries for loss of qualified workers have proved impractical (GCIM, 2005: 25).

Development agencies and international organizations therefore suggest that it is better to try to channel skilled migration in positive ways, rather than trying to curtail it. Policy suggestions include:

- Programmes to support health systems and improve working conditions in developing countries (DFID, 2007: 29)
- Coinvestment programmes between labour-rich and labour-poor countries to upgrade education and training facilities in the former (GCIM, 2005: 25)
- More investment by rich countries in education and training of their own citizens, to reduce the need for importing skills (GCIM, 2005: 26)
- Creating databases of skilled nationals working abroad, as the basis for schemes to get them to return temporarily for specific activities or projects. The United Nations Development Programme (UNDP) and the IOM both organize programmes of temporary return of skilled personnel (IOM, 2005: 177)
- Establishing transnational links with diasporas, to tap their skills and talents.

Such measures are designed to make skilled migration into a benefit for both source and destination countries. However, it must be remembered that the developed countries have the market power to strip the human resources of the South, and that it has up to now been profitable for them to do. What hope is there of a major change of heart?

An interesting light is thrown on this by an important EU policy document: the European Commission's *Policy Plan on Legal Migration* of December 2005 (CEC, 2005b). The main emphasis in the Policy Plan is on attracting highly skilled workers. This group is to be given preferential admission conditions and easy access to permanent residence. This fits in with the existing practice of many EU Member States. The Policy Plan does also stress the need to improve collaboration with 'third countries' (i.e. countries of origin and transit) to develop 'win-win opportunities' for both the migrants and the countries concerned. Identifying and addressing the negative effects of specific cases of brain drain is one aspect of this.

However, it is far from clear that the EU Member States are prepared to make substantial changes in this area (Castles, 2006a; 2006b).

Skilled migration represents a transfer of human capital from poor to rich countries: it tends to benefit the labour-importing countries and to hamper the development of countries of origin. However, current initiatives by development agencies and international organizations show ways in which skilled migration could be transformed into a global circulation of talents, which might benefit receiving countries, migrants and source countries. Whether this will happen depends on the willingness of the states concerned to cooperate for development: receiving countries will have give up some of the economic advantages of the current situation, while source countries will have to seek ways of improving the working and living conditions of the highly qualified, to encourage them to stay in or return to their homelands. Despite some positive signs in recent years, it remains to be seen whether the will for change is strong enough to overcome short-term interests on both sides.

Circular migration

A central theme in policy debates about migration and development is *circular migration*. This is a fairly new term but refers to a long-established phenomenon: *temporary migration*, in which migrants come to a receiving area for a few months or years, and then return to their homelands. The key questions are whether temporary migration can be made to work today, when it has often failed in the past; and whether it can really benefit countries of origin.

In the 1960s, temporary migration was the basis of the 'guestworker' recruitment systems used by Germany, the Netherlands and other European countries to obtain temporary workers, who were not allowed to bring in their families or settle permanently (see Chapter 5 below). However, following the economic downturn of the mid-1970s, many former guestworkers settled and brought in dependents, eventually forming new ethnic minorities. Guestworker systems proved hard to enforce in democratic countries where constitutions and legal systems ensure basic rights for all. However, temporary recruitment has continued through the contract labour systems used by the Gulf oil states and by some Asian countries. Where human rights rules are relatively weak, it is easier to enforce bans on family reunion and settlement.

In Europe and North America, the recent revival of interest in temporary migration is based on the idea that it can lead to 'win-win-win situations' (see CEC, 2005a; IDC, 2004). The GCIM recommends that: 'States and the private sector should consider the option of introducing carefully designed temporary migration programs as a means of addressing the economic needs of both countries of origin and destination' (GCIM, 2005: 16). The destination countries are supposed to gain because they can obtain workers without problems of integration and community relations. The countries of origin hope to gain through remittances, and transfer of skills and knowledge. The third set of winners are said to be the migrants themselves, who gain jobs, income and experience.

Several industrial countries have reintroduced temporary and seasonal labour schemes, mainly for specific sectors such as agriculture, catering and construction. By the late 1990s Germany's 'new guestworker programs' (Rudolph, 1996) had led to temporary employment of around 350 000 foreigners a year (Martin, 2004: 239). Temporary labour migration schemes have also been tried by the Netherlands, Norway, UK, Ireland, Belgium, Sweden, Greece, Italy and Spain (Plewa and Miller, 2005; see also OECD, 2005: 103–105). An important mechanism for temporary migration is free movement within regional economic communities such as the EU (see Chapter 8). Free movement in the EU has not led to mass permanent population shifts (despite initial fears) because of the Community's commitment to long-run equalization of the economic and social levels of its member states. Moreover, the right of free movement encourages migrants to return, because they can migrate again if they are unable to earn a decent living at home.

However, 'many and perhaps most of the world's migrant workers are outside legal admissions channels' (Martin, 2005). Some employers prefer undocumented workers, because they can be easily exploited, while governments may like them because they fill labour needs without the need for difficult political decisions on legal migration policies. The USA and Japan have large undocumented migrant labour forces. Southern European countries have systematically used undocumented migration followed by regularization as a recruitment system, while many emerging economies in Asia have large irregular workforces. Even Western European countries that claim to strongly enforce migration rules – like Germany and the UK – depend on illegal migrants in such sectors as fruit-picking, catering and cleaning. A shift to policies of legal circular migration would therefore require major changes in attitudes and policies.

There are some signs that this may be happening, due to a growing awareness. in developed countries that border control alone does not prevent labour migration, but rather drives it underground. Since 11 September 2001, governments believe that undocumented migration can be a security problem: if migration is going to take place anyway, it is better to monitor and control entries. At the same time, there is a growing belief that appropriate policy settings could avoid the pitfalls of the past. The GCIM Report notes the danger that temporary migration programmes can lead to worker exploitation and unplanned settlement, but argues that such outcomes can be prevented by appropriate policies designed to secure equal treatment of migrant workers while abroad, enforce sanctions against both employers and migrant workers who violate the terms of the programs, encourage migrants to return home, and assist in their reintegration (GCIM, 2005: 17–18).

But how can return home of temporary workers be enforced? Ruhs argues that any temporary worker programme will involve 'some trade-off between the economic gains ... and restrictions of some of the individual rights of migrants while employed abroad' (Ruhs, 2005: 14). One possible type of enforcement is termination of work and residence permits after a fixed period (presumably followed by deportation of those unwilling to leave). Another suggestion is that employers should deposit a share of migrants' wages into savings accounts, which could only be accessed upon return home. A third idea is the required purchase of special bonds by workers or their employers, with the money to be used for enforcement or integration assistance (Agunias, 2007). This raises legal issues, since compulsory savings would violate the rights of migrant workers. There is also the pragmatic question: what is to stop migrants from slipping into the informal sector and taking irregular employment?

If, on the other hand, return is to be truly voluntary, how can incentives be created? A British Parliamentary report suggests that 'if migrants feel that a decision to return home is not irreversible, they will be more likely to make such a decision'. This can be achieved through 'the introduction of flexible citizenship or residence rights'. The idea is that migrants could then undertake repeated short periods of work abroad, increasing labour-market flexibility and reducing permanent settlement (IDC, 2004: 48). Other possible incentives include preferential interest rates on savings in approved home-country accounts, and portability of pensions and other social security rights (Agunias, 2007). Circular migration could be linked to vocational training appropriate to the home-country context, as well as business and investment advice.

One idea for increasing temporary migration is to use the WTO's General Agreement on Trade in Services (GATS) Mode 4, which covers the 'movement of natural persons' to provide services in other countries. Such service providers are seen as independent contractors, rather than employees, and may therefore not be covered by labour law, although migration regulations still do apply. Although originally envisaged for professionals (such as accountants or architects) offering short-term special services, some origin countries (such as India) have suggested that all service sector workers should be allowed to move in this way. Since up to 80 per cent of employment in developed economies is in the services, freedom of movement of service providers might lead to a big expansion of migration, which could benefit both origin and destination countries (DRC Sussex, 2005). Critics argue, however, that this could lead to exploitative conditions for migrants and the undermining of wages and conditions for local workers. Negotiations are still in progress at the WTO on this matter.

It is far from clear whether the official enthusiasm for circular migration represents a genuine desire to link migration to development, or whether it is mainly motivated by the desire to enlist country of origin governments in migration management strategies. This ambiguity is obvious with regard to the concept of *codevelopment*, launched by France in the late 1990s in connection with programmes of voluntary assisted return, and subsequently taken up by Spain and Italy (Nyberg-Sørensen et al., 2002). The central idea was to finance development projects to encourage unwanted migrants to leave the receiving country – development appeared to be an instrument of migration policy, rather than an end in itself (De Haas, 2006b). More recently, the EU has favoured *mobility partnerships* with sending countries (Schrank, 2007). For instance, in 2006 an EU job centre was set up in Mali to recruit young workers and thus reduce the incentive to migrate illegally. A more typical approach is the Italian Government's system of legal admission quotas for some 15 countries whose governments have agreed to sign readmission agreements, guaranteeing the acceptance of persons deported from Italy.

Perhaps the British business magazine, *The Economist,* was close to the truth when it said of the EU's circular migration plan: 'At last the penny drops: this is a spiffy new name to distance it from past Gastarbeiter programmes ...' *The Economist* was favourably impressed by the mixture of sticks and carrots, such as preferential visas, European money to help pay for border guards and fancier passports, and readmission agreements. The magazine enthused: 'If only a few African countries were to sign up to deals like this, there could be a big rise in deportations from Europe' (Schrank, 2007). The implication is that circular migration is above all a legitimation device for stricter border control. Circular migration shares many of the problems of past temporary worker programmes, and seems unlikely to bring about the major changes needed to make migration into a powerful force for the development of the countries of origin.

Mobilizing the diaspora for development

A core idea in current debates on migration and development is that governments and international agencies should work with diasporas (see IDC, 2004; GCIM, 2005). Diasporas are seen as having the potential to channel financial remittances, social remittances, technology transfer and circulation of skills. In Chapter 2 we discussed transnational theory, which argues that technological and cultural shifts linked to globalization allow migrants to maintain close and durable links with their places of origin. Many recent studies and reports address this issue, mainly using the term *diasporas*, rather than transnational communities. According to (Van Hear et al., 2004: 3):

Diasporas are defined as populations of migrant origin who are scattered among two or more destinations, between which there develop multifarious links involving flows and exchanges of people and resources: between the homeland and destination countries, and among destination countries.

In the past, diasporas were largely regarded as undesirable. Receiving states saw them as a form of long-distance nationalism, which could bring in threatening political and religious ideologies. States of origin saw them as potential sources of subversion and support for armed conflict (DFID, 2007). For instance the Moroccan and Turkish governments set up regime-friendly associations for workers in Western Europe in the 1960s to counter left-wing and trade union influence. Suspicion was greatest where the diasporas were the result of political exile or flight from civil war (Van Hear, 1998; Nyberg-Sørensen et al., 2002). Some insurgent movements (e.g. in Eritrea and Sri Lanka) have tried to exert control over diasporas, and to tax their incomes to fund political and military activities. However, with increasing complexity of migration flows, diasporas now generally consist of a mixture of economic and forced migrants, as well as a mixture of different social classes. Women play an increasingly significant part, by remitting their earnings, coordinating social networks and maintaining cultural links (Nyberg-Sørensen et al., 2002: 13).

Until recently, development-relevant activities of diasporas have been based on migrants' own initiatives. Now, with the 'sudden "rediscovery" of the migration and development issue and the rapid shift from pessimistic to optimistic views' (De Haas, 2006b: 11–12), states have tended to focus on diaspora associations – presumably because they are easier to influence than individual migrants. Migrant associations are set up initially to help migrants cope with legal and material issues in the receiving country, as well as to provide a focus for social and cultural activities. Some associations also take on a more overtly political role, often initially concerned with affairs in the home-country, and later on with rights, social conditions and citizenship in the receiving country (Wihtol de Wenden, 1995; Wihtol de Wenden and Leveau, 2001). Explicit involvement in development issues is in most cases a recent development. For instance, a study in the UK found that 'only a very small percentage of the 6,000 to 15,000 black and ethnic minority organizations define themselves as oriented towards international development' (De Haas, 2006b: 62).

There has been a remarkable change in the last 10–20 years: in countries of origin the new emphasis is on migrants as 'heroes of development' and efforts have been made to 'court the diaspora', that is, to channel remittances, skills and business knowledge back to the homeland. India's Ministry for Indians Overseas supports the Diaspora Knowledge Network, designed to connect highly skilled emigrants with opportunities at home. Mexico's government supports community investments through HTAs. Morocco set up the Banque Al Amal in 1989, to encourage legal transfer of remittances and to support migrants' projects. In the Philippines, the Commission for Filipinos Overseas (CFO) supports LINKAPIL (Link for Philippine Development) to mobilize the resources of the diaspora. By contrast, the Turkish Government seems to see the diaspora mainly in terms of maintaining national identity, through state support for religious, cultural and social activities (Castles and Delgado Wise, 2008).

Perhaps the most significant step for states of origin is to include the diaspora in domestic political processes through dual citizenship and the right to vote. India has introduced such measures for persons of Indian origin abroad (except in Pakistan and Bangladesh, for reasons connected with the 1947 partition of India). Mexico created dual nationality for Mexicans abroad in 1996, while voting rights were introduced for presidential elections in 2005. Since 2005 Moroccan migrants have been allowed to vote and to be elected to parliament. The Philippine Government introduced both dual citizenship and the right to vote for Filipinos abroad in 2003 (Castles and Delgado Wise, 2008). Such initiatives in some of the world's main emigration countries show a remarkable convergence (see also Portes et al., 2007).

Efforts by receiving-country governments and international agencies to 'mobilize the diaspora for development' are also quite recent. The first significant statement seems to have been in the UK's White Paper on *Eliminating World Poverty* tabled by the newly elected Labour Government in 1997 (DFID, 1997). This committed DFID 'to build on the talents of migrants and other members of ethnic minorities within the UK to promote the development of their countries of origin' (quoted from De Haas, 2006b: 61). Later documents from the House of Commons and DFID (IDC, 2004; DFID, 2007) have reiterated this approach, and it has also been taken up in statements from several other European governments (see De Haas, 2006b).

Programmes by international agencies to facilitate return of migrants have been in operation for many years (see above), but have only recently been linked to the potential role of diasporas. In 2001, the IOM and the Organization for African Unity (OAU) set up the Migration for Development in Africa (MIDA) Programme to facilitate the transfer of skills and resources of the African diaspora to their countries of origin. The projects carried out so far have been fairly small in scale, and have had mixed results (De Haas, 2006b: 18–21). The European Commission's Communication on *Migration and Development* (CEC, 2005c) recognizes diasporas as potential development actors. The measures suggested by the Commission are mainly concerned with building up databases of appropriate diaspora organizations, and helping them to find a mechanism for representation at the EU level.

The GCIM recommended that 'diasporas should be encouraged to promote development by saving and investing in their countries of origin and participating in transnational knowledge networks' (GCIM, 2005: Section 2, Paragraph 32). GCIM drew attention to the important role of HTAs, diaspora knowledge networks and other associations. However, the Commission also warned against exaggerated expectations of the development potential of diasporas. Development requires 'a healthy business environment characterized by sound legal frameworks, effective banking systems, honest public administration and a functioning physical and financial infrastructure' (GCIM, 2005: 2/38). 'Development must begin at home' and should be based on the talents of people who had remained in their country of origin (GCIM, 2005: 2/40).

Governments and international agencies have introduced a range of measures for working with diasporas, but an Oxfam report finds that 'in terms of formulation and implementation of *concrete* policies, surprisingly little has been achieved at the international level' (De Haas, 2006b: 31, emphasis in original). As for measures by national governments and NGOs, they seem to be small in scale, piecemeal in approach and at a fairly early stage, so that evaluation is not yet possible. The overwhelming problem, however, lies in the genesis of many such programmes in governmental attempts at managing migration. Where governments put their main efforts and resources into border control and readmission agreements with countries of origin, migrant associations may well be sceptical about the intentions of programmes that claim to support diasporas.

Does development reduce migration?

So far the focus has been on the question of whether migration is conducive to development of countries of origin. However, there is another underlying issue: can development (and development policy) help reduce emigration from poorer countries? This is not a new idea: back in the 1970s, when Western European countries had stopped labour migration, governments and international agencies claimed that expanded world trade could speed up development and make migration unnecessary (Hiemenz and Schatz, 1979). This was linked to the strategy of exporting mass-production industries to low-wage economies (Froebel et al., 1980).

This approach was revived in the context of increasing hostility to immigration in Europe. In 1994, the European Ministers for Development Cooperation requested the European Commission to investigate the possibility of using development aid to diminish migration pressures. The idea was summed up in a statement by former Danish Prime Minister Rasmussen in 1995: 'if you don't help the third world ... then you will have these poor people in our society' (De Haas, 2006c). The connection was stressed at the 2002 European Council meeting in Seville, when the British and Spanish governments proposed to make development aid conditional on readmission agreements obliging countries of origin to take back failed asylum seekers (Castles et al., 2003).

Plans for using development to reduce migration are based on the idea that migration is driven by poverty, underdevelopment and unemployment, and that tackling these 'root causes' can keep people at home. This leads on to the notion of a 'virtuous circle' of migration and development, in which circular migration is used to support development efforts, which will in the end reduce emigration (Bakewell, 2007). However, migration researchers have long questioned such simple linkages, and pointed out that development is likely to lead initially to increased emigration rather than to reduce it (e.g. Tapinos, 1990).

This is because people need resources to migrate. Most of the main emigration countries are not amongst the world's poorest. For instance, Mexico has reached the World Bank's 'upper middle' income group, while Turkey, Morocco and the Philippines are considered to be lower-middle income countries (World Bank, 2006). Emigrants from poor countries in Africa or South Asia generally come from families with incomes above the local average, which can pool resources to fund mobility. The very poor usually only migrate if forced to by conflict or disasters, and then mainly move to neighbouring countries. Migrants come mainly from areas already caught up in a process of economic and social transformation. Development actually helps provide the resources needed for migration.

A theoretical explanation is provided through the notion of the 'migration transition' (Abella, 1994). According to (Zelinsky, 1971), at the beginning of a process of modernization and industrialization there is frequently an increase in emigration, due to population growth, a decline in rural employment and low-wage levels. This was the case in early nineteenth-century Britain, just as it was in late nineteenth-century Japan, or Korea in the 1970s. As industrialization proceeds, labour supply declines and domestic wage levels rise; as a result emigration falls and labour immigration begins to take its place. This process parallels the 'fertility transition' through which populations grow fast as public health and hygiene improves, and then stabilize as fertility falls in industrial countries. Thus industrializing countries tend to move through an initial stage of emigration, followed by a stage of both in- and outflows, until finally there is a transition to being predominantly a country of immigration (Martin et al., 1996: 171–172). A more recent concept used to describe this pattern is the 'migration hump': a chart of emigration shows a rising line as economic growth takes off, then a flattening curve, followed in the long run by a decline, as a mature industrial economy emerges (Martin and Taylor, 2001).

However, case studies of specific emigration countries cast doubt on the validity of such theories of evolutionary stages (Castles and Delgado Wise, 2008). Changes seem to take more complex paths and to have uneven effects. For instance, in India economic change shows a marked dualism: the emergence of a high-technology sector seems to have had little effect on the impoverished rural majority. Emigration is too low relative to population to have significant effects on overall development. In the case of the Philippines, migration has been very high relative to population for many years (see Chapter 6), but there is little sign of sustained economic development, and emigration continues to grow. The Mexican experience shows that mass labour emigration may not necessarily contribute to economic development at all. Both remittances and growth of the *maquiladora* industry (factories within Mexico producing for the US market) seem to do more to deepen Mexican dependency on the USA than to bring about genuine development (Delgado Wise and Guarnizo, 2007). Clearly, each emigration country needs to be considered in detail.

The key point here is that the relationship between migration and development is too complex for easy generalizations. In the short run, development is likely to cause more migration – the opposite of what many policy-makers seem to think. In the long run development may lead to a 'migration transition', but this is far from certain and depends on many factors (Nayar, 1994). Indeed, the causality seems to be the other way round: rather than migration leading to development, it is political reform, institutional modernization, demographic shifts and social change that are needed to create the conditions for sustained economic growth. This may in turn make it less necessary for people to migrate in search of adequate livelihoods – but that does not mean that emigration will necessarily decline: where people have resources and choices they are likely to be quite mobile, as is shown by the high level of professional migration between developed countries.

Conclusions

Until recently, views on the relationship between migration and development were predominantly pessimistic: as an ILO official interviewed in the 1990s commented: 'migration and development – nobody believes that anymore' (Massey et al., 1998: 260). In the early twenty-first century, there has been a remarkable turn-around. After years of seeing South–North migrants as a problem for national identity and social cohesion, and more recently even as a threat to national security, powerful politicians and officials now emphasize the potential of international migration to bring about economic and social development in the countries of origin.

The usual explanation for this change is the realization that remittances are now the main source of external income for many countries, exceeding both foreign aid and even foreign direct investment. Moreover, remittances are a reliable source of funds that goes straight to families and contributes directly to poverty reduction, and potentially also to investment and enhanced productivity. This has led to what has been called 'the remittance mantra': the idea that remittances can be channelled into economic investments that will overcome underdevelopment.

However, behind the mantra lie other factors: developed countries desperately need workers, both the highly skilled like doctors and IT specialists, and the lower-skilled who will harvest fruit and vegetables, clean hospitals, serve in restaurants and care for the elderly. At the same time, migrants from the South (especially the low-skilled and asylum seekers) are perceived as a problem – even a threat – in Northern countries. If migration cannot be prevented, policy-makers want to control movements and maximize the benefits. However, successful migration management requires the cooperation of the governments of countries of origin and transit. This will only be forthcoming if migration also brings benefits for them. Linking migration to development is a way of addressing this dilemma.

The new discourse on migration and development goes beyond economic remittances. There is increasing emphasis on social remittances: migrants' transfers home of attitudes and capabilities conducive to development. The reality is more ambiguous: social remittances can have both positive and negative effects. Moreover, they bear disturbing echoes of the modernization theories of the 1950 and 1960s: that transfer of the 'right' (i.e. Western) values and attitudes can overcome the backwardness of the cultures of postcolonial nations.

Governments and international agencies also focus on changing what was previously seen as a damaging brain drain into more positive forms of brain circulation or brain gain. However, there is a large gap between official declarations and the reality that rich countries still make great efforts to attract and retain qualified personnel (especially in the fields of medicine, education and information technology) from developing countries. Moreover, brain circulation is closely linked to ideas on the importance of return migration. There is a strong ambiguity here: developed-country governments want low-skilled migrants to return home permanently, yet want to retain the highly skilled. Programmes for temporary 'return of talents' are unlikely to meet the long-term needs of poorer countries for qualified personnel.

The ambivalence of migration and development policies is perhaps clearest with regard to the renewed enthusiasm for temporary migration – now under the more positive label of circular migration. This is said to benefit the countries of origin, but in reality these would have an interest in permanent emigration of surplus low-skilled workers and temporary emigration of the highly skilled. The interests of labour-importing countries are the opposite, and these have so far prevailed in international debates: lower-skilled migrants are welcome in Europe, North America and the new industrial countries only as temporary 'guestworkers'. Where this proves politically difficult, employers rely on undocumented workers. The ready availability of low-skilled labour in a situation of global surplus gives all the market power to the demand side.

Finally, this chapter examined the hope of labour-importing countries that development of sending countries might reduce emigration pressures. We saw that such ideas are both theoretically and empirically flawed, and that development is likely to lead to more rather than less migration. If 'development instead of migration' policies are bound to fail (De Haas, 2006c), what are the implications for policy? In fact these are spelled out convincingly in some recent official documents. The GCIM Report makes it clear that migration policies cannot be a substitute for much broader policies designed to address underdevelopment and inequality. The world's most prosperous states need to acknowledge the impact of their own policies on the dynamics of international migration – for instance through trade reform to give developing countries fairer access to global markets (GCIM, 2005: 1/49). One might add the need to stop arms exports to conflict regions, as well as measures to build human rights standards into aid and trade agreements.

As for countries of origin, reliance on migrant remittances to fund development can be misguided. Migration alone cannot bring about development. Where political and economic reform is absent, remittances are more likely to lead to inflation and greater inequality than to positive change. On the other hand, where migration takes place at the same time as improvements in governance, creation of effective institutions, construction of infrastructure and the emergence of an investment-friendly climate, then it can be part of the solution. Policies to maximize the benefits of migration for countries of origin must thus be part of much broader strategies designed to reduce poverty and achieve development (DFID, 2007: 37–40).

That is why it is mistaken to see migration and development in isolation from wider issues of global power, wealth and inequality. Mobility of people is an integral part of the major transformations currently affecting all regions of the world. Increasing economic and political integration involves cross-border flows of capital, commodities, ideas and people. In recent years it has been the growing environmental challenges that have made us realize that we live in one world, and that national approaches on their own are inadequate. The same principle applies to migration: global cooperation is essential, and this requires new approaches that abandon short-term national interests in favour of long-term cooperation between rich and poor nations. Fairer forms of migration must be an integral part of comprehensive development strategies designed to reduce global inequality.

Guide to further reading

Amongst the many works on globalization and social transformation, the following are useful as introductions: Castells (1996, 1997, 1998), Held et al. (1999), Bauman (1998) and Cohen and Kennedy (2000). Held and Kaya (2007) is a key text on global inequality. Freeman and Kagarlitsky (2004) provides a useful critique. However, many useful discussions of globalization are to be found in journal articles, some of which are cited in this chapter.

It is difficult to find comprehensive works on migration and development, perhaps because the debate has only recently gained prominence. Chapters 8 and 9 of Massey et al. (1998) are good on the economic theory. A very useful introduction is provided by the February 2007 special issue of the Migration Information Source: http://www.migrationinformation.

org/issue_feb07.cfm (see also Newland (2007) and other citations above). Castles and Delgado Wise (2008) examines the experience of five major emigration countries. GCIM (2005) contains many insights, and is available on http://www.gcim.org/en/finalreport.html – a website that also has many useful papers. World Bank (2006) and Ghosh (2006) provide good analyses of remittance issues, and the IOM's World Migration Reports outline the broader picture (e.g. IOM, 2005). The World Bank website contains many useful papers, including Ellerman (2003); Kapur (2004); Ratha and Shaw (2007): http://www.worldbank.org/

Chapter 4

International Migration before 1945

The post-1945 migrations may be new in scale and scope, but population movements in response to demographic growth, climatic change and the development of production and trade have always been part of human history. Warfare, conquest, formation of nations and the emergence of states and empires have all led to migrations, both voluntary and forced. The enslavement and deportation of conquered people was a frequent early form of labour migration. From the end of the Middle Ages, the development of European states and their colonization of the rest of the world gave a new impetus to international migrations of many different kinds.

In Western Europe, 'migration was a long-standing and important facet of social life and the political economy' from about 1650 onwards, playing a vital role in modernization and industrialization (Moch, 1995: 126; see also Moch, 1992 and Bade, 2003). The centrality of migration is not adequately reflected in prevailing views on the past: as Gérard Noiriel (1988: 15–67) has pointed out, the history of immigration has been a 'blind spot' of historical research in France. This applies equally elsewhere, as shown by 'historians' repeated neglect of the scale and impact of immigration on European societies from the Middle Ages onwards' (Lucassen et al., 2006: 7). Denial of the role of immigrants in nation-building has been crucial to the creation of myths of national homogeneity. It is only recently that a new generation of European historians (like Bade, Noiriel and Jan and Leo Lucassen) have questioned the nationalist orthodoxy of the past. Such approaches were obviously impossible in classical countries of immigration such as the USA and Australia (Archdeacon, 1983; Jupp, 2001; 2002).

Individual liberty is portrayed as one of the great moral achievements of capitalism, in contrast with earlier societies where liberty was restricted by traditional bondage and servitude. Neoclassical theorists portray the capitalist economy as being based on free markets, including the labour market, where employers and workers encounter each other as free legal subjects, with equal rights to make contracts. International migration is portrayed as a market in which workers make the free choice to move to the area where they will receive the highest income (compare Borjas, 1990: 9–18). But this harmonious picture often fails to match reality. As Cohen (1987) has shown, capitalism has made use of both *free* and *unfree workers* in every phase of its development. Labour migrants have frequently been unfree workers, either because they are taken by force to the place where their labour is needed, or because they are denied rights enjoyed by other workers, and cannot therefore compete under equal conditions. Even where migration is voluntary and unregulated, institutional and informal discrimination may limit the real freedom and equality of the workers concerned.

Since economic power is usually linked to political power, mobilization of labour often has an element of coercion, sometimes involving violence, military force and bureaucratic control. Examples are the slave economies of the Americas; indentured colonial labour in Asia, Africa and the Americas; mineworkers in southern Africa in the nineteenth and twentieth centuries; foreign workers in Germany and France before World War II; forced labourers in the Nazi war economy; 'guestworkers' in post-1945 Europe; and 'illegals' denied the protection of law in many countries today. Trafficking of migrants – especially of women and children for sexual exploitation – is often a form of modern slavery, which is to be found throughout the world.

One important theme is not dealt with here because it requires more intensive treatment than is possible in the present work: the devastating effects of international migration on the indigenous peoples of colonized countries. European conquest of Africa, Asia, America and Oceania led either to the domination and exploitation of native peoples or to genocide, both physical and cultural. Nation-building – particularly in the Americas and Oceania – was based on the importation of new populations. Thus immigration contributed to the exclusion and marginalization of aboriginal peoples. One starting point for the construction of new national identities was the idealization of the destruction of indigenous societies: images such as 'how the West was won' or the struggle of Australian pioneers against the Aborigines became powerful myths. The roots of racist stereotypes – today directed against new immigrant groups – often lie in historical treatment of colonized peoples. Nowadays there is increasing realization that appropriate models for intergroup relations have to address the needs of indigenous populations, as well as those of immigrant groups.

Colonialism

European colonialism gave rise to various types of migration (see Map 4.1). One was the large *outward movement from Europe*, first to Africa and Asia, then to the Americas, and later to Oceania. Europeans migrated, either permanently or temporarily, as sailors, soldiers, farmers, traders, priests and administrators. Some of them had already migrated within Europe: Jan Lucassen (1995) has shown that around half the soldiers and sailors of the Dutch East India Company in the seventeenth and eighteenth centuries were not Dutch but 'transmigrants', mainly from poor areas of Germany.

Map 4.1 Colonial migrations from the seventeenth to nineteenth centuries

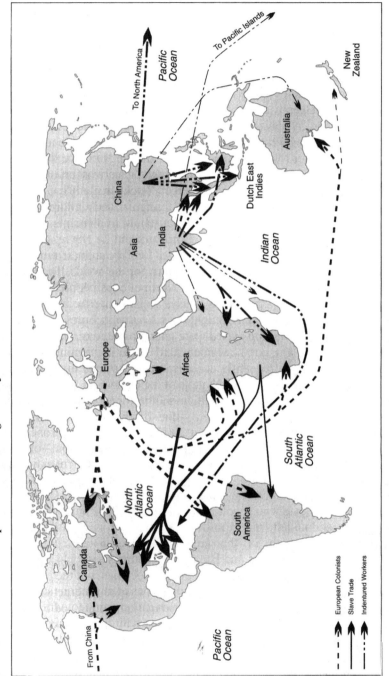

Note: The arrow dimensions give an approximate indication of the volume of flows. Exact figures are often unavailable.

The mortality of these migrant workers through shipwreck, warfare and tropical illnesses was very high, but service in the colonies was often the only chance to escape from poverty. Such overseas migrations helped to bring about major changes in the economic structures and the cultures of both the European sending countries and the colonies.

An important antecedent of modern labour migration is the system of *chattel slavery*, which formed the basis of commodity production in the plantations and mines of the New World from the late seventeenth century to the mid-nineteenth century. The production of sugar, tobacco, coffee, cotton and gold by slave labour was crucial to the economic and political power of Britain and France – the dominant states of the eighteenth century – and played a major role for Spain, Portugal and the Netherlands as well. By 1770 there were nearly 2.5 million slaves in the Americas, producing a third of the total value of European commerce (Blackburn, 1988: 5). The slave system was organized in the notorious 'triangular trade': ships laden with manufactured goods, such as guns or household implements, sailed from ports such as Bristol and Liverpool, Bordeaux and Le Havre, to the coasts of West Africa. There Africans were either forcibly abducted or were purchased from local chiefs or traders in return for the goods. Then the ships sailed to the Caribbean or the coasts of North or South America, where the slaves were sold for cash. This was used to purchase the products of the plantations, which were then brought back for sale in Europe.

An estimated 15 million slaves were taken to the Americas before 1850 (Appleyard, 1991: 11). For the women, hard labour in the mines, plantations and households was frequently accompanied by sexual exploitation. The children of slaves remained the chattels of the owners. In 1807, following a humanitarian campaign led by William Wilberforce, slave trafficking was abolished within the British Empire – the 200th anniversary of abolition was celebrated with great fanfare in 2007 – while other European states followed suit by 1815. A number of slave rebellions broke out – notably in Saint Domingue (later to become Haiti) (Schama, 2006). Yet slavery itself was not abolished until 1834 in British colonies, 1863 in Dutch colonies and 1865 in the southern states of the USA (Cohen, 1991: 9). Slavery actually grew in extent and economic significance. The number of slaves in the Americas doubled from 3 million in 1800 to 6 million in 1860, with corresponding growth in the area of plantation agriculture in the South-Western USA, Cuba and Brazil (Blackburn, 1988: 544).

Slavery had existed in many precapitalist societies, but the colonial system was new in character. Its motive force was the emergence of global empires, which began to construct a world market, dominated by merchant capital. Slaves were transported great distances by specialized traders, and bought and sold as commodities. Slaves were economic property and were subjected to harsh forms of control to maximize their output. The great majority were exploited in plantations which produced for export, as part of an internationally integrated agricultural and manufacturing system (Fox-Genovese and Genovese, 1983; Blackburn, 1988).

In the latter half of the nineteenth century, slaves were replaced by *indentured workers* as the main source of plantation labour. Indenture (or the 'coolie system') involved recruitment of large groups of workers, sometimes by force, and their transportation to another area for work. British colonial authorities recruited workers from the Indian subcontinent for the sugar plantations of Trinidad, British Guiana and other Caribbean countries. Others were employed in plantations, mines and railway construction in Malaya, East Africa and Fiji. The British also recruited Chinese 'coolies' for Malaya and other colonies. Dutch colonial authorities used Chinese labour on construction projects in the Dutch East Indies. Up to 1 million indentured workers were recruited in Japan, mainly for work in Hawaii, the USA, Brazil and Peru (Shimpo, 1995).

According to Potts (1990: 63–103), indentured workers were used in 40 countries by all the major colonial powers. She estimates that the system involved from 12 to 37 million workers between 1834 and 1941, when indentureship was finally abolished in the Dutch colonies. Indentured workers were bound by strict labour contracts for a period of several years. Wages and conditions were generally very poor, workers were subject to rigid discipline and breaches of contract were severely punished. Indentured workers were often cheaper for their employers than slaves (Cohen, 1991: 9–11). On the other hand, work overseas offered an opportunity to escape poverty and repressive situations, such as the Indian caste system. Many workers remained as free settlers in East Africa, the Caribbean, Fiji and elsewhere, where they could obtain land or set up businesses (Cohen, 1995: 46).

Indenture epitomized the principle of divide and rule, and a number of postcolonial conflicts (for example, hostility against Indians in Africa and Fiji, and against Chinese in South-East Asia) have their roots in such divisions. The Caribbean experience shows the effect of changing colonial labour practices on dominated peoples: the original inhabitants, the Caribs and Arawaks, were wiped out completely by European diseases and violence. With the development of the sugar industry in the eighteenth century, Africans were brought in as slaves. After emancipation in the nineteenth century, these generally became small-scale subsistence farmers, and were replaced with indentured workers from India. Upon completion of their indentures, many Indians settled in the Caribbean, bringing in dependants. Some remained labourers on large estates, while others became established as a trading class, mediating between the white and mixed-race ruling class and the black majority.

Industrialization and migration to North America and Oceania before 1914

The wealth accumulated in Western Europe through colonial exploitation provided much of the capital which was to unleash the industrial revolutions of the eighteenth and nineteenth centuries. In Britain, profits from the colonies were invested in new forms of manufacture, as well as encouraging commercial farming and speeding up the enclosure of arable land for pasture. The displaced tenant farmers swelled the impoverished urban masses available as labour for the new factories. This emerging class of wage-labourers was soon joined by destitute artisans, such as hand-loom weavers, who had lost their livelihood through competition from the new manufacturers. Herein lay the basis of the new class which was crucial for the British industrial economy: the 'free proletariat', which was free of traditional bonds, but also of ownership of the means of production.

However, from the outset, *unfree labour* played an important part. Throughout Europe, draconian poor laws were introduced to control the displaced farmers and artisans, the 'hordes of beggars' who threatened public order. Workhouses and poorhouses were often the first form of manufacture, where the disciplinary instruments of the future factory system were developed and tested (Marx, 1976: chapter 28). In Britain, 'parish apprentices', orphan children under the care of local authorities, were hired out to factories as cheap unskilled labour. This was a form of forced labour, with severe punishments for insubordination or refusal to work.

The peak of the industrial revolution was the main period of British migration to America: between 1800 and 1860, 66 per cent of migrants to the USA were from Britain, and a further 22 per cent were from Germany. From 1850 to 1914 most migrants came from Ireland, Italy, Spain and Eastern Europe, areas in which industrialization came later. America offered the dream of becoming an independent farmer or trader in new lands of opportunity. Often this dream led to disappointment: the migrants became wage-labourers building roads and railways across the vast expanses of the New World; 'cowboys', gauchos or stockmen on large ranches; or factory workers in the emerging industries of the North-Eastern USA. However, many settlers did eventually realize their dream, becoming farmers, white-collar workers or business people, while others were at least able to see their children achieve education and upward social mobility.

The *USA* is generally seen as the most important of all immigration countries and epitomises the notion of *free migration*. An estimated 54 million people entered between 1820 and 1987 (Borjas, 1990: 3). The peak period was from 1861 to 1920, during which 30 million people came. Mass migration is seen by some economic historians as a crucial feature of the 'greater Atlantic economy' (Hatton and Williamson, 1998). Until the 1880s, migration was unregulated: anyone who could afford the ocean passage could come to seek a new life in America. An important US Supreme Court decision of 1849 affirmed the 'plenary power' of the federal government to regulate international migration, thereby thwarting attempts by Eastern seaboard municipalities to prevent the arrival of Irish migrants (Daniels, 2004). However, American employers did organize campaigns to attract potential workers, and a multitude of agencies and shipping companies helped organize movements. Many of the migrants

Map 4.2 *Labour migrations connected with industrialization, 1850–1920*

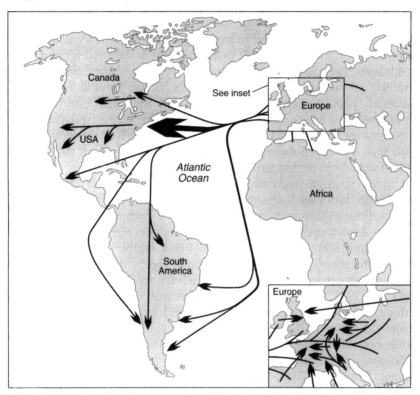

Note: The arrow dimensions give an approximate indication of the volume of flows. Exact figures are often unavailable.

were young single men, hoping to save enough to return home and start a family. But there were also single women, couples and families. Racist campaigns led to exclusionary laws to keep out Chinese and other Asians from the 1880s. For Europeans and Latin Americans, entry remained free until 1920 (Borjas, 1990: 27). The census of that year showed that there were 13.9 million foreign-born people in the USA, making up 13.2 per cent of the total population (Briggs, 1984: 77).

Slavery had been a major source of capital accumulation in the early USA, but the industrial take-off after the Civil War (1861–1865) was fuelled by mass immigration from Europe. At the same time the racist 'Jim Crow' system was used to keep the now nominally free African–Americans in the plantations of the southern states, since cheap cotton and other agricultural products were central to industrialization. The largest immigrant groups from 1860 to 1920 were Irish, Italians and Jews from Eastern Europe, but there were people from just about every other European country, as well as from Mexico. Patterns of settlement were closely linked to the emerging industrial economy. Labour recruitment by canal and railway companies led to settlements of Irish and Italians along the construction routes. Some groups of Irish, Italians and Jews settled in the East coast ports of arrival, where work was available in construction, transport and factories. Chinese immigrants settled initially on the West coast, but moved inland following recruitment by railway construction companies. Similarly, early Mexican migrants were concentrated in the South-west, close to the Mexican border, but many moved northwards in response to recruitment by the railroads. Some Central and Eastern European peoples became concentrated in the Midwest, where the development of heavy industry at the turn of the century provided work opportunities (Portes and Rumbaut, 2006: 38–40). The American working class thus developed through processes of chain migration which led to patterns of ethnic segmentation.

Canada received many loyalists of British origin after the American Revolution. From the late eighteenth century there was immigration from Britain, France, Germany and other Northern European countries. Many African–Americans came across the long frontier from the USA to escape slavery: by 1860, there were 40,000 black people in Canada. In the nineteenth century, immigration was stimulated by the gold rushes, while rural immigrants were encouraged to settle the vast prairie areas. Between 1871 and 1931, Canada's population increased from 3.6 million to 10.3 million. Immigration from China, Japan and India also began in the late nineteenth century. Chinese came to the West coast, particularly to British Columbia, where they helped build the Canadian Pacific Railway. From 1886 a series of measures was introduced to stop Asian immigration (Kubat, 1987: 229–235). Canada received a large influx from Southern and Eastern Europe over the 1895 to 1914 period. In 1931, however, four preferred classes of immigrants were designated: British subjects with adequate financial means from the UK, Ireland and four other domains of the crown; US citizens; dependants of permanent residents of Canada; and agriculturists. Canada discouraged migration from Southern and Eastern Europe, while Asian immigration was prohibited from 1923 to 1947.

For *Australia*, immigration has been a crucial factor in economic development and nation-building ever since British colonization started in 1788. The Australian colonies were integrated into the British Empire as suppliers of raw materials such as wool, wheat and gold. The imperial state took an active role in providing workers for expansion through convict transportation (another form of unfree labour) and the encouragement of free settlement. Initially there were large male surpluses, especially in the frontier areas, which were often societies of 'men without women'. But many female convicts were transported, and there were special schemes to bring out single women as domestic servants and as wives for settlers.

When the surplus population of Britain became inadequate for labour needs from the mid-nineteenth century, Britain supported Australian employers in their demand for cheap labour from elsewhere in the Empire: China, India and the South Pacific Islands. The economic interests of Britain came into conflict with the demands of the nascent Australian labour movement. The call for decent wages came to be formulated in racist (and sexist) terms, as a demand for wages 'fit for white men'. Hostility towards Chinese and other Asian workers became violent. The exclusionary boundaries of the emerging Australian nation were drawn on racial lines, and one of the first Acts of the new Federal Parliament in 1901 was the introduction of the White Australia Policy (see de Lepervanche, 1975).

New Zealand was settled by British migrants from the 1830s. The 1840 Treaty of Waitangi between the British Crown and some 540 chiefs of the indigenous Maori people was the prelude to dispossession and marginalization of the Maori. Entry of British settlers (including white British subjects from elsewhere in the Empire) was to remain unrestricted until 1974. The government provided assisted passages virtually only for Britons, while 'non-Britons' required a special permit to enter. When quite small numbers of Chinese workers were recruited as miners and labourers from the 1860s onwards, public agitation led to strict control measures and a 'white New Zealand' policy. The great majority of the population considered themselves British rather than New Zealanders. British migrants were regarded as 'kin', and a sharp distinction was drawn between 'kin' and 'foreigners'. Maori, of course, were not 'foreigners', as the Treaty of Waitangi made them British subjects (McKinnon, 1996).

Labour migration within Europe

In Europe, *overseas migration* and *intra-European migration* took place side by side. Of the 15 million Italians who emigrated between 1876 and 1920, nearly half (6.8 million) went to other European countries (mainly France, Switzerland and Germany: see Cinanni, 1968: 29). As Western Europeans went overseas in the (often vain) attempt to escape proletarianization, workers from peripheral areas, such as Poland, Ireland and Italy, were drawn in as replacement labour for large-scale agriculture and industry.

As the earliest industrial country, Britain was the first to experience large-scale labour immigration. The new factory towns quickly absorbed labour surpluses from the countryside. Atrocious working and living conditions led to poor health, high infant mortality and short life expectancy. Low wage levels forced both women and children to work, with disastrous results for the family. Natural increase was inadequate to meet labour needs, so Britain's closest colony, Ireland, became a labour source. The devastation of Irish peasant agriculture through absentee landlords and enclosures, combined with the ruin of domestic industry through British competition, had led to widespread poverty. The famines of 1822 and 1846–1847 triggered massive migrations to Britain, the USA and Australia.

By 1851 there were over 700,000 Irish in Britain, making up 3 per cent of the population of England and Wales and 7 per cent of the population of Scotland (Jackson, 1963). They were concentrated in the industrial cities, especially in the textile factories and the building trades. Irish 'navvies' (a slang term derived from 'navigators') dug Britain's canals and built its railways. Engels (1962) described the appalling situation of Irish workers, arguing that Irish immigration was a threat to the wages and living conditions of English workers (see also Castles and Kosack, 1973: 16–17; Lucassen, 2005). Hostility and discrimination against the Irish was marked right into the twentieth century. This was true of Australia too, where Irish immigration accompanied British settlement from the outset. In both countries it was the active role played by Irish workers in the labour movement which was finally to overcome this split in the working class just in time for its replacement by new divisions after 1945, when black workers came to Britain and Southern Europeans to Australia.

The next major migration to Britain was of 120,000 Jews, who came as refugees from the pogroms of Russia between 1875 and 1914. Most settled initially in the East End of London, where many became workers in the clothing industry. Jewish settlement became the focus of racist campaigns, leading to the first restrictive legislation on immigration: the Aliens Act of 1905 and the Aliens Restriction Act of 1914 (Foot, 1965; Garrard, 1971). The Jewish experience of social mobility is often given as an example of migrant success. Many of the first generation managed to shift out of wage employment to become small entrepreneurs in the 'rag trade' (clothing manufacturing) or the retail sector. They placed strong emphasis on education for their children. Many of the second generation were able to move into business or white-collar employment, paving the way for professional careers for the third generation. Interestingly, one of Britain's newer immigrant groups – Bengalis from Bangladesh – now live in the same areas of the East End, often working in the same sweatshops, and worshipping in the same buildings (synagogues converted to mosques). However, they are isolated by racism and violence, and show little sign at present of repeating the Jewish trajectory. It seems that British racism today is more rigid than a century ago.

Irish and Jewish migrant workers cannot be categorized as 'unfree workers'. The Irish were British subjects, with the same formal rights as other workers, while the Jews rapidly became British subjects. The constraints on their labour market freedom were not legal but economic (poverty and lack of resources made them accept inferior jobs and conditions) and social (discrimination and racism restricted their freedom of movement). It is in Germany and France that one finds the first large-scale use of the status of foreigner to restrict workers' rights.

In Germany, the heavy industries of the Ruhr, which emerged in the mid-nineteenth century, attracted agricultural workers away from the large estates of Eastern Prussia. Conditions in the mines were hard, but still preferable to semi-feudal oppression under the Junkers (large landowners). The workers who moved west were of Polish ethnic background, but had Prussian (and later German) citizenship, since Poland was at that time divided up between Prussia, the Austro-Hungarian Empire and Russia. By 1913, it was estimated that 164,000 of the 410,000 Ruhr miners were of Polish background (Stirn, 1964: 27). The Junkers compensated for the resulting labour shortages by recruiting 'foreign Poles' and Ukrainians as agricultural workers. Often workers were recruited in pairs – a man as cutter and a woman as binder – leading to so-called 'harvest marriages'. However, there was fear that settlement of Poles might weaken German control of the eastern provinces. In 1885, the Prussian government deported some 40,000 Poles and closed the frontier. The landowners protested at the loss of up to two-thirds of their labour force (Dohse, 1981: 29–32), arguing that it threatened their economic survival (see also Lucassen, 2005: 50–73).

By 1890, a compromise between political and economic interests emerged in the shape of a system of rigid control. 'Foreign Poles' were recruited as temporary seasonal workers only, not allowed to bring dependants and forced to leave German territory for several months each year. At first they were restricted to agricultural work, but later were permitted to take industrial jobs in Silesia and Thuringia (but not in western areas such as the Ruhr). Their work contracts provided pay and conditions inferior to those of German workers. Special police sections were established to deal with 'violation of contracts' (that is, workers leaving for better-paid jobs) through forcible return of workers to their employers, imprisonment or deportation. Thus police measures against foreigners were deliberately used as a method to keep wages low and to create a split labour market (Dohse, 1981: 33–83).

Foreign labour played a major role in German industrialization, with Italian, Belgian and Dutch workers alongside the Poles. In 1907, there were 950,000 foreign workers in the German Reich, of whom nearly 300,000 were in agriculture, 500,000 in industry and 86,000 in trade and transport (Dohse, 1981: 50). The authorities did their best to prevent family reunion and permanent settlement. Both in fact took place, but the exact extent is unclear. The system developed to control and exploit foreign labour was a precursor both of forced labour in the Nazi war economy and of the 'guestworker system' in the German Federal Republic after 1955.

The number of foreigners in France increased rapidly from 381,000 in 1851 (1.1 per cent of total population) to 1 million (2.7 per cent) in 1881, and then more slowly to 1.2 million (3 per cent) in 1911 (Weil, 1991b: Appendix, Table 4).The majority came from neighbouring countries: Italy, Belgium, Germany and Switzerland, and later from Spain and Portugal. Movements were relatively spontaneous, though some recruitment was carried out by farmers' associations and mines (Cross, 1983: chapter 2). The foreign workers were mainly men who carried out unskilled manual work in agriculture, mines and steelworks (the heavy, unpleasant jobs that French workers were unwilling to take) (see also Rosenberg, 2006).

The peculiarity of the French case lies in the reasons for the shortage of labour during industrialization. Birth rates fell sharply after 1860. Peasants, shopkeepers and artisans followed 'Malthusian' birth control practices, which led to small families earlier than anywhere else (Cross, 1983: 5–7). According to Noiriel (1988: 297–312) this grève des ventres (belly strike) was motivated by resistance to proletarianization. Keeping the family small meant that property could be passed on intact from generation to generation, and that there would be sufficient resources to permit a decent education for the children. Unlike Britain and Germany, France therefore saw relatively little overseas emigration during industrialization. The only important exception was the movement of settlers to Algeria, which France invaded in 1830. Rural–urban migration was also fairly limited. The 'peasant worker' developed: the small farmer who supplemented subsistence agriculture through sporadic work in local industries. Where people did leave the countryside it was often to move straight into the new government jobs that proliferated in the late nineteenth century: straight from the primary to the tertiary sector.

In these circumstances, the shift from small to large-scale enterprises, made necessary by international competition from about the 1880s, could only be made through the employment of foreign workers. Thus labour immigration played a vital role in the emergence of modern industry and the constitution of the working class in France. Immigration was also seen as important for military reasons. The nationality law of 1889 was designed to turn immigrants and their sons into conscripts for the impending conflict with Germany (Schnapper, 1994: 66). From the mid-nineteenth century to the present, the labour market has been regularly fed by foreign immigration, making up, on average, 10–15 per cent of the working class. Noiriel estimated that, without immigration, the French population in the mid-1980s would have been only 35 million instead of over 50 million (Noiriel, 1988: 308–318).

The interwar period

At the onset of World War I, many migrants returned home to participate in military service or munitions production. However, labour shortages soon developed in the combatant countries. The German authorities prevented 'foreign Polish' workers from leaving the country, and recruited labour by force in occupied areas of Russia and Belgium (Dohse, 1981: 77–81). The French government set up recruitment systems for workers and soldiers from its North African, West African and Indo-Chinese colonies, and from China (about 225,000 in all). They were housed in barracks, paid minimal wages and supervised by former colonial overseers. Workers were also recruited in Portugal, Spain, Italy and Greece for French factories and agriculture (Cross, 1983: 34–42). Britain, too, brought soldiers and workers to Europe from its African and South Asian colonies during the conflict, although in smaller numbers. All the warring countries also made use of the forced labour of prisoners of war. Many Africans were pressed into service as soldiers and 'carriers' within Africa by Germany, Britain and other European countries. Official British figures put the military death toll in East Africa at 11,189, while 95,000 carriers died. The estimates for civilian casualties go far higher – for instance at least 650,000 in Germany's East African colonies (Paice, 2006).

The period from 1918 to 1945 was one of reduced international labour migration. This was partly because of economic stagnation and crisis, and partly because of increased hostility towards immigrants in many countries. Migration to Australia, for example, fell to low levels as early as 1891, and did not grow substantially until after 1945. An exception was the encouragement of Southern Italian migration to Queensland in the 1920s: Sicilians and Calabrians were seen as capable of backbreaking work in the sugar cane plantations, where they could replace South Pacific Islanders deported under the White Australia Policy. However, Southern Europeans were treated with suspicion. Immigrant ships were refused permission to land and there were 'anti-Dago' riots in the 1930s. Queensland passed special laws, prohibiting foreigners from owning land, and restricting them to certain industries (de Lepervanche, 1975).

In the USA, 'nativist' groups claimed that Southern and Eastern Europeans were 'unassimilable' and that they presented threats to public order and American values. Congress enacted a series of laws in the 1920s designed to limit drastically entries from any area except Northwest Europe (Borjas, 1990: 28–29). This national-origins quota system stopped large-scale immigration to the USA until the 1960s. But the new mass production industries of the Fordist era had a substitute labour force at hand: black workers from the South. The period from about 1914 to the 1950s was that of the *Great Migration*, in which African–Americans fled segregation and exploitation in the Southern states for better wages and – they hoped – equal rights in the North-east, Midwest and West. Often they simply encountered new forms of segregation in the ghettoes of New York or Chicago, and new forms of discrimination, such as exclusion from the unions of the American Federation of Labor.

Meanwhile, Americanization campaigns were launched to ensure that immigrants learned English and became loyal US citizens. During the Great Depression, Mexican immigrants were repatriated by local governments and civic organizations, with some cooperation from the Mexican and US governments (Kiser and Kiser, 1979: 33–66). Many of the nearly 500,000 Mexicans who returned home were constrained to leave, while others left because there was no work. In these circumstances, little was done to help Jews fleeing the rise of Hitler. There was no concept of the refugee in US law, and it was difficult to build support for admission of Jewish refugees when millions of US citizens were unemployed. Anti-Semitism was also a factor, and there was never much of a prospect for large numbers of European Jews to find safe haven before World War II.

France was the only Western European country to experience substantial immigration in the interwar years. The 'demographic deficit' had been exacerbated by war losses: 1.4 million men had been killed and 1.5 million permanently handicapped (Prost, 1966: 538). There was no return to the prewar free movement policy; instead the government and employers refined the foreign labour systems established during the war. Recruitment agreements were concluded with Poland, Italy and Czechoslovakia. Much of the recruitment was organized by the Société générale d'immigration (SGI), a private body set up by farm and mining interests. North African migration to France was also developing. In addition. a 1914 law had removed barriers to movement of Algerian Muslims to Metropolitan France. Although they remained noncitizens, their numbers increased from 600 in 1912 to 60,000–80,000 by 1928 (Rosenberg, 2006: 130–131).

Foreign workers were controlled through a system of identity cards and work contracts, and were channelled into jobs in farming, construction and heavy industry. However, most foreign workers probably arrived spontaneously outside the recruiting system. The noncommunist trade union movement cooperated with immigration, in return for measures designed to protect French workers from displacement and wage cutting (Cross, 1983: 51–63; Weil, 1991b: 24–27).

Just under 2 million foreign workers entered France from 1920 to 1930, about 567,000 of them recruited by the SGI (Cross, 1983: 60). Some 75 per cent of French population growth between 1921 and 1931 is estimated to have resulted from immigration (Decloîtres, 1967: 23). In view of the large female surplus in France, mainly men were recruited, and a fair degree of intermarriage took place. By 1931, there were 2.7 million foreigners in France (6.6 per cent of the total population). The largest group were Italians (808,000), followed by Poles (508,000), Spaniards (352,000) and Belgians (254,000) (Weil, 1991b: Appendix, Table 4). North African migration to France was also developing. Large colonies of Italians and Poles sprang up in the mining and heavy industrial towns of the north and east of France: in some towns, foreigners made up a third or more of the total population. There were Spanish and Italian agricultural settlements in the South-west.

In the depression of the 1930s, hostility towards foreigners increased, leading to a policy of discrimination in favour of French workers. In 1932 maximum quotas for foreign workers in firms were fixed. They were followed by laws permitting dismissal of foreign workers in sectors where there was unemployment. Many migrants were sacked and deported, and the foreign population dropped by half a million by 1936 (Weil, 1991b: 27–30). Cross concludes that in the 1920s foreign workers 'provided a cheap and flexible workforce necessary for capital accumulation and economic growth; at the same time, aliens allowed the French worker a degree of economic mobility'. In the 1930s, on the other hand, immigration 'attenuated and provided a scapegoat for the economic crisis' (Cross, 1983: 218).

Box 4.1 Forced foreign labour in the Nazi war economy

The Nazi regime recruited enormous numbers of foreign workers – mainly by force – to replace the 11 million German workers conscripted for military service. The occupation of Poland, Germany's traditional labour reserve, was partly motivated by the need for labour. Labour recruitment offices were set up within weeks of the invasion, and the police and army rounded up thousands of young men and women (Dohse, 1981: 121). Forcible recruitment took place in all the countries invaded by Germany, while some voluntary labour was obtained from Italy, Croatia, Spain and other 'friendly or neutral countries'. By the end of the war, there were 7.5 million foreign workers in the Reich, of whom 1.8 million were prisoners of war. It is estimated that a quarter of industrial production was carried out by foreign workers in 1944 (Pfahlmann, 1968: 232). The Nazi war machine would have collapsed far earlier without foreign labour.

The basic principle for treating foreign workers declared by Sauckel, the Plenipotentiary for Labour, was that: 'All the men must be fed, sheltered and treated in such a way as to exploit them to the highest possible extent at the lowest conceivable degree of expenditure' (Homze, 1967: 113). This meant housing workers in barracks under military control, the lowest possible wages (or none at all), appalling social and health conditions, and complete deprivation of civil rights. Poles and Russians were compelled, like the Jews, to wear special badges showing their origin. Many foreign workers died through harsh treatment and cruel punishments. These were systematic; in a speech to employers, Sauckel emphasized the need for strict discipline: 'I don't care about them [the foreign workers] one bit. If they commit the most minor offence at work, report them to the police at once, hang them, shoot them. I don't care. If they are dangerous, they must be liquidated' (Dohse, 1981: 127).

The Nazis took exploitation of rightless migrants to an extreme which can only be compared with slavery, yet its legal core – the sharp division between the status of national and foreigner – was to be found in both earlier and later foreign labour systems.

In *Germany*, the crisis-ridden Weimar Republic had little need of foreign workers: by 1932 their number was down to about 100,000, compared with nearly a million in 1907 (Dohse, 1981: 112). Nonetheless, a new system of regulation of foreign labour developed. Its principles were: strict state control of labour recruitment; employment preference for nationals; sanctions against employers of illegal migrants; and unrestricted police power to deport unwanted foreigners (Dohse, 1981: 114–117). This system was partly attributable to the influence of the strong labour movement, which wanted measures to protect German workers, but it confirmed the weak legal position of migrant workers. Box 4.1 describes the use of forced foreign labour during World War II.

Conclusions

Contemporary migratory movements and policies are often profoundly influenced by historical precedents. This chapter has described the key role of labour migration in colonialism and industrialization. Labour migration has always been a major factor in the construction of a capitalist world market. In the USA, Canada, Australia, the UK, Germany and France (as well as in other countries not discussed here) migrant workers have played a role which varies in character according to economic, social and political conditions. But in every case the contribution of migration to industrialization and population-building was important and sometimes even decisive.

To what extent does the theoretical model of the migratory process suggested in Chapter 2 apply to the historical examples given? Involuntary movements of slaves and indentured workers do not easily fit the model, for the intentions of the participants played little part. Nonetheless some aspects apply: labour recruitment as the initial impetus, predominance of young males in the early stages, family formation, long-term settlement and emergence of ethnic minorities. Worker migrations to England, Germany and France in the nineteenth and twentieth centuries fit the model well. Their original intention was temporary, but they led to family reunion and settlement. As for migrations to America and Oceania in the nineteenth and early twentieth centuries, it is generally believed that most migrants went with the intention of permanent settlement. But many young men and women went in order to work for a few years and then return home. Some did return, but in the long run the majority remained in the New World, often forming new ethnic communities. Here, too, the model seems to fit.

As we have seen, many of the migrants moved under difficult and dangerous conditions. Sometimes their hopes of a better life were dashed. Yet they had good reasons to take the risk, because the situation was usually even worse in the place of origin: poverty, domination by landlords, exposure to arbitrary violence – these were all powerful reasons to leave. And many – indeed most – migrants succeeded in building a better life in the new country – if not for themselves, then for their children. Thus we can see important parallels with today's migrations: migrants still experience many hardships but they often do succeed in escaping poverty and hope-lessness in their place of origin and finding new opportunities elsewhere. Being a migrant can be very tough but staying at home can be worse.

Clearly the study of migrant labour is not the only way of looking at the history of migration. Movements caused by political or religious persecution have always been important, playing a major part in the development of countries as diverse as the USA and Germany. It is often impossible to draw strict lines between the various types of migration. Migrant labour systems have always led to some degree of settlement, just as settler and refugee movement have always been bound up with the political economy of capitalist development.

The period from about 1850 to 1914 was an era of mass migration in Europe and North America. Industrialization was a cause of both emigration and immigration (sometimes in the same country, as the British case shows). After 1914, war, xenophobia and economic stagnation caused a considerable decline in migration, and the large-scale movements of the preceding period seemed to have been the results of a unique and unrepeatable constellation. When rapid and sustained economic growth got under way after World War II, the new age of migration was to take the world by surprise.

Guide to further reading

Additional texts 4.1 'migration and nation in French history' and 4.2 'migrations shaping African history' are to be found on *The Age of Migration* website at www.age-of-migration.com.

Cohen (1987) provides a valuable overview of migrant labour in the international division of labour, while Potts (1990) presents a history of migration from slavery and indentured labour up to modern guestworker systems. Blackburn (1988) and Fox-Genovese and Genovese (1983) analyse slavery and its role in capitalist development, while Schama charts the history of abolition and its meaning for British and US politics (Schama, 2006).

Archdeacon (1983) examines immigration in US history, showing how successive waves of entrants have 'become American'. Hatton and Williamson (1998) present an economic analysis of 'mass migration' to the USA, while their later work (Hatton and Williamson, 2005) compares pre-1920 migration with more recent patterns. Portes and Rumbaut (2006) analyse historical patterns of entry and their long-term results.

Bade (2003) and Lucassen (2005) analyse the role of migration in European history. Moch (1992) is good on earlier European migration experiences, while many contributions in Cohen (1995) are on the history of migration. Lucassen et al. (2006) examine the history of immigrant integration in Western European societies. Homze (1967) describes the extreme exploitation of migrant labour practised by the Nazi war machine. Cross (1983) gives a detailed account of the role of migrant workers in French industrialization. French readers are referred to the excellent accounts by Noiriel (1988, 2007). Jupp (2001, 2002) provides detailed accounts of the Australian experience.

Chapter 5

Migration to Europe, North America and Oceania since 1945

Since the end of World War II, international migrations have grown in volume and changed in character. There have been two main phases. In the first, from 1945 to the early 1970s, the chief economic strategy of large-scale capital was concentration of investment and expansion of production in the existing highly developed countries. As a result, large numbers of migrant workers were drawn from less developed countries into the fast-expanding industrial areas of Western Europe, North America and Oceania. The end of this phase was marked by the 'oil crisis' of 1973–1974. The ensuing recession gave impetus to a restructuring of the world economy, involving capital investment in new industrial areas, altered patterns of world trade, and introduction of new technologies. The result was a second phase of international migration, starting in the mid-1970s and gaining momentum in the late twentieth and early twenty-first centuries. This phase involved complex new patterns of migration. For instance, former emigration areas like Southern Europe experienced large-scale immigration, while Eastern and Central European countries – long cut off from the rest of Europe – now became areas of emigration, transit and immigration, all at once.

This chapter will discuss migratory movements since 1945 to the highly developed countries of Europe, North America and Oceania (Australia and New Zealand). Labour migration to Japan, which did not become significant until the mid-1980s, will be discussed in Chapter 6, in the context of Asian regional migration. This chapter will *not* discuss the long-term impacts of migration on receiving societies, which will be the theme of later chapters, especially 10, 11 and 12. For better understanding of the data presented in this chapter, see the *Note on Migration Statistics* at the beginning of this book.

Migration in the long boom

Between 1945 and the early 1970s, three main types of migration led to the formation of new, ethnically distinct populations in advanced industrial countries:

- migration of workers from the European periphery to Western Europe, often through 'guestworker systems';
- migration of 'colonial workers' to the former colonial powers;
- permanent migration to North America and Oceania, at first from Europe and later from Asia and Latin America.

The precise timing of these movements varied: they started later in Germany and ended earlier in the UK, while migration to the USA grew rapidly after the immigration reforms of 1965 and, unlike migrations to Western Europe and Australia, did not decline at all in the mid-1970s. These three types, which all led to family reunion and other kinds of chain migration, will be examined here. There were also other types of migration which will not be dealt with here, since they did not contribute decisively to the formation of ethnic minorities:

- mass movements of European refugees at the end of World War II (post-1945 refugee movements were most significant in the case of Germany);
- return migrations of former colonists to their countries of origin as colonies gained their independence.

One further type of migration became increasingly significant after 1968:

- intra-European Community free movement of workers, which from 1993 was to become intra-European Union free movement of EU citizens.

This will be covered in Chapter 8 (see also Schierup et al., 2006: Chapter 3). The account in this section is based mainly on the literature listed in the *Guide to further reading* at the end of this Chapter: precise references are given where necessary. Map 5.1 gives an idea of some of the main migratory flows of this period.

Foreign workers and 'guestworker' systems

All the highly industrialized countries of Western Europe used temporary labour recruitment at some stage between 1945 and 1973, although this sometimes played a smaller role than spontaneous entry of foreign workers. The rapidly expanding economies were able to utilize the labour reserves of the less developed European periphery: the Mediterranean countries, Ireland and Finland. In some cases the economic backwardness was the result of former colonization (Ireland, Finland, North Africa). In the case of Southern Europe, underdevelopment resulted from antiquated political and social structures, reinforced by wartime devastation.

Map 5.1 *Global migrations, 1945–1973*

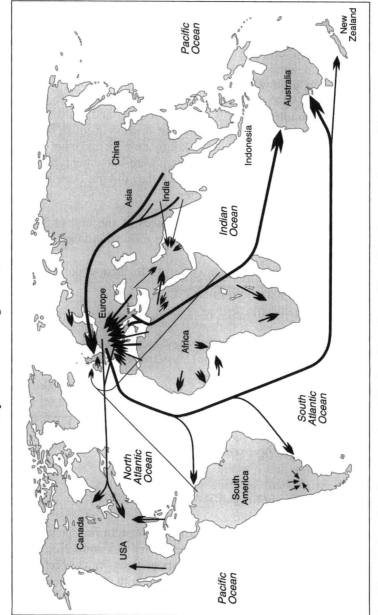

Note: The arrow dimensions give an approximate indication of the volume of flows. Exact figures are often unavailable.

Immediately after World War II, the *British* government brought in 90,000 mainly male workers from refugee camps and from Italy through the European Voluntary Worker (EVW) scheme. EVWs were tied to designated jobs, had no right to family reunion, and could be deported for indiscipline. The scheme was fairly small and only operated until 1951, because it was easier to make use of colonial workers (see below). A further 100,000 Europeans entered Britain on work permits between 1946 and 1951, and some European migration continued subsequently, though it was not a major flow (Kay and Miles, 1992).

Belgium also started recruiting foreign workers immediately after the war. They were mainly Italian men, and were employed in the coal mines and the iron and steel industry. The system operated until 1963, after which foreign work-seekers were allowed to come of their own accord. Many brought in dependants and settled permanently, changing the ethnic composition of Belgium's industrial areas.

France established an Office National d'Immigration (ONI) in 1945 to organize recruitment of workers from Southern Europe. Migration was seen as a solution to postwar labour shortages and to what the French termed their 'demographic insufficiency'. In view of continuing low birth rates and war losses, massive family settlement was envisaged. ONI also coordinated the employment of up to 150,000 seasonal agricultural workers per year, mainly from Spain. By 1970, 2 million foreign workers and 690,000 dependants resided in France. Many found it easier to come as 'tourists', get a job and then regularize their situation. This applied particularly to Portuguese and Spanish workers, escaping their respective dictatorships, who generally lacked passports. By 1968, ONI statistics revealed that 82 per cent of the aliens admitted by the ONI came as 'clandestines'. In any case, ONI had no jurisdiction over French citizens from overseas departments and territories, or from certain former colonies (see below).

Switzerland pursued a policy of large-scale labour import from 1945 to 1974. Foreign workers were recruited abroad by employers, while admission and residence were controlled by the government. Job changing, permanent settlement and family reunion were forbidden to seasonal workers until the mid-1960s. Considerable use was also made of cross-frontier commuters. Swiss statistics include both these groups as part of the labour force but not of the population: 'guestworkers' par excellence. Swiss industry became highly dependent on foreign workers, who made up nearly a third of the labour force by the early 1970s. The need to attract and retain workers, coupled with diplomatic pressure from Italy, led to relaxations on family reunion and permanent stay, so that Switzerland, too, experienced settlement and the formation of migrant communities.

The examples could be continued: the Netherlands brought in 'guestworkers' in the 1960s and early 1970s, Luxembourg's industries were highly dependent on foreign labour, and Sweden employed workers

Box 5.1 The German 'guestworker system'

The German Government started recruiting foreign workers in the mid-1950s. The Federal Labour Office (Bundesanstalt für Arbeit, or BfA) set up recruitment offices in the Mediterranean countries. Employers requiring foreign labour paid a fee to the BfA, which selected workers, testing occupational skills, providing medical examinations and screening police records. The workers were brought in groups to Germany, where employers had to provide initial accommodation. Recruitment, working conditions and social security were regulated by bilateral agreements between the FRG and the sending countries: first Italy, then Spain, Greece, Turkey, Morocco, Portugal, Tunisia and Yugoslavia.

The number of foreign workers in the FRG rose from 95,000 in 1956 to 1.3 million in 1966 and 2.6 million in 1973. This massive migration was the result of rapid industrial expansion and the shift to new methods of mass production, which required large numbers of low-skilled workers. Foreign women workers played a major part, especially in the later years: their labour was in high demand in textiles and clothing, electrical goods and other manufacturing sectors.

German policies conceived migrant workers as temporary labour units, which could be recruited, utilized and sent away again as employers required. To enter and remain in the FRG, a migrant needed a residence permit and a labour permit. These were granted for restricted periods, and were often valid only for specific jobs and areas. Entry of dependants was discouraged. A worker could be deprived of his or her permit for a variety of reasons, leading to deportation.

However, it was impossible to prevent family reunion and settlement. Often officially recruited migrants were able to get employers to request their wives or husbands as workers. Competition with other labour-importing countries for labour led to relaxation of restrictions on entry of dependants in the 1960s. Families became established and children were born. Foreign labour was beginning to lose its mobility, and social costs (for housing, education and healthcare) could no longer be avoided. When the Federal Government stopped labour recruitment in November 1973, the motivation was not only the looming 'oil crisis', but also the belated realization that permanent immigration was taking place.

from Finland and from Southern European countries. Another case worth mentioning is that of Italy, in which migration from the underdeveloped south was crucial to the economic takeoff of the northern industrial triangle between Milan, Turin and Genoa in the 1960s: this was internal migration, but very similar in its economic and social character to foreign worker movements in other European countries. The key case for understanding the 'guestworker system' was the Federal Republic of Germany (FRG), which set up a highly organized state recruitment apparatus (see Box 5.1).

In the FRG we see in the most developed form all the principles – but also the contradictions – of temporary foreign labour recruitment systems. These include the belief in temporary sojourn, the restriction of labour market and civil rights, the recruitment of single workers (men at first, but with increasing numbers of women as time went on), the inability to prevent family reunion completely, the gradual move towards longer stay, the inexorable pressures for settlement and community formation. The FRG took the system furthest, but its central element – the legal distinction between the status of citizen and of foreigner as a criterion for determining political and social rights – was to be found throughout Europe (see Hammar, 1985).

Multinational agreements were also used to facilitate labour migration. Free movement of workers within the EC, which came into force in 1968, was relevant mainly for Italian workers going to Germany, while the Nordic Labour Market affected Finns going to Sweden. The EC arrangements were the first step towards creating a 'European labour market', which was to become a reality in 1993. However, in the 1960s and early 1970s labour movement within the Community was actually declining, owing to gradual equalization of wages and living standards within the EC, while migration from outside the Community was increasing. Table 5.1 shows the development of minority populations arising from migration in selected Western European countries up to 1975.

Colonial workers

Migration from former colonies was important for Britain, France and the Netherlands. *Britain* had a net inflow of about 350,000 from Ireland, its

Table 5.1   *Minority population in the main Western European countries of immigration (1950–1975) (thousands)*

Country	1950	1960	1970	1975	Per cent of total population 1975
Belgium	354	444	716	835	8.5
France	2,128	2,663	3,339	4,196	7.9
Germany (FRG)	548	686	2,977	4,090	6.6
Netherlands	77	101	236	370	2.6
Sweden	124	191	411	410	5.0
Switzerland	279	585	983	1,012	16.0
UK	1,573	2,205	3,968	4,153	7.8

Notes: Figures for all countries except the UK are for foreign residents. They exclude naturalized persons and immigrants from the Dutch and French colonies. UK data are Census figures for 1951, 1961 and 1971 and estimates for 1975. The 1951 and 1961 data are for overseas-born persons, and exclude children born to immigrants in the UK. The 1971 and 1975 figures include children born in the UK, with both parents born abroad.

Source: Castles et al., 1984: 87–88 (where detailed sources are given).

traditional labour reserve, between 1946 and 1959. Irish workers provided manual labour for industry and construction, and many brought in their families and settled permanently. Irish residents in Britain enjoyed all civil rights, including the right to vote. Immigration of workers from the New Commonwealth (former British colonies in the Caribbean, the Indian subcontinent and Africa) started after 1945 and grew during the 1950s. Some workers came as a result of recruitment by London Transport, but most migrated spontaneously in response to labour demand. By 1951, there were 218,000 people of New Commonwealth origin (including Pakistan, which subsequently left the Commonwealth), a figure which increased to 541,000 in 1961. Entry of workers from the New Commonwealth almost stopped after 1962, partly due to the introduction of severe restrictions through the Commonwealth Immigrants Act of 1962, and partly as the result of the early onset of economic stagnation in Britain.

However, most of the Commonwealth immigrants had come to stay, and family reunion continued, until it in turn was restricted by the 1971 Immigration Act. The population of New Commonwealth origin increased to 1.2 million in 1971 and 1.5 million in 1981. Most Afro-Caribbean and Asian immigrants and their children in Britain enjoyed formal citizenship (although this no longer applies to those admitted since the 1981 Nationality Act). Their minority status was not defined by being foreign, but by widespread institutional and informal discrimination. Most black and Asian workers found unskilled manual jobs in industry and the services, and a high degree of residential segregation emerged in the inner cities. Educational and social disadvantage became a further obstacle to mobility out of initial low-status positions. By the 1970s, the emergence of ethnic minorities was inescapable.

France experienced large-scale spontaneous immigration from its former colonies, as well as from Southern Europe. By 1970 there were over 600,000 Algerians, 140,000 Moroccans and 90,000 Tunisians. Many black workers were also coming in from the former West African colonies of Senegal, Mali and Mauritania. Some of these migrants came before independence, while they were still French citizens. Others came later through preferential migration arrangements, or illegally. Migration from Algeria was regulated by bilateral agreements which accorded Algerian migrants a unique status. Moroccans and Tunisians, by contrast, were admitted through ONI. Many people also came from the overseas departments and territories such as Guadeloupe, Martinique and Réunion. They were French citizens, so there were no migration statistics, though estimates put their number at 250,000 to 300,000 in 1972. All these migrations were initially male-dominated, but with increasing proportions of women as the movement matured. Non-European immigrants in France were relegated to the bottom of the labour market, often working in highly exploitative conditions. Housing was frequently segregated, and very poor in quality; indeed, shanty towns (known as *bidonvilles*) appeared in France in the 1960s. Extreme-right groups began to subject non-European immigrants to a campaign of racial violence: 32 North Africans were murdered in 1973.

The Netherlands had two main inflows from former colonies. Between 1945 and the early 1960s up to 300,000 'repatriates' from the former Dutch East Indies (now Indonesia) entered the Netherlands. Although most had been born overseas and many were of mixed Dutch and Indonesian parentage, they were Dutch citizens. The official policy of assimilation appears to have worked well in this case, and there is little evidence of racism or discrimination against this group. The exception is the roughly 32,000 Moluccans, who wanted to return to their homeland if it could achieve independence from Indonesia. They remained segregated in camps, and rejected integration into Dutch society. In the late 1970s, their disaffection led to several violent incidents. After 1965, increasing numbers of black workers came to the Netherlands from the Caribbean territory of Surinam. A peak was reached in the two years leading up to independence in 1975, at which time the Surinamese (except those already living in the Netherlands) lost their Dutch citizenship. By the late 1970s there were estimated to be 160,000 Surinamese in the Netherlands.

Permanent migration to North America and Oceania

Large-scale migration to the *USA* developed later than in Western Europe, due to the restrictive legislation enacted in the 1920s. Intakes averaged 250,000 persons annually in the 1951–1960 period, and 330,000 annually during 1961–1970: a far cry from the average of 880,000 immigrants per year from 1901 to 1910. The 1970 Census showed that the number of overseas-born people had declined to 9.6 million, only 4.7 per cent of the population (Briggs, 1984: 7). The 1965 amendments to the Immigration and Nationality Act were seen as part of the civil rights legislation of the period, designed to remove the discriminatory national-origins quota system. They were not expected or intended to lead to large-scale non-European immigration (Borjas, 1990: 29–33). In fact, the amendments created a system of worldwide immigration, in which the most important criterion for admission was kinship with US citizens or residents. The result was a dramatic upsurge in migration from Asia and Latin America.

US employers, particularly in agriculture, also recruited temporary migrant workers, mainly men, in Mexico and the Caribbean. Organized labour was highly critical, arguing that domestic workers would be displaced and wages held down. Government policies varied: at times, systems of temporary labour recruitment, such as the Mexican *Bracero* Programme of the 1940s, were introduced. In other periods recruitment was formally prohibited, but tacitly tolerated, leading to the presence of a large number of illegal workers. Significantly, the 1952 amendments to US immigration law included the so-called 'Texas Proviso', which was interpreted as barring punishment of employers who hired unauthorized foreign labour.

Canada followed policies of mass immigration after 1945. At first only Europeans were admitted. Most entrants were British, but Eastern and Southern Europeans soon played an increasing role. The largest immigrant streams in the 1950s and 1960s were of Germans, Italians and Dutch. The introduction of a nondiscriminatory 'points system' for screening potential migrants after the 1966 White Paper opened the door for non-European migrants. The main source countries in the 1970s were Jamaica, India, Portugal, the Philippines, Greece, Italy and Trinidad (Breton et al., 1990: 14–16). Throughout the period, family entry was encouraged, and immigrants were seen as settlers and future citizens.

Australia initiated a mass immigration programme after 1945, because policy-makers believed that the population of 7.5 million needed to be increased for both economic and strategic reasons. (see Collins, 1991; Castles et al., 1992). The policy, summed up in the popular slogan 'populate or perish', was one of permanent, family immigration. The initial target was 70,000 migrants per year and a ratio of 10 British migrants to every 'foreigner'. However, it proved impossible to attract enough British migrants. The Department of Immigration began recruiting refugees from the Baltic and Slavic countries, who were perceived as both 'racially acceptable' and anticommunist. Gradually the concept of 'acceptable European races' widened to include Northern Europeans and then Southern Europeans. By the 1950s, the largest sources of migrants were Italy, Greece and Malta. Non-Europeans were not admitted at all, as the White Australia Policy was still in force. There was a male surplus among entrants, leading to schemes to encourage single women to come from Britain and elsewhere. It was not until 1975 that women were allowed to migrate as heads of families.

Immigration was widely regarded as the motor of postwar growth: from 1947 to 1973 it provided 50 per cent of labour force growth. By the late 1960s, it was becoming hard to attract Southern European migrants, and many were returning to their homelands in response to economic developments there. The response was further liberalization of family reunions, recruitment in Yugoslavia and Latin America, and some relaxations of the White Australia Policy. By the 1970s, Australian manufacturing industry relied heavily on migrant labour and factory jobs were popularly known as 'migrant work'.

New Zealand continued its policy of 'kin immigration' from Britain after 1945, with between 9,000 and 16,000 coming each year through the 1950s and 1960s. Britons could enter freely, and could register for New Zealand citizenship (only created in 1949) after one year (although most did not bother to do so). Some white foreigners were admitted too, mainly from the Netherlands or displaced persons originally from Eastern Europe. Entry of Pacific Islanders gradually increased, but many of these came from New Zealand territories and were not considered foreigners. The 1966 Census showed that, of the one-sixth of the population who had been born overseas, about 60 per cent were from Britain, and another

15 per cent from Ireland or Australia. The economic boom of the early 1970s led to government efforts to increase immigration, with a record influx of 70,000 persons in 1973–1974 (McKinnon, 1996).

Comparative perspectives

One common feature in the migratory movements of the 1945–1973 period is the predominance of economic motivations. Foreign worker migrations to Western Europe were caused primarily by economic considerations on the part of migrants, employers and governments. The same is true of temporary worker recruitment for US agriculture. Economic motives played a major part in Australia's postwar migration programme, although population building was also a consideration. The colonial workers who migrated to Britain, France and the Netherlands generally had economic reasons, although for the governments political considerations (such as the desire to maintain links with former colonies) also played a part. Permanent migration to the USA was probably the movement in which economic factors were least dominant. Yet the migrants themselves often had economic motivations, and their labour played a major role in US economic growth. Of course there were also refugee migrations, in which economic motivations were secondary. The overwhelmingly economic motivation for migration was to become less clear-cut in the post-1973 period.

How important was labour migration for the economies of the receiving countries? Some economists have argued that it was crucial to expansion. Migrants replaced local workers, who were able to obtain more highly skilled jobs during the boom. Without the flexibility provided by immigration, bottlenecks in production and inflationary tendencies would have developed. However, other economists have argued that immigration reduced the incentive for rationalization, keeping low-productivity firms viable and holding back the shift to more capital-intensive forms of production. Such observers also claim that social capital expenditure on housing and social services for immigrants reduced the capital available for productive investment. Overall there is little doubt that the high net immigration countries, like the FRG, Switzerland, France and Australia, had the highest economic growth rates in the 1945–1973 period. Countries with relatively low net immigration (like the UK and the USA at this time) had much lower growth rates (see Castles and Kosack, 1973: Chapter 9 and Castles et al., 1984: Chapter 2). Thus the argument that immigration was economically beneficial in this period is convincing.

Another general feature of the 1945–1973 period was growing diversity of areas of origin, and increasing cultural difference between migrants and receiving populations. At the beginning of the period, most migrants to all main receiving countries came from various parts of Europe. As time went on, increasing proportions came from Asia, Africa and Latin America. This trend was to become even more marked in the following period.

A comparison of the situation of colonial workers with that of guestworkers is instructive. The differences are obvious: colonial workers were citizens of the former colonial power, or had some preferential entitlement to enter and live there. They usually came spontaneously, often following lines of communication built up in the colonial period. Once they came in, they generally had civil and political rights; most (though by no means all) intended to stay permanently. On the other hand, guestworkers and other foreign workers were noncitizens. Their rights were severely restricted. Most came because they were recruited; some came spontaneously and were able to regularize their situation; others came illegally and worked without documentation. Generally they were seen as temporary workers who were expected to leave after a few years.

There are also similarities, however, especially in the economic and social situations of the two categories. Both became overwhelmingly concentrated in low-skilled manual work, mainly in industry and construction. Both tended to suffer substandard housing, poor social conditions and educational disadvantage. Over time, there was a convergence of legal situations, with family reunion and social rights of foreign workers improving, while the colonial migrants lost many of their privileges. Finally, both groups were affected by similar processes of marginalization, leading to a degree of separation from the rest of the population and an ethnic minority position.

Migrations in the period of global economic restructuring

The curbing of organized recruitment of manual workers by industrialized countries in the early 1970s was a reaction to a fundamental restructuring of the world economy. The subsequent period – often characterized as the epoch of *globalization* (see Chapter 3) – has been marked by:

(a) changes in global investment patterns: increased capital export from developed countries in the 1970s and 1980s led to the establishment of manufacturing industries in some previously underdeveloped areas; by the 1990s new centres of economic dynamism had emerged in the Gulf oil states as well as parts of Asia and Latin America;

(b) the micro-electronic revolution, which has reduced the need for manual workers in manufacturing;

(c) erosion of traditional skilled manual occupations in highly developed countries;

(d) expansion in the services sector, with demand for both highly skilled and low-skilled workers;

(e) growing informal sectors in the economies of developed countries;
(f) casualization of employment, growth in part-time work, increasingly insecure conditions of employment;
(g) increased differentiation of labour forces on the basis of gender, age and ethnicity, through mechanisms which push many women, young people and members of minorities into casual or informal-sector work, and which force workers with outmoded skills to retire early.

As outlined in Chapter 3, these transformations have had dramatic effects in Africa, Asia and Latin America. In some places, rapid industrialization and social change have taken place. But in large areas postcolonial development strategies have failed. Many countries are marked by rapid population growth, overuse and destruction of natural resources, uncontrolled urbanization, political instability, falling living standards, poverty and even famine. The result is an increase in inequality both within and between regions. Globalization brings about complementary social transformations in North and South that increase the pressure to migrate and generate new forms of mobility. The main trends include:

(a) a decline of government-organized labour migration to Western Europe followed by emergence of a second generation of temporary foreign worker policies in the 1990s;
(b) family reunion of former foreign workers and colonial workers, and formation of new ethnic minorities;
(c) transition of many Southern and Central European countries from countries of emigration to countries of transit and immigration;
(d) continuation of migration to the 'classical immigration countries' of North America and Oceania, but with shifts in the areas of origin and the forms of migration;
(e) new migratory movements (both internal and international) connected with economic and social change in the new industrial countries;
(f) recruitment of foreign labour, mainly from less developed countries, by oil-rich countries;
(g) development of mass movements of refugees and asylum seekers, generally moving from South to North, but also (especially after the collapse of the Soviet Bloc) from East to West;
(h) increasing international mobility of highly qualified personnel, in both temporary and permanent flows;
(i) proliferation of illegal migration and legalization policies.

These movements will be examined in more detail in the next few chapters. The main population flows of the post-1973 period are shown in Map 1.1. in Chapter 1.

Migrants and minorities in Western Europe

Consolidation 1974–1985

The immediate post-1973 period was one of consolidation and demographic normalization of immigrant populations in Western Europe. Recruitment of both foreign workers and colonial workers largely ceased. For colonial migrants in Britain, France and the Netherlands, trends to family reunion and permanent settlement continued. The settlement process, and the emergence of second and third generations born in Western Europe, led to internal differentiation and the development of community structures and consciousness. By the 1980s, colonial migrants and their descendants had become clearly visible social groups.

When the German government stopped recruitment in 1973 and other governments followed suit, they hoped that the now unwanted 'guests' would go away. Many Western European states proclaimed themselves 'zero immigration countries'. In fact some foreign workers did go home, but many stayed. Those who left were mainly from the more developed countries, where there was some prospect of work for returnees. Those who stayed were from less developed areas, in particular Turkey and North Africa. It was above all these non-European groups who experienced socioeconomic exclusion through discrimination and racism, like the former colonial worker groups. Governments initially tried to prevent family reunion, but with little success. In several countries, the law courts played a major role in preventing policies deemed to violate the protection of the family contained in national constitutions.

Foreign populations changed in structure. In Germany, for instance, the number of foreign men declined slightly between 1974 and 1981, but the number of foreign women increased by 12 per cent, while the number of children aged up to 15 grew by 52 per cent (Castles, Booth and Wallace, 1984: 102). Instead of declining, as policy-makers had expected, the total *foreign resident population* of Germany remained fairly constant at about 4 million in the late 1970s, only to increase again to 4.5 million in the early 1980s.

New migrations in the 1980s and 1990s

The brief consolidation was a mere prelude to a new period of rapid change and diversification. By the mid-1980s Southern European countries – the labour reserve for Western Europe, North America, South America and Australia for over a century – were experiencing a migration transition. Economic growth, combined with a sharp fall in birth rates, led to serious labour shortages. Italy, Spain, Portugal, and Greece all became countries of immigration, using labour from North Africa, Latin America, Asia and – later – Eastern Europe for low-skilled jobs (King et al., 2000) (see below).

Change became even more rapid after the fall of the Berlin Wall in 1989. The collapse of the Soviet Union and the Eastern European socialist states led to instability in Central Europe and undermined many of the barriers that had kept population mobility in check. Populist politicians and sensationalist media spoke of a 'migration crisis' (Baldwin-Edwards and Schain, 1994), and warned that 'floods' of desperate migrants would 'swamp' Western European welfare systems and drag down living standards (Thränhardt, 1996).

But by the mid-1990s it was clear that the 'invasion' was not going to take place. Asylum-seeker entries to European OECD countries peaked at 695,000 in 1992 in response to the Yugoslav civil wars and then declined (although they were to increase again around 2000). East–West movements did increase, but most migrants were members of ethnic minorities moving to so-called ancestral homelands, where they had a right to entry and citizenship: ethnic Germans (*Aussiedler*) to Germ: ay (Levy, 1999; Thränhardt, 1996: 237), Russian Jews to Israel, Bulgarian Turks to Turkey, and Pontian Greeks to Greece. Millions of people moved within and between the successor states of the former Soviet Union (UNHCR, 1995: 24–25). Russia thus became a major country of immigration, with around 2 million ethnic Russians leaving or being displaced from the Baltic states, new Central Asian states, and other parts of the former Soviet Union (Münz, 1996: 206). Movements of Poles, Russians, and other East Europeans to Western Europe in search of work also increased in the 1990s, but did not reach the extreme levels originally predicted.

It soon became clear that the end of the Cold War was not the only factor changing migration patterns. This geopolitical shift coincided with an acceleration of economic globalization, as well as an increase in violence and human rights violations in Africa, the Middle East, Asia and Latin America. Economic change, social transformation and political upheavals all triggered migrations. The new migrants coming to Western and Southern Europe varied widely in their levels of education, and in their economic, political and cultural resources. Many were asylum seekers or irregular workers, but others were highly qualified personnel in search of higher salaries or better opportunities. The result was an ever-greater diversity in the geographical, ethnic, social and cultural backgrounds of migrant populations.

The combination of the unexpected settlement of former guestworkers and their families after 1973, and the new migrations of the 1990s, reinforced the politicization of migration. In the 1990s, asylum seekers were portrayed by the media as economic migrants in disguise, and became the target of widespread hostility. Governments vied with each other in introducing tougher asylum rules. They also believed that admission of migrant workers should be avoided since it would inevitably lead to settlement and unpredictable social impacts. Policy-makers tightened up national immigration restrictions and increased European cooperation on border control (see Chapters 8 and 9 below).

Migration trends of the new millennium

Migration movements steadied for a while in the mid-1990s due both to restrictive migration rules and to economic and political stabilization in Eastern Europe. But at the beginning of the new millennium migration movements again increased sharply. There were several reasons. Economic globalization continued to increase commercial and employment opportunities, especially for the highly skilled. Many governments introduced preferential entry rules for this category. Yet governments continued to deny the need for low-skilled labour migrants, so demand was met through limited temporary and seasonal recruitment schemes, or, increasingly, by irregular migration. The EU expansion of 2004 brought in 10 new members, while the expansion of 2007 added Romania and Bulgaria. Many nationals of the new member states moved to seek work, especially in the UK and Ireland (see section on Central and Eastern Europe below).

However, despite official rhetoric giving priority to economic migration, the largest single immigration category in the great majority of European countries remains *family reunion*. In 2004, for example, family reunion made up over 60 per cent of all legal long-term inflows in France, Italy and Sweden, and around half in the Netherlands and Germany (OECD, 2006: Part IV). Asylum and other humanitarian entry, by contrast, was well below 10 per cent of all inflows in 2004 for most countries, although it was higher (15–23 per cent) for Sweden, UK and the Netherlands. Asylum entries rose from the late 1990s, peaking at 471,000 for Western Europe in 2001, but had declined to 243,000 by 2005 (OECD, 2006: 253) (see Chapter 8).

Total inflows into European OECD countries (that is, EU25 plus Switzerland and Norway) have been above 2 million for each year since 2000. The trend is upward: the highest recorded year was 2004, with 2.8 million new entrants (OECD, 2006: 233). However, new entries to some of the earlier main immigration countries – like Germany and France – are stagnating or even declining. Germany now has large outflows, so that net migration in 2004 was only 82,000. The UK had its highest-ever inflow in 2004 – 494,000 persons (OECD, 2006: 30) – and net migration was 202,000. The biggest increases in the number of legal migrants occurred in Southern Europe, with 645,800 in Spain and 319,300 in Italy (OECD, 2006: 233). However, most of these apparent newcomers were probably persons already living in the country, who became legal residents through regularization.

One of the biggest public issues in European migration today is irregular immigration and employment. Irregular migration is driven both by labour market demand for lower-skilled workers, and by differentials in potential income compared with poorer countries of origin in Eastern Europe, African and Asia. The exact numbers are unknown. Düvell notes estimates of between 0.5 and 1.1 million irregular immigrants in Germany, from 50,000 to 0.5 million in the UK and similar fluctuations elsewhere. Overall he estimates the irregular migrant population of the EU25 at 4.1 – 7.3 million (Düvell, 2005: Table 2.1).

Southern Europe

The first decades of the post-Cold War period transformed Southern European societies. Italy, Spain, Portugal and Greece comprise a distinctive subgroup of EU states. Until 1973, they were viewed as lands of emigration. Then, at somewhat different junctures, they underwent migration transitions, becoming significant lands of both emigration and immigration. In the post-Cold War period, their roles as lands of emigration have diminished, whereas their roles as lands of immigration have become more pronounced. They have come to share many of the concerns and characteristics of their EU partner states to the north, yet remain demarcated by the key role played by the underground economy in shaping inflows, the preponderance of illegal migration in overall migration and by weak governmental capacity to regulate international migration (Reyneri, 2001).

In *Italy*, numbers of foreigners with residence permits doubled between 1981 and 1991, from 300,000 to 600,000. Inclusive of foreigners under 18 who live with their parents and therefore do not hold residence permits, the total legally resident foreign population reached an estimated 1.5 million or 2.6 per cent of Italy's resident population by 2001 (Strozza and Venturini, 2002: 265). In 2004, 320,000 first-time residence permits were issued with Romanians, Albanians and Moroccans comprising the principal beneficiaries. The total foreign population increased to 2.4 million with the largest net growth among Romanians (OECD, 2006: 190).

Most resident foreigners arrived illegally or violated visa conditions, and subsequently were legalized. The most recent of the recurrent legalizations since 1986 began in 2002 and ended in 2004. It resulted in 650,000 legalizations (OECD, 2006). The upsurge in immigration has coincided with persistently high levels of unemployment at the national level, a dramatic decrease in fertility and acute crises in neighbouring areas like Bosnia, Kosovo and Albania. Nevertheless, the prevalent pattern appears employer demand-driven from the underground economy, which is assumed to be much more pervasive in Italy and other Southern European countries than in Northern Europe. Most immigrants move to areas of Italy where employment is available, not to areas with high unemployment (Reyneri, 2001).

Migration looms very large in Italy's foreign and national security policies. Trafficking of migrants across the Mediterranean to Italy's far-flung coasts has resulted in a large toll of deaths since 1990. Working with EU and NATO partner states, Italy has played a key role in linking cooperation in prevention of such migration with concrete measures of assistance to governments and societies along the Mediterranean littoral. Cooperation with Albania, Egypt and Turkey in particular led to a drop in illegal arrivals on the coast as numbers of aliens intercepted declined to 14,000 in 2004 from 24,000 in 2002 (OECD, 2006; Pastore, 2006: 118–119). Trafficking from Libya, however, remained very problematic.

Spain went through a similar transformation with profound implications for foreign and national security policies. Prior to 1980, Spain remained a land of emigration and a transit zone for migrants from Africa to Northern Europe. That status quo began to change with post-Franco democratization and rapprochement with the then European Community. The foreign population in Spain grew from 279,000 in 1990 to 801,000 in 1999. By 2005, it stood at 2.6 million, roughly the size of Spain's expatriate population (OECD, 2006).

Virtually all legally resident aliens either entered Spain unlawfully or overstayed visas. Between 1985 and 2005, Spain authorized 12 legalizations (Plewa, 2006: 247). 560,000 persons were legalized in 2005 (OECD, 2006: 216). The recurrent legalizations in Spain and elsewhere in Southern Europe have drawn criticism from other member states of the EU (Kreienbrink, 2006: 192). Unusually, even illegal residents can register with Spanish municipalities (for purposes of education or welfare). Municipal data, which includes both legal and illegally resident aliens, suggested that 350,000 Ecuadorians and 200,000 Romanians registered between 2000 and 2004. Africans tend to work in agriculture, Latin Americans in construction and Europeans in industry (OECD, 2006).

Like the other Southern European states, Spain became part of the new generation of states authorizing temporary foreign worker recruitment policies. Admissions fluctuated in the range of 20,000 to 30,000 foreigners admitted annually and several of the contingents, as they are called, served a backdoor legalization function. That is, foreign workers were not recruited from abroad. Instead, illegal aliens on Spanish soil were given employment and residency authorization (Plewa and Miller, 2005).

Spain's efforts to deter illegal migration and human trafficking from Africa played an important part in foreign and national security policies. The involvement of scores of migrants and persons of migrant background in the bombings in Madrid in 2004 constituted one wellspring (Benjamin and Simon, 2005). Spain's Canary Islands became a major target of human traffickers, especially after Moroccan authorities, at the behest of Spain and the EU, made it more difficult for *pateras* (small boats carrying migrants) to depart. Spain signed a series of bilateral agreements with African states as part of the broader efforts. The agreements typically included a provision for legal recruitment of workers from the African states (see Chapter 7).

Portugal's migration history evolved through three stages. From the mid-nineteenth century to the mid-1970s, Portuguese emigrated, leaving a legacy of some 5 million Portuguese and their descendants living abroad (OECD, 2004: 254). The revolution of 1974 marked the beginning of significant migration from former Portuguese possessions in Africa. The current stage began in the late 1980s with the prospect of Portugal's accession to what became the EU (Cordeiro, 2006: 235–237). Most recent immigrants arrived illegally or overstayed visas. Again, there have been recurrent legalizations, dating back to 1992 when 38,000 aliens received permits (Cordeiro, 2006: 242). The legalization begun in 2001 ended in early 2004 with 184,000 aliens granted 'stay permits', which grant fewer rights than residence permits. About 40 per cent of Portugal's legally resident aliens have such permits. Another legalization was authorized in 2004–2005 for non-EU foreign workers employed prior to March 2003. Many of those legalized were Brazilians (OECD, 2007: 276).

Migrants from Eastern Europe, Brazil and Africa comprised the bulk of the foreign population. By 2005, there were as many Ukrainians as there were Brazilians and Cape Verdeans (OECD, 2006: 210). Many of the Ukrainians had been smuggled in. As in Italy and Spain, Portuguese authorities struggled to achieve control. Cordeiro wrote: 'Like other EU countries, Portugal hardened its policy of regularization of immigration flows and border control, but without the expected success, which proves the weakness of the state power facing such a complex phenomenon' (Cordeiro, 2006: 243).

Until 1990, international migration to *Greece* mainly involved repatriation of ethnic Greeks from abroad and arrivals of refugees in transit. In the post-Cold War period, immigration soared and foreigners constituted 8 per cent of the total population of nearly 11 million and 13 per cent of the workforce by 2001 (Fakiolas, 2002: 281). In 2005, 1.1 million foreign-born persons were enumerated, of whom 656,000 were foreigners and 105,000 foreigners born in Greece. Residence permit data from 2004 indicated that there were 686,000 foreigners legally resident, of whom 60 per cent were Albanians (OECD, 2006). Statistical data on international migration to Greece are deficient and should be viewed sceptically (Baldwin-Edwards, 2005). Within two decades, despite high unemployment and public hostility to immigrants, Greece became one of the EU states most affected by international migration that was mainly illegal.

Central and Eastern Europe

This vast and heterogeneous region extends from the Oder–Neisse boundary between Germany and Poland to the Eurasian steppes of the Russian Federation, and from the Baltic states southeastward to the Mediterranean and the Black Sea. As the area formerly comprised a large swath of the Warsaw Bloc, the transition from Communist rule to democracy and market economies has transformed states and societies. Migration figured centrally in the crisis and collapse of Communist regimes, and the early

1990s witnessed significant outflows. Ethnic Germans from the Volga basin and other areas of German settlement migrated to a reunited Germany. Nearly 1 million so-called Soviet Jews went mainly to Israel but also to the USA. The bulk of the population, however, did not share the migration opportunities afforded such minorities.

Instead, these populations endured transitions to democracy and market economies that often increased unemployment, socioeconomic hardship and interethnic tensions. A major goal in the emergent Common Foreign and Security Policy of the EU involved aiding consolidation of democratic institutions and economic reforms in Central and Eastern Europe. Prevention of illegal migration westward ranked high among priorities. Germany resumed recruitment of temporary foreign workers, mainly from Poland. Citizens of Poland, the Czech Republic and Hungary received visa-free entry into the European Union in return for cooperation on immigration control matters, such as readmission treaties wherein the signatories undertook to accept back illegal entrants. After 1993, emigration from Central and Eastern Europe to the EU declined, although significant outflows of temporary foreign workers and of 'tourists' who took up temporary employment in the EU continued. Total numbers of officially admitted temporary foreign workers from Central and Eastern Europe in Germany fluctuated between 200,000 and 300,000 per year (Hönekopp, 1999: 22).

At the same time, more economically advanced states like Poland, Hungary and the Czech Republic became immigration lands almost overnight. They were generally poorly prepared to regulate international migration, lacking appropriate laws and administrative agencies. Official statistics did not reflect unregistered migration of 'tourists' who found employment in the informal economy. Poland was thought to have received an estimated 800,000 Ukrainians who took up employment by 1995 (Okólski, 2001: 115). Ukrainians mainly worked in agriculture and construction but were also engaged in trading activities. Disparities in levels of economic development, wages and opportunity played a major role in intraregional migrations. Unemployment in states like Belarus and the Ukraine ran very high: perhaps half of the Ukrainian labour force was unemployed (Bedzir, 2001). Many employed persons were unable to live on the income derived from their jobs in Belarus or Romania. Hence they sought to supplement their incomes through temporary employment abroad (Wallace and Stola, 2001: 8).

Most of the states in the region recorded huge increases in border crossings in the 1990s. Transit migration of third-country nationals moving through Central and Eastern Europe to points west grew fast. There were three major streams:

1.   Citizens from countries of the former Warsaw Pact who, until recently, could enter legally without a visa and then attempt to migrate illegally to the EU. Many Gypsies (or Roma) from countries like Romania participated.

2. Refugees from conflicts in the Western Balkans, especially in Bosnia and Croatia (1991–1993) and Kosovo (1999). Hungary and the Czech Republic received many more refugees than Poland.
3. Africans and Asians. The USSR had served as a barrier. When it disintegrated, its successor states became an easy-to-cross bridge between poles of economic inequality (Stola, 2001: 89). People smugglers and traffickers proliferated in this environment and became deeply entrenched, despite countermeasures (IOM, 2000a).

Within the area of the former Soviet Union there were also significant movements of populations between successor states. By 1996 4.2 million persons had repatriated, mainly ethnic Russians going to the Russian Federation. Additionally, there were nearly 1 million refugees from various conflicts and some 700,000 ecological displacees, mainly from areas affected by the Chernobyl disaster (Wallace and Stola, 2001: 15).

Overall, the first 15 years of the post-Cold War period resulted in extremely complex migration patterns. Most migratory movements were thought to be short-term or 'pendular' in nature, as is not unusual in early stages of migration processes. The key question was what would happen to migration after EU enlargement.

On 1 May 2004, 10 new member states gained accession to the EU: the Czech Republic, Cyprus, Estonia, Hungary, Latvia, Lithuania, Malta, Poland, Slovakia and Slovenia (known as the A10). Most of the existing member states (the EU15) decided to restrict migration from the new Eastern and Central European member states (the A8) over the transition period, but Ireland, the UK and Sweden opted not to. This resulted in major influxes of Poles and of citizens of Baltic republics, especially Lithuanians, to the UK and Ireland, but not to Sweden (due to labour market conditions). By 30 June 2006, 447,000 A8 citizens had applied to the Worker Registration Scheme (WRS), which gave them access to employment in the UK (Home Office, 2006: 1). The vast majority of new workers were young and had no dependants living with them.

In Ireland, by 2006, non-nationals employed represented 8 per cent of the entire work force. 31 per cent of non-nationals came from the A8 countries. Non-nationals comprised 9 per cent of the total work force in construction, and more than half came from A8 states (Beggs and Pollock, 2006). Historically, enlargements of what is now the EU have not led to major influxes of workers from the new member states. The pattern was for capital mobility to substitute for worker mobility (Koslowski, 2000: 117). Should this wisdom be revisited in light of the results of the 2004 enlargement? Apparently not: a European Commission report noted that workers from new member states represented less than 1 per cent of the working-age population in all member countries except Austria and Ireland (OECD, 2006: 107–108).

Nevertheless, the enlargement process appeared to have a significant legalization effect for A8 workers employed illegally in the EU 15 states prior to 1 May 1 2004: several hundred thousand benefited from de facto legalization (Tomas and Münz, 2006). Münz held that the accession to the EU of Bulgaria and Romania on 1 January 2007 had a similar legalization effect (Münz et al., 2007). However, the British Government, under pressure from negative media reports, decided to opt out of free movement for workers from Bulgaria and Romania in 2007.

Assessment of the period was less rosy in Poland. One million Poles emigrated between 1 May 2004 and April 2007, principally to the UK, Ireland and Germany. The size of the outflow led to a comprehensive governmental response, which included creation of new consulates. By mid-2007, the euphoria that had accompanied accession and the potential for emigration had given way to growing concerns about migration. A pay strike by medical workers underlined the depletion of the ranks of skilled personnel. Concerns also mounted over abusive treatment of Polish workers abroad, especially in Italy. The Foreign Ministry began to warn Poles about potential risks of emigration.

As the most populous of the A8 states, Poland exemplified the complexities of the migration transition. In 1997, adoption of a new Aliens Law made it more difficult for Ukrainians, Russians and others to shuttle back and forth across Poland's eastern borders. As a result, more migrants took up employment in agriculture and construction. By 2003, when Poland imposed visa requirements upon citizens of Ukraine, Belarus and the Russian Federation, some Polish employers had become dependent on migrant workers. The exodus of Polish workers after 1 May 2004 increased employer fears of labour shortages. Poland, like other Eastern and Central European countries, was experiencing declining fertility and an ageing population. By 2007, the governments of these countries were beginning to see themselves as future immigration lands, and were planning to establish the necessary legal and institutional arrangements.

Poland, like most other A8 states, received vast influxes of foreign direct investments (FDI), especially in the manufacturing sector, as firms moved eastward to benefit from much lower pay than in Germany or France. By 2007, perceived shortages of skilled labour became a concern as the Polish unemployment rate declined to 13.8 per cent. Regionwide, five of the eight states recorded net population losses in 2006 (Perry and Power, 2007). It was in this context that Poland lifted restrictions on short-term workers from Belarus and Ukraine. In 2007, several hundred workers from Uzbekistan and Tajikistan arrived (Perry and Power, 2007).

Ukraine and the Russian Federation have emerged as major source countries for migration to OECD member states since 2000 (OECD, 2006: 34). However, they too face dramatic demographic decline in the future. The bifurcation of the region into EU member states and those on the outside looking in seemed durable, especially after the failed referenda on a constitution for the EU in 2005. While the referenda did not pertain to migration per se, the outcomes reflected voter fear of increased labour migration from A8 countries as well as from Turkey. The question of whether international migration could become a theme of increased bilateral and regional cooperation stood starkly posed. A major issue in Ukraine–EU relations, for example, concerned Ukraine's reluctance to sign a readmission treaty for fear of becoming a 'dumping ground' for illegal entrants apprehended in the EU space (Pankevych, 2006: 205–206). Much appeared to hinge on whether the EU could introduce the European migration policy called for by the 1997 Treaty of Amsterdam but which so far remains unachieved (Straubhaar, 2006).

Europe's changing population

Over half a century of immigration has transformed European populations. Germany (reunited in 1990 following the collapse of the GDR) is a good example. By 1996, the total *foreign resident population* was 7.3 million – a figure that was to remain fairly constant until 2003. However, in 2004 the figure fell sharply to 6.7 million (OECD, 2006: 274). This was due to a mixture of factors: administrative measures to delete foreigners who had left Germany from the Central Aliens Register, the decline of net migration to Germany, and the decline in the number of births of foreign children, following the 2000 Naturalization Law (OECD, 2006: 182). By contrast, the *foreign-born population* (which includes naturalized immigrants, but excludes German-born children with foreign nationality) increased from 9.4 million in 1995 to 10.6 million in 2003 (OECD, 2006: 262). Thus the foreign resident population made up 8.9 per cent of Germany's total population, while the foreign-born population made up 12.9 per cent.

Such complications underline the fact that migration statistics depend very much on administrative rules and practices. Table 5.2 gives information on the growth of foreign resident populations in some European immigration countries, while Table 5.3 gives information on foreign-born populations.

In 1995 the foreign resident populations of European OECD countries totalled 19.4 million. (OECD, 1997: 30). By 2005, this total came to over 24 million. However, the foreign-born population of these countries was 39 million persons. The foreign resident population of the European OECD countries made up about 5 per cent of the total population, while the foreign-born population accounted for over 8 per cent. If one adds the non-European OECD countries in Table 5.3 (USA, Australia, Canada and New Zealand), the OECD was home to about 89 million foreign-born persons – close to half the world's migrants. Significantly, many European countries now have immigrant population shares on a par with the USA – historically viewed as the most significant immigration country (see IOM, 2005: 139–144).

Such trends have important demographic and economic implications. EU countries are characterised by a low total fertility rate: a lifetime average of 1.5 children per woman – well below the replacement rate of 2.1. Life expectancy is increasing, and populations are ageing, so that fewer people of working age will in future have to support more elderly people (UN,

Table 5.2   *Foreign resident population in selected European OECD countries (thousands)*

Country	1980	1985	1990	1995	2000	2005	Per cent of total population 2005
Austria	283	272	413	724	702	801	9.7
Belgium	–	845	905	910	862	901	8.6
Czech Rep.	–	–	–	159	201	278	2.7
Denmark	102	117	161	223	259	270	5.0
Finland	–	–	–	69	91	114	2.2
France	3,714[a]	–	3,597	–	3,263[b]	–	5.6[b]
Germany	4,453	4,379	5,242	7,174	7,297	6,756	8.8
Greece	–	–	–	–	305	553	5.2
Hungary	–	–	–	140	110	154	1.5
Ireland	–	79	80	94	126	259	6.3
Italy	299	423	781	991	1,380	2,670	4.6
Luxembourg	94	98	–	138	165	189	40.0
Netherlands	521	553	692	757	668	691	4.2
Norway	83	102	143	161	184	223	4.8
Poland	–	–	–	–	49[c]	–	0.1[c]
Portugal	–	–	108	168	208	432	4.1
Slovak Rep.	–	–	–	22	29	26	0.5
Spain	–	242	279	500	896	2,739	6.2
Sweden	422	389	484	532	477	480	5.3
Switzerland	893	940	1,100	1,331	1,384	1,512	20.3
UK	–	1,731	1,875	2,060	2,342	3,035	5.2

Notes: For the differences between foreign resident population and foreign-born population, see *Note on Migration Statistics* at the front of this book.
The figures for the UK in this table are not comparable with the birthplace figures given in Table 5.1.
The figures for Germany refer to the area of the old Federal Republic up to 1990, and to the whole of united Germany thereafter.
– data not available
[a] Figure for 1982
[b] Figure for 1999, for metropolitan France only
[c] Figure for 2002

Sources: OECD (1992: 131; 1997: 29; 2000; 2001; 2007: 343).

2000). Eurostat projections show that the population of the EU25 as a whole is likely to fall slightly from 457 million in 2004 to 450 million by 2050 (a decline of 1.5 per cent). However, the decline will be much sharper in Germany (9.6 per cent), Italy (8.9 per cent) and the Eastern and Central European states, which joined the EU in 2004 (11.7 per cent). More serious still is the decline in population of working age (15–64): currently in the EU25, 67 per cent of the population are of working age, compared with 16 per cent who are 65 and over. By 2050, a working-age population of 57 per cent will have to support 30 per cent aged 65 and over (CEC, 2005a: Annexe Tables 1 and 2; see also Holzmann and Münz, 2006).

Table 5.3   *Foreign-born population in selected OECD countries (thousands)*

Country	1995	2000	2005	Share in total population 2005, per cent
Australia	4,164	4,417	4,826	23.8
Austria	–	843	1,101	13.5
Belgium	983	1,059	1,269	12.1
Canada	4,867	5,327	5,896	19.1
Czech Republic	–	434	523	5.1
Denmark	250	309	350	6.5
Finland	106	136	177	3.4
France	–	4,306[a]	4,926	8.1
Germany	9,378	10,256	10,621[b]	12.9[b]
Greece	–	–	1,122[c]	10.3[c]
Hungary	284	295	332	3.3
Ireland	–	329	487	11.0
Italy	–	–	1,147[c]	2.5[c]
Luxembourg	128	145	152	33.4
Netherlands	1,407	1,615	1,735	10.6
New Zealand	–	663	796	19.4
Norway	240	305	380	8.2
Poland	–	–	776[d]	1.6[d]
Portugal	533	523	661	6.3
Slovak Republic	–	119[c]	249	3.9[e]
Spain	–	–	2,172[c]	5.3[c]
Sweden	936	1,004	1,126	12.4
Switzerland	1,503	1,571	1,773	23.8
UK	4,031	4,667	5,842	9.7
USA	24,648	31,108	38,343	12.9

Notes: For the differences between foreign resident population and foreign-born population, see *Note on Migration Statistics* at the front of this book.
[a] Figure for 1999
[b] Figure for 2003
[c] Figure for 2001
[d] Figure for 2002
[e] Figure for 2004

Sources: (OECD, 2006: 262; 2007: 330).

As a result, nearly all population growth now comes through immigration. Münz *et al* (2007) put population growth for the EU27 at 1.9 million persons in 2005, of which 1.6 million was through immigration and 300,000 through natural increase. Many European countries would already have a declining population today if it were not for immigration. The total population of the EU27 in 2006 was 491 million, of whom 40.6 million were legally resident foreign-born persons. Of these, 13.2 million (2.7 per cent of total EU population) were from other EU states, while 27.3 million (5.6 per cent) were from non-EU states (Münz et al., 2007: 2–4).

This represents an important historical shift: Europe went from an area of mass emigration in the nineteenth and early twentieth centuries, to an area of mainly intra-European labour movement from 1945–1974. Today Europe is an area of large-scale inflows from all over the world. Moreover, this inflow increasingly concerns the whole of Europe – not just the older industrial areas of Northwestern Europe as in the past. This has enormous implications for European society and politics, as will be discussed in later chapters.

North America and Oceania

Migration to the *USA* grew steadily after 1970. Total immigration, which refers to aliens granted legal permanent resident status, rose from 4.5 million in 1971–1980, to 7.3 million in 1981–1990 and to 9.1 million in 1991–2000. In 2006, 1.3 million Permanent Resident Aliens were admitted. Mexicans, Chinese and Filipinos comprised the largest groups. Most of the new residents already lived in the USA and most had relatives in the USA. Naturalizations rose to 702,587 in 2006 from 604,280. Mexicans, Indians and Filipinos were the most numerous amongst the new US citizens (DHS, 2006a and 2006b).

As for refugees, the Department of Homeland Security (DHS), which incorporated the former Immigration and Naturalization Service (INS), reported that 41,150 had been admitted in 2006 as compared with 53,813 in 2005. Refugee admissions plummeted in the wake of 9/11 due to more stringent security requirements in processing. Middle Eastern and African refugees were particularly adversely affected. An additional 26,113 persons were granted asylum in 2006, up from 25,257 in 2005. Chinese, Haitians and Columbians formed the largest groups.

Total admissions of temporary foreign workers/trainees and their families have increased markedly in recent years (Martin, 2006). In 2005, 883,706 were admitted but among them only 7,011 were H-2A foreign agricultural workers. This figure compared with 22,141 in 2004 and 14,094 in 2003 (DHS, 2006b).The decline reflected employer dissatisfaction with the programme and the widespread availability of undocumented agricultural workers. Farm workers are the worst-paid group in the US economy and most are Mexicans.

Canada remains one of the few countries in the world with an active and expansive permanent immigration policy, which aims to admit the equivalent of 1 per cent of its total population of about 30 million each year. The 5.4 million foreign-born residents made up 18.4 per cent of the Canadian population at the 2001 Census (Statistics Canada, 2007) – one of the highest shares in any developed country. There is a broad political consensus behind this policy, contrasting sharply with the lack of consensus on immigration policy in the USA.

Canada recorded 251,649 landings, as the Canadians term them, in 2006, of which half went to the province of Ontario. Entries from Asia,

Africa and the Middle East have grown, while European migration has declined. In 2004, the top four countries of origin of permanent immigrants were China, India, the Philippines and Pakistan, followed by the USA, Iran and UK (OECD, 2006: 236). Of the 60,975 new immigrants whose skill level was identified, 31,214 were professional and 23,214 were skilled and technical. These figures reflected a shift in the Canadian system for rating applicants for immigration to award more points for educational and technical skills. Nevertheless, there was concern in Canada that the shift had contributed to growing unemployment and underemployment of immigrants, despite their impressive credentials (Reitz, 2007a, 2007b).

Canada has witnessed a steady increase in temporary foreign workers since 1993. There were 64,871 in 1993 and 112,658 in 2006. Among those were 13,933 Mexican workers in 2006 as compared with 6,133 in 1997 (CIC, 2006). Since 1974, the Mexican and Canadian governments have cooperated on a programme bringing Mexicans to work in Canadian agriculture, particularly the hothouse-based tomato industry in Ontario. Recruitment used to be limited to married men, but recently some women have been recruited as well. The average stay in Canada is 5 months, the minimum 6 weeks. Half to two-thirds of the workers return to the same employer each season.

Immigration has been one the main factors shaping *Australia's* population and society. The long-term result has been the shift from a predominantly white population of mainly British identity to one of the most diverse multiethnic populations in the world. The abandonment of the White Australia Policy in 1973 coincided with a new official rhetoric that redefined Australia as a multicultural society, built through worldwide immigration. Australia has also maintained its traditional role as a resettlement country for refugees, through its Humanitarian Program. Significant Asian immigration began in the late 1970s with the arrival of Indo-Chinese refugees. Australia also attracted Latin Americans (both workers and refugees) and Africans (in fairly small numbers). New Zealanders (who can enter freely) came in increasing numbers. In the 1990s, economic and political crises brought about new inflows from the former Soviet Union, former Yugoslavia, the Middle East and South Africa. All legal immigrants (including refugees) have the right to family reunion, which has been the largest admission category.

The climate changed in 1996, with the election of a centre-right coalition government sceptical of immigration and multiculturalism. The Howard Government set out to orient immigration policy more strongly to economic needs. Public concern about irregular entry of 'boat people' (actually never more than 4,000 persons a year) led to strict border control measures, including compulsory detention of asylum seekers (often in remote camps). Yet a buoyant economy and labour shortages in many sectors actually led to a growth in planned immigration in the early twenty-first century (Castles and Vasta, 2004).

Permanent nonhumanitarian inflows in 2005–2006 totalled 142,930, the highest for over a decade (Australian migration statistics relate to financial years, from July to June) (DIAC, 2007c). In addition, 14,144 persons were admitted under the Humanitarian Program(also the highest figure for years) (DIAC, 2007b). Temporary migration is also growing: in 2004–2005, 93,513 temporary work visas were granted. Overseas students were also important, with 116,716 visas. Overseas students provide a source of part-time labour while studying, and are now permitted to shift to permanent employment after graduation, if they have skills in demand. Another important source of temporary labour is working holidaymakers (generally young people from other developed countries, with 104,353 visas in 2004–2005 (DIAC, 2007a). It remains to be seen how the Australian Labor Party Government elected in November 2007 will cope with challenges of new types of migration.

New Zealand has also experienced sustained immigration, increasing diversity of origins and a trend towards temporary migration. Permanent immigrant inflows grew in waves, with peaks in the early 1990s (55,600 in 1995), then again in the new century (54,400 in 2001), but declined to 36,200 in 2004. As New Zealand emigration (especially to Australia) has also increased, net permanent migration was only 7,000 in 2004–2005. Temporary migration, including temporary workers, students and working holidaymakers, was 145,100 in 2004–2005. Recent policy changes have been concerned with increasing skilled migration and encouraging students to stay on for employment after graduation (OECD, 2006: 202–203, 233).

In 2004, New Zealand's total immigrant population was estimated at 763,600 – 18.8 per cent of the total population. Non-Europeans now predominate as a result of increased entries from Asia and the Pacific since the 1980s. In the 2001 Census, UK-born persons made up only 31 per cent of the immigrant population, followed by the Australian-born (8 per cent). Next came Samoa, China, South Africa, Fiji, Netherlands, India, Tonga and Korea (OECD, 2006: 262, 268). In New Zealand too, migration has led to fundamental changes, with important consequences for culture, identity and politics.

Conclusions

This overview of international migration to Europe, North America and Oceania since 1945 can lay no claim to completeness. The upsurge in migratory movements in the post-1945 period, and particularly since the mid-1980s, indicates that international migration has become a crucial part of global transformations. It is linked to the internationalization of production, distribution and investment and, equally important, to the globalization of culture. The end of the Cold War and the collapse of the Soviet bloc added new dimensions to global restructuring. One was the redirection of some investment of the advanced capitalist countries away from the South towards Eastern Europe. Another dimension was the growth of East–West migration, with previously isolated countries entering global migratory flows.

Many large-scale migrations have been primarily economic in their motivations. Labour migration was particularly significant in the 1945–1973 period. In the following years, other types of migration, such as family reunion and refugee and asylum-seeker movements, took on greater importance. Even migrations in which noneconomic motivations have been predominant have had significant effects on the labour markets and economies of both sending and receiving areas. But no migration can ever be adequately understood solely on the basis of economic criteria. Economic causes of migration have their roots in processes of social, cultural and political change. Furthermore, the effect on both sending and receiving societies is always more than just economic: immigration changes demographic and social structures, affects political institutions and helps to reshape cultures.

In the early 1990s, Western Europe was gripped by fears of uncontrolled influxes from the East and South. By 1995 this scenario had receded, due both to changes in sending countries, and to the tightening of entry rules and border controls. In the second edition of this book (published in 1998) we noted a slowdown in migration to developed countries, but argued that this might be a passing phase, like that of the late 1970s. This indeed proved the case, with significant increases in entry from about 1997, as well as diversification of migratory types. As we noted in the third edition (2003), the main growth at this time was in asylum, irregular migration, and skilled migration. Since then, rich countries have vied with each other to attract skilled migrants, while asylum applications have declined significantly – partly as a result of more restrictive rules in receiving countries. Yet strict border controls, the building of walls (as on the US–Mexico border) and increased marine surveillance (in the Caribbean and Mediterranean) seem to have done little to stop inflows of irregular labour migrants. This conflict between migratory pressures and state measures will be the theme of Chapter 8.

Guide to further reading

The *Age of Migration* website www.age-of-migration.com includes text 5.1, which provides some additional detail on migration to Greece. The website material related to Chapter 11, on Australia, Germany, Canada, the Netherlands and Sweden, is also useful for understanding migration patterns to these countries.

For current data on migration flows, it is best to consult the online sources listed at the end of Chapter 1. For a general overview and analysis for developed countries, the annual *International Migration Outlook* of the OECD is invaluable. The *World Migration Reports* of the IOM and the regularly updated material provided by the *Migration Information Source* are also highly recommended.

Castles and Kosack (1973) is a comparative study of immigrant workers in France, Germany, Switzerland and the UK from 1945 to 1973, while Miller (1981) provides an early analysis of the political effects of migration. Castles et al. (1984) continue the story for the period following the ending of recruitment in 1973–1974. Portes and Rumbaut (2006) provide a detailed account of migration and settlement in the USA, while Collins (1991) and Jupp (2002) examine postwar migration to Australia. A history of migration to New Zealand can be found in McKinnon (1996).

The recent explosion of literature on migration to developed countries makes it hard to single out reading. A useful global comparative study on migration policy is Cornelius et al. (2004). Geddes (2003) is good on recent politics of migration, Schierup et al. (2006) examine the 'European dilemma' of migration and increasing diversity, Green (2004) gives an account of recent changes in Germany, while Düvell (2005) provides a good overview of irregular migration. Other useful books include, for Western Europe, Messina (2002), for Central Europe Wallace and Stola (2001), and for Southern Europe Baganha (1997), Luso-American Development Foundation (1999), King et al. (2000) and King (2001). Horowitz and Noiriel (1992) and Togman (2002) provide comparisons between France and the USA.

Chapter 6

Migration in the Asia–Pacific Region

Over half the world's population lives in the Asia–Pacific region. In 2000, Asia hosted 53 million out of the world's 191 million migrants (UNDESA, 2004). Strictly speaking, the Asia–Pacific region includes the Gulf oil states, Turkey and the rest of the Middle East. However, that area is covered in Chapter 7, so this Chapter will be concerned mainly with South Asia (the Indian subcontinent), East Asia and South-East Asia. Also part of the Asia–Pacific region is Oceania: Australia, New Zealand and many Pacific islands. Some aspects of this subregion will be discussed here, and others in the chapters on highly developed immigration countries.

In the 1970s and 1980s international migration from Asia grew dramatically. The main destinations were North America, Australia and the oil economies of the Middle East. Since the 1990s, the major growth has been in migration within Asia, particularly from less developed countries with massive labour surpluses to fast-growing newly industrializing countries (NICs). The international movements are often linked to internal migration. Skeldon has shown the complexity of the relationship between internal and international migration, and argued that both should be analysed as a reaction to the penetration of external forces such as colonialism and globalization (Skeldon, 1997, 2006a) (as discussed in Chapter 3). India is experiencing large-scale internal migration and urbanization. In China, massive flows from rural areas in the centre and west to the new industrial areas of the east (especially Beijing, Shanghai and the Pearl River Delta) have created a 'floating population' of 100–150 million people. Indonesia's *transmigrasi* programme has shifted about 1.7 million families from densely populated Java to more sparsely populated islands like Sumatra, Sulawesi and Irian Jaya since 1969 (Tirtosudarmo, 2001: 211). Other countries in the region are undergoing similar changes.

Forced internal displacement is also a major problem (Cohen and Deng, 1998): in 2006, there were 3 million internally displaced persons (IDPs) in Asia – not including the 2.7 million in the Middle East (IDMC, 2007: 43). The main causes were conflict, violence or human rights abuses. Millions more are displaced by development projects, such as large dams, while others flee environmental change and natural disasters, like volcanoes and floods. In some places, vulnerable groups (especially indigenous peoples or ethnic minorities) may experience multiple types, as in Sri Lanka, where people have been repeatedly displaced by large dam projects, civil war and then the 2004 tsunami. Internal migration will not be dealt with here, but it is important to realize that it is often the first step in a process that leads to international movement.

Asian governments seek to control migration strictly, and migrants' rights are often very limited. Policy-makers encourage temporary labour migration, but prohibit family reunion and permanent settlement. Most migration in the region is temporary, although trends towards long-term stay are becoming evident in some cases. However, strict entry controls may (as in other parts of the world) prove counterproductive, leading to increased irregular migration, and even to unplanned settlement, as irregular migrants prefer to stay on rather than run the risks of multiple border crossings (Hugo, 2005).

The development of Asian migration

Asian migration is not new: westward movements from Central Asia helped shape European history in the Middle Ages, while Chinese migration to South-East Asia goes back centuries. In the colonial period, millions of indentured workers were recruited, often by force (see Chapter 4). Chinese settlers in South-East Asian countries (Sinn, 1998) and South Asians in Africa became trading minorities with an important intermediary role for colonialism. This often led to hostility – and even mass expulsions – after independence. However, it also helped create the ethnic networks that encouraged more recent migrations (IOM, 2000b: 69). In the nineteenth century there was considerable migration from China and Japan to the USA, Canada and Australia. In all three countries, discriminatory legislation was enacted to prevent these movements.

Migration from Asia was low in the early part of the twentieth century owing to restrictive policies by immigration countries and colonial powers. However, movements within Asia continued, often connected with political struggles. Japan recruited 40,000 workers from its then colony, Korea, between 1921 and 1941. Japan also made extensive use of forced labour in World War II. Some 25 million people migrated from densely populated Chinese provinces to Manchuria between the 1890s to the 1930s, with about 8 million staying on 'to reaffirm China's national territory in the face of Japanese expansionism' (Skeldon, 2006a: 23). In the often violent mass population transfers following Indian Independence in 1947, about 5 million Hindus and Sikhs left Pakistan for India and about 6 million Muslims moved into Pakistan from India (Khadria, 2008).

External movements started to grow from the 1960s. The reasons were complex (Fawcett and Cariño, 1987; Skeldon, 1992: 20–22). Discriminatory rules against Asian entries were repealed in Canada (1962 and 1976), the USA (1965) and Australia (1966 and 1973). Increased foreign investment and trade helped create the communicative networks needed for migration. The US military presence in Korea, Vietnam and other Asian countries forged transnational links, as well as directly stimulating movement in the shape of brides of US personnel. The Vietnam War caused large-scale refugee movements. The openness of the USA, Canada and Australia to family migration meant that primary movements, whatever their cause, gave rise to further entries of permanent settlers. The huge construction projects in the Gulf oil countries caused mass recruitment of temporary contract workers. Rapid economic growth in several Asian countries led to movements of both highly skilled and unskilled workers.

Asia's massive entry onto the world migration stage in the mid-twentieth century can be seen as the result of the opening up of the continent to economic and political relationships with the industrialized countries in the postcolonial period. Western penetration through trade, aid and investment created the material means and the cultural capital necessary for migration. At the same time, the dislocation of existing forms of production and social structures through industrialization, the 'green revolution' and wars (often encouraged by major powers as part of the Cold War) forced people to leave the countryside in search of better conditions in the growing cities or overseas. Later on, the rapid industrial takeoff of some areas and the continuing stagnation or decline of others created new pressures for migration.

In the early twenty-first century, there were some 6.1 million Asians employed outside their own countries within the Asian region, and about 8.7 million in the Middle East. Hugo estimates that there may be over 20 million Asian migrant workers worldwide (Hugo, 2005). Over the last 30 years, migration has grown in volume and become much more diverse. The Asian financial crisis of 1997–1999 caused only a temporary slow-down (Abella, 2002). Economic migrants can be found at all skill levels, with flows of highly qualified personnel from, to and within the region. Feminization of migration is another important trend (Huang et al., 2005), while family reunion is increasing, and refugee movements continue. Emigration for employment from countries within the region has grown at about 6 per cent a year over the last two decades, with about 2.6 million people leaving their homes in search of work each year (ILO, 2006: 37).

All countries in the region experience both emigration and immigration (and often transit migration too), but it is possible to differentiate between mainly immigration countries (Brunei, Hong Kong, Japan, Singapore, South Korea, Taiwan), countries with both significant immigration and emigration (Malaysia, Thailand), and mainly emigration countries (Bangladesh, Burma, Cambodia, China, India, Indonesia, Laos, Nepal, Pakistan, Philippines, Sri Lanka, Vietnam) (Hugo, 2005: 8). (Official names for some countries differ from customary usage. We use Taiwan for what the UN refers to as Chinese Taipei, and Hong Kong for what became the Hong Kong Special Administrative Region (SAR) of China in 1997. The Republic of Korea (South Korea) is called Korea, unless there is any risk of confusion with North Korea. We use Burma, rather than Myanmar.)

Map 6.1 Migrations within and from the Asia–Pacific region

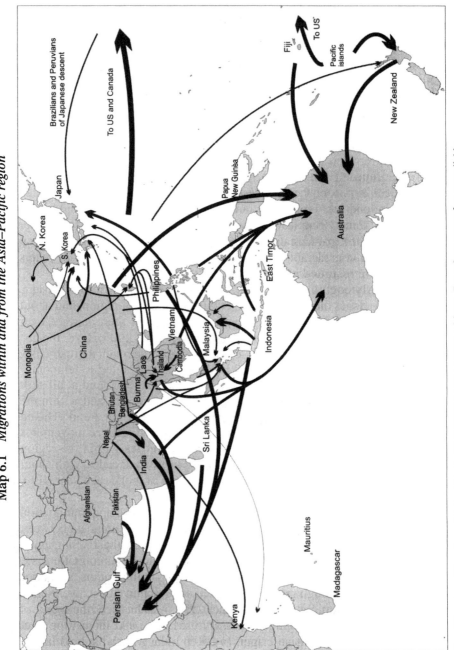

Note: The arrow dimensions give an approximate indication of the volume of flows. Exact figures are often unavailable.

In this chapter, we will examine the main Asian migration systems: movement to Western countries, contract labour to the Middle East, intra-Asian labour migration, movement of highly skilled workers, student mobility and refugee movements. Most of these movements include substantial irregular migration. This often takes the form of tourist visa-holders overstaying their permits, but smuggling and trafficking of people are also frequent. Hugo quotes estimates of irregular migrants in SE Asia countries in the early 2000s totalling about 3.8 million (Hugo, 2005: 22), although this figure is very approximate.

Asian migration to Western Europe, North America and Oceania

Three European countries experienced large Asian migrations connected with decolonization: the Netherlands from the former Netherlands East Indies (Indonesia); France from Vietnam; and Britain from the Indian subcontinent and Hong Kong. There were also some smaller movements, like those from Goa, Macau and East Timor to Portugal. Such movements had declined considerably by the late 1970s. In the 1980s, Vietnamese workers were recruited by the Soviet Union and the German Democratic Republic. Although often called trainees, these migrants shared many of the characteristics of contract workers. After German reunification in 1990, many stayed on, often moving into small business, sometimes initially in illicit cigarette trading, and then in more mainstream enterprises.

Most Asian migrants are in the traditional immigration countries (USA, Canada, Australia and New Zealand), but a recent trend is the growth of Asian migration to Europe: China, India, Japan, the Philippines, Vietnam and Thailand are all significant sources (OECD, 2007: 40). The migrants include medical and information technology personnel, female domestic workers (especially in Southern Europe), and manual workers (often moving irregularly). Censuses in OECD countries around 2000 showed the presence of around 2 million migrants (aged 15 and over) from China and a similar number from India, making up about 5.5 per cent of all immigrants in OECD countries (OECD, 2007: 44).

The largest Asian movement was that to the USA after the 1965 Immigration Act. The number of migrants from Asia increased from 17,000 in 1965 to an average of more than 250,000 annually in the 1980s (Arnold et al., 1987) and over 350,000 per year in the early 1990s (OECD, 1995: 236). Most Asians came to the USA through the family reunion provisions of the 1965 Act, though refugee or skilled worker movements were often the first link in the migratory chain. Since 1992, Asia has been the source of about one-third of all immigrants, and by March 2000 there were over 7 million residents of Asian origin. In 2005, India was the second largest source of new immigrants, with 84,700 (following Mexico with 161,400). China came third with 70,000, while the Philippines, Vietnam and Korea were also among the top 10 source countries (OECD, 2007: 316).

Asian immigration to Australia developed after the repeal of the White Australia Policy, with additional stimulus from the Indo-Chinese refugee movement at the end of the 1970s. Among Australia's top 10 source countries in 2005 were China (third after New Zealand and the UK), India, the Philippines, Malaysia, Sri Lanka and Hong Kong (OECD, 2007: 303). The 2001 Census put the Asia-born population at over 1.2 million (about a quarter of all immigrants), while 2005 estimates put the Asian-born at about 7 per cent of the total population of 20.1 million (Migration Information Source, 2007a).

In Canada, it was the 1976 Immigration Act, with its nondiscriminatory selection criteria and its emphasis on family and refugee entry, which opened the door to Asian migration. Since 1993, over half of all immigrants have come from Asia. In 2005, the top four source countries for new entrants were China, India, the Philippines and Pakistan, followed by the USA (OECD, 2007: 239). By the 2001 Census, the roughly 2.1 million residents of Asian origin made up over a third of the total immigrant population of 5.6 million (Migration Information Source, 2007b).

New Zealand also abandoned its traditional racially selective entry policies. From the 1950s, economic and political links with nearby Pacific islands gave rise to new inflows (Trlin, 1987). From 1991, policies encouraged immigration of people with professional skills and capital for investment. Most of these came from Hong Kong, Taiwan, Korea and Japan (Lidgard, 1996: 6). In 2005, China was the second largest source country (after the UK). India, Korea and Philippines were also in the top 10, as were the Pacific islands of Samoa, Fiji and Tonga (OECD, 2007: 273). New Zealand's ethnic composition has become more complex: by 2001, Maori people had grown to 14.7 per cent of the total population of 3.6 million, Pacific Islanders made up 6.5 per cent and Asians 6.6 per cent (Ministry of Social Development, 2006). This has led to heated public debates and electoral campaigns focusing on immigration policy (IOM, 2000b: 282–283).

Migrations from Asia to North America and Oceania have certain common features. Unexpectedly large movements have developed mainly through use of family reunion provisions. The countries of origin have become more diverse. Vietnamese and other Indo-Chinese refugees were a dominant flow in the 1970s and 1980s; Hong Kong became a major source in the run-up to incorporation into China in 1997, although there has been some return migration since. Movements from these countries continue and have been joined by flows from the Philippines, India, Japan and Korea. The most important trend is the growth in migration from China. All the immigration countries have changed their rules to encourage entry of skilled and business migrants. A global labour market for highly skilled personnel has emerged, with Asia as the main source.

Contract labour migration to the Middle East

Labour migration from Asia to the Middle East developed rapidly after the oil price rises of 1973. Labour was imported by oil-rich countries first from India and Pakistan, then from the Philippines, Indonesia, Thailand and Korea, and later from Bangladesh and Sri Lanka. In the 1970s, most migrants were male workers employed as manual workers in the many construction projects. Governments of sending countries like India, Pakistan and the Philippines actively marketed their labour abroad, and made labour-supply agreements with Gulf countries. Korean construction companies were encouraged to take on contracts in the Arab region, which included provision of labour. The Asian labour-sending countries also allowed private agencies to organize recruitment (Abella, 1995).

By 1985, there were 3.2 million Asian workers in the Gulf states, but the Iraqi invasion of Kuwait and the Gulf War in 1990–1991 led to the forced return of some 450,000 Asians to their countries of origin. After the war, recruitment of Asian workers increased again, partly due to reconstruction needs but also through the replacement of 'politically unreliable' Palestinians in Kuwait and Yemenis in Saudi Arabia (Abella, 1995). Israel began to recruit Thais and Filipinos for agriculture, construction and domestic work, after security measures blocked entry of Palestinians from the West Bank and Gaza.

The temporary decline of the construction sector after 1985 encouraged more diverse employment of contract workers, particularly a shift into services. There was an upsurge in demand for domestic workers, nurses, sales staff and other service personnel, leading to a marked feminization of migrant labour flows, with Sri Lanka and Indonesia as the main sources. In later years, other countries in the Middle East – Lebanon, Jordan and Israel – also became labour-importing countries (Asis, 2008). Women domestic workers are highly vulnerable to exploitation and sexual abuse, and it is difficult for the authorities of their countries of origin to provide protection (Gamburd, 2005). The governments of Bangladesh, Iran, Nepal and Pakistan banned some types of female migration to the Gulf, but found the ban impossible to enforce, due to the activities of illegal recruitment agents. The bans have mostly been lifted, although some limitations remain – especially in the case of Pakistan and Bangladesh. Only Sri Lanka actively encourages female migration to the Gulf (IOM, 2005: 110).

Asian migration to the Middle East has become more differentiated over time. While many migrants remain low-skilled labourers, others have semi-skilled or skilled jobs as drivers, mechanics or building tradesmen. Others came with professional or para-professional qualifications (engineers, nurses and medical practitioners). Many managerial and technical posts are filled by Asians, although sometimes they come second in job hierarchies to senior personnel recruited in Europe or North America. In many cases, Asian labour migrants were not part of the unemployed rural and urban poor at home, but people with above-average education, whose departure could have a negative effect on the economy (Skeldon, 1992: 38).

Labour demand is the key driver of migration. The small national labour forces of the six countries of the Gulf Cooperation Council (GCC) are concentrated in the public sector, leaving huge gaps in the private sector. The result is extreme dependence on foreign labour. By the late 1990s, Saudi Arabia, with a population of 20 million, had a foreign labour share of 28 per cent. The smaller GCC states had even higher foreign shares: Kuwait 65 per cent, Bahrain 37 per cent, Qatar 77 per cent, United Arab Emirates (UAE) 73 per cent and Oman 27 per cent. As flows became more diverse, undocumented migration grew sharply (IOM, 2000b: 107–115). Around 2002, Asian workers in the Middle East were estimated at 3 million Indians, 1 million Pakistanis, 1.8 million Bangladeshis, 0.9 million Sri Lankans, 1.5 million Filipinos and 0.4 million Indonesians (Hugo, 2005: 10).

The strategy of the Gulf states from the 1970s to the 1990s was to recruit the labour needed for accelerated capital investment through rigid contract (or guestworker) systems. These had strict rules designed to prevent long-term residence and family reunion (Abella, 1995). Yet structural dependence on migrant labour and the desire of employers to retain trained workers make it hard to completely prevent longer-term stay. Moreover, the strikes and demonstrations by migrant workers in Dubai in early 2006 (BBC News, 2006) show the difficulty of permanently suppressing worker rights. From the late 1990s, Gulf states introduced strategies to reduce dependence on Asian labour, through recruitment of local workers, restricting new entries, and deporting irregular migrants. The completion of some large construction projects was a further factor reducing labour inflows (especially of male manual workers) (IOM, 2005: 105).

Asians in Arab countries encounter difficult conditions, due both to the lack of worker rights and the very different cultural values. Workers are not allowed to settle or bring in dependants, and are often segregated in barracks. Employers may retain migrants' passports, and sometime trade (illegally) in work visas. Migrants can be deported for misconduct and often have to work very long hours. The big attraction is the wages: unskilled workers from Sri Lanka can earn eight times more in the Middle East than at home, while Bangladeshis earn 13 times more (IOM, 2000b: 119). Many migrant workers are exploited by agents and brokers, who take large fees (up to 25 per cent of wages) and often fail to provide the jobs and conditions promised.

Labour migration within Asia

Since the mid-1980s, rapid economic growth and declining fertility have led to strong demand for labour in the new industrial economies of East and South-East Asia. Labour migration within Asia grew exponentially in the first half of the 1990s. There was some return migration during the Asian financial crisis of 1997–1999, but labour migration resumed quickly. While existing flows from countries like Bangladesh, Indonesia and the Philippines continued, new source countries like Vietnam, Cambodia, Laos and Burma became more significant. In all the 'tiger economies', migrant workers are doing the '3D jobs' (dirty, dangerous and difficult – or just low-skilled and poorly paid) that nationals can increasingly afford to reject. It is impossible to deal in detail here with the complex experience of each Asian country. Instead we will discuss some general trends and look briefly at a number of countries.

The most obvious trend is the increase in intra-Asian labour migration. However, in relative terms, the contribution to labour forces in receiving countries is still quite low: Asian migrant workers make up 40–70 per cent of the workforce in Gulf states, but only about 4 per cent in East and South-East Asia. In Japan, for instance, fewer than 2 per cent of all employees are migrants. However, the situation is different in Singapore and Malaysia, where migrants make up 28 and 12 per cent of the respective workforces (ILO, 2006: 40). Another important trend is increasing diversity: early flows were mainly low-skilled. In recent years flows of the highly skilled have increased throughout the region, and demand for health and care workers is increasing.

Feminization of migration

A key recent development is the feminization of migration (IOM, 2005: 109–110). There was little female labour migration in Asia before the late 1970s. Then demand for female domestic workers surged, first in the Middle East, and, from the 1990s, within Asia. In 2004, 81 per cent of registered new migrant workers leaving Indonesia were women (ILO, 2007). The main official flows from Indonesia were to Malaysia and Saudi Arabia; in the former women were only in a slight majority, while in the latter they outnumbered men 12 to one (Hugo, 2005). The female share among first-time migrant workers from the Philippines rose from 50 per cent in 1992 to 61 per cent in 1998 (Go, 2002: 66), and to 72 per cent by 2006 (ILO, 2007).

Most migrant women are concentrated in jobs regarded as 'typically female': domestic workers, entertainers (often a euphemism for prostitutes), restaurant and hotel staff and assembly-line workers in clothing and electronics. These jobs offer poor pay, conditions and status, and are associated with patriarchal stereotypes of female docility, obedience and willingness to give personal service. Demand for caregivers is likely to be a major factor in the future, due to population ageing in many destination countries. Female migration has considerable effects on family and community dynamics in the place of origin. Married women have to leave their children in the care of others, and long absences affect relationships and gender roles. The increase in domestic service reflects the growth of dual-career professional households in Asia's new industrial countries.

Another form of female migration is for marriage. Asian women moved as brides of US servicemen from the 1940s – first from Japan, then Korea and then Vietnam. From the 1980s, a new phenomenon emerged: so-called 'mail order' brides to Europe and Australia (Cahill, 1990). Since the 1990s, foreign brides have been sought by farmers in rural areas of Japan and Taiwan, due to the exodus of local women to more attractive urban settings. This is one of the few forms of permanent immigration permitted in Asia. The young women involved (from the Philippines, Vietnam and Thailand) can experience severe social isolation (IOM, 2000b: 65).

By the early twenty-first century, marriage migration to Korea was increasing, and brides for Indian men were being recruited in Bangladesh. Chinese farmers called for wives from Vietnam, Laos and Burma – China's one-child policy has led to severe gender imbalances, with 118 male versus 100 female births (IOM, 2005: 112). International marriages accounted for almost 14 per cent of all marriages in Korea in 2005, with even higher percentages in rural areas. Marriages are often arranged by agencies (OECD, 2007: 260). By 2003, 32 per cent of brides in Taiwan were from the Chinese mainland or other countries, and births to immigrant mothers made up 13 per cent of all births (Skeldon, 2006b: 281). This has important cultural implications: the countryside is frequently seen as the cradle of traditional values, and the high proportion of foreign mothers is seen by some as a threat to national identity.

Migration agents and irregular migration

A further feature of Asian labour migration is the major role played by the 'migration industry'. Most recruitment of migrant workers both to the Gulf and within Asia is organized by migration agents and labour brokers:

> This scheme has given rise to irregularities and abuses at all stages of the migration process, exacting costs on migrants and their families. Excessive placement fees, contract substitutions, contract violations, low wages, non-payment of wages are widespread, especially among women migrants in domestic work and entertainment. Unauthorized migrants and trafficked persons are rendered more vulnerable because they are seen as immigration violators and have limited or no access to support and redress of grievances. (Asis, 2005: 18)

According to an ILO study: 'the high degree of commercialization of migration processes in Asia not found in other regions explains the rapid expansion and relative efficiency of the system. But there have been serious problems with fraud and abuse, making migration a costly and risky undertaking' (ILO, 2006: 43). The dominance of private agents is partly due to the unwillingness of receiving states to make bilateral agreements on labour-supply with countries of origin. Where the latter try to set minimum wages for their nationals, these workers may be priced out of the market.

While some agents carry out legitimate activities, others deceive and exploit workers. There is sometimes no clear division between organizations providing legitimate recruitment and travel services, and those indulging in people-smuggling or trafficking (IOM, 2005: 112–114). *Smuggling* means helping migrants obtain illegal entry to a state, by assisting in transportation and border crossing. People-smuggling organizations sometimes include former migrants and officials of both sending and receiving countries, as well as middlemen along the route, and may be motivated by the desire to help migrants, as well as by profit. *Trafficking* involves the use of violence, coercion or deception to exploit workers, treating people as commodities to be traded (compare ILO, 2006: 42). Trafficking may involve forcing both men and women into new forms of slavery, but applies particularly to providing women and children for the sex industry. Trafficking often involves organized criminal gangs (see Chapter 8 below).

Irregular (or undocumented) migration has grown rapidly and affects many countries in the region. Labour flows from Indonesia to Malaysia have been largely undocumented. Thai workers move irregularly to Malaysia and other countries for work, while Thailand itself hosts up to 1.7 million undocumented workers, mainly from Burma (IOM, 2005: 110–112). Hugo points to the complexity of irregular migration, arguing that there is a continuum from voluntary individual movement, through use of middlemen, to trafficking and bonded labour (Hugo, 2005: 25). The growth of irregular migration is linked to the unwillingness of governments to effectively manage migration and to the desire of employers for easily available and exploitable workers. Spontaneous undocumented migration can meet labour needs effectively, but creates a situation of insecurity and rightlessness for workers. Moreover, they can become scapegoats for social problems like crime, disease and unemployment. Recently, governments' enhanced desire to combat drug trafficking and terrorism has led to attempts at multilateral cooperation to prevent irregular migration (IOM, 2005: 111–112).

Length of stay

As already pointed out, intra-Asian migration is perceived by policy-makers as temporary labour migration, and is not expected to lead to settlement. This understanding matches the wishes of the main actors. Employers want low-skilled workers to meet immediate labour needs. Many migrant workers wish to work abroad for a limited period to improve the situation of their families at home. Sending-country governments do not want to lose nationals permanently. Ideas from Europe, North America or Oceania on the benefits of multiculturalism are unpopular in most Asian countries, while turning immigrants into citizens is unthinkable. The dominant policy in Asian countries can be summed up in the principles: immigration is not good for the nation-state and should only be a temporary expedient; migration policies should be concerned mainly with restriction not migration management; immigrants should not be allowed to settle; foreign residents should not normally be offered citizenship; national culture and identity should not be modified in response to external influences (see Castles, 2004b; Hugo, 2005). A key question for the future is whether this exclusionary model can be sustained. We will return to this below.

East Asia

In East Asia the combination of rapid economic growth, fertility decline, ageing populations and growing undocumented migration has led to serious contradictions, most evident in Japan, but also emerging in Korea, Hong Kong, Taiwan and China (the latter will be discussed below in the section on countries of emigration).

Japan has experienced considerable and varied labour immigration since the mid-1980s. The foreign population of Japan increased from 817,000 in 1983 to 2 million in 2005 (OECD, 2007: 349). About 39 per cent are permanent residents (MOJ, 2006), mainly descendants of Koreans, who were recruited (sometimes by force) as workers before and during World War II. In 2005 there were 599,000 Koreans. Other main groups, mainly resulting from more recent labour migration, were Chinese (520,000), Brazilians (302,000), Filipinos (187,000) and Peruvians (58,000) (OECD, 2007). However, government policies and public attitudes remain opposed to recruitment of foreign labour and to long-term stay, for fear of diluting the perceived ethnic homogeneity of the population. In view of the continuing inflows, this policy leads to considerable strains.

Korea exported labour to the Gulf in the 1970s and 1980s, but has since passed through a migration transition: by 1995, the GDP per capita was US$10,000 and labour departures had fallen sharply. In 1994 the government introduced the 'industrial trainee system' as a disguised framework for import of low-skilled labour. 'Trainees' did not enjoy the legal rights of workers and were paid below the minimum wage. In a situation of labour scarcity, trainees left their posts and found irregular work, with better pay and conditions. In response, the Korean Government introduced an employment permit system in 2004, which gives migrants the same rights and treatment on the labour market as Koreans, including the right to change jobs. However, permits are only for three years, and only from countries with which Korea has bilateral agreements (China plus several South-east and Central Asian countries). An amnesty gave legal status to existing irregular workers (IOM, 2005; OECD, 2007: 260). Korea's foreign resident population of 485,000 surpassed 1 per cent of total population for the first time in 2005. Apart from migrant workers, this includes foreign brides (see above) and Chinese of Korean ethnic origin. The government set up a Foreigner Policy Commission in 2006 to address discrimination against foreigners, seen as a source of potential social conflict. Legal measures are planned to regulate marriage agents and to allow entry and employment of ethnic Koreans with Chinese nationality (OECD, 2007). Such measures represent major shifts for a country very concerned about ethnic homogeneity.

Between the 1950s and reunification with China in 1997, *Hong Kong* was transformed from a labour-intensive industrial economy to a postindustrial economy based on trade, services and investment. Highly qualified expatriate workers from North America, Western Europe and India were recruited for finance, management and education. Unskilled workers from China entered illegally in large numbers. Due to fears about reunification, many highly skilled Hong Kong workers emigrated to the USA, Canada and Australia in the 1990s (Skeldon, 1994), though many returned once they had gained overseas residence rights or citizenship (Pe-Pua et al., 1996). After reunification, Hong Kong became a Special Administrative Region (SAR) with its own laws and institutions. The 2006 Census showed a total population of 6.9 million, of whom 60 per cent were Hong Kong-born, 34 per cent born elsewhere in China and 6 per cent in other countries (HKCSD, 2007). Low-skilled workers from the Mainland are not admitted to Hong Kong, but some 380,000 mainlanders were allowed in from 1997–2004 through family reunion provisions – nearly all women and children. Most of the women are employed as cleaners and restaurant workers (Sze, 2007). In October 2005, there were 223,394 foreign maids in Hong Kong, 53 per cent from the Philippines, 43 per cent from Indonesia and 2 per cent from Thailand. Foreign maids are guaranteed the minimum wage, but have limited-duration permits, and are not permitted to change jobs (HKG, 2006).

Taiwan introduced a foreign labour policy in 1992, permitting recruitment of migrant workers for occupations with severe labour shortages. Duration of employment was limited to two years. Workers came mainly from Thailand, the Philippines, Malaysia and Indonesia. Most recruitment was carried out by labour brokers. Many workers stay on illegally after two years, or change jobs to get higher wages and to escape repayments to brokers (Lee and Wang, 1996). Today, statistics vary widely: official figures show 322,771 legal workers in 2005 (Skeldon, 2006b: 279), while Hugo quotes an estimate of 600,000 foreign workers in total for 2004 (Hugo, 2005: 10). The Taiwanese Government has signed labour agreements with Vietnam, Thailand, Indonesia, Mongolia and the Philippines, in an effort to regulate the activities of recruitment agencies. However, the complex network of agencies spanning Taiwan and the origin countries adds greatly to the costs of recruitment (Skeldon, 2006b: 290).

South-East Asia

South-East Asia is characterized by enormous ethnic, cultural and religious diversity, as well as by considerable disparities in economic development.

Governments of immigration countries are concerned about maintaining complex ethnic balances, and combating possible threats to security.

Singapore is a country lacking in natural resources, which has success-fully built a first-world economy through specialization in modern service industries. It relies heavily on import of labour at all skill levels. The 2000 Census revealed a total population of 4 million, of whom 3.3 million (81.2 per cent) were residents and 754,000 (18.8 per cent) nonresidents. Between 1990 and 2006, the nonresident workforce grew from 248,000 to 670,000 and is now nearly a third of the total workforce. About 580,000 migrants were classified as lower-skilled in 2006 (Yeoh, 2007). They come from Malaysia, Thailand, Indonesia, the Philippines, Sri Lanka, India and China. Foreign men work in construction, shipbuilding, transport and services; women are mainly in domestic and other services. The government imposes a foreign worker levy to encourage employers to invest in new technology rather than hiring migrants. However, this has led to downward pressure on migrants' wages, rather than reductions in foreign employment. Unskilled workers are not permitted to settle or to bring in their families. Migrants usually work long hours, six days a week, and live in barracks. However, the government favours entry of skilled workers and professionals and gives them a privileged status (IOM, 2000b: 82). There were 90,000 skilled-employment pass holders in 2006 (Yeoh, 2007). Such migrants – especially those of Chinese ethnicity – are encouraged to settle permanently.

Malaysia is another industrializing economy in SE Asia that has become heavily dependent on immigration. Rapid economic growth since the 1980s had made Malaysia into a 'second-wave tiger economy' with severe labour shortages, especially in the plantation sector. The estimated total foreign labour force was recently put at 2.6 million (Skeldon, 2006b), of whom nearly half are irregular workers. Due to Malaysia's complex ethnic composition, immigration has been an area of particular controversy, and successive governments have struggled to find appropriate approaches.

Thailand became a major exporter of workers to the Gulf in the 1980s and then to Taiwan, Malaysia, Japan and Singapore in the early 1990s. Fast economic growth in the 1990s initiated a migration transition. Construction, agricultural and manufacturing jobs have attracted large numbers of workers from Burma, Cambodia, Laos and Bangladesh. Many of the Burmese are fleeing violence in their homeland and it is hard to distinguish clearly between migrant workers and refugees. Most of the migrants are irregular: Skeldon quotes estimates of 100,000 legal foreign workers in 1999–2000, and perhaps another 1 million irregulars. The total number of foreign workers in Thailand in 2004 was put at 2 million, and the Thai authorities had created a category of 'registered workers' to allow migrants who entered irregularly to work legally (Skeldon, 2006b: 285). Some Thais still go to other countries in search of work, and trafficking of Thai women for the sex industry remains a problem (Hugo, 2005: 24–25). Yet with falling fertility and fast economic growth, many Thais are no longer willing to do 3D jobs, and Thailand's transition to an immigration country is well underway (Skeldon, 2006b: 285).

Countries of emigration

Just as the Mediterranean periphery fuelled Western European industrial expansion up to the 1970s, industrializing Asia has its own labour reserve areas: China, the South Asian countries, the Philippines, Indonesia, Vietnam, Cambodia, Laos and Burma have all become major labour providers for the region and indeed for the rest of the world. Asian sending-country governments have set up special departments to manage recruitment and to protect workers, such as Bangladesh's Bureau of Manpower, Employment and Training (BMET) and India's Office of the Protector of Emigrants – recently incorporated into a new Ministry for Indians Overseas. The governments of labour-sending countries see migration as economically vital, partly because they hope it will reduce unemployment and provide training and industrial experience, but mainly because of the worker remittances (see Chapter 3 above; and Hugo, 2005: 28–33). However, by the early twenty-first century, change was apparent: industrial development was spreading to new regions, and migration patterns were gaining in complexity. Some sending countries were also attracting migrants – such as highly skilled personnel or spouses – to make up for demographic imbalances.

China is a vast country with major internal migration – especially from the agricultural regions of the west and centre to the fast-industrializing eastern seaboard. With regard to international migration, China is still mainly seen as an area of emigration, with streams to North America, Europe and – most recently – Africa. The latter is strongly linked to China's emerging trading interests in countries like Mozambique, Zambia, Zimbabwe and Sudan. However, it must be noted that 'the era of cheap labour in China is ending' (Skeldon, 2006b: 282). The rapid economic expansion and the sharp decline in fertility due to the one-child policy mean that China's rural labour reserves are being depleted. Labour shortages have been reported in the industrial cities of the East coast, especially for highly skilled personnel. Professional mobility from Hong Kong, Taiwan and other countries is helping to fill the gap, while emigration of workers from China continues. In the long run China may well become a significant immigration destination for economic migrants as well as brides.

India too has experienced large-scale emigration, and today the 'Indian diaspora' is estimated at around 20 million persons (including persons of Indian origin now holding other citizenships). Indians still go in large numbers to the Gulf as manual workers, and to the USA and other developed countries as highly skilled personnel (IT professionals, medical practitioners etc.). However, export of the highly skilled has been matched by return flows of skills and capital, which are contributing to the development of modern manufacturing and service industries in some parts of India (Khadria, 2008).

The Philippines is a major emigration country. Eight million Filipinos are abroad, roughly 10 per cent of the country's 85 million people, and they are to be found all over the world. Labour export has been an official policy since the 1970s, and a 'culture of emigration' has developed, so that going abroad to work and live has become a normal expectation for many people. The Philippines has developed strong institutions to manage labour export and to maintain links with the diaspora. Nonetheless, migration is a topic of controversy within the Philippines, and it is far from clear that it has contributed to economic and social development of the country (Asis, 2008).

Highly qualified migrants and students

Most Asian migration is of low-skilled workers, but mobility of professionals, executives, technicians and other highly skilled personnel is growing. Since the 1960s, university-trained people have been moving from less developed countries in the South to take up jobs – and often to settle permanently – in North America, Oceania and Europe. This 'brain drain' can mean a serious loss of human capital in medicine, science, engineering, management and education, and be a major obstacle to development. Student migrants often already have bachelor's degrees, and go to more developed countries for graduate studies. Many of them remain there after graduation and are lost to their home countries.

However, in recent years, perceptions of skilled migration have changed, with analysts identifying potential positive effects of the international mobility of skilled personnel, based on the development of diasporas. These can be a source of remittances and investment for countries of origin, and help homeland producers gain new markets abroad. Diasporas can transmit knowledge and skills, and can facilitate temporary or permanent return of experts (see Hugo, 2005: 33–37). Today, a key debate centres on what can be done (especially by states) to minimize 'brain drain' and to facilitate 'brain circulation'. Yet policies of developed countries are still designed to attract the scarce human resources of the South. These issues were examined in Chapter 3 above. Here we will merely look at some of the Asian trends.

Country studies show substantial skill losses for Asian countries in the 1980s and 1990s. In the case of the Philippines, 40 per cent of permanent emigrants had a college education, and 30 per cent of IT workers and 60 per cent of physicians emigrated. For Sri Lanka, academically qualified professionals comprised up to one-third of outflows (Lowell et al., 2002). The opposite side of the coin is reliance on immigrant professionals in the North. The US Census showed that 4.3 million foreign-born persons were college graduates, making up 13 per cent of all college graduates in the USA. Half of the graduates who arrived in the 1990s were from Asia, with India and China as the largest sources. Almost one-third worked in natural and social sciences, engineering and computer-related occupations. The college-educated foreign-born were almost twice as likely as the native-born to be physicians and surgeons (Batalova, 2005). Indian and Chinese IT experts played a key role in the rise of Silicon Valley. Today, European countries like the UK, Germany and France are competing with the USA, Australia and Canada to attract the highly skilled.

Another form of highly qualified migration concerns executives and experts transferred within multinational enterprises, or officials posted abroad by international organizations. Capital investment in less developed countries may be seen as an alternative to low-skilled migration to developed countries, but it leads to movements of skilled personnel in the opposite direction. China had some 200,000 foreign specialists in 2000, while Malaysia had 32,000 and Vietnam about 30,000. They came from other Asian countries, but also from the USA, Europe and Australia (Abella, 2002). Capital investment from overseas is a catalyst for socioeconomic change and urbanization, while professional transients are not only agents of economic change, but also bearers of new cultural values. The links they create may encourage people from the developing country to move to the investing country in search of training or work. The returning professional transients bring new experiences and values with them, which can lead to significant changes at home.

Student mobility is often a precursor to skilled migration. Between 1998 and 2003, 2.6 million Asian students went to study in other countries. The 471,000 Chinese were the largest group, followed by South Koreans (214,000), Indians (207,000) and Japanese (191,000) (Hugo, 2005: 12). There is considerable competition among developed countries to attract fee-paying students. Many former students stay on in developed countries upon graduation, especially those with PhDs (Abella, 2002). Australia changed its immigration rules in 1999: in the past, students had to leave Australia on graduation and wait at least two years before applying to migrate to Australia. Now they are allowed to remain in the country as they pursue their immigration applications.

An important emerging trend is the growth of highly skilled mobility within Asia. Regional migration flows are becoming far more diverse, and India, Japan, Singapore, Taiwan, Korea and Malaysia are all trying hard to attract overseas professionals – either on a temporary or a permanent basis. Like Northern countries, they have introduced privileged immigration and residence regimes for this category. Often Asian countries are seeking to lure back their own diasporas – the professionals and students who left in the past when there were few opportunities at home. Taiwan has been especially successful in maintaining contacts with expatriates and drawing them back as industrialization progressed (Hugo, 2005: 35–37), and other countries are now trying to follow this example. The Chinese diaspora has been a crucial source of capital and expertise in the Chinese economic takeoff.

The changing face of skilled migration is a reflection of the major shifts taking place in Asia. For instance, the annual number of Chinese travelling abroad (for both business and tourism) shot up from less than a million in 1990 to about 15 million by 2003 (Hugo, 2005: 11). A corresponding change is the increasing quality of tertiary education within the region, with Japan, China and Korea all competing for foreign students. Fewer Chinese students are going abroad, while foreign student inflows (especially from Thailand) are increasing. Japan has had substantial growth in foreign students: by 2003, 109,508 were enrolled (IOM, 2005). North America, Oceania and Europe are beginning to lose their dominant position within the international education industry.

Refugees

At the end of 2004, UNHCR counted 3.4 million refugees in the Asia–Pacific, 33 per cent of the global total of 9.2 million. This was a substantial reduction compared with 2000, when there were 5.4 million refugees in Asia, 44 per cent of the global total of 12.1 million (UNHCR, 2006b: 213). The decline reflects a political stabilization since the latter half of the twentieth century, when Asia was affected by violent turmoil arising from colonial liberation struggles and the Cold War. In the wider sense of forced migration (see Chapter 8), millions of people are displaced by violence, disasters and development projects, but the majority remain in their own countries. Here our concern is with those who cross international boundaries. At the end of 2006, Afghanistan remained the biggest global source of refugees, with 2.1 million (21 per cent of the global refugee population) in 71 different asylum countries. Iraq came second with 1.5 million refugees, mainly in Jordan and Syria. In fact, global refugee numbers grew in 2006 for the first time since 2002, mainly due to the Iraq War (UNHCR, 2007a). However, East Asia and the Pacific were relatively peaceful compared with the Middle East and Central Asia.

Asia's three largest refugee emergencies resulted from the 1947 Partition of India, and later from the wars in Indo-China and Afghanistan. Over 3 million people fled from Vietnam, Laos and Cambodia following the end of the Vietnam War in 1975. Many left as 'boat people', sailing long distances in overcrowded small boats, at risk of shipwreck and pirate attacks. Over the next 20 years, 2.5 million found new homes elsewhere, while 0.5 million returned. Over a million were resettled in the USA, with smaller numbers in Australia, Canada and Western Europe. China accepted about 300,000 refugees, mainly of ethnic Chinese origin. Other Asian countries were unwilling to accept settlers. In 1989, a 'Comprehensive Plan of Action' was adopted by all the countries concerned. People already in the camps were to be resettled, while any new asylum seekers were to be screened to see if they were really victims of persecution. Those found to be economic migrants were to be repatriated. In 1979 Vietnam introduced an 'Orderly Departure Programme' to permit legal emigration, particularly of people with relatives overseas. By 1995, most of the camps were closed and the emergency was considered over (UNHCR, 2000b: 79–103).

Up to a third of Afghanistan's 18 million people fled the country following the Soviet military intervention in 1979. The overwhelming majority found refuge in the neighbouring countries of Pakistan (3.3 million in 1990) and Iran (3.1 million) (UNHCR, 2000b: 119). There was hardly any official resettlement overseas. The Afghan emergency came just after the Indo-Chinese exodus, and there was little willingness in Western countries to provide homes for new waves of refugees. Moreover the *mujahedin* (Islamic armed resistance) leaders wanted to use the refugee camps as bases for recruitment and training. For political, humanitarian, religious and cultural reasons, Pakistan and Iran were willing to provide refuge for extended periods. Pakistan received substantial military, economic and diplomatic support from the USA. Iran, on the other hand, received very little external assistance, despite being one of the world's principal havens for refugees (UNHCR, 2000b: 118).

The different handling of the Vietnamese and Afghan cases is an example of the way refugee movements can become part of wider foreign policy considerations for major powers (Suhrke and Klink, 1987). With the end of the Soviet intervention in 1992, about 1.5 million Afghan refugees returned home. However, the seizure of power by the fundamentalist Taliban, a four-year drought and the devastated condition of the country delayed the return of the rest. To help fund the costs of rebuilding their villages, increasing numbers of Afghans went to work in the Gulf states, while others sought asylum in Western countries (UNHCR, 1995: 182–183).

The events of 11 September 2001 made the world aware of the consequences of protracted situations of conflict. Afghanistan had become the centre of the global Al-Qaida terrorist network. It was also the world's leading producer of heroin. The huge Afghan refugee diaspora came to be seen as one component of a threat to global security. The US-led invasion of Afghanistan was designed to destroy Al-Qaida and the Taliban, establish a legitimate government, and permit the return of the refugees. In March 2002, the Afghan Transitional Authority and UNHCR started a mass return programme. By July, more than 1.3 million Afghans had returned, 1.2 million from Pakistan and 100,000 from Iran. This unexpectedly rapid repatriation put severe strain on UNHCR finances (UNHCR, 2002). Western countries – willing to spend billions on armed intervention – were not ready to top up relief funds. Meanwhile, the governments of Australia, the UK and other Western countries began sending back Afghan asylum seekers, even though it was far from clear that conditions were safe in Afghanistan. The intensification of hostilities between the US-led forces and the Taliban from 2005 hindered further returns. Pakistan and Iran continued to host the largest refugee populations in the world – around a million each (UNHCR, 2007a).

Apart from these two huge refugee movements, there have been many exoduses smaller in numbers, but no less traumatic for those concerned. After the failure of the democracy movement in 1989, thousands of Chinese sought asylum overseas. Conflicts linked to the break-up of the former Soviet Union led to mass displacements in the 1990s affecting many new states, including Georgia, Chechnya, Armenia, Azerbaijan and Tajikistan. At least 50,000 North Koreans have fled to China. Other long-standing refugee populations include Tibetans and Bhutanese in India and Nepal, and Burmese in Thailand and Bangladesh. In 2005–2006 Muslims from both southern Thailand and southern Philippines fled to Malaysia to escape persistent internal conflict. The long civil war in Sri Lanka has led to mass internal displacement as well as refugee outflows. In 2001, an estimated 144,000 Sri Lankan Tamils were living in camps in India, while other Tamils were dispersed around the world. The resurgence of fighting in 2006 led to new displacements of some 200,000. The majority of the population of East Timor was forced to flee by violence at the time of the vote for independence in 1999. Most were able to return after the UN peacekeeping mission, but new violence forced 150,000 from their homes in 2006. The major political shifts in Indonesia after 1998 led to massive internal displacements, as well as refugee flows from areas of civil war, such as Aceh. Again, recent peace settlements have allowed many people to return (UNHCR, 2006a).

The Asian experience shows the complexity of refugee situations in situations of rapid regional change: they are hardly ever a simple matter of individual political persecution. Almost invariably, economic and environmental pressures play a major part. Refugee movements, like mass labour migration, are the result of the massive social transformations currently taking place in Asia (Van Hear, 1998). Long-standing ethnic and religious differences exacerbate conflicts and often motivate high levels of violence. Resolution of refugee-producing situations and the return home of refugees are hampered by scarcity of economic resources and lack of guarantees for human rights in weak and despotic states. Western countries have often become involved in struggles about state and nation formation in Asia, and responses to asylum seekers have been conditioned by such experiences.

Conclusions: perspectives for Asian migration

Recent Asian migration got under way through permanent settlement flows to North America, Oceania and Europe from the 1950s, and then grew rapidly from the 1970s, driven by labour demand in the Gulf region and then by rapid but uneven industrial expansion within the region. Most governments still see Asian migration primarily in economic terms – receiving countries emphasize the importance of temporary labour supplies, while sending countries look at the economic benefits of remittances or the development potential of diasporas. But Asian migration is rapidly moving beyond purely economic impacts, and is on the way to becoming a major element of demographic, social and political change.

The early twenty-first century has been a period of growing diversity in Asian migration. Economic migrants can be found at all skill levels: the lower-skilled still migrate out of the region but increasingly also within it; many highly skilled people move to Northern countries, but increasing numbers go to other Asian countries, while expatriates from other world regions are attracted to areas of economic growth. Feminization of migration is highly significant: Asian women are in increasing demand in many occupations, while migration for the purpose of marriage is growing fast, mainly as the result of demographic change in East and South Asia. Increased length of stay of economic migrants appears to be leading to family reunion and formation. Refugee and other forced migrant populations still remain large and vulnerable.

Greater diversity also applies at the national and subregional levels. The old distinction between predominantly emigration and predominantly immigration countries is breaking down: virtually all Asian countries now experience simultaneous in- and outflows of varying types, and many have transit flows as well. Some of the labour-surplus countries of a generation ago – like Korea, Thailand and Malaysia – are now poles of attraction. Some former source countries of highly skilled migrants – notably Taiwan, but also Korea and incipiently China – have successfully reversed the brain drain, and are profiting from the skills of their returnees.

Asian migration has become much more complex, yet some general features remain. One is the lack of long-term planning: movements have been shaped not only by government labour policies, but also by the actions of employers, migrants and the migration industry. Irregular migration is very high, and agents and brokers play a major role. The weakness of migration management in some countries contrasts with the dominant Asian model of migration, based on strict control of foreign workers, prohibition of settlement and family reunion, and denial of worker rights. Asian governments refer explicitly to the European experience, in which temporary guestworkers turned into settlers and new ethnic minorities, leading to significant changes in national cultures and identities. East Asian authorities emphasize the importance of maintaining ethnic homogeneity, while South-east Asian governments wish to safeguard existing ethnic balances. Yet the globalization of migration is bringing about rapid changes and it is far from clear that Asian governments will be able to prevent unforeseen shifts.

When Western Europeans tried to reduce foreign populations in the 1970s, they found it difficult for several reasons: their economies had become structurally dependent on foreign labour, employers wanted stable labour forces, immigrants were protected by strong legal systems, and the welfare state tended to include noncitizens. Such pressures are beginning to make themselves felt in Asia too. There are signs of increasing dependence on foreign workers for the '3D jobs' as labour force growth slows in industrializing countries and local workers reject menial tasks. In these circumstance employers seek to retain 'good workers', migrants prolong their stays, and family reunion or formation of new families in the receiving country takes place. This applies particularly when migrants have scarce skills – the privileged entry and residence rules for the highly skilled may well become a factor encouraging permanent settlement and greater cultural diversity.

The feminization of migration is likely to have important long-term effects on demographic patterns and cultural values. Trends towards democracy and the rule of law also make it hard to ignore human rights. The growth of NGOs working for migrants' rights in Japan, Malaysia and the Philippines indicates the growing strength of civil society. It therefore seems reasonable to predict that settlement and increased cultural diversity will affect many Asian labour-importing countries; yet Asian governments are just beginning to think about the need for plans to deal with long-term effects of migration.

Despite the rapid growth, movements are still quite small in comparison with Asia's vast population. Migrant workers make up a far smaller proportion of the labour force in countries like Japan and Korea than in European countries (although the proportion is large in Singapore and Malaysia). However, the potential for growth is obvious. The fast-growing economies of East and South-east Asia seem certain to pull in large numbers of migrant workers in the future. This may have far-reaching social and political consequences. The twenty-first century has been dubbed the 'Pacific century' in terms of economic and political development, but it will also be an epoch of rapidly growing migration and population diversity in the Asian region.

Guide to further reading

Asia is half the world and generalizations are extremely difficult. Our account here is inevitably fragmented and superficial. *The Age of Migration website* www.age-of-migration.com includes additional text 6.1 on the situation of foreign maids in Singapore and provides brief case studies of the migration experiences of Japan (6.2), Malaysia (6.3) and the Philippines (6.4).

Literature on Asian migration has grown exponentially in the last few years, yet there still seems to be no single work that provides a comprehensive treatment. Overview articles by Asis (2005), Hugo (2005) and Skeldon (2006b) are a useful beginning, and the IOM *World Migration Reports* (e.g. IOM, 2005) have useful regional overviews. The publications of the Scalabrini Migration Center (Quezon City, Philippines) (http://www.smc. org.ph/Cuerpo.htm) provide ongoing and varied sources of information and analysis, especially the *Asian and Pacific Migration Journal* (APMJ), and the magazine, *Asian Migrant.* The Asia Pacific Migration Research Network (http://apmrn.anu.edu.au) is useful for contacts and information. Appleyard (1998) is good on emigration from South Asia. Huang et al. (2005) is very useful on domestic work and more generally on female migration. On Japan, Komai (1995), Mori (1997) and Weiner and Hanami (1998) provide good studies in English. The chapters on Japan and Korea in Cornelius et al. (2004) present useful summaries. For most other countries, journal articles are still the best sources.

Chapter 7

Migration in Sub-Saharan Africa, the Middle East and North Africa, and Latin America

Most global population growth in coming decades will occur in the three regions covered in this chapter, together with Asia (Chamie, 2007). Nevertheless, much of North Africa and Mexico are going through demographic transitions resulting in plummeting birth rates which will likely reduce the levels of future emigration. International migration involving each of the three regions has become more varied, complex and politically and diplomatically relevant in recent decades. The following sections can only highlight the key historical and contemporary patterns, though the six key trends demarcating the age of migration, presented in Chapter 1, are amply evidenced in each of them.

Sub-Saharan Africa: mobility within the continent and beyond

Africans are a global people. Every human being can trace his or her genetic roots to the first humans who migrated from Tanzania's Great Rift Valley up to 200,000 years ago. Some historical and contemporary studies claim that Africa – with 25 percent of the world's landmass and 10 percent of its total population – is the continent with the world's most mobile population (Curtin, 1997). Although the evidence for such claims is far from conclusive, they help shape current perceptions of Africa as a 'continent on the move', which have given rise to myths of mass illegal flows across the Sahara and the Mediterranean to Europe. In fact the great majority of African migrants move within the continent. Flows to Europe have increased, but are still quite small compared with intracontinental movements (Bakewell and de Haas, 2007).

In precolonial times, frequent migrations resulted from the ancient traditions of small ethnic groups whose primary sustenance came from hunting, gathering, agriculture and pastoralism. As these lifestyles were tied closely to the whims of nature, people had to relocate whenever herds moved in search of grazing, vegetation was lacking, or land lost fertility. More permanent migrations were driven by warfare, population growth and economic factors. One of the greatest migrations in human history was that of the Bantu people, who left the area now encompassing Nigeria and Cameroon and formed settlements throughout the entire southern half of the continent, bringing their languages and joining with indigenous groups along the way. Beginning in the sixteenth century, 400 years of the Atlantic slave trade resulted in upwards of 15 million forced migrants from the continent, and the legacies of European colonialism laid the groundwork for many of the migration patterns that followed.

Today, some groups maintain traditional ways of life that include seasonal and cyclical mobility for pastoralism and agriculture. But, increasingly, migration is driven by economic, political and social change (Mafukidze, 2006). Millions of people move within their own states in search of work or better living conditions. Others are displaced internally by violence or persecution. Many Africans move across international borders as migrant workers, professionals, refugees or as family members of all of these categories. Both internal and international movements are often, at the same time, rural–urban migration. However, migration of Africans is becoming more globalized. Whereas the population of Europe was three times that of Africa in 1950, the two were roughly equal by 2007. Africa's population is expected to triple that of Europe by the year 2050 (Chamie, 2007). Flows to Europe and beyond have become major political themes, even though they are far lower in volume than migrations within the continent.

In 2006, 39 of the world's 50 least developed countries were in Africa (UNDP, 2006). With over 70 percent of citizens in some states living on less than the equivalent of $1US per day, migration has become a way to escape crushing poverty. In 2005, there were an estimated 17 million international migrants in Africa (ECOSOC, 2006). Refugees represented 18 percent of international migrants (approximately 3 million), a higher proportion than in any other continent (UNFPA, 2006). The number of internally displaced persons (IDPs) was estimated at over 11 million throughout sub-Saharan Africa in 2006 (IDMC, 2006). (Categories of forced migration are discussed in Chapter 8 below.)

It is very difficult to acquire reliable data on African migrants (especially forced migrants). Some states have never conducted a proper census, many individuals possess no identification documentation, and laws regarding immigration, emigration, and citizenship vary considerably. For example, the Ivory Coast views children born of immigrants within its borders as immigrants, whereas many other African countries would find such a child to be a citizen due to the place of birth (Kress, 2006).

In this section we will discuss migration affecting sub-Saharan Africa, while North Africa will be examined in the next section, along with the Middle East. However, it should be noted that recent scholarship is questioning the idea that the African continent is split in two by the Sahara:

> Throughout known history, there has been intensive population mobility between both sides of the Sahara through the trans-Saharan (caravan)

Map 7.1   *Migrations within and from Africa*

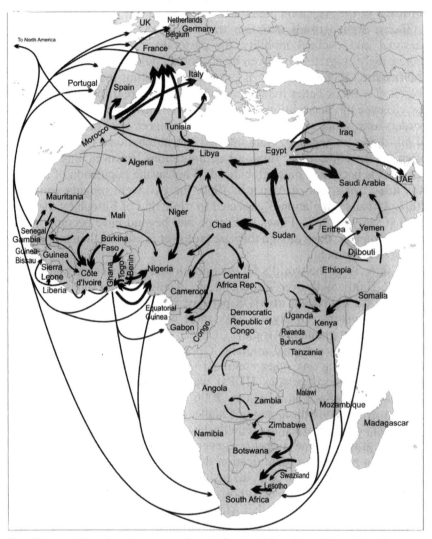

Note: The arrow dimensions give an approximate indication of the volume of flows. Exact figures are often unavailable.

trade, conquest, pilgrimage, and religious education. The Sahara itself is a huge transition zone, and the diverse ethnic composition of Saharan oases testifies to this long history of population mobility. (Bakewell and de Haas, 2007: 96)

Today, ancient caravan routes are once again migration routes as many Africans cross the Sahara. However, for many, the final destination is Libya, Egypt or Morocco, and only a minority seek to move on across the Mediterranean.

Colonial roots of migration

African mobility has been shaped in many ways by colonial practices. The nineteenth-century 'cutting of the African cake' into politico-administrative entities often imposed arbitrary borders, dividing established African nations. As a result, members of a single ethnic group could become citizens of two or more states and most African societies included members of several ethnic groups. Many individuals continued to regularly cross colonial boundaries. Today, African states often have very porous borders.

The colonial period brought European administrators and farmers throughout the continent, as well as Syro-Lebanese merchants to West Africa, and merchants and labourers from the Indian subcontinent to East and Southern Africa. In the postindependence period, these populations generally became privileged but vulnerable minorities, often with a key role in trade. In the 1970s, Ugandan residents of Indian origin were expelled by the Idi Amin regime, eventually finding refuge in the UK. In Sierra Leone, individuals of Lebanese descent whose families have been in the country for generations are still not allowed to vote because they are not African by bloodline (USDS, 2006).

Colonialism was always concerned with control of mobility, in order to provide African labour for European-owned plantations and mines (Bakewell, 2007). Colonial labour recruitment was based on temporary migration, since permanent concentrations were seen as a potential threat to order, yet colonialism in fact started processes of rapid urbanization that continue today. In 2007, cities in sub-Saharan Africa were growing at a rate of 4.6 percent annually. By 2030, it is estimated that 54 percent of Africans will live in cities due to migration from rural areas (UN-HABITAT, 2007). The growth of cities has resulted in increased populations of slum dwellers, homeless people, and the impoverished. Extreme poverty coupled with high population density has fostered the spread of diseases in cities.

Outflows of intercontinental migrants, mainly to Western Europe, have traditionally been to former colonial powers, such as Congolese emigrating to Belgium, Senegalese to France or Nigerians to the UK. In the 1990s, the transition from white minority to black majority rule in Southern Africa resulted in an exodus of whites, mirroring the outpourings of the

1960s during the independence era. A quarter of a million white South Africans have emigrated since the end of Apartheid in 1994; however, the Republic of South Africa remains home to 80 percent of the continent's 5 million whites (SAMP, 2005). Such emigration has had serious economic consequences, as whites played key roles in agriculture, business, and government.

Forced migration

Most African countries experience both economic and forced migration. In some regions, forced migration has been the main form of mobility, as a result of long-drawn-out and recurring wars, both internal and external. This has applied throughout the postcolonial period to the Horn of Africa, East Africa, the Great Lakes Region and Central Africa – especially the Democratic Republic of Congo (DRC). In West Africa and Southern Africa, economic migration has predominated most of the time, but with large refugee flows during the liberation wars in Mozambique, Angola, Zimbabwe and South Africa from the 1960s to the 1990s, and during civil wars in Nigeria in the 1960s and in Sierra Leone, Liberia and Côte d'Ivoire in the 1990s and the early 2000s (Mafukidze, 2006).

During the period of colonial liberation, millions of people fled brutal conflicts with colonial powers reluctant to relinquish control (Algeria, Kenya, Congo, etc.) or with white settler groups determined to cling to their privileges (e.g. Zimbabwe, South Africa). Yet, the defeat of old-style colonialism and the establishment of independent states often did not mean a return to peaceful conditions. During the Cold War, East and West fought proxy wars in Africa. Political and economic pressures, arms supplies, mercenaries and even direct military intervention were factors causing new conflicts or the continuation of old ones (Zolberg et al., 1989). Struggles for domination in Angola, Mozambique and Ethiopia involved massive external involvement, with great human costs for local populations. The large refugee flows of this period remained mainly within Africa. In the post-Cold War period, several of the conflicts continued. Violence mainly took the form of internal warfare and persecution of minorities, although sometimes spilling over into cross-border conflicts or international interventions (Duffield, 2001; Kaldor, 2001).

Over half of Africa's refugees have been displaced from the Horn of Africa and East Africa regions (Bakewell and de Haas, 2007: 100; Oucho, 2006: 132). The Horn of Africa has been an area of turbulence, with protracted and repeated armed struggles concerning Ethiopia, Eritrea and Somalia. The failed US-led military intervention of 1992–1993 in Somalia only made matters worse, while the new US-backed intervention by Ethiopia in 2006 has also failed to restore stability. Large numbers of Somalis have fled to Kenya, Yemen, Europe and North America, and remittances have become crucial to the survival of many Somalis (Lindley,

2007). In addition to warfare, the Horn of Africa region has experienced drought, famine and government schemes to shift people for economic and political reasons. All of these upheavals have led to internal displacement and refugee flows – often under appalling conditions (Turton, 2006).

In East Africa the Great Lakes Region has been particularly violent: long-drawn-out civil wars in Rwanda, Burundi, Uganda and DRC have led to millions of deaths and mass displacement. The Rwanda genocide of 1994 is particularly notorious. Sudan has lived through over 30 years of warfare and massive internal and international displacement. In early 2008, political and ethnic violence came to Kenya too, in the wake of a disputed presidential election. However, most East African countries have received refugees, even in the middle of their own conflicts: Uganda has admitted Rwandans, Burundians and Sudanese; Ugandans have gone to Sudan. Tanzania has had between 400,000 and 800,000 refugees for the last 40 years – they have come from South Africa, Zimbabwe, Mozambique, Malawi, Uganda, Rwanda, Burundi and DR Congo. The international community came to rely on this 'African hospitality' to restrict flows of refugees to the North, but the expulsion of Rwandan refugees by Tanzania in 1996 signalled a shift. Since then African states have become more restrictive in hosting refugees (Bakewell and de Haas, 2007).

Today, the overall security situation in Africa has improved, and the number of refugees recorded by UNHCR has declined from 6.8 million in 1995 (UNHCR, 1995) to 2.4 million in 2006 (UNHCR, 2006d). However, many of those remaining are in what UNHCR calls 'protracted refugee situations' (UNHCR, 2004) – that is, they have been living in camps for five years or more, and have little hope of returning home or improving their often isolated and impoverished life situations. However, where peace agreements have been successfully implemented, large-scale repatriations of refugees and resettlements of IDPs have occurred. The end of the apartheid regime in South Africa removed a major cause of conflict. In Mozambique, South Africa had funded and armed the RENAMO rebel movement, and by the early 1990s there were an estimated 5.7 million uprooted Mozambicans, including 1.7 million refugees and 4 million internally displaced persons. By 1996, most had returned home (USCR, 2001).

The twenty-first century has seen the end of brutal conflicts in Angola, Liberia, Sierra Leone, and the Great Lakes Region. Each is now at a different stage of postconflict development and reconciliation, but the mass return of people to their homes reflects growing stability. However, states that have experienced the uprooting of large numbers of people are poorly equipped socially, economically, politically, and physically to deal with the mass return of these persons, making stability difficult to maintain.

In other places new conflicts have broken out. The tenuous peace agreement between Northern and Southern Sudan in 2005, which ended 22 years of civil war, heightened focus on the violence in the western province of Darfur, where an estimated 400,000 Sudanese have died. The conflict has spilled over into neighbouring Chad. By 2006, 648,000 refugees had fled from Sudan to other countries, while 5.3 million persons were internally displaced within the country. Yet Sudan was also host to 231,000 refugees, mainly from Eritrea (USCRI, 2006). The strain of these huge forced migrations on the population of a very poor country stands in stark contrast to the much lower refugee numbers in the rich countries of the North (see Chapter 8). Another recent case of mass flight concerns Zimbabwe: millions of people have fled deteriorating economic conditions as well as political repression, with the majority seeking work and refuge in South Africa.

Economic migration within Africa

Economic migration is important throughout Africa – even in areas strongly affected by forced migration. As Akokpari points out (Akokpari, 2000: 3–4), in situations of stress and conflict, it is extremely hard to differentiate between refugees escaping violence and migrants who move because their livelihoods are destroyed by economic collapse. He suggests that the latter should be regarded as 'economic refugees' – which questions the neat categories that underlie official asylum rules. However, in many parts of Africa, economic migration is dominant, and important migration systems have evolved, centring on areas of economic growth such as Libya in the North, Côte d'Ivoire, Ghana and Gabon in the West, and South Africa and Botswana in the South (Bakewell and de Haas, 2007: 96).

West Africa is often seen as the most mobile part of the continent. A UN study showed an international migrant population of 6.8 million (2.7 per cent of West Africa's total population) in 2000 (Zlotnik, 2004). Precolonial circular and seasonal mobility for farming, trade and religion was replaced in the colonial period first by the transatlantic slave trade and then by recruitment for mines, plantations, police and army. Migration based on cycles of rainfall and drought persists today in the Sahel region (Mali, Burkina Faso, Niger and Chad). The largest contemporary movements are from the northern inland to the southern coastal regions, where migrants seek work in factories, mines and plantations, or in the service economies (both formal and informal) of fast-growing cities like Lagos, Dakar and Accra.

International migration has largely been spontaneous. In periods of rapid growth, governments have often welcomed labour migrants, while in times of economic crisis migrants have often been expelled in large numbers. For instance, in the 1950s and 1960s large numbers of migrants from Togo and Nigeria were attracted to Ghana. After the 1966 coup in Ghana and the subsequent economic decline, the government ordered a mass expulsion of some 200,000 migrants, mainly Nigerians. With Nigeria's new oil wealth after 1973, millions of Ghanaians and other West Africans sought work there – including many teachers, doctors and administrators. But corruption and misguided economic policies precipitated a crisis, and in 1983–1985 an estimated 2 million low-skilled West

Africans were deported, including over one million Ghanaians (Bakewell and de Haas, 2007: 104). One scholar has enumerated 23 mass expulsions of migrants conducted by 16 different African states between 1958 and 1996 (Adepoju, 2001).

West African migration patterns changed dramatically due to economic decline in the 1980s and civil wars in Sierra Leone (1991–2001), Liberia (1989–1996 and 1999–2003), Guinea (1999–2000) and Côte d'Ivoire (since 2002) (Bakewell and de Haas, 2007). Mass flows of refugees and IDPs took place, and labour migration patterns were disrupted. For instance, the seasonal labour migration of many Burkina Faso citizens to Côte d'Ivoire had been important since before French colonization in 1886. However, instability and the launch of an anti-foreigner campaign resulted in over 365,000 persons returning to Burkina Faso in 2006 and 2007 (Kress, 2006).

Today, multidirectional patterns of labour migration within the region persist – often of a temporary nature. However, increasing numbers of West Africans, both highly skilled and less-skilled, now seek work outside the region. Many are attracted by the new migration poles in the north (Libya) and south (South Africa, Botwana) of the continent. Others seek opportunities in Europe, North America and even Japan and China.

Post-apartheid South Africa is the economic powerhouse of sub-Saharan Africa, and draws in migrants from the rest of the continent. The roots of migration go back to the mine labour system developed between 1890 and 1920 to provide workers for the gold and diamond mines. Workers were recruited during the apartheid period from Mozambique, Botswana, Lesotho, Swaziland and Malawi. Mainly young men were hired. They had to live in squalid hostels, and were required to return home after one or two years of work. The absence of economic opportunities in their home countries made employment in South African mines the only possibility for many, despite the high risk of injury or death. There was also considerable illegal immigration from neighbouring countries. Security measures, including an electrified fence along the border with Mozambique, made illegal entry dangerous.

After 1994, unauthorized entry grew enormously. At the same time, many South African refugees came back. Widespread unemployment and lawlessness further complicated the picture. An Immigration Act was passed in 2002, but proved difficult to implement. Emphasis was placed on recruiting people with high skill levels, but it also continued the system of temporary labour recruitment for mines and farms, and introduced heavy penalties for unauthorized immigration. Recruitment of mineworkers from Mozambique, Botswana, Lesotho and Swaziland grew: the share of foreign workers in the mine labour force was 60 percent by the late 1990s. The economic dependence of neighbouring states also continues: some 81 percent of the citizens of Lesotho (a small state surrounded by South African territory) have worked in South Africa, while the figures for Mozambique and Zimbabwe were 20 and 23 percent respectively (Crush, 2003).

Since the 1990s Africans from as far away as Ghana, Nigeria and DR Congo have flocked to the South African 'Eldorado'. Many brought with them qualifications and experience in medicine, education, administration and business. Others joined the informal economy as hawkers, street food-sellers or petty traders. Over a million migrants have been deported since 1994 (Crush, 2003). Most irregular migrants enter legally, although some risk injury crossing the border fence illegally. Large inflows from neighbouring Zimbabwe have occurred recently. Once in the country, work is available in both the formal and informal sectors, but hostility to immigration has hindered the development of legal mechanisms for employment and regularization. Xenophobia has become a major problem. In the first eight months of 2006, no less than 28 Somalis were murdered in Western Cape Province (*Cape Times* 1 September 2006). In May 2008, there was an explosion of violence against immigrants: many were killed, beaten, raped or forced to flee, by gangs of youths from the poor townships.

African migration to Europe and other regions

Historically, African migration has been predominantly intracontinental, with populations crossing borders into neighbouring countries or circulating throughout the region. This remains the case today: even in West Africa, the part of sub-Saharan Africa with the highest rate of migration to industrialized countries, regional migration is at least seven times higher than movement to the rest of the world (Bakewell and de Haas, 2007: 111). Despite the media hysteria on the growth of African migration to Europe, actual numbers seem quite small – although there is a surprising lack of data. According to an IOM study, there were about 3.5 million Africans in Europe in 2000 (IOM, 2003: Table 12.1, p. 219). On this basis, the 'African diaspora in Europe' would be equivalent to just 0.5 percent of Europe's population.

However, the period of accelerated globalization since the 1980s has created the conditions for increased movement from Africa to developed countries. The increased role of global capital in Africa has not improved average incomes, but has instead led to an income decline for many – both in absolute terms and relative to the rest of the world (Akokpari, 2000). The structural adjustment polices of the IMF and the World Bank have not brought the expected stimulus to industry and trade, but have often reduced middle-class employment in the health, education and administrative sectors (Adepoju, 2006). These factors have increased motivation for migration northwards, while technological advances – cheaper transport and communications – have facilitated movement.

The intercontinental migration of Africans to Europe and the Middle East has increasingly involved poorly educated labour migrants and irregular migration. The areas receiving the most international attention include those closest to the African Mediterranean coast – namely Spain, the Canary Islands, Italy, and Malta. Tighter control measures and naval patrols by EU countries have forced irregular migrants to take longer sea routes, increasing the risks and the death rate. An estimated 31,000 illegal migrants arrived in the Canary Islands in 2006, a 600 percent increase from 2005. At least 6,000 others were thought to have died in their attempts to reach the islands (BBC News Online, 2006). In an effort to stop boats before they start, Frontex, the EU's border control agency, has been patrolling the shores of Senegal and Mauritania. However, while some West African nations have increased security measures, others – such as Gambia – have opened up smuggling ports (Fleming, 2006). African nationals who successfully reach Europe often face unemployment, racism, and homelessness, but these are risks they are willing to take to escape the lack of opportunity faced at home. Some low-skilled Africans have gone as far afield as Russia and Japan in search of work, while Ghanaian traders have been reported in China.

EU and African Union (AU) nations are now working together to combat illegal immigration. The Spanish government signed several bilateral immigration treaties with West African nations in 2006. Senegal, Guinea, Guinea-Bissau, Mali, and Gambia agreed to help stop potential illegal migrants before they left and to facilitate the repatriation of those caught once they arrived on Spanish shores. In return, Spain agreed to provide each nation with several million Euros in aid over a five-year period and authorized some recruitment of skilled and unskilled African labourers. In addition, the EU has drafted treaties aimed at reducing illegal migration and trafficking, attracting skilled labour, and creating a brain circulation rather than a brain drain. The EU also allocated 40 million Euros to foster job creation within West Africa.

Many of the Africans migrating to developed countries are highly educated, and one of the major issues in African development is the brain drain (see Chapter 3 above). In the USA, Africans possess the highest average level of education of any immigrant group: 49 percent of African immigrants hold a bachelor's degree, 19 percent have earned their master's degree and 30,000 have their PhD before entry into the USA ('African Immigrants...', 1999–2000). Many Africans entering developed nations are attracted by 'the good life' portrayed in international media which promises success based on individual merit. Many of their home nations, rife with patronage and corruption, no longer hold such promise. However, a 'brain waste'– underutilization of skills accompanied by underpayment in employment – is often experienced. Annual household incomes of Africans in the USA are still reportedly an average of US$11,600 less than those of Asian immigrants ('African Immigrants...' 1999–2000). Education, training, and job experience abroad often hold little value in immigration countries, and immigrants are forced to work at jobs far below their skill level.

One of the most troubling aspects of the brain drain involves the healthcare sector. Developed nations are scooping up the most promising African doctors and nurses (whether trained in Africa or in the receiving country) with incentives like the potential to earn up to 20 times their current salaries (Kaba, 2006) and international recruitment drives (Batata, 2005). The World Health Organization's minimum standard for basic healthcare is one doctor for every 5,000 people. In sub-Saharan Africa, 38 countries fall short of this standard, and 13 have one or fewer doctors for every 20,000 people. Niger, the nation with the lowest Human Development Index in 2006, had only three doctors for every 100,000 people (UNDP, 2006). Increased morbidity and mortality rates of diseases such as HIV/AIDS, tuberculosis, and malaria throughout the continent have compounded this problem, resulting in a 'dual brain drain' – of emigration and death. Malawi, for example, has one nurse for every 5,900 people (Hamilton and Yau, 2004) and a 14.2 percent HIV infection rate (CIA, 2007).

Remittances

Africans abroad – whether within the continent or outside, high or low-skilled, regular or irregular migrants, refugees or economic migrants – send money home to their families. Remittances provide a crucial form of income to millions of people. According to the World Bank, remittance flows to Africa in 2007 totalled US$10.8 billion (Ratha and Zhimei, 2008). Remittances often reach poor households more readily than other forms of aid and help to boost disposable incomes, to provide for children's education, to build homes, and to start small businesses (see Chapter 3 above). Remittances have become so important in some areas that mobile phone companies in Kenya and Tanzania started working in 2007 to allow migrants to send money transfers via text message (Mwakugu, 2007). Remittances are a central theme in debates on migration and development (see Ghosh, 2006; Lindley, 2007; Ratha and Shaw, 2007; World Bank, 2007).

Regional organizations

Sub-Saharan Africa has witnessed the creation of numerous international organizations for the purpose of removing barriers to trade and the free movement of goods, capital, and people. The Economic Community of West African States (ECOWAS), the South African Development Community (SADC), the East African Community (EAC) and the Common Market for East and Southern Africa (COMESA) have all introduced rules for free movement of nationals between their member states. Opinions vary on the effectiveness of such measures. Generally, these agreements have been poorly implemented or contradicted by the policies and practices of member states (Ricca, 1990; Adepoju, 2001). Despite the existence of many zones in which there is nominally freedom of movement, there is nonetheless a great deal of irregular migration. South Africa still restricts migration from other SADC states. ECOWAS did facilitate movement of Nigerians and Ghanaians in the 1970s and 1980s, but did not prevent mass deportations when governments deemed it expedient (Akokpari, 2000: 77). Today free movement between the 16 ECOWAS states does seem to be leading to more mobility and better protection of migrants in that region. Oucho draws attention to visa-free movement and common passports in East Africa, but mentions the challenges of harmonizing national legislation, policies and practices (Oucho, 2006: 131).

The Middle East and North Africa: A geostrategically critical region

This region stretches from the Atlantic beaches of Morocco to the western border of Pakistan. It includes both the Arab states and non-Arab states such as Turkey, Iran and Israel. It comprises an area where enormous political, cultural and economic diversity has resulted in many varied types of migration and mobility. Yet, for all the heterogeneity, the Middle East and North Africa (MENA) can also be seen as an area united by certain commonalities of history, geography, religion and culture, which have given rise to some shared migration experiences. At the same time, as pointed out above, North Africa and sub-Saharan Africa are strongly linked through political and economic relationships, which have led to mobility across the Sahara (de Haas, 2006d). Regional boundaries have never been rigid, and are becoming even more porous in the age of migration.

Provision of a comprehensive overview of migration in the MENA is challenging for two main reasons. The first arises from a lack of research. Existing literature focuses mainly on emigration from the MENA to Western countries, overshadowing the more complex networks of migration within the region. Until recently, migration in the MENA has been viewed mainly through the lens of economic push-pull factors. More recent literature calls for research to reflect systematic fieldwork, better theoretical frameworks (such as networks theory) and use of new social scientific tools such as analysis of social and cultural capital. In addition, information is rather uneven: there is much literature on certain cases, like Jordan, but other important migration areas, like Libya, are little studied.

The second reason is the complex pattern of migration both within and from the region. The official categories often do not correspond to the human realities. A pilgrimage to Mecca can also be the opportunity to foster contact with trading partners; Palestinian migrants to the Gulf are often both refugees and labour migrants. Until 1990, it was fairly easy to distinguish 'receiving states' from 'sending states' – usually oil-rich countries as receiving states and non-oil-producer countries as sending states. However, over the last two decades, it has become more difficult to distinguish between the two, as receiving states have tended to restrict immigration while former sending states now receive immigrants or transit migrants (Fargues, 2007).

Current migrations in the MENA include six major types: traditional forms of mobility; migration for settlement within the MENA; emigration

Map 7.2 *Migrations within and from the Middle East and North Africa*

Note: The arrow dimensions give an approximate indication of the volume of flows. Exact figures are often unavailable.

from the MENA to other parts of the world; labour migration within the region; flows of refugees within the region; and transit migration. Analysis of these different types requires understanding of related issues that affect the region, such as weak political systems, demographic change, deprivation of basic rights, globalization, and poverty in some places compared with abundant resources and wealth in others.

Traditional forms of mobility: nomads, traders and pilgrims

The MENA has historically been a region of high mobility. Reasons for this include the existence of desert or semi-desert areas allowing the persistence of nomadic ways of life, the presence of numerous holy places encouraging pilgrimages (Chiffoleau, 2003), and a long history of large empires and loose borders which have fostered the exchange of goods and knowledge (Laurens, 2005: 25–27). During the nineteenth and twentieth centuries, mobility decreased due to increased state regulation. Nomadic populations became the primary victims of stronger structures as states implemented forced sedentarization policies in order to control and tax such groups. Likewise, states regulated the movement of pilgrims and traders. For example, Saudi Arabia limits the number of pilgrims travelling to Mecca and Medina by means of country of origin quotas (Chiffoleau, 2003).

Despite increased state regulation, traditional forms of mobility have persisted due to the ability of migrants to adapt and reinvent their practices within a new context. States have also lacked the logistical capability to fully control population movements. There has been a revival of pilgrimage mobility due primarily to an increase in Muslim pilgrims from the former Soviet countries, as well as from the US and Europe (Balci, 2003; Chiffoleau, 2003). Furthermore, modern traders have replaced former caravan traders. These 'suitcase' migrants, who come from the former Soviet Union and North Africa, are particularly attracted to the new economic hub that has sprung up in the Gulf countries such as Dubai (Jaber, 2005: 20).

Settlement immigration

For centuries, the various empires of the region used migration and population displacement as strategic tools to stabilize newly conquered lands. For instance, as the Ottoman Empire expanded, the government ordered Muslim subjects to settle in recently acquired lands, a process known as 'surgun' (Tekeli, 1994: 204–206). With the contraction of the Ottoman Empire and the creation of new nation-states in its wake, policies of national preference developed. The concurrent expulsion of 'non-nationals' and welcoming of 'nationals' reflected a national approach to migration which resulted in population transfers such as the 1923–1924 population exchange between Greece and Turkey that resettled hundreds of thousands of displaced people (Mutluer, 2003: 88–94).

The tendency to view migration along national lines became institutionalized in the immigration policies of states in the MENA region. In 1934, Turkey promulgated the Law of Resettlement, which authorized ethnic Turks from areas formerly comprising the Ottoman Empire to emigrate to and settle in the Turkish Republic (Tekeli, 1994: 217). This policy continued throughout the twentieth century: as recently as the 1980s, 310,000 ethnic Turks from Bulgaria fled to Turkey to avoid persecution, though many of them later returned to Bulgaria. Conflicts in the Western Balkans also led Muslims to seek refuge in Turkey: approximately 25,000 Bosnians in 1992, 20,000 Kosovars in 1999 and 20,000 Albanians in 2001 (Içduygu, 2000: 362–363: Danis and Pérouse, 2005: 97).

However, Turkey is not the only country to apply national criteria to its immigration policy. Israel's Law of Return encourages the 'return' of Jewish populations to Israel. During the 1990s, Israel received approximately 1 million new immigrants from the former Soviet Union. This wave of immigration by the 'Russians,' as they are commonly called, has had important demographic and political effects (see Chapter 12 below). Overall, Israel's population grew from 800,000 in 1947 to 6 million in 1998, with immigration accounting for 40 percent of the total population growth (Kop and Litan, 2002: 23–25).

Like Turkey and Israel, some Arab states have adopted national preference policies. In general, Arab countries have exclusively granted the right to settle and to gain citizenship to persons with historic or ethnic ties to the country. The concept of the 'Arab nation' has had little impact on immigration policy, except in the 1960s and 1970s when Arab labour migrants were preferred to non-Arab migrants in oil-rich countries like Iraq (Lavergne, 2003). The large and recurrent influxes of refugees, especially Palestinians but also Kurds and Iraqis, have challenged the immigration and naturalization policies of Arab countries.

By the early twenty-first century, Turkey had revised its immigration and asylum policies due, in large part, to pressure from the EU and has gradually been moving away from the traditional preference given to ethnic Turks from abroad (Kirişci, 2006). In the Gulf countries, a still rather rigid conception of the national is having contradictory effects on migration patterns as Arab labour migrants are often seen as a threat to the national order, which, in turn, encourages the immigration of non-Arab migrants, often from South or South-east Asia (Lavergne, 2003; Laurens, 2005: 33).

Emigration from the MENA

The most thoroughly documented type of migration involves emigration from the MENA region to other parts of the world, especially Western countries. Emigration from Turkey and the North African countries has been well researched due to the large numbers of immigrants from these countries in Germany, Netherlands and France. The statistics are impressive. In 2005, it was estimated that the Mediterranean MENA countries (Algeria, Egypt, Israel, Jordan, Lebanon, Morocco, the Palestinian Territories, Syria, Tunisia and Turkey) counted between 12 and 15 million first-generation emigrants. The principal destination is Europe, which has about 6 million migrants of MENA origin (mainly Turks and North Africans). The second most popular destination is the Gulf oil states, where most intraregional migrants come from Egypt, Palestine, Syria and Jordan. It is estimated that emigration from the Mediterranean MENA countries is on the rise, with the notable exception of Turkey, where emigration levels have declined (Fargues, 2007).

The underlying reasons for the high levels of emigration were an explosive increase in the under-30 population coupled with high unemployment and underemployment. The area from Morocco to Turkey was, until recently, a region of enormous population growth. Places like Beirut, Gaza and the lower Nile Valley are densely populated areas where the gap between job creation and the entry of new cohorts into the labour market has helped to propel emigration. Nearby are lightly populated desert wastelands and zones of rapid economic growth made possible only through the massive recruitment of foreign labour. However, the demography of the MENA has dramatically changed during the last two decades, with a sharp decline in birth rates. As a result, it seems likely that there will be less pressure on employment markets and, perhaps, less emigration by 2010–2015 (Fargues, 2007). In recent years, research on emigration from the MENA countries has tended to place less stress on economic factors and more on psychological and social factors such as the subjective level of satisfaction towards the country of origin and the expectations of the host country; the so-called 'Western lure' (De Bel-Air, 2003; Mutluer, 2003). Others have insisted on the centrality of social capital and migratory networks that create and maintain patterns of migration (Roussel, 2003; Hanafi, 2003).

The consequences of this emigration are considerable. Remittances have a major economic impact on countries of origin. In 2007 Morocco received US$5.5 billion in remittances, 9.5 percent of its GDP (Ratha and Zhimei, 2008). Migrant remittances similarly had an important effect on the economies of Tunisia and Algeria, although many cash flows to Algeria go unrecorded. In 2004, Saudi Arabia paid out US$13.5 billion in international worker remittances (Adams, 2006).

Emigration can cause or exacerbate political conflicts between sending and receiving states. For instance, in 1973, Algeria unilaterally suspended emigration of its citizens for employment in France following a wave of violence against Arabs in southern France. When migration resumed, French President Giscard d'Estaing (1974–1981) sought to deny renewal of residency and employment authorization to several hundred thousand Algerians. Algerian President Boumedienne declared that nothing could stop migration northward to Europe, but Boumedienne's prophecy did not hold true. Even during the violent conflict in Algeria in the 1990s, relatively few Algerians were able to move to Europe. Nevertheless, migration remained a source of considerable tension, especially when the strife in Algeria spilled over into France. Turkey and Morocco have experienced similar problems; the former due to German attempts to limit the inflow of Turkish migrants in the 1970s and 1980s; Morocco due to recent Spanish attempts to deter irregular migration of Moroccans and sub-Saharan Africans.

Labour migration within the MENA region

The 1973 oil crisis had a substantial impact on migration patterns in the MENA region. The sudden rise in the price of oil generated financial resources to undertake costly construction projects in oil-exporting countries. However, this construction boom required the hiring of thousands of foreign workers, generating sizeable population movements. From the mid-1960s to the mid-1970s, most migrants were Arabs, mainly Egyptians, Yemenis, Palestinians, Jordanians, Lebanese and Sudanese. Today, the share of non-Arab workers is much higher. The United Arab Emirates (UAE) have an estimated combined population of over 3 million, of whom at least 75 percent are migrants. Three-fifths of migrants are from South Asia while approximately one-quarter are from the MENA (Rycs, 2005) (see Chapter 6).

Migrants have often been used by their host countries or countries of origin to further political agendas. Libya provides an extreme example. In the 1970s and 1980s, Libya admitted large numbers of Egyptians, Tunisians and Palestinians, but Libya expelled thousands of Egyptians when diplomatic relations soured as a result of Egyptian President Anwar al-Sadat's reorientation of foreign policy towards the West (Farrag, 1999: 74). A similar fate befell Tunisian workers during a period of tension between Tunisia and Libya. Likewise, after Yasser Arafat signed the Oslo Accords in 1993, Libya ordered thousands of Palestinian migrants to leave. Since 1989, citizens of the four other Maghreb Union states (Morocco, Tunisia, Mauritania and Algeria) have theoretically been able to enter Libya freely, but the regional integration framework has had little effect (Safir, 1999: 89). From the early 1990s, President Gaddafi positioned himself as an African leader and encouraged entry of workers from Sudan, Chad and Niger. These countries became transit regions for migrants from further south. However, since 2000, black Africans in Libya have experienced xenophobia, violent anti-immigrant riots and mass expulsions. Libya remains both a destination for migrant workers and a transit area for Africans seeking to move on to Europe (Bakewell and de Haas, 2007: 98–99).

During the 1970s, the Gulf monarchies grew increasingly worried about the possible political repercussions of their migrant populations. Palestinians, in particular, were viewed as subversive. They were involved in efforts to organize strikes in Saudi oil fields and in civil

Box 7.1 The system of sponsorship (*Kafala*) in the Gulf

The sponsorship system has been a central feature of immigration policy in Gulf countries. Originally, the sponsorship system was based on an agreement between the local *emir* and foreign oil companies in which a *kafil* (sponsor) would find trustworthy men (usually Bedouins) to work on the oil sites. With the oil industry taking off and the national workforce insufficient to fulfil the needs for manpower, the *kafils* had to recruit men from abroad. With time, recruiting and 'sponsoring' foreign workers became the main activities of the *Kafala*. Today, in order to enter a Gulf country, each migrant must find a sponsor. This requirement applies to various forms of migration including construction workers, domestic servants, foreign tradesmen and businessmen. The *kafil* is the official intermediary between the foreigner and the administration, authorities and local society. The *Kafala* system structures the relationship between the state, national *kafils,* and foreigners. Granting *kafil* status to nationals permits the state to delegate some administrative work, to control the foreign population and to reward nationals for their services. But *kafils* often exploit migrants by denying them proper wages and conditions, and retaining their passports, or threatening to report them to the police. Employment contracts are often illegally sold on to other employers. However, Gulf states have begun to abandon the *Kafala* system in order to gain more control over foreign populations.

Source: Rycs, 2005.

strife in Jordan and Lebanon. Yemenis were implicated in various anti-regime activities in Saudi Arabia (Halliday, 1985: 674). Non-Saudi Arabs were involved in the bloody 1979 attack on Mecca, which was subdued only after the intervention of French troops. One result of these political repercussions was the increased recruitment of workers from South and South-East Asia, who were seen as less likely to get involved in politics and easier to control. The politicization of migration came to a head during the first Gulf War.

Reports of precarious conditions, absence of rights, mass expulsions, violence and abuse are regularly made in MENA countries such as Abu Dhabi, Bahrain, Israel and Libya. As the Moroccan scholar Boudahrain has argued, disregard for the rights of migrants is commonplace despite the existence of treaties designed to ensure protection (Boudahrain, 1985: 103–164). The feminization of migration resulting from the growth of foreign domestic servant employment is also contributing to the fragile and vulnerable situation of labour migrants in the MENA (Jureidini, 2003; Baldwin-Edwards, 2005). Unfortunately, the increase in the numbers of South and South-East Asian migrants in MENA countries has developed in parallel with the deterioration of the working conditions of these migrants. In most Gulf countries, the use of the Kafala system (see Box 7.1) reinforces the vulnerability of migrants (Lavergne, 2003).

The trends identified above – the replacement of Middle Eastern workers by Asian workers, the feminization of labour migration flows, the vulnerability and exploitation of migrants and the dependency upon labour migration – are also relevant to labour migrant flows to non-oil-producing states. In Jordan during the mid-1970s, approximately 40 percent of the domestic workforce was employed abroad, primarily in the Gulf (Seccombe, 1986: 378). This outflow prompted a replacement migration of foreign workers into Jordan. However, much of the Jordanian labour abroad was skilled. While the majority of the labour that Jordan received was also skilled, there were major inflows of unskilled Egyptians and Syrians. By the 1980s, these inflows were thought to have contributed to the higher unemployment levels among Jordanian citizens and resident aliens. Wages in industries heavily affected by foreign workers also declined (Seccombe, 1986: 384–385).

On the other side of the Jordan River, the Israeli labour market was opened up to workers from Gaza and the West Bank after the 1967 war, as part of a strategy to integrate the occupied territories into the Israeli economy (Aronson, 1990). Most of the workers had to commute daily to work in Israel and were required to leave each evening. Palestinians found jobs primarily in construction, agriculture, hotels, restaurants and domestic services (Semyonov and Lewin-Epstein, 1987). Illegal employment of Palestinians from the territories was fairly widespread (Binur, 1990). In 1984, some 87,000 people, roughly 36 percent of the total workforce of the Occupied Territories, were employed in Israel. However, by 1991, immigration from the former Soviet Union began to limit employment opportunities for Palestinians. The Israeli government sought to replace Palestinian labour in construction and agriculture, yet its efforts to employ Soviet Jewish immigrants met with little success, since many of them wanted different jobs or found the pay and working conditions unsatisfactory (Bartram, 1999: 157–161).

It was difficult to measure the displacement of Palestinians because other factors were also at work. A wave of attacks by Palestinians from the Occupied Territories on Jews in Israel during the first *Intifada* (the uprising of Palestinians in the West Bank and Gaza that began in 1987), and the First Gulf War, heightened tension in Israel. Israeli authorities introduced restrictive regulations aimed at weakening the *Intifada*, as well as ensuring greater security. As a result, there was a sharp decline in Palestinian employment in Israel after 1991. Increasingly, foreign workers from Romania, the Philippines and Thailand were recruited to replace Palestinian labour. Concurrently, the closure of Gulf state labour markets to Palestinians worsened the economic plight of Palestinians. This threatened the leadership of the Palestinian Authority and the entire regional peace process.

In 2002, the Israeli government 'declared war' on the illegal employment of foreigners, but measures like employer sanctions and deportation appeared to have little deterrent effect, in part because fines were too low. The sharp contrast between the governmental generosity afforded to Jewish immigrants and the lot of foreign workers in Israel prompted soul-searching and calls for a phase-out of foreign worker recruitment (Kop and Litan, 2002: 108). Faced with the day-to-day reality of coping with issues like the education of the children of illegally resident migrants, some municipal governments, such as Tel Aviv, took steps to foster integration of the growing non-Jewish, non-Arab population comprised of legally admitted foreign workers, illegally resident foreign workers and families, as well as non-Jewish family members of the so-called Soviet Jews. About 20 percent of the 'Russians,' in fact, were not Jewish (Bartram, 2005).

Forced migration

The recurrent political instability in the region, due to a combination of wars, internal conflict and repressive governments, has regularly caused large flows of forced migration within and from the MENA. Historically, the region has created, as well as received, diverse flows of refugees. During the last century of the Ottoman Empire from the 1820s to the 1920s, approximately 5 million people sought refuge in the Empire while several million people fled from it (McCarthy, 1995).

Today, the issue of refugees remains centred on the Palestinians. As of 2006, the United Nations Works and Relief Agency for Palestine Refugees in the Near East (UNWRA) reports that some 4.3 million Palestinian refugees are scattered throughout the region and the world. The Israeli–Palestinian peace accords of the 1990s have done very little to alter their plight, although thousands of Palestine Liberation Organization officials and military or police personnel have been authorized to return to the area under the control of the Palestinian Authority. The status of Gaza remains unsettled after factional fighting in 2007. Negotiations concerning refugees, repatriation, compensation, reparations and access to the territory are among the most difficult aspects of the Peace Process. Israeli and Palestinian viewpoints and positions differ enormously, starting with the estimated number of refugees. With the Palestinian population of the West Bank and Gaza in dire economic straits, prospects appear bleak for the mass repatriation of Palestinian refugees from Lebanon and Syria. Since the beginning of the second *Intifada* in 2000, roughly 100,000 Palestinians have fled from the West Bank and Gaza Strip. Additionally, most Palestinian refugees living in Iraq had to flee in 2006 after many refugees were killed (Fargues, 2007).

Since 1990, another mass population of refugees has appeared in the MENA region. Between 1990 and 2002, some 1.5 million Iraqis left their country due to the First Gulf War and Saddam Hussein's repressive regime. In the following years, about 500,000 Iraqis left Iraq through Turkey and Jordan, and tens of thousands left through Iran and Syria. The US-led invasion of Iraq in 2003 and its aftermath have triggered a second wave of Iraqi displacement. The UNHCR reports that there are over 4 million displaced Iraqis around the world, including 1.9 million displaced within Iraq and 2 million in neighbouring MENA countries, primarily in Syria and Jordan (UNHCR, 2007c).

In addition to Palestinian and Iraqi refugees, the UNHCR is particularly concerned with the unabated flow of asylum seekers and migrants from the Horn of Africa (Somalia, Eritrea, and Ethiopia) to Yemen and with the growing number of Sudanese refugees in Egypt, Syria, Jordan and Israel. Moreover, events in Lebanon in 2005 and 2006 have reactivated flows of forced migration. In 2005, several hundred thousand Syrian workers fled Lebanon following the assassination of former Prime Minister Rafiq Hariri, the subsequent withdrawal of Syrian armed forces from Lebanon and a series of attacks on Syrian workers. Israel's bombing of Lebanon in 2006 led to the repatriation of several thousand foreign workers (mainly Asian female domestic workers). An unknown number of Lebanese, probably close to 1 million, also fled Lebanon (Fargues, 2007). Most of these Lebanese refugees found temporary refuge in Syria and then returned home after hostilities had come to an end.

Some countries have been particularly affected by the large influx of refugees. By the early 1990s, Iran had become the world's most important haven for refugees. Most came from Afghanistan, but Iran also received large numbers of Azeris fleeing advancing Armenian forces in Azerbaijan. Despite attempts at repatriation (USCR, 1996: 111), 1.5 million Afghan refugees remained in 2000 and their numbers increased during the US-led invasion of Afghanistan in 2001 (USCR, 2001: 174). Today many Afghans remain mainly because they have jobs in Iran, but no employment chances at home: the distinction between refugees and economic migrants has become blurred.

Turkey and Egypt have also become central crossroads for refugee flows. Turkey received substantial flows of Balkan, Iraqi, Iranian and Central Asian populations while Egypt has been host to many Palestinian, Sudanese and other population flows from Africa. Turkey is also a country of origin for the many Kurdish refugees who have fled to Greece, Germany, Sweden and other countries to escape ethnic conflicts.

Transit migration through the MENA

Transit migration through MENA countries has grown significantly in recent years. The main pole of attraction is Europe, while transit migration involves Algeria, Morocco, Tunisia and Mauritania for sub-Saharan migration flows, and Lebanon and Syria for Middle Eastern and Central Asian migration flows. Additionally, Yemen has become a transit country for migrants from Africa eager to reach the rich countries in the Gulf. Accurate figures on the number of transit migrants are lacking.

The fate of transit migrants is sometimes tragic, as many fail to reach their destinations in Europe. Many live under difficult conditions illegally in a transit country while others take perilous risks to enter Europe (Fargues, 2007). However, in view of the difficulties of onward migration, many sub-Saharan African migrants decide to settle in North African countries like Morocco and Egypt, which have previously been seen as transit countries. Libya has been an important destination for labour migrants for many years, but has recently also become a transit country for onward movement to Europe. Thus a rigid distinction between transit and destination areas is increasingly untenable. Transit migration is a source of considerable tension. European states and the EU pressure MENA countries to control their borders and to curb illegal migration, while the MENA countries complain of having to bear the burden of these illegal migrants alone.

Migration policies in the MENA

The proliferation of migration flows, as well as the growing awareness of their political and economic importance, has led several MENA states to take measures to regulate migration. However, the results have been mixed. Many MENA countries view emigration as a 'solution' that reduces unemployment and increases revenue through remittances. Such countries have implemented policies promoting emigration as well as attempting to mobilize diasporas to support national development. Turkey, Morocco, Tunisia, Algeria, Egypt, Jordan and Yemen have all improved their banking systems to better channel remittances, have included emigration and remittance issues in diplomatic negotiations with host countries, and have instituted special organizations to manage emigration (De Bel-Air, 2003; Fargues, 2006). These countries have also instituted cultural policies to maintain the link between migrants and their country of origin, including mother tongue classes, return travel and religious education (Castles and Delgado Wise, 2008).

By contrast, public policies to regulate immigration and labour migration have been less developed. Initially, oil-rich countries did little to regulate the entry and living conditions of foreign labour. Recent developments have included protectionist measures seeking to give nationals first priority for employment. Some countries, such as Turkey and Morocco, have taken major steps to curb illegal immigration due to pressure from the EU. Most measures remain restrictive and often raise humanitarian concerns (Fargues, 2006).

Currently, many MENA countries lack refugee policies, and only a few are party to the 1951 Geneva Refugee Convention. There are few domestic laws concerning the right of asylum, and this often remains unclear and discretionary. Some governments are aware of the need to resolve refugee issues. However, the relationship between the UNHCR and local authorities remains tense, leading one commentator to characterize the current situation of refugee policy in the Middle East as one of deadlock (Zaiotti, 2005).

An important future issue is likely to be the integration of migrants into host countries. Most MENA countries have a very strict, often national or ethnic understanding of citizenship. The rising trend of immigrants remaining for longer periods of time renders discussion of increased societal diversity and multiculturalism urgent (Fargues, 2006). Greater protection and the granting of basic rights to migrants have entered the national discourse of MENA countries even if such reforms have yet to be achieved. Recently, the government of Dubai announced its intention to implement reforms in this direction (DeParle, 2007). Granting of citizenship to foreigners is rejected by most governments, but may become a significant issue, especially in Gulf oil states, where migrants outnumber nationals.

Latin America and the Caribbean: from immigration to emigration region

The vast and highly diverse region south of the USA is sometimes portrayed as consisting of four principal areas. A number of countries do not fit neatly into these four areas, but the categorization serves to underscore how immigration since 1492 has differentially affected the area as a whole:

1. The Southern Cone includes Brazil, Argentina, Chile, Uruguay and Paraguay. These countries have substantial populations of European origin due to massive immigrant settlement from Europe. There were also inflows from elsewhere: for example, Brazil received African slaves into the nineteenth century and Japanese workers from the late nineteenth century until the 1950s.
2. The Andean area to the north and west differs in that Indians and *mestizos* (persons of mixed European–Indian background) comprise the bulk of the population. Immigration from Europe during the nineteenth and twentieth centuries was less significant.
3. Central American societies are largely comprised of persons of Indian and *mestizo* background, although there are exceptions, such as Costa Rica, where 94 percent of the population is white and *mestizo*.
4. Caribbean societies predominantly consist of people of African origin, but there are also many people of Asian and European descent.

From European settlement to intraregional migration

De Lattes and de Lattes (1991) estimate that Latin America and the Caribbean received approximately 21 million immigrants from 1800 to 1970. The bulk of immigrants came from Spain, Italy and Portugal, and most migrated to the Southern Cone. The single largest migration was the estimated 3 million Italians who settled in Argentina. Argentina and Uruguay encouraged immigration until the interwar period, when the

Map 7.3 *Migration within and from Latin America*

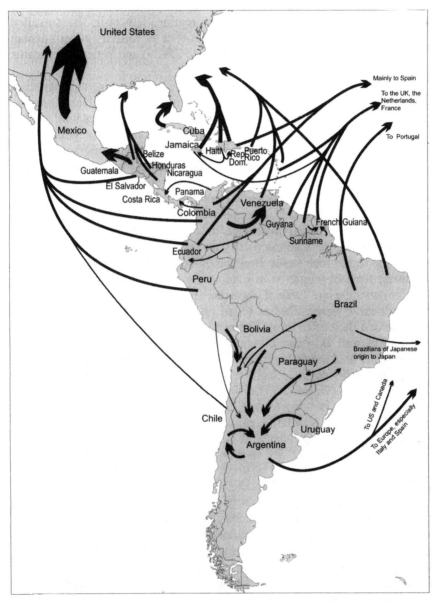

Note: The arrow dimensions give an approximate indication of the volume of flows. Exact figures are often unavailable.

economic depression of the 1930s brought significant changes in policies. Mass immigration from Europe declined sharply by the 1930s (Barlán, 1988: 6–7). A significant exception to this general pattern was Venezuela, which had received few European-origin immigrants until the rule of Perez Jiminez, from 1950 to 1958. About 332,000 persons, mainly of Italian origin, settled in Venezuela under his regime. However, the so-called open-door policy stopped with the overthrow of the military government in 1958 (Picquet, Pelligrino and Papail, 1986: 25–29) and Venezuela became a country of emigration.

As intercontinental inflows from Europe waned, intracontinental migrations developed. Labour migration predominated. In 1935, seasonal labour migration from Bolivia to Argentina commenced, lasting for decades until mechanization reduced labour needs. This labour flow was largely unregulated until the signing of a 1958 bilateral agreement protecting Bolivian migrants (Barlán, 1988: 8–9). Similarly, Paraguayan and Chilean labour migrants began to find employment in Northeastern Argentina and Patagonia in the 1950s and 1960s respectively. Foreign workers spread from agricultural areas to major urban centres. Single, mainly male, migrants were soon joined by families, creating neighbourhoods of illegal immigrants in some cities. Beginning in 1948, the Argentine government adjusted laws and policies to enable illegal foreign workers to rectify their status. Irregular or illegal migration has been the predominant form of migration in Latin America, but it was not viewed as a problem until the late 1960s (Lohrmann, 1987: 258).

Historically, Venezuela has relied on Colombian seasonal workers to help harvest the coffee crop. The reduction of immigration from Europe after 1958 and oil-related economic growth resulted in millions of Colombians flocking to Venezuela. In 1979, the Andean Pact was signed, obliging member states to legalize illegally resident nationals from other member states (Picquet, Pelligrino and Papail, 1986: 30). However, despite estimates ranging from 1.2 to 3.5 million illegal residents out of a total Venezuelan population of some 13.5 million, only some 280,000 to 350,000 aliens were legalized in 1980 (Meissner, Papademetriou and North, 1987: 11). By 1995, 2 million persons were thought to be residing illegally in Venezuela, most of them Colombian (Kratochwil, 1995: 33). Additionally, another 2 million aliens resided legally (Dávila, 1998: 18).

In Venezuela, the early twenty-first century was characterized by continued political and economic instability. The unrest encouraged further emigration from Venezuela, particularly to the USA, which saw an increase in the number of Venezuelan immigrants from 2,630 in 1995 to 5,259 in 2002 (IOM, 2005: 93). Spain also became a major destination country for Venezuelan immigrants, mainly from rural areas. However, Venezuela continued to receive significant migration flows from neighbouring countries whose economies and political environment were suffering, especially Colombia (O'Neil, Hamilton and Papademetriou, 2005: 4).

Argentina remains a country of both immigration and emigration. Most of Argentina's immigration is intraregional, and over 65 percent of the foreign-born population are from other South American countries (Jachimowicz, 2006). Most unauthorized migrants in Argentina work in domestic service, construction, and textile factories. In 2006, Argentina announced a new regularization programme with the potential to benefit an estimated 750,000 undocumented residents, mostly Paraguayans and Bolivians. This followed a tragic fire in a textile factory in which six Bolivians died, including four children. Afterwards, thousands of people marched in the streets of Buenos Aires in protest at poor migrant working conditions (BBC Mundo, 2006). Successful applicants to the programme received two-year work permits. After five years, they would get the opportunity to apply for permanent residence (Migration News, 2006). Argentina also instituted a regularization programme for non-MERCOSUR citizens, mostly Chinese and Koreans. By November 2005, over 900 people had participated in the programme (Jachimowicz, 2006).

The legalization policies implemented in Argentina and Venezuela provide evidence of the changing character of migration within Latin America. Intraregional migration has continued in the early twenty-first century. However, trends to emigration from the region also started emerging from the 1970s, and have become much more marked in recent times (see below).

Regional initiatives

The post-Cold War period in Latin America and the Caribbean has been marked by efforts to reinvigorate and expand the many regional integration organizations such as MERCOSUR and the Andean Group (GRAN) (Derisbourg, 2002). MERCOSUR includes Argentina, Brazil, Paraguay, Uruguay, and Venezuela and encompasses a total population of 250 million. More than three-quarters of the economic activity in South America involves the MERCOSUR region (BBC News, 2007). The Andean Group includes Bolivia, Colombia, and Peru, with a total population of 98 million (Comunidad Andina, 2006). The movement of persons across national borders within these regional blocs has been an important concern. However, inadequate information has stymied coordination and cooperation (Maguid, 1993). After analysing earlier efforts within the Andean Group to regulate labour migration, Kratochwil concluded that a 'significant amount of work has been ultimately ineffective and the administrative agencies have collapsed erratically' (Kratochwil, 1995: 17). As in the MENA and sub-Saharan Africa, Latin American and Caribbean regional integration projects have had a weak record of managing international migration.

Forced migration

A second significant feature of the post-Cold War period in Latin America and the Caribbean also echoed developments elsewhere: there were significant repatriations of refugees subsequent to peace accords in some countries, but the eruption of new conflicts in the region produced new refugee flows. The most significant peace accords were reached in Central America where fighting in El Salvador, Nicaragua and Guatemala abated. In the 1980s, approximately 2 million Central Americans were uprooted, but only some 150,000 were recognized by the UNHCR as refugees (Gallagher and Diller, 1990: 3). The 1990s saw significant repatriations of Guatemalans from Mexico, Nicaraguans from the US and Costa Rica, and Salvadorans from the USA.

However, the political situation in all three countries remained tense. Several killings of returning Guatemalans, many of whom were Indians, were reported. Guatemalan migrants continued to come to the USA and their presence became increasingly evident in labour-intensive agriculture and poultry-processing. Most Guatemalans, Salvadorans and Nicaraguans in the USA did not repatriate, despite the peace accords. Between 1984 and 1994, over 440,000 Central Americans applied for asylum in the USA. The majority of applications were denied, but most applicants stayed nonetheless (Martin and Widgren, 1996: 35). The adoption of a 1986 law to curb illegal immigration prompted then President of El Salvador, Napoleon Duarte, to write a complaint to the US president that the US law threatened El Salvador's stability, since remittances from Salvadorans in the USA were vital to the Salvadoran economy (Mitchell, 1992: 120–123). Similarly, while there was some repatriation of Nicaraguans from Costa Rica, many stayed put.

The USA remained a common destination for fleeing Haitians and Cubans, who often travelled illegally by boat. In 2002, the number of Cubans entering the USA reached 28,270. Haiti suffered further political unrest in 2004, when a rebel uprising forced President Jean-Bertrand Aristide to flee the country. However, contrary to expectations, there was no significant refugee outflow from the crisis. This may have been due to the restrictive immigration policies of the USA and several Caribbean countries, rather than a lack of desire to leave Haiti (IOM, 2005: 93–95). A key motive behind the US-led invasion of Haiti in 2004 was the prevention of mass emigration.

Emigration from the region

The Haitian outflow to the USA was part of the broader shift in Latin America and the Caribbean from a region of immigration to one of emigration. By the 1970s, the Caribbean subregion was a net exporter of people. The underlying reasons for this historic change are many, and the transition did not occur overnight. Since the colonial period, Caribbean migrants had been arriving on the eastern and southern shores of what is now the USA. These northward flows were accentuated during World War II, when Caribbean workers were recruited for defence-related employment and agricultural work. The origins of the British West

Indies Temporary Foreign Worker Programme, which continued into the twenty-first century as the H-2A programme, were not unlike the far larger temporary foreign worker programme established between Mexico and the US from 1942 to 1964.

Temporary labour recruitment helped set in motion the massive northward flows of legal and illegal immigrants from Latin America and the Caribbean to the USA and Canada after 1970. But the causes of the shift are to be found in other factors as well: the declining economic fortunes of the region, its demographic explosion, rural–urban migration, political instability and warfare. Many of these additional factors cannot be viewed as strictly internal. Policies pursued by the USA, such as its political and military intervention in Central America, clearly played a role. The linkage was clearest in the case of the Dominican Republic, where US involvement in the assassination of the Dominican president Trujillo in 1961 led to a mass issuance of visas to Dominicans to forestall a Cuban-style revolution (Mitchell, 1992: 96–101).

The most important factor behind the rise in emigration from the region (apart from demand for foreign labour in the USA, Europe and Japan) was the economic woes of Latin America: GDP per capita declined sharply in the 1980s, which some called the 'decade lost to debt' (Fregosi, 2002: 443). Democratic renewal and a trend toward liberalization in the early and mid-1990s briefly buoyed Latin American economies before a succession of economic crises ravaged the area. According to a UN report, 209 million people (40 percent of the region's population) were living below the poverty line in 2005 (ECLAC, 2006). Moreover, in Latin America and the Caribbean, 10 percent of the population earned less than $1 per day (GCIM, 2005). Economic liberalization policies increased already severe inequality in countries like Mexico and Argentina. One consequence was that, according to a 2001 poll, 21 percent of all Argentineans wanted to emigrate. That applied to one-third of persons between 18 and 24 years of age (Fregosi, 2002: 436).

Although intraregional migration remains important in the early twenty-first century, increasing numbers of Latin Americans emigrate to other continents. This is reflected in both the accelerating flows of migrants to the USA and an increasing number of 'return migrants', people who return to their own or their ancestors' country of origin in Europe or Asia, often under preferential agreements (IOM, 2005: 91). Dominican migrants, for instance, used to go mainly to Venezuela. However, increased political and economic instability there has caused a shift in migration flows to the USA and Spain.

Brazilian emigrants are increasingly travelling outside of Latin America, especially to Portugal, the USA, and Japan. Reflecting historical and colonial ties, Portugal is a top destination of Brazilians, who comprise the largest foreign group – 11 percent of Portugal's 191,000 legal immigrants. In 2003, Portugal implemented a regularization programme specifically for irregular Brazilian residents to encourage further immigration (Padilla and Peixoto, 2007). Most are skilled and middle-class, although there are also increasing numbers of medium and low-skilled Brazilians, who find employment in retail, construction and the hotel industry (Pellegrino, 2004: 36) (see also Chapter 5 above).

The Brazilian population in the USA rose from 82,500 legal residents in 1995 to 212,400 in 2000. The primary destinations were Florida, Massachusetts, and New York (IOM, 2005: 93). Brazilians are also moving to Japan along with other Latin Americans of Japanese descent. In 2005, the 302,000 Brazilians represented Japan's second largest foreign-born group, after the Chinese. Peruvians were the fourth largest with 58,000 (OECD, 2007). Migration from Latin America to Japan was facilitated by the 1990 revision of Japan's Immigration Control Act, which established a preferential agreement for Japanese descendants and improved training and employment opportunities for skilled migrants (O'Neil, Hamilton, and Papdemetriou, 2005: 20).

Traditionally a country of immigration, Argentina, since the 1990s, has seen a new wave of emigration to the USA, Spain, Italy, and Israel fuelled by low employment at home, strong labour demand abroad, and preferential agreements in destination countries. Emigration from Argentina during the recent economic crisis also included return migration to countries that had high levels of migration to Argentina during the 1990s, including Chile, Bolivia, Paraguay, and Peru (IOM, 2005: 92). By 2005, it was estimated that more than 1 million Argentineans lived abroad – double the 1985 figure. In the USA, most Argentine migrants live in California, Florida, and New York, and, while some are temporary workers, many come under family reunification programmes.

Spain and Italy have particularly favourable citizenship policies for Argentineans. Under Italy's dual-citizenship policy, foreign citizens who can prove Italian descent can apply for Italian citizenship (Padilla and Peixoto, 2007). By 2004, there were 157,323 native-born Argentineans living in Spain. In Italy, there was a marked increase in immigration of Argentineans from 5,725 in 1999 to 11,266 in 2003 (Jachimowicz, 2006). However, after Argentina's economy recovered, emigration slowed and returned to pre-crisis rates of approximately 1500 departures per year (O'Neil, Hamilton, and Papdemetriou, 2005: 18–19).

Europe has become a major destination for Latin American migrants. Reasons include high unemployment and economic and political instability at home, demand for labour and governmental worker recruitment in European countries, and increasingly strong social networks. In addition, stricter immigration controls introduced in the USA after 11 September 2001 stimulated a shift in migration to Europe (Pellegrino, 2004: 40–45).

Spain signed bilateral labour recruitment agreements with several countries and now hosts the largest Latin American population in Europe. The over 1 million Latin Americans account for 35 percent of Spain's foreign population. Ecuadorians make up the second largest foreign group with 376,000 citizens, second only to Moroccans (Padilla and

Peixoto, 2007). Other European countries with large Latin American and Caribbean populations are Italy, Portugal, the UK, Switzerland, and Sweden (Pellegrino, 2004: 7). In Italy, the largest Latin American populations are Peruvians and Ecuadorians. There are also significant numbers of Brazilians, reflecting historic migration ties between the two countries (Padilla and Peixoto, 2007). Another notable trend in Europe is the feminization of Latin American migration, especially from the Dominican Republic and Colombia (Pellegrino, 2004: 38). In Spain, the majority of Latin American immigrants are women. This reflects a growing labour demand in the domestic sector (Pellegrino, 2004: 28–30).

Recent trends

The Inter-American Bank estimated that remittances to Latin America were US$62.3 billion in 2006, up from US$52 billion in 2005. An estimated 65 percent of the 25 million Latin Americans living outside their country of origin sent remittances home on a regular basis (Economist Intelligence, 2006). Most remittances came from the USA, but there were also significant inflows from Spain, Canada, and Italy. Mexico received US$23 billion in remittances, the highest amount in the region and 3 percent of its GDP. World Bank Economist Humberto Lopez estimated that remittances alone were responsible for the reduction in the share of Latin Americans living in poverty from 28 percent in 1991 to 25 percent in 2005 (Migration News, 2006). Remittances are likely to continue to be stable sources of income for many Latin American households.

Growing trafficking of persons was in evidence throughout Latin America. Many countries served as transit points for trafficking mainly to the USA and Canada and, with increasing frequency, to Europe. The CIA estimated that approximately 50,000 women and children are trafficked to the USA each year, many of them from Latin America and the Caribbean. The Dominican Republic was a major source and transit location, and many women were trafficked to Europe and South America through Santo Domingo. Furthermore, 50,000–70,000 women from the Dominican Republic were working abroad in the sex trade. Trafficking throughout the region was expected to continue increasing.

However, many Latin American countries began cooperating with each other and international organizations to reduce trafficking (IOM, 2005: 97–98). Combating irregular migration was a major goal of the Puebla Process, formally the Regional Conference on Migration, begun in 1996. Eleven North American and Latin American states had become participants by 2000 and five other states were observers. Of the 11 regional consultative processes monitored by the IOM, the Puebla Process was regarded as one of the most successful (Klekowski von Koppenfels, 2001: 34–38). However, bilateral and regional cooperation on many issues related to irregular migration remained very problematic.

In 2007, the government of Mexico estimated that at least 4500 migrants had died on Mexico's side of the border since the US Government drastically increased border controls in 1994 (Emmott, 2007). An additional 3000 known deaths were recorded on the US side from 1998 to 2005 (Lomonoco, 2006; Marosi, 2005). Yearly deaths have at least doubled since 1995. US Border Patrol measures like 1994's Operation Gatekeeper include deployment of supplementary border-monitoring personnel, physical barriers and enhanced surveillance equipment (Cornelius, 2001). This has led migrants to rely on traffickers who often attempted to cross into the US through remote, dangerous areas (Andreas, 2001): Arizona's deserts became the busiest illegal migrant corridor. Exposure to the desert's extreme heat and cold, lack of adequate food and water, drowning, and car accidents were the leading causes of migrant deaths. In addition, several cases of killings by Border Patrol Agents, vigilantes, and 'coyotes' (migrant smugglers) were recorded. There were 13,500 border patrol agents in 2007, compared with fewer than 4000 in 1993. The US government plans to add 9,600 more patrol agents by 2012. A 700 mile-long border fence is planned, and 'virtual fences' with cameras, drones, sensors, vehicle barriers, and satellites are being constructed in desert areas (Emmott, 2007). (See Box 1.1 in Chapter 1 and Chapter 5 above.)

Overall trends and patterns in Latin American migrations already discernible in the 1990s seemed likely to endure. Most emigration will continue to go to the USA and to Canada and the scale of intraregional migrations will pale in comparison. The frequency of legalizations in Argentina rivalled those in Southern Europe. Further growth of emigration to Europe also appeared likely.

Conclusions

This chapter has dealt with three vast and diverse regions that are undergoing rapid change. Generalization is even more difficult than in the case of Asia (see Chapter 6). We hope our account here will whet the reader's appetite to go into greater depth – perhaps initially by following up the cited literature on specific areas and populations.

Yet for all the differences, Africa, the Middle East and Latin America do reflect some of the general tendencies in global migration mentioned in Chapter 1. They all show trends to globalization and acceleration of migration – that is, more countries are affected more profoundly by growing flows of migrants, to and from an increasing variety of destinations. Differentiation of migration is obvious too, with new types of mobility and the blurring of boundaries between bureaucratic categories. Feminization of migration is inescapable: women play an increasing part in both economic and forced migration, and are often the initiators and the majority in specific flows. Politicization of migration continues: it has become a key issue in both popular mobilization and elite discourses everywhere. The tendency to migration transition is increasingly significant: North Africa, large parts of the Middle East (e.g. Iran and Turkey) and Central America can no longer be seen simply as regions of origin for migrants. They are also transit and destination areas. Some of the oil-rich states (Saudi Arabia, UAE, Libya, Venezuela) are principally immigration zones today.

Each area has its specific historical and cultural experiences, yet all reflect global trends – albeit in specific ways. In a long historical perspective it is possible to see that all the migratory movements of the South have common roots. Western penetration triggered profound changes, first through colonization, then through military involvement, political links, the Cold War, trade and investment. The recent upsurge in migration is due to rapid processes of economic, demographic, social, political, cultural and environmental change, which arise from decolonization, modernization and uneven development. These processes seem set to accelerate in the future, leading to even greater dislocations and changes in societies, and hence to even larger migrations. Thus the entry of the countries of the South into the international migration arena may be seen as an inevitable consequence of the increasing integration of these areas into the world economy and into global systems of international relations and cultural interchange.

Guide to further reading

The Age of Migration website www.age-of-migration.com includes additional text on 'migrations shaping African history' (4.2), 'remittances to Somalia' (7.1), 'the Gulf War Crisis of 1990–1991' (7.2), 'major events affecting refugees and refugee policies in the Middle East (1990–2003)' (7.3), and 'Haitian Migrant Labour and Trafficking in the Dominican Republic' (7.4).

Up-to-date information on forced migration all over the world can be found at http://www.forcedmigration.org/. Remittance data for all regions and countries can be found in Ratha and Zhimei (2008), accessible at www. worldbank.org/prospects/migrationandremittances. For experiences and strategies of emigration countries see Castles and Delgado Wise (2008). Useful overviews of African migration include Adepoju (2006); Bakewell and de Haas (2007); Cross et al. (2006); Curtin (1997); Mafukidze (2006); Manuh (2005); and Zlotnik (2004). See http://www.imi.ox.ac.uk/ for information and links on African migration.

Concerning the MENA, a very useful website is www.carim.org. Baldwin-Edwards' report to the GCIM is also extremely useful with an extensive and up-to-date bibliography. The 2003 special issue of the Revue Europeenne des Migrations Internationales contains both French and English-language articles which can be accessed at http://remi.revues.org/ sommaire167.html. On remittances and MENA see Adams (2006). On Turkey, see Kirişci (2006) and Mutluer (2003). On Israel, see Bartram (2005).

On Latin America, the 2005 report written by O'Neil et al. for the GCIM provides an overview and can be accessed at www.gcim.org/en. IOM country reports are also helpful. For example, Venezuelan Facts and Figures can be accessed at www.IOM.int/jahia/Jahia/pid/451. Philip L. Martin's Migration News also is a very good source on Latin America as elsewhere. On Latin American migration to Europe, see Padilla and Peixoto (2006) and Pellegrino (2004). On Argentina, see Jachomiowicz (2006). The Economic Commission for Latin America and the Caribbean (ECLAC) also remains a valuable resource. Its Social Panorama of Latin America 2006 report can be accessed at www.eclac.cl/id.asp?id=27484.

Chapter 8

The State and International Migration: The Quest for Control

International migration to highly developed states entered a new phase during the global economic recession of the early 1970s. To combat illegal immigration, postindustrial democracies such as France, Germany, and the USA embarked on what can be termed a 'quest for control' over cross-border movements. This quest entailed sustained efforts to prevent illegal migration and the abuse or circumvention of immigration regulations and policies.

This chapter appraises key components of governmental strategies designed to better regulate immigration flows. Although focusing on transatlantic states, many of the issues addressed in this chapter are relevant to, and have implications for, other regions discussed in Chapters 6 and 7. The policies examined include employer sanctions enforcement, legalization or amnesty programmes (also called regularizations), temporary foreign-worker admission programmes, asylum and refugee policies, regional integration approaches, and measures against human smuggling and trafficking. Testifying to the growing significance of migration, cooperation on such issues has become a central feature of international politics. Migration policy has evolved over time from reflecting national-based and often short-term economic and political interests to broader and more comprehensive international (if not global) management strategies.

Employer sanctions

Since the 1970s, the USA and most European states have implemented laws punishing employers for the unauthorized hiring of undocumented aliens. Known as employer sanctions, they are often coupled with legalization programmes which give work and residence permits to undocumented workers who meet certain criteria. These carrot-and-stick measures, it is argued, remove the motivation for undocumented work since employers may be punished for hiring illegal aliens while formerly undocumented workers will regularize their legal status. However, in practice, these programmes have met resistance as employers often had the political clout to prevent effective enforcement of employer sanctions while many migrant workers failed to regularize due to fear of losing their job or being unable to find a new one.

Despite the political consensus behind many of these policies, effective enforcement was often lacking due to insufficient personnel, poor coordination between various agencies, inadequate judicial follow-up and the adaptation of employers and illegal employees to enforcement measures. Symptomatic of the progressive regionalization of immigration policies in Europe, the European Commission adopted in May 2007 a directive on employer sanctions designed to crackdown on the demand side of irregular migrant labour (CEC, 2007b). The directive's aim was to provide minimum standards and to harmonize preventive measures, employer sanctions, and enforcement policies across EU member states. The measures included employer verification of the identity and employment authorization of third-country nationals, as well as compulsory notification to competent governmental authorities of the intention to hire prior to the actual hiring of employees. Those employers who did not follow these measures would expose themselves to heavy fines and other costs including deportation costs and the repayment of wages, unpaid taxes and social security. Furthermore, other administrative penalties included the possibility of being barred from EU subsidies and business for a period of five years. Nevertheless, disagreements over the directive between EU member states persisted into 2008 (Goldriva, 2008).

Unlike many Western European states, the USA lacked an employer sanctions policy prior to 1986. The termination of the *Bracero* programme with Mexico in 1964 led to growing concerns over illegal migration to the USA during the 1960s and 1970s. However, these concerns were assuaged by the creation of *Maquiladores* (assembly plants just south of the US–Mexico border) which were established to provide alternative employment opportunities for former *Braceros* (migrant labourers). Nevertheless, many migrant labourers continued to enter the USA to seek employment. Such movement reflected the substantial levels of illegal migration during the *Bracero* programme from 1942 to 1964, during which some 5 million Mexicans were authorized to perform temporary labour services in the USA. In 1954, approximately 1 million Mexicans were deported during Operation Wetback.

Continued illegal migration from Mexico to the USA led to the appointment in 1978 of the Select Committee on Immigration and Refugee Policy (SCIRP). In 1981, SCIRP recommended the implementation of an employer sanctions policy, a legalization programme, and the introduction of a counterfeit-resistant employment identification document (SCIRP, 1981). In 1986, President Reagan signed into law the Immigration Reform and Control Act (IRCA) which made the hiring of unauthorized aliens a punishable offence. IRCA required employers to fill out an I-9 form for each new hire in order to prove the employee's employment eligibility. However, the IRCA permitted an assortment of documents, many of which could be easily forged or fraudulently obtained. The Commission for Immigration Reform concluded by 1994 that the employer sanctions system adopted in 1986 had failed because many unauthorized foreign workers could simply present false documents to employers (Martin and Miller, 2000b: 46).

The enforcement of employer sanctions was further hampered by political opposition within the USA. Several Hispanic advocacy groups alleged that employer sanctions would increase employment discrimination of minorities, while business interests viewed the I-9 requirement as another government-imposed burden. Others feared that enforcement would disrupt entire industries, such as labour-intensive agriculture, which would result in crops rotting in the fields and higher food costs. Even the AFL-CIO, the major confederation of unions, which had been a major proponent of punishing the illegal employment of undocumented aliens since the early 1980s, announced in 2000 that it no longer supported enforcement of employer sanctions. The AFL-CIO was under new leadership, which emerged from unions with large numbers of immigrant members including many undocumented workers. This faction had close ties to the US Conference of Catholic Bishops, which supported a broad legalization of the millions of illegally resident aliens. This diverse opposition ensured that there would be no political consensus in support of the enforcement of employer sanctions in the USA.

The overall record of employer sanctions enforcement has not been strong. In 1999, the US government announced that it was suspending enforcement, which resulted in a reduction of the number of INS employer investigations from 7,537 cases completed and 17,552 arrests in 1997 to 3,898 cases completed and 2,849 arrests in 1999 (INS, 2002: 214). The events of 11 September 2001 and the successive reorganization of the INS under the Department of Homeland Security (DHS) in 2003 signified a substantial shift in the mission of worksite inspectors. Enforcement took on a 'National Security focus', which resulted in the diversion of funds and resources from workplaces lacking security relevance to employers in key strategic areas, such as airports (Brownell, 2005).

The continued growth of the illegal alien population triggered the divisive immigration debate that has been at the forefront of US politics since 2004. This debate has renewed interest in the necessity of employer sanctions and counterfeit-proof work identification. Several proposals sought the establishment of a counterfeit-resistant identification card, the participation of employers in an electronic-based verification system, an increase in fines for contravening employers, an increase in border security, the creation of a guestworker programme, and the possibility for most migrants to benefit from a legal pathway to residency through earned legalization.

In 2007, the Bush Administration announced a major enforcement initiative centred on so-called no-match letters. Such letters are sent by the Social Security Administration to employers advising them that an employee's name or social security number do not match the agency's records. In response to a no-match letter, employers have 14 or 90 days to resolve the discrepancy or to fire the unauthorized worker or risk fines up to US$10,000. Prior to 2007, such no-match letters generally had not been followed-up with enforcement; however, a Department of Homeland Security spokesman has declared, '[w]e are tough and we are going to be even tougher' (Preston, 2007). The initiative appeared to confirm that the US never truly had a credible employer sanctions regime due, in part, to the ease of circumventing the 1986 law.

Legalization programmes

Prior to the 1970s, many national migration policies used 'back door' rather than 'front door' immigration to remedy labour or demographic shortages. In the USA, the de facto legalization of illegally employed Mexican workers was standard practice from 1942 to 1964, when it was commonly referred to as 'drying out wetbacks.' In France, aliens who took up employment in contravention of ONI procedures after 1947 were routinely legalized and, between 1945 and 1970, legalization comprised the major mode of legal entry into France (Miller, 1999: 40–41). Thereafter, the French government declared that legalization would be exceptional, but there were recurrent legalizations throughout the 1970s (Miller, 2002).

In 1981, the election of a Socialist President and a Leftist majority in the National Assembly set the stage for a new French approach to legalization to help combat illegal migration and employment. Unlike previous legalizations, trade unions and immigrant associations participated in the legalization effort and additional governmental personnel were mobilized to facilitate the processing of applications. As a result, approximately 120,000 of 150,000 applicants were legalized. However, assessments of the legalization programme varied; many eligible aliens did not know about the legalization programme or feared to participate in it. Furthermore, there was reason to believe that this legalization had a magnet effect that attracted additional illegal immigrants to France. Consequently, the legalization benefited its participants but did not alter the underlying labour-market dynamics fostering illegal migration and employment. Application deadlines were repeatedly extended and the criteria for eligibility evolved. But for French government officials the legalization of 1981–1983 constituted a major success, one fit for emulation elsewhere.

The legalization provisions in the US IRCA of 1986 differed in several key respects from its French counterpart. First, the IRCA had a five-year period between the cutoff date for eligibility (1 January 1982) and the effective starting date of the general programme (4 May 1987) known as I-687. The general programme was open to all aliens who could prove residency prior to 1 January 1982. Almost 1.7 million aliens applied for legal status under I-687 and 97 per cent were approved. A congressional bid to extend the deadline for application was defeated. The IRCA also had a programme for Special Agricultural Workers (SAW), which targeted aliens who could demonstrate evidence of seasonal employment for 90 days between 1 May 1985 and 1 May 1986. A total of 1.3 million aliens applied but widespread fraud contributed to a much lower approval rate than the I-687 programme. In all, approximately 2.7 million undocumented migrants underwent legalization under IRCA provisions (Kramer, 1999: 43; GAO, 2006; OECD, 2006).

The second major difference between the French and US legalization programmes involved the treatment of immediate family members of successful applicants. After prodding by the US Conference of Catholic Bishops, the US Government promulgated a 'family fairness doctrine', empowering INS district commissioners to grant temporary, protected legal status to illegally resident dependants of legalizing aliens out of humanitarian considerations. This doctrine was further developed under the Immigration Act of 1990, which enabled the spouses and children of legalized aliens to become permanent resident aliens (Miller, 1989: 143–144).

The migration transition of Southern European states during the 1980s led to a wave of mass legalizations under which more than 3.2 million aliens benefited. Since 1986, Italy has had five legalization programmes resulting in the regularization of about 1.4 million migrants, including 650,000 during the 2002–2004 programme. In 2005, Spain's *Normalisacíon* programme granted 549,000 visas (OECD, 2006: 82). However, many migrants reverted to illegal status due to expired visas and administrative backlogs, forcing governments to address the problem through subsequent legalizations (also see Chapter 5).

In 2000, Switzerland enacted a legalization programme to regularize approximately 15,000 aliens who had entered the country prior to 31 December 1992, mainly Sri Lankan citizens who had been denied refugee status but who could not be repatriated due to the continued conflict in Sri Lanka (OECD, 2001: 251). Similarly, legalization advocacy grew in Germany where authorities had long viewed legalization as a policy likely to backfire and encourage further illegal migration. Roman Catholic Cardinal Stazinsky of Berlin called for a German legalization policy in 2001, as did the German trade-union confederation (Appenzeller et al., 2001). In 2007, the lower house of the German parliament adopted legislation granting the possibility of legalization to employed aliens who had been denied refugee status but who could not be repatriated.

Paradoxically, as a new generation of European countries embraced mass legalizations, France, once Europe's leading advocate of legalization, began to shun such policies. In 2006, then Minister of the Interior Nicolas Sarkozy introduced a procedure to process the illegally resident parents of children in French schools on an individual basis. A total of 6,924 visas were conferred (*Le Monde*, 6 April 2007). This measure, along with an increase in deportation orders and the cancelling of a provision granting undocumented migrants legal status after 10 years of residency, marked a tightening of French immigration policy. Nevertheless, France recorded a 55 per cent increase in the number of migrants legalized from 2005 to 2006.

The debate concerning the wisdom of legalization as sound immigration policy also resonated across the Atlantic. In 2006 and 2007, several proposals emerged to meet the challenges posed by the growing undocumented population in the USA. Several of these proposals advocated 'earned legalization' which would permit undocumented migrants to benefit from a legal pathway to citizenship upon demonstration of English proficiency, uninterrupted employment, payment of taxes, and a clean criminal record. In 2006, President Bush advocated such a proposal along with increased border control. One year later, a bipartisan committee of Congress reached an agreement known as the 'great compromise', under which undocumented aliens would be given the opportunity to legalize if certain conditions were met, including the payment of administrative fees. Additionally, the bill would have established a guestworker programme and a points system emphasizing skills and credentials rather than family ties for future immigrants. However, the legislation faced opposition across the political spectrum and its defeat in June 2007 postponed any chance of comprehensive immigration reform in the USA until after the 2008 general election.

Assessments of legalization programmes on both sides of the Atlantic have varied. Legalizations can be interpreted as evidence of governmental inability to prevent illegal migration or as evidence that sovereign states can adapt to, and cope with, international population movements in the era of globalization. Opponents of legalization typically contend that such policies undermine the rule of law. Proponents of legalization point out that legalized aliens generally experience improvements in their overall socio-economic and employment prospects, though major transatlantic disparities have been observed as to the impact of such policies on migrants' lives (Laacher, 2002: 66; Levinson, 2005: 9–10).

Temporary foreign worker admission programmes

The post-Cold War era has witnessed the re-emergence of temporary foreign worker (TFW) programmes, which had been curtailed in Western Europe after 1973. This has occurred in states with a history of guestworker programmes, such as Germany and the Netherlands, as well as in states with little or no previous guestworker experience, such as Italy. Post-Cold War TFW programmes have differed in many respects from their predecessors in the 1960s and 1970s. For one thing, the number of admitted foreign workers has declined. In 2002, Germany granted nearly 375,000 temporary visas, of which 298,000 were for seasonal workers. However, this figure is low compared with the approximately 646,000 new foreign workers who entered Germany in 1969 (Castles and Kosack, 1973: 40). Other major differences include the separate treatment of highly skilled and low-skilled foreign labour, and host countries' claims of contributing to the economic development of sending nations through remittances (Castles, 2006b: 741).

Germany's resumption of TFW admissions was, in part, an effort to support the new democratic governments in Central and Eastern Europe and to secure their cooperation on combating illegal migration and human trafficking. Since the mid-1970s, representatives of influential German employer groups such as hotels, restaurants and agriculture had supported the adoption of a seasonal worker programme similar to the Swiss programme of the 1960s and 1970s. However, the Swiss government had changed its policy by the 1980s, as former seasonal workers and their families had come to comprise the single largest component of resident aliens in Switzerland. By 1999, only 10,000 seasonal workers were admitted to Switzerland, as compared with over 200,000 in 1964 (Miller, 1986: 71; OECD, 2001: 50). Like France, which admitted only 7,612 seasonal workers in 1999 as compared to a past average of 100,000 per year, the Swiss had largely phased out their seasonal foreign worker policy (Tapinos, 1984: 47). Hence, the German advocacy of emulation of Swiss seasonal foreign worker policy reflected a lapse in historical memory.

In Southern Europe, guestworker programmes remained essentially marginal policies (Reyneri, 2003; Castles, 2006b: 754). In Spain, many of the visas initially allotted for the recruitment of foreign workers were granted instead to illegal aliens undergoing legalization (Lopez-Garcia, 2001: 114–115). To complicate matters, some employers preferred illegal aliens to legal foreign workers in order to avoid social security payments (Lluch, 2002: 87–88). By 2002, most foreigners were required to return home in order to obtain a visa (Plewa and Miller, 2005:73). Nevertheless, backdoor immigration continued, resulting in the 2005 *Normalisacion* programme (see above). The recurring possibility of achieving long-term residence through mass legalization weakened the viability of TFW policies in Spain and other Mediterranean countries (Plewa and Miller, 2005; Castles, 2006b: 754).

In the USA, temporary foreign worker proposals have been championed as an effective way to legalize millions of illegally employed foreigners. However, it is doubtful that a TFW programme would reduce the employment of illegal aliens, as evidenced by the failure of such programmes in Europe. A recent Pew Hispanic poll revealed that, while showing strong support for a proposed guestworker programme, more than half of the Mexicans surveyed expressed a desire to remain permanently in the USA and most would likely stay upon the expiration of their proposed six-year renewable visa (Martin, 2005a: 47). Nevertheless, states and non-state actors alike have stressed that the return of guestworkers to their home countries through intelligently designed TFW programmes can reduce possible negative effects of international migration and ensure a win-win situation for both sending and receiving states (Castles, 2006b: 748).

The re-emergence of TFW programmes in the last decade has led to a dualistic approach to migration. Many states seek to settle and integrate highly skilled workers into their societies while restricting the length of stay of unskilled labourers. States have also placed greater emphasis on attracting international students and researchers with ties to the host country since such individuals constitute a pool of readily available (and desirable) migrants (OECD, 2006: 80–81).

Refugees and asylum

The number of refugees and asylum seekers worldwide has risen this century following a relative decline during the mid-1990s. As a result, asylum has increasingly become a major political issue in many Western countries. Sensationalist journalists and right-wing politicians map out dire consequences such as rocketing crime rates, fundamentalist terrorism and overstretched welfare systems. Calls for strict border control, the detention of asylum seekers and the deportation of illegal aliens abound. The public appeal of such polemics is obvious: right-wing electoral successes in countries as disparate as Denmark, the Netherlands, Belgium, Austria, France and Australia can be linked to fears of mass influxes from the south and east. Yet the reality is that the overwhelming majority of refugees remain in poor countries in Africa, Asia, the Middle East and Latin America.

Defining forced migration

Refugees and asylum seekers are *forced migrants* who flee their homes to escape persecution or conflict, rather than *voluntary migrants* who move for economic or other benefits. Popular usage tends to refer to all kinds of forced migrants as 'refugees', but most forced migrants flee for reasons not recognized by international refugee law, often remaining within their country of origin. Here we are mainly concerned with those who cross international borders, but all forms of forced migration are connected in both causes and effects (for more detail see Castles and Van Hear, 2005).

A *refugee* (or Convention refugee) is defined by the 1951 *United Nations Convention Relating to the Status of Refugees* as a person residing outside his or her country of nationality, who is unable or unwilling to return because of a 'well-founded fear of persecution on account of race, religion, nationality, membership in a particular social group, or political opinion.' By 2006, 147 of the UN's 192 member states had signed the Convention or its 1967 Protocol. Signatories undertake to protect refugees and to respect the principle of *non-refoulement* (not to return them to a country where they may be persecuted). UNHCR counted 9.9 million refugees by the end of 2006 (UNHCR, 2007a).

Resettlement refers to refugees permitted to move from countries of first asylum to countries able to offer long-term protection and assistance. Such persons are usually selected by UNHCR in cooperation with the governments of resettlement countries – mainly the USA, Canada, Australia and New Zealand, and to a lesser extent EU member states.

Asylum seekers are people who have crossed an international border in search of protection, but whose claims for refugee status have not yet been decided. Determination procedures may take many years. Host countries offer varying types of protection – typically full refugee status for those who fulfil the 1951 Convention criteria, temporary protection for war refugees, and humanitarian protection for people not considered refugees, but who might be endangered by return. In some European countries 90 per cent of asylum applications are rejected, yet many rejected applicants stay on. Without any clear legal status, they lead a marginalized existence. During 2006, 503,600 new asylum applications were made worldwide (UNHCR, 2007a).

Internally displaced persons (IDPs) 'have been forced to flee their homes because their lives were in danger, but unlike refugees they have not crossed an international border. Many IDPs remain exposed to violence, hunger and disease during their displacement and are subject to a multitude of human rights violations' (IDMC, 2007: 9). There are no international legal instruments or institutions specifically designed to protect IDPs, although they are covered by general human rights conventions. As it became harder for people displaced by violence to cross frontiers, IDP numbers grew worldwide to a total of 24.5 million people in 2006. IDPs are to be found in 52 countries (IDMC, 2007: 11).

Development displacees are people compelled to move by large-scale development projects, such as dams, airports, roads and urban housing. The World Bank – which funds many development projects – estimates that development projects displace 10–15 million people per year. Many development displacees experience permanent impoverishment and social marginalization (Cernea and McDowell, 2000).

Environmental and disaster displacees are people displaced by environmental change (desertification, deforestation, land degradation, rising sea levels), natural disasters (floods, volcanoes, landslides, earthquakes), and man-made disasters (industrial accidents, radioactivity). This category is controversial (Castles, 2002): some environmentalists claim that there are already tens of millions of 'environmental refugees' and that, with global warming, hundreds of millions may eventually be at risk of displacement (Myers and Kent, 1995; Myers, 1997). Refugee experts question such views, noting that, while environmental factors do play a part in forced migration, displacement is always closely linked to other factors, such as social and ethnic conflict, weak states, inequitable distribution of resources and abuse of human rights (Black, 1998; 2001).

Finally, the concept of *persons of concern* to the UNHCR includes Convention refugees plus all persons who receive protection or assistance from

UNHCR: asylum seekers, internally displaced persons, returnees and stateless persons.

Global forced migration trends

The global refugee population grew from 2.4 million in 1975 to 14.9 million in 1990. A peak was reached after the end of the Cold War with 18.2 million refugees in 1993 (UNHCR, 1995: 2000a). By 2000, the global refugee population had declined to 12.1 million, and in 2005 it was down to 8.7 million – the lowest figure since 1980. But the trend reversed in 2006 with refugee numbers jumping to 9.9 million, mainly due to the flight of 1.2 million Iraqis to Jordan and Syria (UNHCR, 2007a: 5).

The number of persons of concern to the UNHCR peaked at 27.4 million in 1995, but had decreased to 17.5 million by 2003. It appeared that global violence was declining (UNHCR, 2006b), but the number of persons of concern rose to a new record of 32.9 million in 2006. Most of the increase was due to UNHCR's enhanced responsibility for IDPs and stateless persons, but some 3 million persons were newly displaced (UNHCR, 2007a).

Refugees come from areas hit by war, violence and chaos. UNHCR listed the world's top refugee-producing countries at the beginning of 2006 as Afghanistan (1.9 million), Sudan (693,000), Burundi (438,700), Democratic Republic of Congo (430,600) and Somalia (394,800). However, these figures only refer to refugees for whom UNHCR takes responsibility. While Pakistan hosted over 1 million recognized refugees and Iran over 700,000, there were another 1.5 million Afghans living outside camps in Pakistan and an unknown number in Iran. Moreover, UNHCR does not cover most Palestinian refugees, who still constitute the world's largest exile population. Some 4.3 million Palestinian refugees come under the mandate of UNRWA (UNHCR, 2006a).

The top 10 host countries for refugees are (in descending order) Pakistan, Iran, USA, Syria, Germany, Jordan, Tanzania, UK, China and Chad. Significantly only three – USA (844,000 refugees), Germany (605,000) and UK (302,000) – are rich countries (UNHCR, 2007a). Refugee flows are generated in regions of poverty and conflict, and mostly remain within these regions. Yet since the 1980s, Western Europe, North America and Australia have been gripped by panic about asylum. Annual asylum applications in these areas rose from 90,400 in 1983 to 323,050 in 1988, and then surged again with the end of the Cold War to 828,645 in 1992 (UNHCR, 1995: 253). Applications fell sharply to 480,000 by 1995 (OECD, 2001: 280). Nearly all this decline was due to a decrease in applications following changes in refugee law in Germany and Sweden. Numbers began to increase again from 1997. For OECD countries as a whole, asylum seeker inflows increased to 594,000 in 2001 and then declined to 298,000 in 2005 (OECD, 2007: 321). Globally, new asylum applications in 2006 totalled 503,000.

South Africa became the main destination for new asylum seekers with 53,400 new applications – more than the USA (UNHCR, 2007a).

Forced migration and global politics

Forced migration has become a major factor in global politics (Loescher, 2001). This is reflected in the changing nature of the *international refugee regime*. This term designates a set of legal norms based on humanitarian and human rights law, as well as a number of institutions designed to protect and assist refugees. The core of the regime is the 1951 Convention, and the key institution is the UNHCR, but many other organizations also play a part: intergovernmental agencies like the International Committee of the Red Cross (ICRC), the World Food Programme (WFP) and the United Nations Children's Fund (UNICEF); as well as hundreds of nongovernmental organizations (NGOs) such as OXFAM, CARE International, Médecins sans Frontiers (MSF) and the International Rescue Committee (IRC).

The refugee regime was shaped by two major international conflicts: World War II and the Cold War (Keely, 2001). Many of the 40 million displaced persons who left Europe in 1945 were resettled in Australia, Canada and other countries, where they made an important contribution to postwar economic growth. During the Cold War, offering asylum to those who 'voted with their feet' against communism was a powerful source of propaganda for the West. Since the 'non-departure regime' of the Iron Curtain kept the overall asylum levels low, the West could afford to offer a warm welcome to those few who made it. Asylum levels remained manageable with occasional spikes following events like the 1956 Hungarian Revolution and the 1968 Prague Spring.

Different refugee situations were developing in the South. The colonial legacy led to weak undemocratic states, underdeveloped economies and widespread poverty in Asia, Africa and Latin America. Northern countries sought to maintain their dominance by influencing new elites, while the Soviet Bloc encouraged revolutionary movements. The escalation of struggles against white colonial or settler regimes in Africa from the 1960s, resistance against US-supported military regimes in Latin America in the 1970s and 1980s, and long-drawn-out political and ethnic struggles in the Middle East and Asia – all led to vast flows of refugees (Zolberg et al., 1989). With the end of the Cold War, from the 1980s, economic globalization led to profound social transformations, population movements and increased inequality, fuelling renewed conflicts (see Chapter 3).

Northern states and international agencies responded by claiming that such situations were qualitatively different from the individual persecution for which the 1951 Convention was designed (Chimni, 1998). The solution of permanent resettlement in developed countries was not seen as appropriate, except for Indo-Chinese and Cuban refugees who fitted the Cold War mould. In 1969, the Organization of African Unity (OAU) introduced its own Refugee Convention, which broadened the refugee definition to include people forced to flee their country by war, human rights violations or generalized violence. A similar definition for Latin America was contained in the Cartagena Declaration of 1984. Today, UNHCR follows this broader approach and has begun to take on new functions as a humanitarian relief organization. It helps run camps and provides food and medical care around the world (Loescher, 2001). This expanding role has made it one of the most powerful UN agencies.

By the 1980s, asylum seekers were coming directly to Europe and North America from conflict zones in Latin America, Africa and Asia. Numbers increased sharply with the collapse of the Soviet Bloc. The most dramatic flows were from Albania to Italy in 1991 and again in 1997, and from former Yugoslavia during the wars in Croatia, Bosnia and Kosovo. Many of the 1.3 million asylum applicants arriving in Germany between 1991 and 1995 were members of ethnic minorities (such as Roma) from Romania, Bulgaria and elsewhere in Eastern Europe. The situation was further complicated by ethnic minorities returning to ancestral homelands as well as undocumented workers from Poland, Ukraine and other post-Soviet states (see Chapter 5).

The early 1990s were thus a period of politicization of asylum. Extreme-right mobilization, arson attacks on asylum-seeker hostels and assaults on foreigners were threatening public order. European states reacted with a series of restrictions, which seemed to herald the construction of a 'Fortress Europe' (UNHCR, 2000a; Keely, 2001):

- Changes in national legislation to restrict access to refugee status.
- Temporary protection regimes instead of permanent refugee status for people fleeing the wars in former Yugoslavia.
- 'Non-arrival policies' to prevent people without adequate documentation from entering Western Europe. Citizens of certain states were required to obtain visas before departure. 'Carrier sanctions' compelled airline personnel to check documents before allowing people to embark.
- Diversion policies: by declaring countries bordering the EU to be 'safe third countries', Western European countries could return asylum seekers to these states, if they had used them as transit routes.
- Restrictive interpretations of the 1951 UN Refugee Convention, for instance, excluding persecution through 'non-state actors' (such as the Taliban in Afghanistan).
- European cooperation on asylum and immigration rules, through the Schengen Convention, the Dublin Convention, and EU agreements.

The US experience was similar: refugee admissions began to decline in the late 1990s as traditional flows from communist countries tailed off with the end of the Cold War. Then the events of 11 September 2001 precipitated a sharp fall in admissions. Restrictive measures in receiving countries – rather than real improvements in human rights – were the main reason for the decrease in the number of officially recognized refugees worldwide after 1995.

The refugee regime of Western countries has been fundamentally transformed over the last 30 years. It has changed from a system designed to welcome Cold War refugees from the East and to resettle them as permanent exiles in new homes, to an exclusionary regime, designed to keep out asylum seekers from the South. The EU's 2005 *Hague Action Programme for Freedom, Justice and Security* continues this trend, with its strong emphasis on migration management, border control and a common asylum policy (CEC, 2005c).

Refugees and asylum seekers in Western countries

Between 1975 and 2000 the USA provided permanent resettlement to over 2 million refugees, including some 1.3 million people from Indochina. The USA accepted more people for resettlement during this period than the rest of the world combined (UNHCR, 2000b). Inflows from Central America and the Caribbean were also important, although many refugees entered 'illegally' as the USA did not consider all such states to be refugee-producing countries. The open door policy towards Cubans, which had been in place since 1959, was restricted in the 1980s, and interdiction at sea commenced in the 1990s. Many Haitians attempting to come to the USA during the 1980s and 1990s were prevented from doing so.

After the terrorist attacks of 11 September 2001, the USA temporarily halted its refugee resettlement programme. Stronger detention powers were introduced for noncitizens suspected of terrorist activities. In 2006, the US Government 'held 2000 to 3000 asylum seekers in detention on any given day, often in remote areas with limited access to legal counsel' (USCRI, 2007c). Detention times of up to three and a half years have been recorded (USCRI, 2007c). Refugee admission fell from an average of 76,000 a year in the 1997–2001 period, to fewer than 29,000 in both 2002 and 2003. Enhanced security checks, increased processing costs and suspicion of applicants of Muslim background made it very difficult to obtain asylum. However, annual numbers recovered to around 50,000 by 2005, partly through programmes to target priority groups in urgent need of resettlement (Martin, 2005a).

Canada, like the USA, accepted large numbers of people from Indochina, some 200,000 between 1975 and 1995. By 1998, resettlement admissions had fallen to under 9,000, only to rise again to 17,000 in 1999 as a result of the humanitarian evacuation programme for Kosovo (UNHCR, 2000b). By 2005, resettlement was again down to 10,400 (UNHCR, 2006b). The number of asylum seekers coming to Canada rose to its highest level ever: 44,000 in 2001. Most were from the Indian subcontinent or China, with Sri Lanka topping the list (USCR, 2001: 261). The 2006 figure of 30,000 new refugees and asylum seekers combined shows a certain shift in origins, with the largest groups coming from Colombia (5,000), Mexico (3,900), Afghanistan (3,000) and China (2,700) (USCRI, 2007b).

Australia also remains a major resettlement country. Its Humanitarian Programme has admitted between 12,000 and 16,000 refugees per year since the early 1990s. Admissions under the programme totalled 14,144 in 2005–2006 (DIAC, 2007b). The number of asylum seekers arriving by boat averaged only a few hundred per year up to the late 1990s, but went up to about 4,000 a year from 1999 to 2001 (Crock and Saul, 2002: 24). Although this was low compared with other parts of the world, it was seen as undermining the tradition of strict government control of entries. This led to a politicization of refugee issues (Castles and Vasta, 2004). Strict laws were passed 'excising' Australia's northern islands from its 'migration zone'. In the 'Pacific solution', asylum seekers arriving by boat from Indonesia (mainly Afghans, Iraqis and Iranians) were to be sent to islands like Nauru and Papua New Guinea to be held in camps. Other asylum seekers, already in Australia, were kept in grim detention centres in remote areas. Some were detained for several years, and even children were kept behind the wire. Such policies evoked considerable protest. By 2005, there were signs of liberalization (USCRI, 2007a), and the new ALP Government elected in 2007 vowed to close the offshore camps.

In the EU, the top five countries of origin for asylum seekers during the 1990–2000 period were the Federal Republic of Yugoslavia (836,000 persons), Romania (400,000), Turkey (356,000), Iraq (211,000) and Afghanistan (155,000). The two peaks of asylum seekers from Yugoslavia coincided with the wars in Croatia and Bosnia in 1991–1993 and the war in Kosovo in 1998–1999. The majority of the Romanians came in the early 1990s, at a time of persecution of Roma and other ethnic minorities. Most refugees from Turkey were Kurds, fleeing violent conflicts involving government forces (Castles et al., 2003).

Asylum applications declined in the latter part of the 1990s before increasing again. The UK had had relatively few asylum applicants earlier on, but by 1999 new applications were running at over 90,000 a year, with a peak of 103,000 in 2002. In 2003, Prime Minister Blair said he wanted to cut asylum seeker entries by 30–40 per cent within a few months (BBC News, 2003). The British Government put forward a 'new vision' for refugee protection. One idea was to set up protection areas for refugees in their region of origin, so that asylum seekers could be safely removed from the EU. Another was to set up 'transit processing centres' outside EU borders: asylum seekers who arrived in the EU would be sent to camps in countries like Libya and Ukraine for determination of their applications (Castles and Van Hear, 2005: 118–119). These proposals raised serious human rights concerns and were not implemented in this form, but they helped create a climate in which asylum seekers were seen as a security threat, justifying ever-tighter legal procedures, and increased use of detention and deportation.

The result was that new asylum applications in the EU15 fell sharply from 393,000 in 2002 to 180,000 in 2006. For the UK, the 2006 inflow was down to 28,000, while France received 31,000 asylum applications. Relative to population size, the highest rates of asylum applications were in Cyprus, Austria and Sweden. By 2006, the effects of the invasion of Iraq were becoming obvious: asylum applications by Iraqis rose 80 per cent to 19,375 persons – the largest asylum inflow to the EU. Next came Russia, Serbia and Montenegro, Afghanistan and Turkey (UNHCR, 2007b).

Protracted refugee situations

Clearly, flight from violence remains a major international challenge, and efforts for prevention of conflicts and for protection and assistance of forced migrants are far from adequate. As rich countries become less and less willing to admit asylum seekers, many are seeking refuge in new destinations like South Africa, Kenya, Egypt, Malaysia and Thailand. Since conflict and impoverishment often go together, it is increasingly difficult to make a clear distinction between economic and forced migration.

The great majority of refugees remain in poor countries, which may lack the capacity to protect them and the resources to provide adequate material assistance. Refugees may spend many years living on subsistence rations in isolated camps, with no prospect of returning home or of resettlement. UNHCR applies the term 'protracted refugee situation' to refugee populations of 25,000 persons or more in exile for five or more years, while the US Committee on Refugees and Immigrants speaks of 'warehoused refugees' (USCR, 2004). UNHCR estimated that there were 6.2 million refugees in such conditions in 2003 – about two-thirds of all refugees. UNHCR identified 38 such situations, of which 22 (affecting 2.3 million refugees) were in sub-Saharan Africa. However, the largest were in the region comprising Central Asia, South West Asia, North Africa and the Middle East, where eight major protracted refugee situations affected 2.7 million refugees (UNHCR, 2004).

Regional integration

States have sought to regulate international migration either through bilateral treaties or through regional agreements. The latter option could only prove to be a viable solution provided that member states of regional organizations committed themselves to the long-term goal of evening out national economies (Castles, 2006a and b: 749). A question remains as to whether regional integration in the post-Cold War period in Europe and North America helped or hindered the quest for migration control. Transatlantic comparisons need to be grounded in history, as the evolution of the two regional integration processes proved quite dissimilar. The European project is much older and more far-reaching than the North America Free Trade Agreement (NAFTA), and there is no inevitable logic that NAFTA will follow the same path as the European Union.

The European Union's governance structure

Stretching back to the European Coal and Steel Community (ECSC) of the early 1950s and the European Community (EC) up to 1992, the EU and its predecessors have comprised a federalist project with an explicit commitment to eventually supersede member-state sovereignty through the creation of European institutions and governance. The project has always been security-driven, as regional integration was above all a strategy to prevent the recurrence of war between member states.

The Single European Act (SEA) of 1986 aimed to achieve a genuine common market and paved the way for signature of the 1992 Treaty on European Union (TEU, also known as the Maastricht Treaty), which resulted in the reinforcement and expansion of federalist European institutions within the then 15-member-state area. The TEU created three pillars related to the single market, Justice and Home Affairs, and the Common Foreign and Security Policy respectively. Governance procedures in the pillars varied, with the first pillar being the most supranational – that is, controlled by decisions at the EU level rather than by member states. The TEU left immigration and asylum matters in the third pillar, that is, in the hands of the member states.

Aiming to secure an 'area of freedom, security, and justice', the 1997 Treaty of Amsterdam integrated into the EU body of law all decisions made by the member states of the Schengen Agreement (see below). Issues concerning 'visas, asylum, immigration, and other policies related to free movement of persons' were brought under the first pillar of the Union. This common immigration and refugee policy introduced a progressive transfer of decisions pertaining to free movement (external border control, asylum, immigration, and rights of third-country nationals) from intergovernmental to supranational authority. This approach was buttressed at the Tampere Summit (Finland), which defined a comprehensive approach to asylum, managed migration, and enhanced partnership with sending regions. The November 2004 Hague programme established goals to expand the 'area of freedom, security, and justice' over the 2005–2010 period.

Freedom of movement within the European Communities and the European Union

Migration has always figured in the history of European integration. The 1951 Treaty of Paris, which created the ECSC, barred employment restrictions based on nationality for citizens of the six member states (Geddes, 2000: 45). The 1957 Treaty of Rome envisaged the creation of a common market between the six signatory states. Under Article 48, workers from member states were to enjoy freedom of movement if they found employment in another member state. In the 1950s, Italy pushed for regional integration in order to foster employment opportunities for its many unemployed citizens (Romero, 1993). Other member states of the EC resisted. By 1968, when Article 48 came into effect, Italy's unemployment problem had eased, due in part to economic development spurred by the infusion of EC structural funds. Italian citizens were nevertheless the major beneficiaries of Article 48, but relatively little intra-EC labour migration occurred, despite expectations of much more (Werner, 1973). It was firmly established that the freedom of labour movement applied only to citizens of EC member states, not to third-country nationals from outside the EC.

The planned accession of Spain and Portugal in the mid-1980s sparked an important debate over the likely effects on labour mobility. Some feared the rest of the enlarged EC would be flooded with Portuguese and Spanish workers. However, at the end of a seven-year transition period, the predicted massive inflow did not occur. Instead, Spain and Portugal had become significant lands of immigration in their own right as EC structural funds and private investments poured in. Intra-European capital mobility substituted for intra-European labour mobility (Koslowski, 2000: 117; see also Chapter 5).

The growing support for the creation of a more genuine common market led France, Germany, Belgium, Luxemburg, and the Netherlands to sign the Schengen Agreement in 1985. They committed themselves to hasten the creation of a border-free Europe in which EU citizens could circulate freely internally with harmonized external frontier controls. The SEA of 1986 defined the single market as 'an area without internal borders in which the free movement of goods, persons, services, and capital is ensured within the provision of this treaty' (Geddes, 2000: 70). Many Europeans, including the governments of several EU member states, balked at the idea of eliminating internal boundaries, fearing that it would lead to further illegal migration and loss of governmental control over entry and stay of aliens. Indeed, anti-immigrant parties such as the *Front National* in France, which were hostile to the EU for nationalist reasons, made opposition to such agreements part of their programmes. However, signatories of the Schengen Agreement retained the prerogative to reimpose frontier control if warranted by circumstances, and several signatories subsequently availed themselves of this option.

In March 1995, the Schengen Agreement finally came into force for those signatory states which had established the necessary procedures: Germany, Belgium, Spain, France, Portugal, Luxemburg, and the Netherlands. This meant complete removal of border controls for people moving between these countries. Border elimination was, however, compensated for by the creation of the Schengen Information System (SIS), a network of information designed to enhance cooperation between states on judicial matters such as transnational crime and terrorism. Effectively, the Agreement created a new class of 'Schengen citizens' to be added to the existing categories of EU citizens and 'third-country' (i.e. non-EU) citizens. Austria joined the Schengen Agreement in 1995, followed by Denmark, Finland, and Sweden in 1996 (Denmark was able to opt out of certain sections). At first, the UK and Ireland refused to join the Schengen Agreement, insisting on their own stricter border controls of people coming from the continent, but eventually agreed to take part in some aspects of the Agreement.

In 2000–2001, negotiations between the EU and the Central and Eastern European Countries plus Malta and Cyprus (A10) over planned accession sparked a debate concerning the potential inflows of Polish labour to Germany and France. Labour-mobility restrictions were placed on the workers of Central and Eastern European states (the A8), which joined the EU in 2004, by most, but not all, of the 15 states already comprising the EU (see Chapter 5). As part of the agreed transition period, Germany could limit free movement and access to its labour market for another two years following the 2009 deadline. In July 2007, the Merkel government announced its decision to lift the restrictions, most likely as a result of the February 2006 report on transitional procedures released by the European Commission (CEC, 2004). The document stressed the positive effects of free movement on the economies and labour markets of the countries that had already relaxed labour movement restrictions. Spain and Portugal also removed restrictions.

Comparable fears surrounded Turkey's candidacy bid. Following a favourable vote of the European Parliament, EU leaders decided to initiate accession talks with Turkey in October 2005 despite the reservations held by several governments. Unlike previous waves of enlargement in which periods of adjustment were established, permanent mechanisms were considered to control the additional migratory fluxes of Turkish workers expected after accession to the EU. There is no doubt that the spectre of further Turkish immigration to Europe together with rising Islamophobia fuelled by politicians played a significant role in the referenda of May 2005 that led to the French and Dutch rejections of the Constitutional Treaty. As attested by the Turkish case, the use of the 'race card' to satisfy political ambitions remains a dangerous tradition in European politics.

European citizenship

Under TEU, resident aliens from other EU states are enfranchised to vote in their country of residence (in local and European, but not national, elections), an important aspect of EU citizenship. Nevertheless, provisions protect EU countries in which the proportion of foreign nationals is greater than 20 per cent, such as Luxembourg. By 2006, 13.2 million residents (2.7 per cent of the total population) of the 27 EU member states were from other EU states (Münz et al., 2007: 2–4).

More problematic has been the status of third-country nationals. By 2006, the third-county national residents of the 27 EU member states had risen to 27.3 million (5.6 per cent of the total population) (Münz et al., 2007: 2–4). These individuals do not benefit from freedom of movement. Instead, member states largely retain their prerogatives over entry, stay, and removal of non-EU citizens. The European Commission, the supranational half of the EU's dual executive, favoured granting freedom of movement within the European space to third-country nationals, but this was opposed in the Council of Ministers, which represents the interests of member states. Among other objections, several EU member states argued that the European Commission Proposal would further devalue the importance of national citizenship. Despite exhortations to harmonize EU policy and facilitate the integration of migrants, political participation in the democratic process of host societies remained a discretionary prerogative of member states and insignificant concessions were granted as regards to intra-EU mobility.

There is no conclusive evidence as to whether the elimination of internal borders within the European space has resulted in a loss of control over international population movements other than those of EU citizens. The overall effect of European regional integration in recent years may have made the European quest for control more credible, as EU states participating in the Schengen group have been able to externalize control functions through the creation of a buffer zone in Central and Eastern Europe and a common border in Southern Europe. The EU remains open to legal migration and porous to illegal migration. But the enlargements, treaties, and institutional changes of recent years have been significantly affected by migration control concerns.

The North American Free Trade Area (NAFTA)

The origins of NAFTA had much to do with the sudden progression of regional integration in Europe in the mid-1980s. Rightly or wrongly, many EC trading-partners feared that Schengen and the SEA would lead to a Fortress Europa, a zone less accessible to exports from outside the EC. This perception helped hasten the signature of a US–Canadian free-trade agreement in 1988. Later, Mexican President Carlos Salinas approached the US administration with the idea of enlarging the US–Canadian free-trade pact to include Mexico. President Bush referred the Mexican proposal to his National Security Council, which supported the idea. The NAFTA treaty was signed in 1993 and came into effect on 1 January 1994. Unlike the EU, NAFTA only created a free-trade area. Nevertheless, this much less ambitious project met with considerable political opposition in the USA and in Mexico, where it helped spark the Zapatista revolt.

Paradoxically, concerns over international migration figured centrally in NAFTA's genesis but such concerns were barely mentioned in the treaty text. US and Mexican views on illegal migration were sharply opposed. To Mexicans, migration to the USA was driven by US labour market demands. For the USA, much migration was in contravention of its laws and was spurred by the paucity of socioeconomic opportunities in Mexico. Simply put, the Mexican economy did not generate sufficient growth and jobs to employ its growing population. Restrictions on mobility remained largely unaltered by the treaty as only certain categories of professionals could move freely across borders.

During the run-up to NAFTA, both President Clinton and President Salinas hailed the pact as a way to reduce illegal migration. Salinas warned that the US would either get Mexican tomatoes or Mexican migrants to pick them in the US. Such presidential optimism over the migration-reducing impact of NAFTA belied the key research finding of droves of studies of international migration after IRCA, namely that trade liberalization would diminish illegal migration only over the long term. Philip L. Martin later refined this finding into his theory of a 'migration hump' (Martin, 1993). Illegal migration from Mexico to the USA in fact grew significantly in the wake of NAFTA. Liberalization of the Mexican economy in the 1990s hit the poor and middle-class very hard. Farmers and their families in the formerly subsidized *Ejido* sector, one-third of Mexico's population, were adversely affected and many moved northwards, just as Martin had predicted. Roughly 3 million authorized and 2.6 million illegal migrants came to the USA from 1995 to 2000, compared with 1.9 and 1.5 million respectively from 1990 to 1994 (Hufbauer et al., 2005: 448). Overall, NAFTA has led to significantly expanded trade between the signatory states and greater socioeconomic interdependence.

The election of Vincente Fox as President of Mexico in 2000 ushered in a new era. President Fox and his newly elected American counterpart, President Bush, sought a fresh departure in US–Mexico relations, specifically on bilateral migration issues. President Fox and his foreign minister repeatedly referred to the European experience and called for freedom of migration within NAFTA. However, the two regional integration projects differed markedly due to the US dominance of the North American economy and the huge economic gap between Mexico and the USA (OECD, 1998: 7). The evocation of a European referent betrayed a misunderstanding of the history of regional integration in Europe. EC member states resisted Italy's efforts to export its unemployed northward in the immediate postwar era. The EU initially decided against accession of Turkey in large part due to concerns that Turkish membership would result in further mass emigration even after a transition period (Martin, 1991).

Curiously, there was little public discussion of what might be the most important European referent to NAFTA, namely possible North American emulation of structural and regional funds, which have had the effect of levelling the socioeconomic playing field within the European space. In European regional integration history, an aspect of the commitment to a federalist project involved the use of European funds to aid less developed areas. Italy and later Ireland, Spain and Portugal were all major beneficiaries. The contrast with the North American situation was stark (Miller and Gabriel, 2008).

Regional integration in North America and Europe has had important implications for governmental control strategies. The historical and institutional contexts of the two projects vary greatly but they comprise a salient dimension of overall strategies to reduce illegal or unwanted migration. It may be that NAFTA will evolve into something more akin to the EU. However, the short-term results of NAFTA have been a significant increase in illegal migration from Mexico to the USA. Nevertheless, at least one study has predicted a deceleration of Mexican migration to the USA by 2010 due to a combination of Mexico's declining fertility rate and improved economic and employment conditions (Hufbauer et al., 2005: 464).

The 'migration industry'

In order to help explain the frequent failure of official migration policies to achieve their objectives, one must examine the emergence of the so-called migration industry. This term embraces a broad spectrum of people who earn their livelihood by organizing migratory movements. Such people include travel agents, labour recruiters, brokers, interpreters, housing agents, immigration lawyers, human smugglers (like the 'coyotes' who guide Mexican workers across the Rio Grande, or the Moroccan fishermen who ferry Africans to Spain), and even counterfeiters who falsify official identification documents and passports. Document forgery constitutes a great concern as irregular migrants increasingly use counterfeit tourist visas to enter countries through airport facilities. Banking institutions have become part of the migration industry as well, as many banks have established special transfer facilities for remittances.

Migration agents also include members of migrant communities such as shopkeepers, priests, teachers and other community leaders who help their compatriots on a voluntary or part-time basis. Others are unscrupulous criminals, out to exploit migrants or asylum seekers by charging them extortionate fees for oftentimes nonexistent jobs. Such criminals vary from isolated individuals to highly structured transnational criminal organizations (TCOs) which have drawn increased attention over the past few years. Yet others are police officers or bureaucrats who seek to make money on the side by showing people loopholes in regulations or issuing false documents. One major impediment to efforts aimed at curbing irregular migration has been that smugglers are often viewed as 'social bandits,' if not heroes, rather than criminals (Kyle and Liang, 2001: 1).

The development of the migration industry is an inevitable aspect of the social networks and the transnational linkages which are part of the migratory process (see Chapter 2). Once a migratory movement is established, a variety of needs for special services arise. Even governments which initiate labour recruitment rarely provide all of the necessary services. While some countries tend to use bilateral treaties, others, as exemplified by the UK, have tended to utilize 'third party entities' or private operators to contract guestworkers (GAO, 2006: 21–23). Third party recruitment is, however, viewed as more prone to abuse and labour exploitation, hence demanding close supervision by governmental authorities. In spontaneous or illegal movements, the need for agents and brokers is all the greater. There is a broad range of entrepreneurial opportunities, which are seized upon by both migrants and nonmigrants alike. The role of the agents and brokers is vital: without them, few migrants would have the information or contacts needed for successful migration.

In time, the migration industry can become the primary motive force in a migratory movement. In such situations, governmental policies aimed at curtailing the migratory movement run counter to the economic interests of the migration agents who foster the continuation of the migration even though the form of the migration may change (for example, from legal worker recruitment to illegal entry facilitation). One observer has characterized migration agents as 'a vast unseen international network underpinning a global labour market; a horde of termites ... boring through the national fortifications against migration and changing whole societies' (Harris, 1996: 135).

Human smuggling and trafficking

A disturbing and increasingly salient feature of the migration industry has been the rise of organizations devoted to the smuggling and trafficking of migrants. It is important to distinguish between people-trafficking and people-smuggling. Formal definitions are embodied in two international treaties, known as the 'Vienna Protocols', adopted by the UN General Assembly in 2000. According to Ann Gallagher (2002) of the UN High Commission for Human Rights:

> Smuggled migrants are moved illegally for profit; they are partners, however unequal, in a commercial transaction ... [b]y contrast, the movement of trafficked persons is based on deception and coercion whose purpose is exploitation. The profit in trafficking comes not from the movement but from the sale of trafficked person's sexual services or labour in the country of destination.

It is impossible to accurately measure the number of people affected by trafficking and smuggling due to the clandestine and criminal nature of such activities. Clients of smuggling gangs include not only economic migrants, but also legitimate refugees unable to make an asylum claim because restrictive border rules prevent them from entering countries of potential asylum (Gibney, 2000). Içduygu's comprehensive study based on official governmental sources highlights the scope of the smuggling industry in Turkey (Içduygu, 2004: 302) As a gateway to the European Union, 200,000 irregular migrants pass through Turkey every year at an estimated cost of $1,600 per person paid to smugglers, hence amounting to a $300 million annual business. A quarter of migrants were known to have used the services of smugglers to enter Turkey, while most expected to resort to such assistance to cross over to Europe. About 400,000 migrants were apprehended while crossing Turkey between 1997 and 2003. The number of smugglers arrested rose from 98 in 1998 to 850 by 2000, and reached 1,157 in 2002.

A US government report revealed that the percentage of aliens smuggled increased from 9 per cent of all border patrol apprehensions in 1997 to 14 per cent in 1999. In the fiscal year 1999, the INS arrested 4,100 smugglers and over 40,000 smuggled aliens. The INS prosecuted 2,000 smugglers, of whom 61 per cent were convicted, receiving an average sentence of 10 months and an average fine of US$140 (GAO, 2000: 2). Approximately 2,400 smugglers were convicted in 2004 in various US courts (DHS, 2006a: 15–16). However, the number of convictions was down to 1,657 in the fiscal year 2005 out of a total of 2,713 arrests (DHS, 2006b: 4). A UN Under-Secretary General held that 200 million persons worldwide were involved in some manner in human trafficking. He stated 'this is the fastest growing criminal market in the world because of the number of people who are involved, the scale of profits being generated for criminal organizations and because of its multifold nature' (Crossette, 2000; see also Parisot, 1998). Other sources advanced much lower figures, ranging from 4 to 27 million persons trafficked. A 2006 US report estimated the number of individuals trafficked across borders to be 800,000 per year (therefore not taking into account the many more trafficked within countries). One study estimated that as many as 50,000 women were trafficked to the USA each year (Richards, 1999: 3). The human trafficking industry may generate profits of US$ 5 to 10 billion per year (Martin and Miller, 2000a: 969). An ILO report estimated the number of victims of any form of forced labour to be 12.3 million at any given time (USDS, 2007: 8).

Women and young girls are particularly vulnerable to trafficking and constitute 80 per cent of all victims (minors in general constitute approximately 50 per cent of all victims) (USDS, 2007: 8). The UN Office on Drugs and Crime confirmed these figures (UNODC, 2006: 33). Seventy per cent of sources in the UN human trafficking database reported cases involving women, 33 per cent children, and only 9 per cent men. Of these cases, 87 per cent involved sexual exploitation while 28 per cent involved forced labour. The IOM, which made combating human trafficking one of its priorities in the 1990s, gave multiple reasons for the post-Cold War upsurge in human trafficking (1999: 4). Migrants driven by war, persecution, violence, and poverty often find themselves in search of better opportunities. They sometimes accept the services of traffickers of their own free will. However, many are deceived by promises of good jobs and salaries into accepting traffickers' services. Possibilities for legal immigration have declined and anti-trafficking legislation is often absent or deficient with inadequate enforcement.

Imprisonment, deportation and even death are the risks faced by illegal migrants, while the leaders of smuggling and trafficking organizations are rarely apprehended. Trafficking is supply-driven: British women's minister Harriet Harman pointed out in July 2007 that 85 per cent of women in British brothels now came from outside the UK, compared with only 15 per cent 10 years earlier. The sex industry had been transformed by global trafficking, yet only 30 men had been prosecuted in Britain for trafficking women for prostitution, and no man had ever been prosecuted for paying for sex with a trafficked woman (Branigan, 2007).

It is still unclear how new laws and regulations have affected human smuggling and trafficking. Some observers have contended that increased restrictive measures in the EU created greater demand for traffickers' services (Morrison, 1998). A number of analysts attributed the deaths of 58 migrants being transported to Dover, England, in 2000 to restrictive laws. The clientele of traffickers and smugglers often include persons who might have valid claims for refugee status, such as Kurds fleeing Iraq (Kyle and Koslowski, 2001: 340).

Similar unintended outcomes were witnessed in the USA (Skerry and Rockwell, 1998; Cornelius, 2001). By disrupting the modus operandi and traditional routes of smugglers, increased border enforcement has contributed to rising fees. Underscoring the false dichotomy that sometimes exists between smuggling and trafficking, insolvent migrants have, upon arrival, been forced into a condition of debt bondage until they reimburse the smuggler. Additionally, increased border enforcement has resulted in mounting deaths as smugglers take greater risks to achieve their mission. In 2005, 472 deaths were reported along the US–Mexico border, an increase from 241 deaths in 1999 (GAO, 2006: 9; see also Chapter 7).

In 2000, the USA enacted the Trafficking Victims Protection Act (TVPA) in order to combat trafficking and assist victims. The US also began to monitor anti-trafficking efforts globally and, in 2006, the US spent more than US$102 million to fight trafficking in persons, of which 72 per cent funded international projects. By the spring of 2007, nearly 1,200 victims had been certified and could claim governmental benefits comparable to those granted to refugees (USDS, 2007: 49). Furthermore, the TVPA created a new category of visas for victims who aided US authorities in the prosecution of traffickers. By spring 2007, 729 'T-visas' had been attributed to emancipated victims and 645 to their family members.

As a country of origin, transit, and destination, the People's Republic of China (PRC) instituted very harsh measures to counter human trafficking, including life imprisonment and capital punishment for convicted criminals (Chin, 1999: 200). Studies of smuggled and trafficked Chinese revealed complex global networks which were difficult to dismantle through law enforcement. Lower-echelon 'snakeheads' might be apprehended and punished but higher-echelon criminals were more elusive. Koslowski assessed the overall picture of the effectiveness of anti-smuggling and human trafficking countermeasures as 'quite dim' (Kyle and Koslowski, 2001: 353). He noted, however, that fear of organized crime might '... galvanize serious international co-operation to curb human smuggling ...'

Conclusions: a quixotic or credible quest for control?

Assessment of the capacity of nation-states to regulate international migration seems both imperative and exceptionally daunting. Western states clearly intervene more now than in the past to regulate migration. The quest for control characteristically includes imposition of employer sanctions, phasing in and out of temporary foreign worker admissions policies, legalizations, measures against human trafficking, and measures concerning refugees and asylum seekers. Concurrently, the migration industry developed, as did seemingly interminable political controversies about how best to achieve the quest for control. Regional integration significantly affected these efforts and, in turn, they spurred regional integration in North America and Europe. In recent years, more comprehensive, indeed global, migration management strategies have been advocated. These are discussed and analysed in Chapters 1, 3 and 12.

The overall assessment that emerges is mixed. Persisting levels of illegal immigration throughout the world should by no means be interpreted as the failure of states to control their borders. What states do *does* in fact matter a great deal. Yet their governments, in the formulation and implementation of such policies, confront powerful transnational forces and domestic interests. In the USA alone, the population of illegally resident aliens expanded to an estimated 12 million by 2007, thereby further validating scepticism that has prevailed over the last three decades about the willingness and capacity of democratic governments to regulate international migration. The events of 11 September 2001 threw into sharp relief shortcomings in US immigration control. The USA, and many other states around the world, began to reform policies and procedures to enhance the security of their homeland, thus raising hopes for more credible and coherent policies in the future (OECD, 2001: 14).

Guide to further reading

The Age of Migration website www.age-of-migration.com includes additional text on 'The French approach to combating illegal employment' (8.1). It also includes a table: 'summary of major legalization programmes in the Transatlantic area' (8.2).

Concerning laws punishing illegal employment of aliens, many governments issue yearly or periodic reports on enforcement. The French government, for instance, began to publish reports by the mid-1970s. The title of the report has evolved from time to time with governmental changes: see Martin and Miller (2000b). Also see GAO (2006) and USDS (2006).

On temporary foreign worker policies, see Castles (2006b), Plewa and Miller (2005), Plewa (2007), and Martin, Abella and Kuptsch (2006). Also see GCIM (2005). Analyses of legalization policies have proliferated in the twenty-first century, especially in France. See De Bruycker (2000), Levinson (2005), Heckmann and Wunderlich (2005) and Miller (2002). Comparison of international migration and regionalization processes constitutes an increasingly important area of inquiry. See Lavenex and Uçarer (2002), Faist and Ette (2007), Geddes (2000 and 2003), Hufbauer et al., (2005), Miller and Stefanova (2006), Koslowski (2000) and Miller and Gabriel (2008).

Laczko and Gozdziak (2005) examine data problems and issues in research on human trafficking. The volume comprises two issues of the journal *International Migration*. The IOM and the International Centre for Migration Policy Development engage in extensive research on human trafficking, which is reported on in their publications. Valuable annual reports on human trafficking include the US Department of State's Trafficking in Persons Report.

Chapter 9

Migration and Security

Prior to 9/11, students of international relations and international security paid scant attention to international migration. Conversely, students of international migration rarely analysed the implications of international migration for security, or for understanding of international relations or world politics (Tirman, 2004). The attacks on 9/11 and the subsequent bombings in Madrid, London and elsewhere greatly altered that state of affairs, resulting in the increased relevance of the security dimension of international migration. Indeed, the new scrutiny given to migration and security is part of the politicization of international migration which was identified as a defining tendency of the age of migration in Chapter 1.

This chapter cannot comprehensively examine the nexus between migration and security. Instead, the first section of this chapter will endeavour to elucidate why migration and security have become a much more salient concern in the post-Cold War period than in the post-World War II era. The fact that international migration is now perceived as a significant or priority issue virtually around the world reflects ideational as well as material transformations. The second section will examine key dimensions of migration and security. Subsequent sections will assess the threat posed by immigrant-background Islamic populations in the transatlantic area and analyse the War on Terrorism.

Why the rediscovery of the international migration and security nexus?

As recounted in Chapter 4, international migration has continuously forged and reforged societies and states since time immemorial. Migrations often proceeded peacefully, but many engendered various conflicts. Suffice it to recall that mass European migrations to the New World resulted in the decimation and subjugation of indigenous populations.

In many respects, the period between 1945 and 1980 was unusual. The horrors of World War II discredited the xenophobia of the extreme right and perceptions of migrants as a security threat. Indeed, international migration was often viewed as an economic phenomenon and a largely beneficial one at that. Moreover, international migration was believed to be a temporary or conjunctural phenomenon, especially in Western Europe.

Box 9.1 Spillover of the PKK insurgency to Germany

During the 1960s and 1970s, the Federal Republic of Germany recruited thousands of Turkish citizens to work in its industries and services. Many of these Turkish citizens were of Kurdish background. This seemed to be of little political consequence during the mass recruitment period, but became a political issue as Kurdish aspirations for independence or autonomy from Turkey were galvanized during the 1980s. The PKK emerged as an important Kurdish separatist organization leading an armed insurrection against the Turkish Republic.

Up to one-third of the over 2 million Turkish citizens resident in Germany by the 1990s were of Kurdish origin. Perhaps 50,000 of these individuals sympathized with the PKK and up to 12,000 became active members of the party or its front organizations (Boulanger, 2000: 23). By striking at Turkish consulates, airlines and businesses, the PKK transformed Germany and other Western European states into a second front. Moreover, Turkish repression of the PKK-led insurgency, which took tens of thousands of lives, complicated diplomatic ties with EU member states. Turkish counterinsurgency measures included mysterious death squads and the uprooting and forced relocation of millions of Kurdish civilians. This backdrop rendered PKK activities on German soil and German and Turkish countermeasures highly emotive and significant. By the mid-1990s, the PKK had become a vital German national security concern, particularly after the PKK leader, Abdallah Öcalan, threatened to send suicide bombers against German targets in retaliation for German assistance to Turkey in its struggle with the PKK.

Despite the German decision to outlaw the PKK and its front organizations, the PKK possessed an extensive organizational infrastructure in Germany and nearby European states. PKK tactics featured protest marches and hunger strikes. Street demonstrations on Kurdish and Turkish issues, though routinely banned by German authorities, were staged and frequently resulted in violent clashes. In 1996, the German government sought to strengthen its

⟶

For mainstream students of international relations, national states constituted the principal actors in international relations, and all other actors paled into insignificance. The key questions in international relations pertained to peace and war. International migration did not appear to bear importantly upon either, hence the nearly total lack of connection between the study of international relations and of international migration. This state of affairs began to evolve in the 1970s. Some students of world politics began to investigate 'low politics' as opposed to the 'high politics' of peace and war. Keohane and Nye broadened the scope of inquiry to include transnational phenomena, political events that affect at least two states concurrently (Keohane and Nye, 1977). A window on the study of international migration and international relations had opened.

The failure of postwar guestworker policies in Western Europe by the mid-1970s resulted in unexpected migrant settlement and family

---

→

ban on PKK street protests by making participation in such events a major offence. Several Kurdish protesters were subsequently apprehended and recommended for deportation, even though hunger strikes in Turkish prisons had cost the lives of numerous prisoners and the torture and ill-treatment of Kurdish prisoners was believed to be commonplace. As a result, the deportation of Kurdish activists raised important legal and human rights issues, which polarized German public opinion.

The arrest of Abdallah Öcalan by Turkish authorities in 1999 sparked a massive wave of Kurdish protests in Europe and as far away as Australia. Three Kurds were killed after trying to enter the Israeli consulate in Berlin and scores of protesters were injured. During his subsequent trial, Öcalan called upon his followers to abandon armed struggle, which resulted in reduced Kurdish militant activities on German soil, but the unresolved Kurdish question remained and, with it, the potential for renewed conflict. Such concerns undoubtedly contributed to Germany's opposition to the US-led attack upon Iraq in 2003, which damaged overall diplomatic relations between the long-time allies. This dramatic turn of events had much to do with differing German and US perspectives on the migration and security nexus in the Middle East.

As the Iraq war evolved into a protracted quagmire for the USA, German apprehensions about the invasion appeared well founded. In addition to the huge toll of killed and wounded, at least 2 million refugees flowed to nearby states, some of whom were resettled in Europe, particularly in Sweden (see Chapter 8). In the largely autonomous Kurdish-ruled enclave in northern Iraq, remnants of the PKK reorganized and, by 2007, launched strikes on Turkish troops within Turkey. Kurdish militants similarly attacked targets in Iran from Iraqi territory. Both Iran and Turkey struck back, and a major escalation of fighting appeared possible as Turkish aircraft and soldiers attacked PKK targets inside Iraqi territory in late 2007 and early 2008.

---

reunification. At this time, the prospects for conventional or nuclear war between NATO and Warsaw bloc-affiliated states had declined significantly (Barnett, 2004). Interstate conflicts had also declined (Kaldor, 2001). The accretion of settlers, swelled by an influx of asylum seekers and unauthorized migrants in the 1980s, resulted in the securitization of migration issues: the linking of migration issues to security studies (Waever et al., 1993; Buzan et al., 1998; Tirman, 2004; Messina, 2007). Concurrently, combating terrorism emerged as a national security priority in many states, not exclusively in the transatlantic area (Laqueur, 2003). However, the understanding of the interface between international migration and terrorism lagged far behind developments in the real world.

Boxes 9.1 and 9.2 recount how conflicts in Turkey and Algeria spilled over into Germany and France respectively during the 1990s. By

Box 9.2 Spillover of insurgency in Algeria to France

In 1992, an offshoot of the Islamic Salvation Front, the Armed Islamic Group (GIA), pursued an insurgency against the Algerian government. Tens of thousands died in a merciless war of terrorism and counterterrorism. France provided military and economic support to the Algerian government, which became the pretext for the extension of GIA operations to French soil. A network of militants waged a bombing campaign, principally in the Paris region in 1995, before being dismantled. In late 1996, the GIA was thought to have been behind another fatal bombing, although no group took responsibility for the attack. Some French journalists and scholars believed that the GIA had been penetrated by Algerian agents who then manipulated GIA militants into attacking targets in France in order to bolster French support for the Algerian government (Aggoun and Rivoire, 2004).

French authorities undertook numerous steps to prevent bombings and to capture the bombers. Persons of North African appearance were routinely subjected to identity checks. Most French citizens and resident aliens of North African background accepted such checks as a necessary inconvenience. Indeed, information supplied by such individuals greatly aided in the dismantling of the terrorist group, several of whom were killed in shoot-outs with French police. Nevertheless, French police rounded up scores of suspected GIA sympathizers on several occasions as apprehension of attacks remained high.

→

mid-decade, both had become key national security concerns. Moreover, both the Kurdish Workers Party (PKK) and the Armed Islamic Group (GIA) had threatened to fly hijacked airplanes into targets. Such threats foreshadowed the attacks of 9/11, which are often interpreted as ushering in a new era in world politics. However, the 9/11 attacks actually reflected trends and patterns in the making for decades. In retrospect, attacks of that nature were predictable (Shenon, 2008), but a confluence of factors masked the threat.

In the postwar era, security studies centred on the assessment of threats emanating from states. Less attention was given to threats posed by non-state actors. Al-Qaida, which literally means 'the base' in Arabic, and its allies constituted such a non-state actor. As documented in the 9/11 Commission Report, US security agencies suffered from poor coordination and legal barriers to information sharing. The very factors that explain the lack of connection between the study of international migration and international relations largely explain why the threat posed by Al-Qaida was insufficiently and belatedly apprehended. International migration affects the security of states in ways that differ from other threats due to its highly complex, diffuse and often contradictory nature (Adamson, 2006: 197).

→

Such fears appeared warranted in the aftermath of 11 September 2001. Scores of GIA and Al-Qaida-linked individuals, mainly of North African background, were detained for involvement in various plots, including one to attack the US embassy in Paris. Several of those arrested were French citizens of North African background like Zacarias Moussaoui, who was accused of plotting with the perpetrators of the 9/11 attacks. At least one French citizen of North African background died during the Allied military campaign against the Taliban and Al-Qaida in Afghanistan. Algerians and other individuals of North African Muslim background with links to the GIA figured prominently in the hundreds of arrests in the transatlantic area. The anti-Western resentment of some of those arrested was linked to perceived injustices endured by migrants and their families. Despite increased vigilance, several French citizens were involved in a series of suicide bombings of Western targets in Casablanca in 2003. Several of the bombers had been recruited into a fundamentalist network in the Parisian suburbs and their involvement was deeply disturbing to the French population, including most of the Islamic community.

Despite an amnesty offer from the Algerian government to Islamic militants who laid down their arms in 2006, many continued to fight. In 2007, these militants renamed themselves Al-Qaida in the Islamic Maghreb and launched a murderous bombing campaign in Algiers. French and other European intelligence officials continue to worry about the potential for spillover to Europe.

Political and security analysts were slow to grasp how political movements inclined to use terrorism, violence directed against a civilian population to achieve political goals, could thrive in migrant and displaced populations. International mobility became a key feature of asymmetric conflicts pitting more technologically advanced and powerful nation-states against insurgent movements. Al-Qaida exemplifies such threats, as it constitutes a network of largely migrant militants engaged in a war against the West (Roy, 2003; Tirman, 2004).

Key dimensions of the international migration and security nexus

Traditionally, security has been viewed through the prism of state security. As a result, relatively few scholars have sought to conceptualize what can be termed the migration and security nexus (Miller, 2000; Tirman, 2004). However, the scope of security concerns is much broader, and is inclusive of human security (Poku and Graham, 1998). International migrants often suffer insecurity; indeed, their insecurity should be a major focus of security studies.

Much migration from the South is driven by the lack of human security that finds expression in impoverishment, violence, lack of human rights and weak states. Such political, social and economic underdevelopment is linked to histories of colonialism and the present condition of global inequality (see Chapter 3). Where states are unable to create legal migration systems for necessary labour, many migrants are also forced to move under conditions of considerable insecurity. Smuggling, trafficking, bonded labour and lack of human and worker rights are the fate of millions of migrants. Even legal migrants may have an insecure residence status and be vulnerable to economic exploitation, discrimination and racist violence. Sometimes legal changes can push existing migrants into illegality, as happened to the *sans papiers* in France in the 1990s. The frequent insecurity of the people of poorer countries is often forgotten in discussions of state security, yet the two phenomena are closely linked.

Frequently, such migrant insecurity is linked to perceived threats, which can be divided into three categories: cultural, socioeconomic and political (Lucassen, 2005). The first perceived threat, the perception of migrant and migrant-background populations as challenging the cultural status quo, may contribute most to migrant insecurity. Such perceptions were commonplace in Europe during the 1980s and have contributed to the aforementioned securitization of migration policies (Messina, 2007). Mexican and other 'Hispanic' migrants to the USA have also been viewed as posing a cultural threat (Huntington, 2004). Oftentimes, the religious identity and linguistic practices of migrants loom large in perceived threats. Examples of the second perceived threat, the perception of migrant populations as socioeconomic threats, include Italians in Third Republic France, ethnic Chinese diasporas in much of Southeast Asia, Syro-Lebanese communities in West Africa, and Chechen and other populations from the Caucasus in the post-Soviet Russian Federation. Lastly, the third perceived threat, perceptions of migrants as potentially politically disloyal or subversive, includes migrant populations such as Palestinians residing in Kuwait prior to the first Gulf War, Yemenites living in Saudi Arabia at the same juncture, ethnic Chinese in Indonesia suspected of political subversion on behalf of Communist China in the 1960s and ethnic Russian populations stranded in Baltic Republics after the collapse of the Soviet Union.

The perceived threats of international migration to national identity and the maintenance of cultural cohesiveness are an important aspect of the challenges posed by international migration to the sovereign state (Adamson, 2006). International migration affects the autonomy of states, their sovereign prerogative of control over all matters transpiring within the territory of the state, and the capacity of states to implement public policies and to enforce laws (Adamson, 2006). Alternatively, international migration can also increase state power. International migration often facilitates economic growth and is frequently viewed as indispensable to a state's economic wellbeing. Influxes of migrants often slow population contraction and the ageing of populations, which can adversely affect economic performance and overall state security. Additionally, many immigrants serve as soldiers, and intelligence services frequently tap immigrant expertise and knowledge of languages. If effective public policies are pursued, international migration can enhance rather than detract from state power (Adamson, 2006: 185).

A state's immigration policies can also contribute to its 'soft power', its ability to achieve foreign policy and security objectives without recourse to military or economic means of persuasion. Nye views the large body of foreign students studying in the USA as an important source of soft power (Nye, 2004). Similarly, treatment of immigrants can affect a state's reputation abroad, a not inconsequential matter for diplomacy and 'smart power', influence that arises from investing in global goods that better enable states to address global challenges (Graham and Poku, 2000; National Commission on Terrorist Attacks upon the United States, 2004).

International migration has also had a significant impact on the changing nature of violent conflicts. Migration flows can interact with other factors to foment violent conflict in three ways: by providing resources that fuel internal conflicts, by facilitating networks of organized crime and by serving as conduits for international terrorism (Adamson, 2006: 190–191). Migrant and diasporic communities often provide financial aid and recruits to groups engaged in conflicts in their homeland. Kosovar Albanian communities in Western Europe and North America, for instance, provided much of the financing and many recruits for the Kosovo Liberation Army which, by the late 1990s, engaged in heavy fighting with Serbian forces in the former Serbian republic which acceded to independence in 2008. Similarly, Tamil Sri Lankans in Europe, Canada, India and elsewhere have aided and abetted the Tamil Tigers' insurrection in Sri Lanka.

Since 1990, the foreign and national security policies of most states around the world have prioritized the combating of human trafficking and other types of transnational crime (see Chapter 8). In some instances, organizations viewed as engaging in terrorism, such as the PKK, have simultaneously been involved in human trafficking. Other such organizations have been engaged in drugs and arms smuggling. While the growing awareness of the security dimensions of international migration since 9/11 has sometimes led to restrictive policy measures, it should be obvious that certain kinds of migration and certain blends of public policies enhance security, rather than undermine it. Strong states capable of implementing public policies successfully and enforcing laws are best positioned to harness the power of international migration (Adamson, 2006: 199). It is also clear that many states, especially in Europe, are relinquishing elements of their autonomy in order to better maintain the ability to regulate the movement of goods, capital, people and ideas across borders (see Chapters 8 and 12). Such measures have enhanced state power rather than diminished it. Alternatively, weak states are oftentimes threatened by international migration-related security issues.

Immigrant and immigrant-background Muslims and transatlantic security

Since 9/11, questions pertaining to the incorporation of Muslim immigrants and their offspring in Western democracies have assumed geostrategic significance. A US Senate hearing in 2006 referred to Europe as the third front in the War on Terrorism and a good number of books, articles and reports have analysed Islamic populations in the transatlantic area since 2001.

Prior to 2001, there had been considerable scholarship on Muslim immigrants and their offspring. Aside from areas like the former Yugoslavia and Bulgaria where large Muslim populations have resided for many centuries, most Muslims in the transatlantic area are post-World War II immigrants or their descendants. France constitutes somewhat of an exception to the pattern due to the fact that the French Republic encompassed Algeria from the nineteenth century until Algerian independence in 1962. Upon independence, many persons of Algerian Muslim background living in metropolitan France retained their French citizenship. Furthermore, tens of thousands of *Harkis*, French troops of Algerian Muslim background, fled to France to avoid reprisals. However, during the interwar period, and even prior to 1914, many Muslim-background persons from French Algeria were recruited for employment in metropolitan France, and some settled. The Algerian Muslim population in interwar France was widely viewed as constituting a security threat (Rosenberg, 2006).

For the most part, post-World War II migration of Muslims to the West was not viewed as a security problem until the 1970s and 1980s. In most instances, Muslim guestworkers and seasonal foreign workers were assumed to be temporary residents who would eventually repatriate. The UK constituted an exception to the pattern as Commonwealth migrants from India, Pakistan and elsewhere could settle. Postwar France pursued a two-pronged immigration policy, welcoming settlement of immigrants from nearby European states like Italy but regarding foreign workers from largely Islamic states like Morocco, Turkey, Tunisia and, after 1962, Algeria as temporary migrants who would repatriate (Tapinos, 1975). By the 1970s, the supposedly temporary foreign worker policies had unravelled.

While there were Islamic fundamentalist movements active in Western Europe in the 1970s, they were not perceived as posing much of a threat. The success of the Islamic Revolution in Iran in 1979 began to change that perception. In many Arab states and Turkey, secular-oriented governments felt threatened by Islamic fundamentalist movements which viewed them as illegitimate. Such governments came to be viewed by some of the more radical Islamic fundamentalists as the 'near enemy' that had to be overthrown and replaced with truly Islamic governance (Gerges, 2005).

Thus, by the 1980s, the growth of Islamic fundamentalism came to affect the transatlantic area in a variety of ways. A massacre of Syrian army cadets led to the brutal repression of Syrian fundamentalists. Many of the survivors ended up as refugees in Germany. The Israeli invasion of Lebanon in 1982 prompted Iranian intervention in the conflict and the creation of Hezbollah, the Party of God. American and French troops deployed to the Beirut area as part of the Multinational Force in 1982 suffered grievous losses in suicide bomb attacks thought to have been perpetrated by Hezbollah or its allies. The war in Afghanistan between the Soviet Union and its Afghan allies and the Mujahadeen, Afghanis who fought the Soviets, began to attract non-Afghan Muslim volunteers, some of whom came from the transatlantic area. This marked the genesis of what would later become Al-Qaida, which Oliver Roy has labelled as a predominantly Western movement (Roy, 2003). A US-led coalition of states, including Pakistan and Saudi Arabia, armed and aided the Mujahadeen. Following the defeat of the Soviet Union in Afghanistan, the Pakistani Inter-Services intelligence agency would help create the Taliban, which recruited heavily amongst the Afghani refugees in Pakistan, another case of refugee–soldiers. By 1996, the Taliban had seized control over most of Afghanistan.

The perpetrators of the 1993 bombing of the World Trade Center in Manhattan were mainly Arab immigrants to the USA. In retrospect, the attack should have galvanized greater alarm and stronger countermeasures. A succession of federal commissions in the USA investigating terrorism warned that additional countermeasures were needed, but the warnings were largely not heeded (National Commission on Terrorist Attacks upon the United States, 2004). On the eve of the new millennium, an alert US customs agent detected the nervousness of Ahmed Ressam, an Algerian Armed Islamic Group member living in Canada, who planned to attack Los Angeles airport. By 2001, a number of US officials feared a catastrophic attack by Al-Qaida upon a target or targets in the USA, but failed to prevent it (Shenon, 2008).

Following the US-led invasion of Iraq in 2003, hundreds, if not thousands, of European Muslims have volunteered to fight the USA in Iraq and many have died or been captured. Thousands of European Muslims have received military training in camps in the Middle East and North Africa (MENA) and have subsequently returned to Europe (Scheuer, 2008). The terrorist attacks in Madrid and London and the numerous planned attacks thwarted by European police and security agencies, who have detained thousands of suspected radical Muslims since 2001, provide ample grounds for concern about Muslims in Europe. There is a struggle for the hearts and minds of Muslims in the West, but the preponderance of evidence suggests that

Al-Qaida-style radicalism holds little appeal for the vast majority of Muslims in the transatlantic area.

The profiles and histories of Islamic populations in North America and Europe are quite divergent. Muslims living in North America are generally more prosperous and well educated than Muslims in Europe, many of whom were recruited as unskilled labour (CSIS, 2006). However, even within Western Europe, Muslim populations typically are highly heterogeneous. Muslims of Turkish background, for example, are very diverse. There are Sunnis and Alevis (orthodox Muslims and a non-orthodox Shíite offshoot respectively), as well as ethnic Kurds and Turks. Many Turks and Kurds are quite secular in orientation. It is true that many Muslim immigrants and their descendants confront incorporation barriers in housing, education and employment and endure prejudice and racism. However, the gist of the huge body of social science research on the incorporation of Muslim immigrants and their offspring suggests that most are slowly incorporating, much like previous waves of immigration in the transatlantic space that have been viewed as problematic or threatening in the past (Lucassen, 2005; also see Chapters 10 and 11).

Perhaps the best analysis of largely MENA-background migrant populations in Europe both prior to and after 9/11 has been conducted in France. One well known study, conducted by Michèle Tribalat, found quite contrasting evidence about the state of incorporation of various national-origin communities from the MENA area (Tribalat, 1995). The evidence revealed the widespread use of French in migrant households and decreasing use of Arabic and other mother tongues. Furthermore, the evidence showed a decline in traditional arranged marriages, a rising intermarriage rate with French citizens and social practices, such as youth dating and cohabitation with French citizens, that suggested an overall pattern of improving incorporation, if not assimilation. The major problem areas were high unemployment, perceived discrimination and educational problems. Tribalat also found that some communities did not fit the general pattern. Persons of Algerian background tended to be less religious and more secular than persons of Moroccan background. Furthermore, the Turkish community in France exhibited a lower proclivity to French usage at home, interacted less with French society and virtually never intermarried with French citizens.

Tribalat's study made obvious the danger of overgeneralization with respect to the incredibly heterogeneous MENA-background populations of France, to say nothing of the rest of Europe or the West. But her key insight, that France's Muslims were incorporating and becoming French like earlier waves of immigrants to France, largely agreed with the insights of other social scientists. France's top experts on radical Islam, Gilles Kepel and Olivier Roy, doubt that extremists will find much support in immigrant-background populations in Europe, although Kepel criticized British toleration of radical Muslims in the London area (Kepel, 2002, 2005; Roy, 2003). Their assessments appear borne out by research on public opinion in the Middle East and North Africa and other predominantly Muslim areas of the world, which evidence scant support for terrorism (Esposito and Mogahed, 2007).

It is difficult to characterize the gist of the burgeoning social science literature concerned with incorporation of migrant-background (especially Muslim) populations in Europe. Incorporation processes are complex. Scholars follow diverse approaches and the evidence appears mixed and variable from one country to the next. The attacks of 9/11 and in Madrid and London have had the effect of transforming the decades-old, indeed centuries-old, question of migrant incorporation in Western countries into an important security issue, not only in Europe but also in North America and Australia. In recent years much has been written about the susceptibility, indeed the likelihood, of migrant Muslim and migrant-background Muslim mobilization into terrorist movements (Ye'or, 2005; Bawer, 2006; Philips, 2006; Berlinski, 2007). For the most part, such articles and books appear often inadequately based upon social science literatures pertaining to migrant incorporation.

A more measured analysis would begin with the acknowledgement that all developed countries are highly vulnerable to the havoc wreaked by violence-prone groups. This vulnerability is heightened by the permeability of developed states to migration ranging from illegal migration to human trafficking. More broadly put, as Robert Cooper has argued, the key security threat to developed countries in the twenty-first century is disorder emanating from failed or failing states external to the developed countries (Cooper, 2003). The very conditions conducive to the emergence of terrorist threats are also those conducive to mass asylum seeking and human trafficking.

In the not so recent past, extreme leftist groups looked to migrant populations for mass support but generally did not succeed in its mobilization. There is little reason not to expect that pattern to hold into the twenty-first century. The new generation of terrorist organizations has thus far succeeded in attracting the support of a fringe of the migrant and migrant-background population. The Madrid and London bombings attest to the seriousness of the threat posed by this fringe. But the key to any successful counterterrorism strategy involves knowing who is and who is not the enemy. The great bulk of migrant and migrant-background populations should not be construed as the enemy. Seen in this light, successful incorporation of migrant and migrant-background populations in Western countries looms as a geostrategic imperative in the War on Terrorism.

Migration, security and the War on Terrorism

What has been termed the War on Terrorism by the George W. Bush Administration involves calculated exaggeration and misleading simplification. After largely ignoring the threat posed by Al-Qaida in its first months in office, the Administration then declared a war and likened it to World War II (Clarke, 2004; Shenon, 2008). In doing so, the Administration exaggerated the threat posed by radical Muslims at a time when overall support for achievement of Islamic fundamentalist goals through political violence had declined significantly and mainstream Islamic fundamentalist movements had rejected violence while embracing incremental reform (Gerges, 2005; Roy, 1994). This is not to suggest that US retaliation against Al-Qaida and the Taliban in Afghanistan in 2001 was somehow unwarranted; on the contrary.

The Administration simultaneously committed a classic error in counterterrorism by misidentifying the enemy and overreacting to terrorist outrages. It did so by incorrectly specifying the terrorist enemy, creating an amalgamation of global terrorist threats that had little or nothing to do with reality, although there are well known ties and contacts between movements that engage in terrorism, say, for example, between the Irish Republican Army and the Armed Forces of the Columbian Revolution (FARC) in South America. It then compounded the error by linking the government of Iraq to Al-Qaida and then using that and an unwarranted claim concerning weapons of mass destruction as a pretext to invade Iraq.

The invasion of Iraq proved counterproductive to the campaign against Al-Qaida and its allies, like the Taliban, in Afghanistan (Ricks, 2007). Nevertheless, the US-led attack on Afghanistan, later supported by a NATO deployment, badly damaged Taliban and Al-Qaida forces in Afghanistan without eliminating them (Miller, 2007). By 2007, Taliban forces in Afghanistan were resurgent, in part due to the ability of Al-Qaida and confederates, like the Taliban, to use frontier areas of Pakistan as a de facto sanctuary to regroup, train and recruit. Thus, by 2008, Al-Qaida remained a very real threat, still capable of striking 'the far enemy' as it had on 11 September 2001.

Al-Qaida probably played some role in the mounting of the attack in Madrid in 2004 and the attacks in London in 2005 and 2007, although these attacks were initially viewed as home-grown but inspired by Al-Qaida (Benjamin and Simon, 2005). In early 2008, French and Spanish authorities thwarted a planned series of attacks in Western Europe, apparently timed again to precede general elections in Spain. Most of the suspects were Pakistani migrants, several of whom had recently arrived from the frontier area of Waziristan in Pakistan. Spain's most important antiterrorism magistrate commented, '... the jihadi threat from Pakistan is the biggest emerging threat we are facing in Europe. Pakistan is an ideological and training hotbed for jihadists, and they are being exported here' (Scoliano et al., 2008). Hence, the US Secretary of Defence correctly claimed that the outcome of the war in Afghanistan directly affected European security (Shanker and Kulish, 2008). However, his exhortation for Europeans '... to fracture and destroy this movement in its infancy – to permanently reduce its ability to strike globally and catastrophically, while deflating its ideology' again appeared to ignore the several decades which have witnessed the rise and ebb of radical Islam (Roy, 1994; Gerges, 2005).

While untoward developments in Pakistan and Afghanistan proved unsettling, it remained imperative to assess accurately the threat posed by Al-Qaida and its allies. Their violence is condemned by most Islamic fundamentalists and the vast majority of Muslims around the world, including Muslims in the West. They constitute a fringe movement in Islamic politics that has little or nothing to do with movements like the Lebanese Hezbollah or the Palestinian Hamas or Fatah. Al-Qaida stokes perceptions of grievance that are widely shared by Muslims. But the conflation of groups like Hamas with Al-Qaida only impedes progress on an all-important issue, the long overdue creation of a Palestinian state that could assuage those perceptions of grievance.

It remains highly unlikely that movements linked to Al-Qaida can achieve strategic victory, the takeover of a country like Pakistan, Algeria or Afghanistan. However, a veteran former CIA analyst with extensive experience on Afghanistan has predicted that the USA and its allies will lose the wars in Afghanistan and Iraq (Scheuer, 2004, 2008). Consolidation of Al-Qaida control over any given area would expose that area to attack by all the means available to the US military. Fundamentalist Muslim insurrections in the 1970–2000 period were crushed. The failure to defeat 'the near enemy', such as regimes in Egypt and Algeria, in part due to US and French assistance, led most Islamic fundamentalists to moderate their politics and to eschew armed struggle. Al-Qaida's strikes against 'the far enemy' thus need to be seen for what they were, acts of desperation by a fringe movement with limited prospects for mobilizing much support from Muslims anywhere. Again, other analysts have made starkly contrasting assessments, especially concerning the progress of radical Islam in the Caucasus, Somalia, Nigeria, Thailand and Bangladesh, where radicalized former migrant workers in the Gulf states have emerged as a new and destabilizing factor (see Scheuer, 2008).

Even the counterproductive course of US foreign and national security policy since 2002 has not fundamentally improved Al-Qaida's long-term prospects. The invasion of Iraq appeared almost providential for Al-Qaida and has had a radicalizing effect upon Muslims in Europe and elsewhere (Gerges, 2005). However, the violent and retrograde politics of Al-Qaida largely doom it to political oblivion (Miller, 2007). Even the Taliban should not be conflated with Al-Qaida.

Hence, measured vigilance and international cooperation on the threat of terrorism posed by Al-Qaida and its allies will be required for some time. It will remain a priority in the accelerating pace of bilateral, regional and multilateral diplomacy concerning international migration and security. The attacks on 9/11 did have the effect of heightening the saliency of migration and security concerns in foreign policy and international relations. And that saliency, while belated, will likely endure rather than diminish irrespective of Al-Qaida's fate.

Conclusions: migration and security in the age of migration

All epochs involve continuities and discontinuities with the past. The centrality and pervasiveness of perceived connections between migration and security demarcate the present era from the Cold War era in which, whether rightly or wrongly, migration did not figure centrally in security thinking. Nevertheless, certain features of the current epoch echo dramas of the distant past. Ethnic cleansing and human trafficking have deeply stained the age of migration, but such tragedies are not without ample precedent. Near-global consciousness and consensus that the phenomena constitute intolerable affronts to human rights differentiate the current era from the past. It remains far from clear, however, whether the emergent global consciousness concerning human rights and democratic values will prove durable (Shaw, 2000; Habermas and Pensky, 2001).

Growing understanding and appreciation of migration and security connections include the realization that the world's most powerful and wealthiest nations cannot afford to be indifferent to mass suffering, chaos and political extremism in distant places. European leaders appeared to grasp this more readily than their American counterparts, in part because of Europe's proximity to the MENA, which means that the human consequences of conflicts there often immediately affect Europe through refugee arrivals. Such European–American divergences, in turn, threatened the cohesion of the key security institution of the post-Cold War era, namely the North Atlantic Treaty Organization (NATO) (Kupchan, 1998; Lindberg, 2005).

Guide to further reading

There has been a remarkable outpouring of scholarship about migration and security since 2002. Key earlier works included Weiner (1993), Waever et al. (1993), Lyon and Ucarer (2001), Poku and Graham (1998), Graham and Poku (2000) and Weiner and Russell (2001). Notable recent contributions include Adamson (2004, 2006), Alexseev (2005), Freedman (2004), Kleinschmidt (2006), Lucassen (2005), Tirman (2004) and Guild and van Selm (2005).

On Muslims in Europe, see CSIS (2006), Benjamin and Simon (2005), Cesari (2004), Derderian (2004), Haddad (2002), Kepel (2002, 2004), Laurence and Vaisse (2006), Leiken (2005), Roy (2003, 2004) and Klausen (2005). On complex security implications of transnational populations see Argun (2003), Ostegaard-Nielsen (2003), Ögelman (2003), Silverstein (2004) and Rosenberg (2006).

Chapter 10

Migrants and Minorities in the Labour Force

People migrate for many reasons. Despite recent government policies focusing on economic migration, most migration to OECD countries is not specifically for economic purposes. The largest entry category for many countries is family reunion. In addition, large numbers come to seek refuge from war and persecution, while others move to enhance their education. The increased ease of mobility in the age of migration is also leading to more movement for marriage, retirement or simply in search of new lifestyles. But a large proportion of migrants do move for explicitly economic reasons: in search of higher incomes, better employment chances or professional advancement. Moreover, all international migration has an economic dimension, and perceptions of economic causes and consequences weigh heavily in public policy-making in both migrant-sending and receiving countries. Sending countries look to remittances, investments and technology transfer by migrants as resources for economic growth, while receiving countries are concerned with the role of migrants in meeting demand for labour and skills.

This chapter focuses on the position of migrants and minorities in the labour force. Assessments of the costs and benefits of migration for various social groups (such as migrants themselves, high- or low-skilled local workers, employers and welfare recipients) are highly controversial, and have become increasingly politicized. The chapter will provide an introduction to such debates, but can only cover a small part of the complex issues. We concentrate on the situation of lower-skilled migrants and their descendants in advanced economies. Highly skilled migration is not discussed in detail, because it was covered in the section on 'brain drain or brain circulation' in Chapter 3.

We explore these issues first by looking at the factors that drive demand for migrant labour in advanced economies, and how migrants meet this demand. The next section presents information on the work situation of migrants, paying attention to both foreign-born workers themselves and their descendants: the 'second generation'. Then we look briefly at the dispute among economists about whether immigration is 'good or bad' for the receiving economy. A further section examines the dynamics of labour market change, and links these to the 'new political economy' of globalization and the social transformation of societies in both North and South.

Labour demand in advanced economies

It is often said that labour migration from poor to rich countries meets *mutual needs* (see CEC, 2005b; GCIM, 2005). Poor countries have too many young labour market entrants for their weak economies to employ, so they 'need' to export surplus workers. Rich countries, by contrast, have declining numbers of young people entering their labour markets and cannot fill the growing numbers of jobs, so they 'need' to import labour. But it is important to realize that such needs are socially constructed. In Chapter 3 we discussed the historical and economic factors that stimulate emigration from the South. Here we are concerned with corresponding processes in the North.

The 'need' for low-skilled labour in northern countries is socially constructed by the poor wages, conditions and social status in certain sectors. A European study showed that 'immigration plays an important role in improving labour market efficiency', because some jobs are avoided by natives:

> dirty, difficult and dangerous jobs, low-paid household service jobs, low skilled jobs in the informal sector of the economy, jobs in sectors with strong seasonal fluctuation, e.g. farming, road repairs and construction, hotel, restaurant and other tourism-related services. (Münz et al., 2007: 7)

If the conditions and status of such jobs were improved, local workers might be more willing to take them while marginal employers might go out of business. The result might be that certain types of work would become unviable, and be relocated in lower-wage economies in the South. Such 'offshoring' or 'outsourcing' has in fact been common since the 1970s in the manufacturing sector, where much of the production has been moved to new industrial economies. Agriculture also seems an obvious choice for outsourcing, since productivity is low. During debates on the NAFTA Treaty in the early 1990s, Mexican President Salinas suggested that it would be better for US consumers to buy tomatoes produced in Mexico than tomatoes produced by Mexicans in California (see Chapter 8). However, both local farm employers and local farm workers would be hurt by moving production offshore, and they have had the political clout to prevent this happening. This explains the persistence of the EU's Common Agricultural Policy and US farm subsidies, both of which are costly to taxpayers, disadvantageous to consumers and highly damaging to agriculture in poor countries.

Rather than a *need* for migrant labour, we should therefore be analysing a *demand*, which is put forward by powerful economic and political interests. Government policies in receiving countries have responded to this demand either by creating recruitment and management systems for legal foreign labour, by tacitly permitting (and sometimes regularizing) irregular employment of migrants, or, often, by allowing a mix of regular and irregular migrant employment.

Recognition of the demand for migrant labour in postindustrial economies represents a shift in approach in recent years. As described in Chapter 5, foreign labour employment in Europe stagnated or declined after 1973 in a period of recession and restructuring. Many European countries adopted 'zero immigration policies', but were unable to prevent family reunion and permanent settlement. The USA changed its immigration rules in 1965, but did not expect a significant increase in entries from nontraditional sources. However, the early 1990s saw an upsurge of migration to developed countries, driven by both economic and political factors.

The reaction of policy-makers was to tighten up national immigration restrictions and to increase international cooperation on border control. An important reason for this restrictiveness (especially in Europe) was the fear that temporary migrants might again turn into new ethnic minorities. There was also another reason. In view of increased demand for highly skilled personnel and offshoring of low-skilled jobs, governments believed that low-skilled migrant workers would not be needed in the future. Restrictive labour migration policies were maintained through the 1990s. Moreover, Southern European countries that had been major sources of migrant workers in the past now became important immigration areas.

In recent years there has been a gradual shift in official views. An important milestone was the *Süssmuth Commission Report* (2001), which argued that Germany had long since become an immigration country and would need to rely on labour migration to fill both skilled and less-skilled jobs in the future. In Britain, after nearly 30 years without any serious economic analysis of migration, the Home Office published a report that highlighted the potential benefits of labour migration (Glover et al., 2001). What led to these changes?

A major *economic factor* was the realization that developed countries could not export all low-skilled work to low-wage countries. The manufacture of cars, computers and clothing could be shifted to China, Brazil or Malaysia, but the construction industry, hotels and restaurants and hospitals had to be where their customers lived.

A major *demographic factor* was the realization that total fertility rates had fallen sharply. Eurostat projections show that the population of the EU25 as a whole is likely to fall by 1.5 per cent from 457 million in 2004 to 450 million by 2050. However, the decline is forecast to be much greater in Germany (9.6 per cent), Italy (8.9 per cent) and the A10 states, which joined the EU in 2004 (11.7 per cent). More serious still is the decline in working age population (15–64): in 2005, 67 per cent of the population of the EU25 were of working age, compared with 16 per cent aged 65 and over. By 2050, a working age population of 57 per cent will have to support 30 per cent aged 65 and over (CEC, 2005a: Annexe Tables 1 and 2). As the European Commission argued (CEC, 2005a: Section 1.2):

In the short to mid-term, labour immigration can ... positively contribute to tackling the effects of this demographic evolution and will prove crucial to satisfying current and future labour market needs and thus ensure economic sustainability and growth.

However, migration is likely to make only a small contribution, since the immigration levels needed to fully counteract ageing would be extremely large. Moreover, the demographic benefit of immigration is a short-term one, because immigrant fertility behaviour tends to take on the patterns of the host society in the long run.

An important *social factor* derives from the economic and demographic shifts. The proportion of children aged 0–14 in the EU25 population is projected to fall from 16.4 per cent in 2005 to 13.4 per cent in 2050 (CEC, 2005a, Annexe Table 2). If there are fewer young people, they will expect better educational opportunities, and few of them will accept low-skilled jobs. European labour market experts now forecast that manual jobs in manufacturing and agriculture may decline, but there is likely to be a growth in unmet demand for low-skilled service workers in household and care jobs (Münz et al., 2007: 9).

How migration meets labour demand

Migrant labour made a crucial contribution to the post-war boom in advanced economies. This role in labour force dynamics was questioned in the 1970s and 1980s, but strongly reasserted from the 1990s. The average number of foreign-born workers increased in OECD countries (the advanced industrial countries of Europe, North America, Oceania, Japan and Korea) by 20 per cent from 2000 to 2005. By 2005, foreign-born workers made up a substantial share of the labour force: 25 in Australia and Switzerland, 20 per cent in Canada and around 15 per cent in the USA, New Zealand, Austria and Germany. The figure for other Western European countries was around 12 per cent. The migrant share was lower only in Japan (0.3 per cent), Korea (0.8 per cent) and some Central and Eastern European countries (OECD, 2007: 63).

From 1995 to 2005 there was sustained growth in OECD economies, leading to strong demand for labour. In the USA, 16 million new jobs were created, of which nearly 9 million (55 per cent) were filled by foreign-born persons. Migrants made up between one-third and two-thirds of new employees in most Western and Southern European countries. Due to demographic factors the number of nationals available for employment actually declined in Germany, and similar declines are forecast for other European countries, making the future contribution of migrant workers all the more important (OECD, 2007: 66).

New immigrants often bring skills with them: the old stereotype of the unskilled migrant coming in to take the least qualified positions is no longer valid (Collins, 2006; Portes and Rumbaut, 2006: 67–68). In Belgium, Luxembourg, Sweden and Denmark, over 40 per cent of the employed migrants who arrived from 1995 to 2005 had tertiary education.

In France the figure was 35 per cent and in the Netherlands 30 per cent. In many cases, migrant workers had higher qualification profiles than local-born workers. Only in Southern European countries did low-skilled labour migration predominate (OECD, 2007: 67–68).

But even in Western Europe migrants were important to employers for low-skilled jobs. For example, a study of UK employers found that migrants were an importance source of less-qualified labour in agriculture; hotels and catering; administration, business and management; and finance. In some cases, employers preferred them to locals because they were 'more reliable, motivated and committed', and 'more prepared to work longer and flexible hours' and 'work harder' than domestic workers (Institute for Employment Studies et al., 2006: iv).

Migrants in the labour market

There are many ways of describing and assessing labour market performance. Here we concentrate on sectoral and occupational distribution, unemployment and self-employment.

The migrant generation

'Sectoral distribution' refers to the industries in which migrants work. Frequent jobs for migrant men in the 1970s were manual work in factories, on building sites, or in low-skilled services such as garbage collection and street cleaning. Women were also to be found in factories (especially textiles and clothing, engineering and food processing) and in services such as cleaning and health. Today migrants can be found right across the economy. However, they remain overrepresented in manufacturing – a sector deserted by many nationals. In Italy, Germany, Finland and Austria, at least one in five foreign-born workers is in manufacturing; in Japan the figure is 54 per cent. Migrant workers are also overrepresented in construction in many countries. However, in the postindustrial OECD economies, services jobs predominate, and most migrant workers are to be found in this sector. Here the foreign-born are overrepresented in hotels and restaurants, and the healthcare and social services sector (OECD, 2007: 72–73).

'Occupational distribution' refers to the jobs people do. Foreign-born persons are overrepresented in cleaning jobs: more than 50 per cent of such jobs are held by migrants in Switzerland, and more than 30 per cent in Austria, Germany, Sweden, Italy, Greece and the USA. They are also overrepresented in jobs as waiters or cooks, and domestic carers. These are typically jobs with poor pay and conditions, and little security. However, foreign-born persons are also overrepresented in some service occupations requiring high-skill levels, such as teachers (in Switzerland and Ireland), doctors and nurses (in the UK) and computer experts (USA). Overall, migrant employment in the tertiary sector seems to be 'dualistic' with concentration at low and high-skill levels and a gap in between (OECD, 2007: 73–74).

In the early stages of migration, most migrants succeed in getting jobs, and are rarely unemployed. The picture today is more mixed, as Table 10.1 shows. In Southern Europe (apart from Italy), unemployment rates for the foreign-born are only slightly higher than for the native-born. But in Western Europe migrant workers have borne the brunt of restructuring and recessions, and have much higher unemployment rates than local workers. The situation is different again in the USA and Australia: legal immigrants have become well integrated into the labour market, and unemployment rates for the foreign-born and natives are very similar (OECD, 2007: 71–72). But it is important to remember that these figures are only for legally registered workers. Undocumented migrants are in a much more precarious situation (see below).

Table 10.1   *Unemployment rates of foreign-born and native-born populations in selected OECD countries (2005)*

| Country | Unemployment rate 2005, per cent | | | |
| | Women | | Men | |
	Native-born	Foreign-born	Native-born	Foreign-born
Austria	4.4	9.8	4.1	11.8
Belgium	7.5	20.3	6.3	14.8
Czech Republic	9.7	16.5	6.2	10.4
Denmark	5.0	12.4	4.0	7.2
Finland	8.3	20.2	8.0	16.6
France	9.2	16.5	8.1	13.3
Germany	10.2	16.3	10.6	17.5
Greece	15.3	15.9	5.9	6.4
Hungary	7.4	7.3	7.0	-
Ireland	3.5	6.0	4.5	6.0
Italy	9.2	14.6	6.2	6.1
Luxembourg	4.5	7.5	3.0	4.2
Netherlands	4.5	9.5	3.6	11.9
Norway	4.3	8.5	4.2	12.5
Portugal	8.4	9.7	6.8	8.5
Slovak Republic	17.0	28.6	15.7	23.0
Spain	12.0	13.5	7.0	9.5
Sweden	7.9	14.1	7.9	15.6
Switzerland	3.7	9.7	2.7	7.7
United Kingdom	3.8	7.1	4.7	7.4
Australia	5.0	5.2	4.7	5.0
Canada	–	–	–	–
United States	5.2	5.2	6.3	5.1

Source: OECD (2007): Annex Table I.A1.1.

Overall, migrants still tend to have lower occupational status and higher unemployment rates than nonmigrant workers. Yet the labour market positions of migrant workers are much more varied than they were 20 or 30 years ago. The averages given in the table may obscure quite big differences between high and low-skilled groups, or between specific occupations. New migrants often come with higher qualifications and gain access to better jobs than their predecessors. Older migrant workers, by contrast, often seem to have got stuck in the manual manufacturing sectors for which they were originally recruited. Restructuring and recessions have often led to unemployment or displacement from the labour force for such groups. One indication of this is the fact that migrants have lower labour force participation rates than natives in many countries (OECD, 2007: Annex table I.A1.2).

However, the OECD material is too general to reveal the complex patterns of differentiation based on ethnicity, gender and legal status. We will look at the UK as just one example (for the US situation see Portes and Rumbaut, 2006: chapter 4). In the UK, ethnic inequality has become a long-term feature of the labour market. An official study based on the 2001 Census showed that Bangladeshi women had the highest unemployment rate at 24 per cent – six times that of white women. Bangladeshi men had a 20 per cent unemployment rate, four times that of white men. Indian men and women had only slightly higher unemployment rates than their white counterparts. All other ethnic minority groups – both men and women – had unemployment rates two to three times higher than whites. Young people under 25 years were far more likely to be out of work. The rate for young Bangladeshi men was 40 per cent, compared with 12 per cent of young white men. Other minority young men had unemployment rates of 25–31 per cent. The picture for young minority women was similar, with unemployment rates considerably higher than for whites (ONS, 2002).

The general picture in the UK in 2001 was of a labour force stratified by ethnicity and gender and with a high degree of youth unemployment. Generally, people of Indian, Chinese, or Irish background tended to have employment situations as good as or sometimes better than the average for white British (see also Dustmann and Fabbri, 2005). By contrast, other groups were worse off, with a descending hierarchy of black Africans, black Caribbeans, Pakistanis, and – at the very bottom – Bangladeshis (ONS, 2004). Gender distinctions vary: young women of black African and black Caribbean ethnicity seem to perform better in both education and employment than men of these groups, while the opposite appears to be the case for Pakistanis and Bangladeshis (see also Schierup et al., 2006: 120–130).

The second generation

Most labour migrants to OECD countries up to the 1970s were workers with low skill levels. As a result of subsequent settlement processes, a new *second generation* (native-born persons with both parents foreign-born) has emerged. In most OECD countries *persons with a migration background* (foreign-born persons plus the second generation) make up a large proportion of young adults – the highest share is in Australia (45 per cent of persons aged 20–29), followed by Switzerland and Canada (30–35 per cent), and then Sweden, USA, the Netherlands, Germany, France and the UK (20–30 per cent) (OECD, 2007: 79).

Since members of the second generation have gained their education in the host country, it is valuable to compare their experience both with migrants of the same age group and with *young people who do not have a migration background* (native-born children of native-born parents). Studies of schooling in immigration countries during the early settlement period predicted that children of immigrants might inherit their parents' low socioeconomic positions (Castles et al., 1984: chapter 6). Has this in fact happened? Studies using national statistics (censuses, labour force surveys etc.) and international comparative studies (such as OECD's Programme for International Student Assessment – PISA) now make it possible to give a provisional answer. For the USA data have been provided by the Current Population Survey and the Children of Immigrants Longitudinal Survey (see Portes and Rumbaut, 2006: chapter 8).

In general, the research shows that the second generation has better average educational outcomes than the migrant parent generation. They also do better than today's young migrants of the same age group (20–29). However, the outcomes of the second generation lag behind those of native-born young people without a migration background. This may be partly explained by the low educational and socioeconomic levels of their parents, since such factors tend to be transmitted across generations. The PISA study assessed performance of 15-year-olds in mathematics, science, reading and cross-curricular competencies. The study showed that, even after allowing for parental background, second generation students remained at a substantial disadvantage. This applied particularly to former guestworker-recruiting countries, like Germany, Belgium, Switzerland and Austria. Second-generation education disadvantage was found to be insignificant in the cases of Sweden, France, Australia and Canada (OECD, 2007: 79–80). This makes it clear that the original mode of labour market incorporation can have effects that cross generations (see also Portes and Rumbaut, 2006: 92–101).

The OECD research also revealed substantial gender differences. In all OECD countries studied (except the USA), second-generation young women did better than their male counterparts at school. This is particularly interesting in view of the fact that young immigrant women often have less education than young immigrant men (OECD, 2007: 81). Schooling in host countries seems to have an important emancipatory effect for second-generation women.

In the long run, the most important question for the second generation is whether they can get decent jobs in the host country. The OECD found that young second-generation members had a higher employment probability than immigrants in the same age group, but still suffered significant disadvantage compared with young people without a migration background. Worryingly, the disadvantage seemed greatest at the top end of the qualification scale, indicating the persistence of a 'glass ceiling' for minorities. Native-born children of immigrants from African countries seemed to have the greatest labour market difficulties: members of the second generation in Europe were up to twice as likely to be unemployed as young people without a migration background. Possible explanations for this included lack of access to informal networks that help in job-finding; lack of knowledge of the labour market; and discrimination on the basis of origin or class (OECD, 2007: 81–85).

Migrant entrepreneurs

Up to the 1970s, migrants (especially) in Europe were seen as wage-workers, and rarely became self-employed or entrepreneurs. In some countries (such as Germany, Switzerland and Austria) their work permits initially prohibited self-employment. The situation was different in the USA, Australia and the UK and France, where migrants began to run small shops and cafés early on. Since the 1980s, migrant self-employment has become far more common everywhere. The OECD notes that foreign-born persons made up 12 per cent of the self-employed in the UK, 13 per cent in Belgium, France and Germany, and 14 per cent in Sweden in 2005. Self-employment does not necessarily mean an improved social position: many migrants choose it as a fall-back solution, because they are unemployed, or find their upward mobility in paid employment blocked (OECD, 2007: 74–75). Nonetheless, a US study in the early 1990s found that self-employed persons do, on average, have higher incomes than employees (Portes and Rumbaut, 2006: 81).

Typical migrant-owned businesses are ethnic restaurants, 'mom and pop' food stores and convenience stores (Waldinger et al., 1990). Immigrant-owned businesses frequently employ family members from the country of origin. Light and Bonacich (1988) traced the origins of the Korean business community in Los Angeles to the Korean War, which led to extensive transnational ties and eventually migration between Korea and the USA. More recently, Ness (2005: 58–95) has shown how Korean entrepreneurs came to dominate the New York greengrocery business, at first employing co-ethnics, then replacing them with Mexican workers at lower wages – and then re-employing Koreans when the Mexicans demanded better pay and conditions (see also Waldinger, 1996).

Immigrant entrepreneurship has been assessed divergently. Some scholars stress the economic dynamism of immigrant entrepreneurs with their positive effects upon economic growth and quality of life for consumers (Fix and Passel, 1994: 53). A more critical viewpoint stresses the human suffering entailed by intense competition, long hours of work, and exploitation of family labour and of illegally employed aliens (Collins et al., 1995; Light and Bonacich, 1988: 425–436). The growth of small business in Europe is strongly linked to neoliberal policies of economic deregulation, which have made it easier to start businesses and to employ workers on a short-term, casual basis. In many such businesses, both the employers and the workers are migrants or members of ethnic minorities.

In the UK, an official study showed that the groups most likely to be self-employed in 2001 were Pakistanis (23 per cent) and Chinese (18 per cent), compared with 12 per cent of white British (see also Dustmann and Fabbri, 2005). Self-employment often reflected desperation to escape a cycle of low-paid insecure jobs and unemployment. The 2000–2001 annual Local Area Labour Force Survey showed that one in six Pakistanis in employment was a cab driver or chauffeur, compared with 1 per cent of white British men. Forty per cent of Bangladeshi men were either cooks or waiters, compared with 1 per cent of white British men. Ten per cent of black African and white Irish women in employment were nurses, compared with 3 per cent of white British women. By contrast Indians, Chinese, white Irish, and other non-British white groups had rates of professional employment of 17–20 per cent, compared with 11 per cent for white British (ONS, 2004a).

The data show a complex pattern of ethnic and gender segmentation, with some ethnic minority groups doing quite well while others are disadvantaged and impoverished. There is no clear status distinction between the employed and the self-employed – the former can include high-status managers as well as low-paid service workers, while the latter range from medical professionals to cab drivers and food-stall operators. Ethnic small business is an important part of the new political economy of the labour force in developed countries (see below and also Light and Gold, 1999; Reitz, 1998; Waldinger and Lichter, 2003).

How does immigration affect host economies and local workers?

Some economists argue that immigration may damage the economy by worsening the balance of payments, causing inflation and reducing the incentive for productivity improvements. It is also claimed that migrants may harm lower-skilled level workers by competing for their jobs and bidding wages down. This has been taken up in headlines such as 'East Europe migrants help to take jobless to six-year high' in Britain's mass-circulation *Daily Mail* (17 August 2006, quoted in TUC, 2007: 10). A British economist summarised his report on labour migration:

> It concludes that the economic consequences of large-scale immigration are mostly minor, negative or transient, that the interests of more

vulnerable sections of the domestic population may well be damaged, and that any economic benefits are unlikely to bear comparison with its substantial impact on population growth. Such findings are in line with those from other developed countries. (Rowthorn, 2004)

By contrast, a British Home Office study found that in theory '... migration is likely to enhance economic growth and the welfare of both natives and migrants' (Glover et al., 2001: vii). According to an early study of post-1945 European expansion, the entry of migrant workers prevents bottlenecks, provides skills and reduces inflationary pressures. These factors allow continued economic expansion, which benefits local workers too. In the absence of a migrant labour supply, stagnation might ensue, leading to lower incomes for all (Kindleberger, 1967). Similarly, a review of the literature on macroeconomic impacts of immigration from the 1970s to the early 1990s found that studies converge 'in concluding that immigration causes no crowding-out on the labour market and does not depress the income of nationals' (OECD, 1994: 164).

However, immigration may have differing effects for different groups of the host population: employers may benefit most while unskilled workers may lose. Hatton and Williamson (2005: 125) affirm that unskilled workers in the USA were adversely affected by international migration prior to World War I. In their view, what Daniels (2004) refers to as the closing of the Golden Door, the enactment of restrictive laws and policies that curtailed immigration to the USA after 1918, reflected a political will to protect unskilled workers (Hatton and Williamson, 2005: 177, 222). To what extent are such historical findings relevant today? In 1997 a report by a National Research Council (NRC) panel of leading US economists and other social scientists found that, while the aggregate impact of immigration on the US economy was quite small, it 'produces net economic gains for domestic residents' (Smith and Edmonston, 1997: 4). But they pointed out that:

> Even when the economy as a whole gains, however, there may be losers as well as gainers among different groups of US residents. Along with immigrants themselves, the gainers are the owners of productive factors that are complementary with the labour of immigrants – that is domestic, higher-skilled workers, and perhaps owners of capital – whose incomes will rise. Those who buy goods and services produced by immigrant labour will also benefit. The losers may be the less-skilled domestic workers who compete with immigrants and whose wages will fall. (Smith and Edmonston, 1997: 5)

The econometric studies carried out by the NRC panel revealed that 'immigration has had a relatively small adverse impact on the wages and employment opportunities of competing native groups' (Smith and Edmonston, 1997: 7). But some US economists argue that negative effects on the receiving economy and the wages of competing workers are much more serious. Hatton and Williamson estimated the effects of immigration to the USA upon earnings between 1979 and 1995 under two scenarios, one in which capital was assumed to be fixed and a second in which capital volume changed as a result of various factors. In the first, immigration reduced the earnings of skilled native-born workers by 2.5 per cent and unskilled by 4.6 per cent. However, in the second scenario, the earnings of skilled workers increased marginally while the earnings of unskilled workers again decreased by 4.6 per cent. (Hatton and Williamson, 2005: 304–306, 317–318).

Borjas claims that there has been a pattern of declining skills in post-1965 immigrant cohorts. As entries from Western Europe were replaced by those from Asia and Latin America, the differences in socioeconomic and educational standards between the regions were reflected in declining skills and rising poverty of post-1965 immigrants (Borjas, 1990; 1999). However, such findings are contested in Portes and Rumbaut's analysis of migrants' educational qualifications (2006: 67–76) More recently, Borjas found that between 1980 and 2000 immigration did not affect average wages of the workforce, but led to a 5–10 per cent decrease in unskilled wages (Borjas, 2006). Borjas also found that the workers most negatively affected by immigration were minorities, especially black low-wage workers (see also Borjas, 2001). By contrast, US economist Card found that immigration had no negative impact on American workers (Card, 2005).

Australian economists have also been studying immigration for many years, as it has been the motor of economic growth in Australia since the 1940s (Wooden, 1994; Foster, 1996). An analysis by Foster concluded:

> that immigration impacts on both demand and supply sides of the economy. Immigrants create jobs as well as fill them; they pay taxes as well as make demands of government; and they bring funds from overseas and contribute to higher exports as well as to imports. ... But beyond their mere presence, the research evidence shows that the demand- and supply-side effects in fact balance each other so closely that no more than marginal impacts can be detected for any of the key economic indicators ... . To the extent that any of the usual measures of economic health have been significantly affected, the evidence is that immigration has been generally beneficial for the Australian economy and for the employment prospects and incomes of Australian residents. (Castles et al., 1998: 73)

A British Home Office study found that 'there is little evidence that native workers are harmed by migration. There is considerable support for the view that migrants create new businesses and jobs and fill labour market gaps, improving productivity and reducing inflationary pressures' (Glover et al., 2001; see also Dustmann and Glitz, 2005). Recently, the Trades Union Congress commissioned a study, which found that

> The overall economic impact of immigration is limited but positive. Migrant workers contribute more in taxes than they receive in benefits, and migration probably leads to higher levels of employment and wages for native workers. Migration may possibly be linked to an increase in wage inequality in this country, but the evidence is not conclusive. … The only adequate response to the small number of specific cases where problems do arise is to demand equal rights for native and migrant workers. (TUC, 2007)

Clearly, economists remain divided over the costs and benefits of migration. However, the positive findings seem to be confirmed by the eagerness of many governments to encourage economic migration. Although the emphasis is on attracting highly skilled migrants, there is also growing demand for the lower-skilled – a demand met in Europe through a mix of mobility within the European Union (especially from Poland, Romania and other new member states), temporary labour recruitment measures, and tacit acceptance of undocumented migration. In the USA, undocumented migration seems to be the main source of low-skilled migrant labour.

The new political economy and the dynamics of labour force change

The discussion presented so far in this chapter indicates the continuing (and indeed growing) importance of migrant labour for advanced economies. It also shows that migrant workers meet special types of labour demand, and often experience economic and social disadvantage. But what analyses of official labour market data fail to reveal is the complex dynamics of labour force change. In Chapter 3 we argued that globalization is the crucial context for twenty-first-century migration. Changes in the work situation and social position of workers in advanced economies can only be fully understood through analysis of the global restructuring of investment, production and trade, and the way this has changed economic and social conditions in migrant-sending, transit and receiving countries.

A recent study provides an overview of the phases in post-war political economy (Schierup et al., 2006: 240–246). A *first phase* of expansion in core industrial economies from 1945 to about 1973 was marked by mass production in large factories, where manual workers were concentrated in their thousands, facilitating strong unions. Trade unions were able to negotiate better wages and conditions, while social democratic political parties could introduce welfare state provisions to protect workers and their families. As employment of migrant workers increased, they tended to get work in unionized factories – albeit usually in the lower positions within these – and enjoyed many of the benefits of high wages and strong welfare provisions.

As long as the economies of Western Europe and North America were expanding and faced little international competition, this approach was successful, but it ran into difficulties in the 1970s: recession, growing competition from Asian economies and a decline in profit margins led to a *second phase* based on a new international division of labour. Labour-intensive production was moved to low-wage economies, while migrant labour recruitment for the North was stopped. This led to the closure of many 'rustbelt factories' with their strong unions. Restructuring was pushed forward by the new-right governments of the 1980s (Thatcher in the UK and Reagan in the USA), opening the way for a rollback of worker rights. Economic deregulation and the 'small state' led to major social changes, such as the emergence of the 'working poor' in the USA – millions of people who were in employment but earned too little to climb out of poverty and were no longer entitled to welfare payments. Zero immigration policies were one aspect of this shift in Europe, although existing immigrants remained, often experiencing unemployment and social exclusion.

However, the very success of neoliberal globalization led to a new *third phase* by the 1990s: the re-creation of sweatshops and other forms of exploitative work in the advanced economies. Social transformation in the South created economic conditions conducive to emigration of both highly skilled and unskilled workers to the North (Schierup et al., 2006: 243–244). This corresponded with the new demand for migrant workers outlined above. The 'contexts of reception' (Portes and Rumbaut, 2006: 92–93) for new migrants were quite different from those of their predecessors in the 1960s and 1970s: a laissez-faire state that offered little protection to workers; weak unions and fragmented labour markets which opened the door for exploitative employment practices; and the existence of ethnic communities with varying capacity to help newcomers in the job search.

It is important not to glorify the past: the migrant workers of the 1960s and 1970s were always in weak economic and legal situations, and vulnerable to exploitation. However, the labour force dynamics of postindustrial economies are based on a proliferation of employment relationships that differentiate workers on the basis of ethnicity, race and gender, leading to complex and often highly disadvantageous forms of work for migrants and minorities.

New employment forms: subcontracting, temporary work and casualization

A key element of neoliberal employment practices has been the drive to turn wage-workers, who enjoyed the protection of labour law and collective agreements, into independent 'contractors', who have no guarantee of work, have to buy their own tools and equipment, and bear all the risks of accident, sickness or lack of jobs (Schierup et al., 2006: chapter 9). The pressure to become independent contractors has affected occupations as diverse as building tradesmen, truck drivers, graphic designers and architects. A striking example from the USA concerns the New York 'black-car drivers', who take executives and tourists to and from the airports. Once paid employees, they now have to buy the expensive luxury vehicles (on credit) and bear all operating costs, with no guarantee of work. The result is low income and extreme working hours. Most of the drivers are South Asians. They were hard-hit after the events of 11 September 2001, not only by the sharp downturn in work, which plunged many drivers into disastrous debt, but also by rising hostility on the part of customers and authorities (Ness, 2005: 130–180).

Employing migrants on a temporary basis is another way of enhancing employer control and reducing demands for better wages and conditions. The OECD found that migrants are more likely to be employed in temporary jobs than natives in all European immigration countries (except Austria and Switzerland). In Spain 56 per cent of the foreign-born have temporary jobs compared with less than 30 per cent of locals. In Portugal, Poland and Finland, temporary employment affects 30 per cent of foreigners (OECD, 2007: 75–76). The old idea of migrants as a subordinate, flexible labour force is clearly not dead.

Economic deregulation has led to the removal of legal controls on employment and the reduction of work-site inspections by labour market authorities. This allowed a big expansion in casual employment: that is, hiring by the hour or for specific tasks, especially of migrants, young people and women. Casualized jobs are typical for cleaning, catering, and other service occupations, but also for the construction, textile and garment industries. Many big firms no longer engage directly in production, but subcontract it to smaller firms in sectors of the labour market with a high degree of informality and scant regulation of working conditions. Through outsourcing to subcontractors they strive for a maximum of flexibility. The frequent celebration of the rise of 'ethnic entrepreneurship' needs to be seen in the context of such trends.

Migrant women workers

In Chapter 2 we summarized some theoretical discussions on gender and migration. As early as 1984, Morokvasic argued that migrant women from peripheral zones living in Western industrial democracies:

> represent a ready made labour supply which is, at once, the most vulnerable, the most flexible and, at least in the beginning, the least demanding work force. They have been incorporated into sexually

segregated labour markets at the lowest stratum in high technology industries or at the 'cheapest' sectors in those industries which are labour intensive and employ the cheapest labour to remain competitive. (Morokvasic, 1984: 886)

The disadvantaged position of migrant women persists today: the OECD found that 'immigrant women are generally the group with the least favourable outcomes in the labour market ..., both in absolute terms and relative to children of natives of the same gender' (OECD, 2007: 81–82). Even female members of the majority population tend to be disadvantaged compared with men, because of a range of factors which include: employers' assumptions that they are not primary breadwinners; the expectation that women are temporary workers who will leave to get married; women's need for part-time work due to family commitments; skill definitions which favour masculine occupations, gender-specific social networks; and gender-based discrimination (compare Schrover et al., 2007). Migrant women face all these factors too, but in addition are disadvantaged by stereotypes on the characteristics of specific ethnic and racial groups, and often also by weak legal status.

Migrant women are thus disadvantaged by two interlocking sets of mechanisms. Migrant men, of course, are also affected by the second set, and may have lower wages and occupational status than majority-group women (Browne and Misra, 2003: 489). The key issue to examine is how factors of gender and ethnicity interact in specific work situations. One approach is to look at the formation of ethnic 'niches' (often used in studying entrepreneurship) and the extent to which gender plays a part in this; a useful review of literature is provided by Schrover et al. (2007). Another way is to examine the 'intersectionality' of the factors, as Browne and Misra (2003) do in their examination of race and gender in the US labour market.

Contrary to neoliberal theories of the labour market, which argue that variations in employment status are due to differing levels of human capital (Browne and Misra, 2003: 506), many studies show the importance of race, gender, class and sexual orientation in allocating positions. The specific (and usually disadvantaged) position of migrant women is crucial to certain sectors such as the garment industry. A US study revealed that 'women of colour are differentially situated in local labour markets compared with White women and co-ethnic men, so that economic restructuring affects each group uniquely' (Browne and Misra, 2003: 497). The study reviewed evidence of increasing wage inequality between Whites, Black and Latinos, as well as between high and low-skilled groups (Browne and Misra, 2003: 496). An analysis of European labour market statistics found that:

there is a demarcation between EU and third-country nationals along national, ethnic and gender lines and legal status. The majority of third-country nationals are employed in vulnerable, low-skilled, low-paid jobs in medium and low segments ... There are sharp differences in pay between men and women, which can be explained in part by women's disproportionate representation in low pay sectors, such as cleaning and domestic work, the casual or part-time nature of many female jobs and their concentration in the informal sector. (Ayres and Barber, 2006: 30)

This study also pointed to the special vulnerability of women and children to trafficking, which can lead to bonded domestic work, care work and employment in sweatshops, but is mainly linked to prostitution. It is estimated that between 120,000 and 170,000 persons are trafficked into the EU each year and that 75–80 per cent of them are involved in sex work. Indeed sex work seems to have become an ethnic niche in Europe today: up to 80 per cent of the roughly 0.5 million sex-workers are thought to be migrants (Ayres and Barber, 2006: 30).

The employment of migrant women domestic workers is a category of gendered and racialized labour that has expanded remarkably in recent years in virtually all advanced industrial economies (Anderson, 2000; Cox, 2000). Here we find the intersection of gendered norms that define childcare and housework as natural tasks for women, with racial stereotypes of ethnic minorities as servants.

Historically, domestic work has been performed by ethnic minorities, and ethnicity, nationality, and citizenship-status construct an idea of domestic workers as 'others', who do not deserve better pay or working conditions. Work conditions are informal, leaving ample room for employers to use personal preferences and biases to enter decisions about hiring, pay and the treatment of their domestic employees. (Browne and Misra, 2003: 502)

Domestic work can become a niche for migrant women (Schrover et al., 2007: 536–537); however bad the conditions, it does offer a chance of a job, often combined with live-in conditions that are perceived by migrant women's families as sheltered. Domestic work is marked by a hierarchy of work tasks, of formal and informal modes of employment, and of groups with varied statuses. For instance, Filipina domestic workers are preferred in some places due to their better education and English, but rejected in others because they are seen as too active in defending their rights. Such hierarchies are often generated and reproduced through the formal practices of recruitment agencies. But they are also increasingly formed through practices of agencies and social networks embedded in a growing underground economy fed by undocumented immigration from Africa, Asia, and Latin America, as well as from Eastern Europe and the former Soviet Union (Jordan and Düvell, 2002).

Domestic work by migrant women can be the result of increased opportunities of professional or white-collar employment for majority-group women: hiring foreign maids can free women in Italy, the USA or Singapore from housework and childcare (Huang et al., 2005). Such transnational care hierarchies sometimes go a stage further, when migrant domestic workers hire a maid in the home country to look after their own children. This may mean higher living standards and better education, but at a high emotional cost.

The growth of the informal economy

One of the most dramatic – and perhaps surprising – trends of the last 20 years has been the growth of informal economies in advanced countries. In the past, informal employment practices were associated with less developed countries in the South, where lack of regular employment in industry and the public sector forced people to scratch a living through petty production and trading. Neoliberalism and economic deregulation have led to a burgeoning of informal work in formerly highly regulated labour markets. All the trends already mentioned – subcontracting, temporary work, casualization, and gendered and racialized work situations – can be summed up through the concept of informalization, defined by Ness as: 'referring to a redistribution of work from regulated sectors of the economy to new unregulated sectors of the underground or informal economy' (Ness, 2005: 22).

Although informal employment can affect natives as well as migrants, irregular migration has been crucial to its growth. This is particularly obvious in the USA, with its officially estimated irregular population of 12 million (Passel, 2006). Most of them are Mexican and other Central American and Caribbean migrants in low-skilled jobs – although the lax regulatory regime in the USA means that irregular migrants are often in legal employment relationships. In Europe estimates of the irregular population are less precise, ranging from 5 to 7.5 million (Ayres and Barber, 2006: 29; Düvell, 2005: Table 2.1). Some European politicians argue that irregular immigration is the cause of informalization, but other observers believe that the causality is the other way round: economic deregulation and employer practices have created informal sector jobs, forming a pull factor for irregular migrants (Reyneri, 2003). This applies most obviously in Southern Europe, but informal work is widespread, for instance in British agriculture, cleaning and catering, but also in the cases of traffic wardens and security work – both services devolved by public authorities to subcontractors.

The regulated German labour market has long been seen as the antithesis of the informal or 'black' economies of Southern Europe. Yet trends towards the growth of small enterprises, deregulation, casualization, and contracting-out have opened up the space for informal employment here too, as one EU-commissioned study found:

> In Germany informal work is not limited to undocumented foreigners, but is also done increasingly by foreigners with legal status, or by young

adults of Turkish origins ... The trend is linked to a general increase in *Schwarzarbeit* ['black work'] ... In some cases in Germany it is perceived as necessary to work in the informal sector to supplement income from low public assistance, and, also to earn money for work and not to be a recipient of public assistance. In other cases working without a permit is a result of a precarious legal status, a permit to stay which does not include an accrued right to a work permit. The informal are often the only jobs which low skilled unemployed persons can find. (Wilpert and Laacher, 1999: 53)

Informal work is a crucial part of the new global political economy, often vital for the survival of certain industries in advanced economies. As Ness points out:

Now the reliable jobs in the established labour market have been replaced by low wage jobs with substandard conditions commonly found underground. Thus, informalization does not represent industrial decline but horizontal restructuring, often done to maintain and increase flexibility and competitiveness in regional, national and international markets'. (Ness, 2005: 23)

Labour market segmentation

Taken together, the various forms of labour force restructuring described in this section add up to a process of *labour market segmentation*. This means that people's chances of getting jobs depend not only on their human capital (i.e. their education and skills) but also on gender, race, ethnicity and legal status. Sometimes, the legally vulnerable status of many foreign workers fosters resentment against them on the part of native workers, who fear that their wages and conditions will be undermined. In addition, migrant workers may belong to racial or ethnic minorities, stigmatized through ideologies of racism and experiences of colonialism. Such factors may be reinforced by resentment of foreign workers for social and cultural reasons (for instance, hostility to Islam).

Labour market segmentation is not new. In Western Europe in the 1960s, the discrimination inherent in the employment and residential restrictions of guestworker policies funnelled immigrants into specific economic sectors and occupations (Castles and Kosack, 1973). Collins regarded the 'impact of post-war immigration on the growth and fragmentation of the Australian working class' as 'one of the most salient aspects of the Australian immigration experience' (Collins, 1991: 87). A 1989 US Department of Labor report found that: 'Newcomers arrive in the United States ... with distinct legal statuses. In turn, this proliferation of legal statuses may become a new source of social and economic stratification' (US Department of Labor, 1989: 18).

However, the character of labour market segmentation is changing in complex ways, linked to a new global social geography. In the 1980s, Sassen (1988) showed how foreign investment and displacement of manufacturing jobs abroad had fostered new migratory streams to the USA. Linkages between global cities and distant hinterlands created paradoxes wherein enormous wealth and highly remunerated professional employment uneasily coexisted with growing unskilled service industry employment and Third-World-like employment conditions in underground industries. The casualization of labour and growing illegal alien employment were characteristic of global cities. Considerable illegal employment of migrants often coincided with high unemployment of citizens and legally resident aliens. The latter were likely to belong to minorities and had often been victims of job losses in industries that had shifted manufacturing operations abroad.

Twenty years on, Ness examined the transformation of the social geography of New York City (Ness, 2005: chapter 2). In the early twentieth century, immigrant labour from Southern and Eastern Europe had been crucial to the emergence of the garment, printing, meatpacking, construction and transportation industries. Industry was concentrated in 'ethnic neighbourhoods' and immigrants came to form the backbone of the city's strong labour movement. In the late twentieth century, these traditional industries were restructured, with most production jobs being moved to nonunionized 'sunbelt' states or offshore to the Caribbean, Latin America and Asia. Many new jobs were created in retailing, personal services, and business services (see also Waldinger, 1996). The new economy is heavily stratified on the basis of ethnicity:

> On the whole, native-born whites have gravitated to high-paying professional service jobs, African Americans and native-born Latinos have occupied jobs that rely on public sector funding ... . Immigrants tend to fill many of the low-wage jobs created in the new sectors of the economy. Low-end jobs in the service sector pay low wages and provide few, if any, benefits. These new jobs include private transportation, hotel and restaurant, delivery, security, building maintenance and other low-wage services. (Ness, 2005: 17)

The new jobs are no longer concentrated in ethnic neighbourhoods and the enterprises are often very small, making union organization difficult (although Ness's study does explore examples of migrant militancy). The new labour market is shaped by government policies:

> In effect, there are two national immigration policies: the official policy of restricting immigration passed to satisfy anti-immigrant political constituencies and the actual policy of allowing a steady flow of immigrants to satisfy the demands of corporate constituencies in search of cheap labour. This creates the best of both worlds for employers. On

the one hand, low-wage immigrant labour is always available. On the other, immigrant workers' illegal status increases employers' leverage in all aspects of the employment relationship. (Ness, 2005: 15)

The 2000 Census found that immigrants made up 2.9 million (36 per cent) of New York City's 8 million people, but no less than 47 per cent of the city's workforce. Moreover, immigrants made up 62 per cent of the low-wage workforce (earning between US5.15 and US$7.10 an hour). The new ethnic workforce is highly diverse, with newcomers from every continent. The Italian and Russian women, who sewed garments on the Lower East Side, have been replaced by women from China and Latin America, who work in new sweatshops in Chinatown and Sunset Park. The worst jobs are done by undocumented migrants from the Dominican Republic, Mexico and French West Africa, who compete for precarious and exploitative posts as supermarket workers, delivery drivers and kitchen workers (Ness, 2005).

Parallels to the changes in New York City can be found everywhere. Each case has specific characteristics, due to economic, social and political conditions in sending and receiving areas, as well as the characteristics of employers and workers. But one can also see recurring patterns that show the connections between specific experiences and global shifts.

Take, for instance, the Berlin construction industry. Following German reunification in 1990 and the move of the government to Berlin, the city experienced an unprecedented building boom. Yet, by 1996, 25 per cent of unemployed persons in Berlin were building workers. Some employers took on workers from Poland, who came through temporary labour schemes. Another option was to subcontract work to Portuguese firms, who could bring their own workers (at lower wages) through EU free movement provisions. In addition, many workers came as daily commuters from the former East German hinterland of Brandenburg. This competition had adverse effects on unionized building workers, many of whom were long-term foreign residents of Berlin. In the old German model of long-term employment, the firm and the trade union had been sites of interethnic communication and integration. Racism against migrants had been less pronounced at work than in other social areas. The decline of this model and its replacement with contract workers thus had negative effects on social integration and intergroup relations. This was no doubt one factor behind the increase in racism and racist violence following German reunification (Hunger and Thränhardt, 2001).

The garment industry provides many national examples of ethnic entrepreneurship and hierarchies based on race and gender (Rath, 2002). In Britain, ethnic and gender-based divisions allowed the revival of clothing production after it seemed doomed to extinction through outsourcing to low-wage economies (see Phizacklea, 1990). From the 1970s, management, design, and marketing of clothing became heavily concentrated in a few big and highly capitalized British retail clothing companies (Mitter, 1986).

Domestic clothing production declined steeply. During the 1960s and 1970s the immigrant workforce in the garment industry had mainly been first-generation male immigrants: Pakistanis, Indians, Bangladeshis and others. Many of these workers lost their jobs, and then became contractors to the big clothing houses, setting up small formally independent sweatshops based on cheap ethnic minority or immigrant family labour – mainly provided by women. Wages and working conditions were very poor, while the rate of accidents and work injuries was high. The industry's state of informality suited both the economic interests of the big retailers and the male ethnic middlemen contractors, who controlled their female workforce through bonds of family and ethnic community allegiance (Mitter, 1986; Schierup et al., 2006: 235–237).

Schierup (2006: 238–240) also shows how the restructuring of the construction industry in Spain has been marked by a profound dualism. On the one hand, a small number of high-tech big firms became centres of financial and legal expertise, design, know-how, and project conception and monitoring. On the other hand, all manual production work and associated employment costs and social security were subcontracted to small firms, which had to bear the risk of market fluctuations. This led to a polarized job setting, marked by requalification and favourable job ladders and wages in the dominant firms, and dequalification, low pay and insecurity in the small firms. These small firms mainly employed non-EU immigrants from Eastern Europe and Africa. Often subcontracting took place through a long chain, with the last link consisting of small firms owned mainly by migrants, employing other migrants on a temporary basis without any formal contract, often in hazardous working environments. The fragmentation was further exacerbated by the proliferation of fake 'self-employment', in which manual workers were forced to become 'independent' subcontractors, bearing all risks of unemployment, accident or illness themselves (Veiga, 1999).

Conclusions

Economic migration is vital for advanced economies. Migrant workers – both highly skilled and less skilled – provide *additional labour* at a time of shortages resulting from economic and demographic shifts. They also provide *special types of labour* to fill gaps that native workers are unavailable or unwilling to fill. Migration thus makes it possible to maintain labour market flexibility, encouraging investment and economic growth.

During the post-1945 boom, migrant workers were steered into subordinate jobs: 'guestworkers' had strictly limited labour market rights, while colonial migrants were often subject to labour market discrimination. In addition, many migrants lacked education and vocational training, and therefore entered the labour market at low levels. A key question was whether long-term residence in developed countries could lead to upward mobility. Even more crucial was the question whether the initial disadvantaged position would be carried over to the migrants' descendants, the second generation.

Recent labour market data show that migrants' work situation has become much more diverse, partly as a result of the shift to service-based economies. But some migrants have tended to get stuck in manufacturing jobs with poor prospects. High unemployment rates – often twice the average for natives – and low activity rates reveal that migrant workers often still have a disadvantaged position. Many migrant workers now have service jobs, some of them in high-skilled positions (like doctors, nurses and teachers), but overwhelmingly in such areas as cleaning, catering, domestic work and care.

As for the second generation, the picture is even more mixed, with important variations by ethnic group and host country. On the whole, children of migrants have done better than their parents, but have generally been less successful in both education and the labour market than young people without a migration background. Moreover, even those young second-generation members who have done well in education sometimes fail to get commensurate jobs. Explanations for the 'glass ceiling' include lack of local knowledge and networks, but also discrimination on the basis of race, ethnicity and class.

One reaction of migrants to this rather negative labour market experience has been to establish their own businesses. However it is not clear that this always represents a better situation: some migrant or ethnic entrepreneurs do gain higher incomes and status, but others establish businesses in marginal sectors, and can only keep going through long hours, poor working conditions and exploiting the labour of other migrants (including family members).

Migrant labour clearly plays an important role in rich countries, but economists cannot agree on the consequences for the economy as a whole. Most studies indicate benefits in terms of economic growth and average per capita income, but some economists argue that competing groups of local workers (especially the less skilled) may be disadvantaged. This debate cannot be easily resolved, but the continued eagerness of employers to hire migrant workers and the willingness of governments either to set up legal entry schemes or to turn a blind eye to irregular entry indicates that powerful groups see labour migration as economically crucial.

The key finding of this chapter is that, over the last 30 years, economic restructuring in rich countries has been linked to a new international division of labour, in which migrant workers play important but varied roles. The shift to neoliberal economic management has reshaped the conditions under which migrant workers are employed. Deregulation of the economy has gone hand-in-hand with the decline of trade unions and the erosion of welfare state protection. Formal employment within large-scale enterprises has in many cases been replaced by a variety of work arrangements that differentiate and separate workers. Temporary and causal employment, chains of subcontracting, informalization and new forms of labour market segmentation affect both native and migrant workers. However, it is disadvantaged and vulnerable groups of workers – migrant women, irregular workers, ethnic and racial minorities – who end up in the most precarious positions. Deprivation of human and worker rights for groups that lack legal status and market power seems to be an integral aspect of all advanced economies today.

Guide to further reading

In this chapter, we can look only at a limited range of studies on the labour market experience of migrants and the economic effects of migration. It would be important to look at other indicators, like wage levels (and how they change over time), income levels, poverty, employment rates and participation rates. Readers are recommended to use the further reading and to follow up the sources we cite for more on these issues.

The Age of Migration website www.age-of-migration.com includes an additional text on the educational and occupational success of the 'second generation' in Germany (10.1), as well as a summary of the debate between economists George Borjas and David Card on whether labour immigration is bad for US workers (10.2). It also includes an analysis of labour market segmentation in the French car and building industries in the 1970s and 1980s (10.3).

Hatton and Williamson's two books (1998; 2005) provide useful overviews of the economics of labour migration. For developed countries in general see the OECD's annual *International Migration Outlook* (e.g. OECD, 2007). For the USA see: Borjas (2001); Daniels (2004); Portes and Rumbaut (2006); and Smith and Edmonston (1997). For early analyses of European labour migration see: Böhning (1984); Castles and Kosack (1973); Castles et al. (1984); and Kindleberger (1967). More recent European work includes: Dustmann and Glitz (2005); Düvell (2005); Glover et al. (2001); Münz et al. (2007); and Straubhaar and Zimmermann (1992). For Australia see: Castles et al. (1998); Collins (1991, 2006); Lever-Tracy and Quinlan (1988); and Wooden (1994); and for Canada Reitz (1998).

On the political economy of migrant labour, Piore (1979); and Sassen (1988; 1991) are still useful, while Stalker (2000) provides a brief overview. Older studies on ethnic entrepreneurs include: Collins et al. (1995); Light and Bonacich (1988); Waldinger et al. (1990). For more recent work see Kloosterman and Rath (2003); Light and Gold (1999); Rath (2002); Waldinger (1996); and Waldinger and Lichter (2003). Gender and migrant labour are examined in: Anderson (2000); Browne and Misra (2003); Pessar and Mahler (2003); Phizacklea (1990, 1998); and Schrover et al. (2007). On irregular migration and the informal sector see: Düvell (2005); Ness (2005); and Reyneri (2003).

Chapter 11

New Ethnic Minorities and Society

Migration since 1945 has led to growing cultural diversity and the formation of new ethnic groups in many countries. Such groups are visible through the presence of different-looking people speaking their own languages, the development of ethnic neighbourhoods, and the establishment of ethnic associations and institutions. In this chapter we will examine the experience of a range of Western societies. The topic would really require detailed description of developments in each immigration country. That is not possible here. Instead, accounts of diversity and minorities in selected countries – the USA, Australia, the UK, France, Germany and Italy – are presented as boxes. These should be read in conjunction with the descriptions of migration in Chapter 5. The *AOM website* provides further material on several immigration countries (see Further Reading at the end of this chapter).

The aim of the chapter is to show similarities and differences in the migratory process, and to discuss why ethnic group formation and growing diversity have been relatively easily accepted in some countries, while in others the result has been marginalization and exclusion. We examine the consequences for the ethnic groups concerned and for society in general. Our argument is that the migratory process works in a similar way everywhere with respect to settlement, labour market segmentation, residential segregation and ethnic group formation. The main differences are to be found in public attitudes and government policies on immigration, settlement, citizenship and cultural pluralism.

This chapter uses a range of statistical concepts. For better understanding of these, please consult The Note on Migration Statistics at the beginning of the book.

Incorporation: how immigrants become part of society

A crucial question is how immigrants and their descendants can become part of receiving societies and nations. A second question is how the state and civil society can and should facilitate this process. Answers have varied in different countries. The process is most commonly referred to as 'integration', but this can refer to a specific idea of where the process should lead, so we prefer the more neutral term 'incorporation'. The key issue is whether immigrants should be incorporated as *individuals* – that is, without taking account of cultural difference or group belonging – or as *communities* – that is, ethnic groups which tend to cluster together and maintain their own cultures, languages and religions.

The starting point for understanding incorporation is historical experiences of nation-state formation: the ways in which emerging states handled difference when dealing with internal ethnic or religious minorities, conquering new territories, incorporating immigrants, or ruling people in their colonies (see Chapter 4). Differing ideas about citizenship developed from these experiences (see Chapter 2). 'National models' for dealing with ethnicity and cultural difference emerged in various European countries (see Brubaker, 1992; Favell, 1998; Bertossi, 2007), and these models helped to determine how states and the public later reacted to immigrants (Castles and Davidson, 2000).

The British history of conquering Wales, Scotland and Ireland and of dealing with religious diversity led to a politically integrated state that accepted difference: the United Kingdom required political loyalty, but a person's group identity could be Welsh or Scottish, Protestant or Catholic. In France, the 1789 Revolution established principles of equality and the rights of man that rejected group cultural identity, and aimed to include individuals as equal political subjects. In both Britain and France, however, it was the expansion of the state that created the nation – political belonging came before national identity. Germany was different: it was not united as a state until 1871, and the nation came before the state. This led to a form of ethnic or folk belonging that was not consistent with incorporation of minorities as citizens. By contrast, the white settler societies of the New World were built through the dispossession of indigenous peoples, and through immigration from Europe. Incorporation of immigrants as citizens was part of their national myths. This led to models of assimilation, such as the US image of the 'melting pot'. Of course, it was thought that only white people could be assimilated: Australia, New Zealand, Canada and the USA all had racially selective immigration laws.

These differing approaches imply different relationships between society and nation, and between civic belonging and national identity. In Britain a person could be a full member of the society and political nation and yet belong to a distinct cultural or religious group. In France, civic identity required a unitary national identity. In Germany, national identity came first, and was the precondition for belonging as a citizen. In the settler societies, civic belonging was thought to lead to national identity, so that differing identities were acceptable as a passing phase on the way to 'Americanization' (or the equivalent).

When immigration started in the post-1945 boom (see Chapter 5), incorporation of the newcomers was not a major issue. The numbers were not expected to be large, and there was a strong belief in the 'controllability of difference'. The 'classical immigration countries' (the USA, Canada, Australia etc.) only wanted white settlers from their 'mother countries' or other Northwestern European countries, and saw no problem in assimilating them. Britain, France and the Netherlands also expected to be able to assimilate fairly small groups of immigrants from their colonies and from other European countries. Germany and other 'guestworker' importers (e.g. Austria and Switzerland) did not anticipate family reunion or settlement, and therefore pursued polices of temporary admission to the labour market.

Assimilation meant that immigrants were to be incorporated into society through a one-sided process of adaptation. They were to give up their distinctive linguistic, cultural or social characteristics and become indistinguishable from the majority population. The 'guestworker' model can be described as *differential exclusion*: migrants were to be temporarily incorporated into certain areas of society (above all the labour market) but denied access to others (especially citizenship and political participation) (Castles, 1995).

But the belief in the controllability of difference proved misplaced in all these cases. In the postwar boom, labour migration grew in volume and became a structural necessity for Western economies. Racially selective immigration rules broke down, and migrants came from more distant and culturally different countries. When the boom faltered in the 1970s, family reunion took place – even in 'guestworker' countries. Then the end of the Cold War and globalization brought new migrations from ever more diverse origins.

In the classical immigration countries, migrants from non-Western European backgrounds tended to have disadvantaged work situations and to become concentrated in specific neighbourhoods. This led to community formation and the maintenance of minority cultures, languages and minorities. Since many immigrants had become citizens, they gained electoral clout in some inner-city areas. Assimilation had clearly failed and new approaches were needed. In European host countries, similar trends were emerging. Even in the 'guestworker' countries, settlement was taking place despite official denials, leading to social exclusion, and an enduring link between class and ethnic background.

Assimilation was replaced (initially at least) by the principle of *integration*, which meant recognizing that adaptation was a gradual process that required some degree of mutual accommodation. Acceptance of cultural maintenance and community formation might be a necessary stage, but the final goal was still absorption into the dominant culture – integration was often simply a slower and gentler form of assimilation. Today, of all the highly developed immigration countries, France comes closest to the assimilationist model (see Box 11.4). Elsewhere, however, there was a shift to an approach that recognized the long-term persistence of group difference.

Multiculturalism meant that immigrants should be able to participate as equals in all spheres of society, without being expected to give up their own culture, religion and language, although usually with an

Box 11.1 Minorities in the USA

US society is a complex ethnic mosaic deriving from five centuries of immigration. The white population is a mixture of the original mainly British colonists and later immigrants, who came from all over Europe in one of the greatest migrations in history from 1850 to 1914. Assimilation of newcomers is part of the 'American creed', but this process has always been racially selective. Native American societies were devastated by white expansion westwards, while millions of African slaves were brought to America to labour in the plantations of the South.

The USA is becoming ever more culturally diverse. Recent immigrants have come mainly from Latin America and Asia. The foreign-born population grew by 5.6 million between 2000 and 2005 to reach 35.7 million. The foreign-born share in population rose from only 4.8 per cent in 1970 to 12.4 per cent in 2005. By 2005, 53 per cent of the foreign-born were from Latin America, 27 per cent from Asia and only 14 per cent from Europe. Until recently over three-quarters of all new immigrants settled in the six 'gateway states' of California, New York, Florida, Texas, New Jersey and Illinois. After 2000, a growing share went to other states where there had been little immigration in the past.

Ethnic minorities now make up over a quarter of the population. The greatest divide in US society remains that between African–Americans and whites. However, the number of Hispanics now exceeds that of African–Americans.

US population by race and Hispanic origin, 2005

	Millions	Per cent
White	215.4	74.7
Black or African–American	34.9	12.1
American Indian and Alaskan Native	2.3	0.8
Asian, Native Hawaiian and other Pacific Islander	11.5	4.4
Some other race	17.3	6.0
Two or more races	5.5	1.9
Total population	288.4	100.0
Hispanic or Latino origin (of any race)	41.8	14.5

Note: Data are for 'household population' (excluding people in institutions like prisons).

Source: American Community Survey in (US Census Bureau, 2005).

$\longrightarrow$

expectation of conformity to certain key values. There have been two main variants. In the USA, cultural diversity and the existence of ethnic communities are officially accepted, but it is not seen as the role of the state to work for social justice or to support the maintenance of ethnic cultures. The second variant is multiculturalism as a public policy. Here,

---

→

Hispanics are the descendants of Mexicans absorbed into the USA through its south-western expansion, as well as recent immigrants from Latin American countries. Hispanics can be of any race, but are seen as a distinct group based on language and culture. The Asian population is also growing fast.

The movement of Europeans and African–Americans into low-skilled industrial jobs in the early twentieth century led to labour market segmentation and residential segregation. In the long run, many 'white ethnics' achieved upward mobility, while African–Americans became increasingly ghettoized. Distinctions between blacks and whites in income, unemployment rates, social conditions and education are still extreme. Members of some recent immigrant groups, especially from Asia, have high educational and occupational levels, while many Latin Americans lack education and are concentrated in unskilled categories.

Incorporation of immigrants into the 'American dream' has been largely left to market forces. Nonetheless, government has played a role by making it easy to obtain US citizenship, and through compulsory public schooling. Legislation and political action following the Civil Rights Movement of the 1950s and 1960s led to an enhanced role for a black middle class. However, commitment to equal opportunities and anti-poverty measures declined from the 1980s, leading to increased inequality and impoverishment of minorities.

Illegal migration and the costs of welfare for immigrants became major political issues in the 1990s. The Clinton Administration's 'Operation Gatekeeper' built fences and surveillance systems along the US–Mexico border. The effect was not to cut migration but to make it more dangerous and expensive: up to 500 migrants a year lost their lives trying to cross the deserts of California, Arizona and Texas, while smugglers were able to increase their fees sharply. In view of the high risks and costs, many Mexican workers decided to stay on in the USA, and to bring their families. Thus border control measures turned temporary labour movement into permanent settlement. Welfare restrictions played a similar role: in 1996, US Congress approved a law which drew a sharp line in welfare entitlements between US citizens and foreign residents. This encouraged many immigrants to apply for naturalization.

Today immigration reform is a central issue in US politics. In 2006, it was estimated that roughly one-third of the 35 million foreign-born residents were naturalized US citizens, another third were legal residents, and one-third were illegal residents. However, efforts at reform were stalled by 2007 (see Box 1.1 above).

Sources: Feagin (1989); OECD (2007); Cornelius (2001); Lyman (2006); Passel (2006); Portes and Rumbaut (2006); US Census Bureau (2005); Wasem (2007).

---

multiculturalism implies both the willingness of the majority group to accept cultural difference and state action to secure equal rights for minorities. Multiculturalism originated in Canada, and was taken up in various forms between the 1970s and the 1990s in Australia, the UK, the Netherlands and Sweden.

Box 11.2 Minorities in Australia

Australia has pursued a programme of planned immigration since 1947: 6.5 million new settlers have arrived (one-tenth of them as refugees). Immigration has helped treble the population from 7 million in 1947 to 20 million today. The 2006 Census counted 4.4 million overseas-born people, 22 per cent of Australia's total population. In addition, a quarter of the population are 'second generation Australians' – that is, they are Australian-born with at least one parent born overseas. In 2006 there were 455,000 Aboriginal people (2.3 per cent of total population).

Historically, Australians have been fearful of migration from Asia. The White Australia Policy was introduced in 1901. Post-1947 migration was designed to be mainly from Britain, with a gradual broadening to the rest of Europe. But the White Australia policy proved unsustainable, and Asian entries grew from the 1980s. In 2001, 51 per cent of the foreign-born population were from Europe (especially from the UK, Italy, Greece, Germany and the Netherlands), while 21 per cent were from Asia (mainly Vietnam, China, the Philippines and India) and 11 per cent from Oceania (mainly New Zealand but also Samoa, Tonga and Fiji). African-born people made up only 4 per cent of the population, but their numbers are growing due to refugee intakes from Sudan and migration from South Africa.

Australia – like the USA and Canada – has seen immigration as vital for nation-building. Family migration has been the norm and the initial five-year waiting period for naturalization was reduced to two years in 1984. Two-thirds of immigrants who have been in Australia over two years now hold Australian citizenship. In the 1950s and 1960s, immigrants were called 'New Australians' and were expected to quickly assimilate into the Australian culture and lifestyle. However, non-British immigrants (especially

$\longrightarrow$

As the rest of this chapter shows, immigrant populations and their relationship with societies and nations have developed in complex and unexpected ways. All of the different approaches to incorporation have proved problematic in one way or another, so that by the early twenty-first century there appeared to be a widespread 'crisis of integration'.

Immigration policies and minority formation

Taking the period since 1945 as a whole, three groups of countries may be distinguished. The 'classical immigration' countries encouraged family reunion and permanent settlement and treated most legal immigrants as future citizens. Sweden, despite its very different historical background, has followed similar policies. The second group includes France, the Netherlands and the UK, where immigrants from former colonies were often citizens at the time of entry. Permanent immigration and family

⟶

Eastern and Southern Europeans) tended to get low-paid manual jobs in manufacturing, construction and transport. This in turn meant clustering in low-income areas, providing the basis for ethnic community formation. The maintenance of homeland languages, religions and cultures, and the emergence of ethnic businesses and associations, made it obvious that assimilation could not succeed. Moreover, once migrants became citizens, they became an important electoral force.

By the 1970s, a policy of multiculturalism had been adopted, with the support of all the main political parties. Australian multiculturalism combines two key principles: recognition of the right of minorities to maintain their own cultures (within a common framework of law), and concern for social inclusion and equity. The Australian approach emphasises the duty of the state to combat racism and to ensure that minorities have equal access to government services, education and the labour market.

Public support for immigration and multiculturalism waned in the 1990s. The Liberal-National Coalition, in government from 1996 to 2007, dismantled many multicultural institutions and services, and promoted principles of integration and social cohesion around 'core cultural values'. This was linked to a tough line on asylum and undocumented entry, and an emphasis on economic migration – especially of the highly skilled. The Australian Citizenship Act of 2007 increased the qualifying period for naturalization from two to four years, and introduced citizenship tests. The Australian Labor Party (ALP) Government elected in November 2007 has indicated that it will maintain existing immigration policies, although citizenship rules are to be re-examined and the test may be scrapped.

Sources: ABS (2007a, b); Castles and Vasta (2004); DIAC (2007a); Jupp (2002); OECD (2007); Collins (1991).

reunion have generally been permitted (though with some exceptions). Immigrants from other countries have had a less favourable situation, although settlement and naturalization have often been allowed. The third group consists of those countries which tried to cling to 'guestworker' models, above all Germany, Austria and Switzerland. Such countries tried to prevent family reunion, were reluctant to grant secure residence status and had highly restrictive naturalization rules.

The distinctions between these three categories are neither absolute nor static. The USA tacitly permitted illegal farmworker migration from Mexico, and denied rights to such workers. France had very restrictive rules on family reunion until the 1970s. Germany and Switzerland gradually improved family reunion rules and residence status. One important change has been the erosion of the privileged status of migrants from former colonies. Making colonized people into subjects of the Dutch or British crown, or citizens of France, was a way of legitimating colonialism, and after 1945 it also seemed a convenient way of bringing in low-skilled labour. In response to permanent settlement and declining labour demand, all three countries removed citizenship from most former colonial subjects and put them on a par with foreigners.

There has been some convergence: former colonial countries have become more restrictive, while former 'guestworker' countries have become less so. But this has gone hand in hand with a new differentiation: the EC countries granted a privileged status to intra-Community migrants in 1968. The establishment of the EU in 1993 was designed to create a unified labour market, with all EU citizens having full rights to take up employment and to obtain work-related social benefits in any member country. The EU enlargements of 2004 and 2007 did indeed lead to large labour movements (see Chapter 5). But entry and residence have become more difficult for non-EU nationals, especially those from outside Europe.

Immigration policies have consequences for immigrants' future status. Policies designed to keep migrants in the status of temporary mobile workers make it likely that settlement will take place under discriminatory conditions. Moreover, official ideologies of temporary (or more recently 'circular') migration create expectations within the receiving population. If a temporary sojourn turns into settlement, then it is the immigrants who are blamed for any problems. Anyone who looks different becomes suspect.

Immigration policies also shape the consciousness of migrants themselves. In countries where permanent immigration is accepted and the settlers are granted secure residence status and civil rights, a long-term perspective is possible. Where the myth of short-term sojourn is maintained, immigrants' perspectives are inevitably contradictory. Return to the country of origin may be difficult or impossible, but permanence in the immigration country is doubtful. Such immigrants settle and form ethnic groups, but they cannot plan a future as part of the wider society. The result is isolation, separatism and emphasis on difference. Thus discriminatory immigration policies cannot stop the completion of the migratory process, but they can be the first step towards the marginalization of the future settlers.

Labour market position

As Chapter 10 showed, labour market segmentation based on ethnicity and gender has developed in all immigration countries. This was intrinsic in the type of labour migration practised until the mid-1970s. The situation has changed; today's migrants are much more diverse in educational and occupational status. Highly skilled personnel are encouraged to enter, either temporarily or permanently, and are an important factor in skill upgrading and technology transfer. Many refugees bring skills

---

Box 11.3 Minorities in the United Kingdom

The UK uses three main categories for its population of immigrant origin: foreign residents, foreign-born people and ethnic minorities. These categories are based on different criteria.

In 2005, there were 3 million *foreign residents* (5.2 per cent of the total population) – a sharp increase from 1.9 million in 1996. The main origins were Ireland (369,000), India (190,000), Poland (110,000), USA (106,000), France (100,000), Germany (100,000), South Africa (100,000), Pakistan (95,000), Italy (88,000) and Portugal (88,000).

The *foreign-born population* in 2006 numbered 5.8 million (9.7 per cent of total population), compared with 4.1 million in 1996. The main countries of origin were: India (570,000), Ireland (417,000), Pakistan (274,000), Germany (269,000), Poland (229,000), Bangladesh (221,000), South Africa (198,000), the USA (169,000), Kenya (138,000) and Jamaica (135,000).

The *ethnic minority population* are mostly British-born descendants of New Commonwealth immigrants who arrived from the 1950s to the 1970s. The 2001 Census recorded 4.6 million ethnic minority members (7.9 per cent of total population). Half were 'Asian or Asian British', a quarter were 'Black or Black British', 14.6 per cent were 'Mixed', 5.2 per cent were Chinese and 5 per cent other ethnic groups. This classification is based on 'race', and does not include Irish (691,000 in 2001) or other white immigrant groups. In 2001, London contained 45 per cent of Britain's ethnic minority population. Twenty-nine per cent of London's population were members of ethnic minorities (ONS, 2004b).

$\longrightarrow$

---

with them, although they are not always allowed to use them. Low-skilled migrants are unwelcome as workers, but enter through family reunion, as asylum seekers or illegally. Their contribution to low-skilled occupations and small business is of great economic importance, but is officially unrecognized.

Labour market segmentation is part of the migratory process. When people come from poor to rich countries, without local knowledge or networks, lacking proficiency in the language and unfamiliar with local ways of working, then their entry point into the labour market is likely to be at a low level. The question is whether there is a fair chance of later upward mobility. The answer often depends on state policies. Some countries (including Australia, Canada, Sweden, the UK, France and Netherlands) have active policies to improve the labour market position of immigrants and minorities through language courses, basic education, vocational training and antidiscrimination legislation.

The 'guestworker' countries initially restricted migrants' labour market rights through work permits that bound foreign workers to specific occupations, jobs or locations. Rules for temporary workers still maintain such restrictions. However, in the late 1970s, Germany and Austria

→

Commonwealth immigrants who came before 1971 were British subjects and enjoyed all citizenship rights. The 1971 Immigration Act and the 1981 British Nationality Act put Commonwealth immigrants on a par with foreigners in most respects. However, legally resident Commonwealth citizens still have full voting rights. Irish immigrants too enjoy virtually all rights. Citizens of other EU states have employment and social rights, and can vote in local and European elections, but not in parliamentary elections. Foreigners can apply for naturalization after five years of legal residence.

The *race relations approach* which emerged in the late 1960s and the 1970s was based on management of intergroup relations by the state. It meant recognizing the existence of distinct groups, defined primarily on the basis of 'race'. Acceptance of cultural and religious diversity was officially labelled as *multiculturalism*, especially in education. The Race Relations Acts of 1965, 1968 and 1976 outlawed discrimination in public places, employment and housing. A Commission for Racial Equality (CRE) was set up in 1976 to enforce these laws and promote good community relations.

However, discrimination and racist violence remained major problems. Black youth discontent exploded into riots in inner-city areas in 1980–1981, 1985–1986 and 1991. The government responded with measures to combat youth unemployment, improve education, rehabilitate urban areas and change police practices. But the 1999 Stephen Lawrence Inquiry (set up to analyse the poor police response after the murder of a young black man by a white gang) revealed the continued strength of institutional racism. The Race Relations (Amendment) Act 2000 required all public bodies to introduce race equality schemes and to work to eliminate discrimination. But in 2001, riots broke out involving youth of Asian origin in the northern cities of Oldham, Burnley and Bradford. The extreme-right British National Party sought to exploit local conflicts, and had some electoral success amongst white voters.

In the early twenty-first century, the main immigration issue was asylum (see Chapter 8). Successive governments introduced five new laws between 1993 and 2006, tightening up entry rules, and introducing deterrent measures such as detention and restrictions on welfare. Asylum applications declined from 103,000 in 2002 to just 28,000 in 2006. However, by then public attention had shifted to a new issue: the growth of Islam. The 1.6 million Muslims in Britain only make up 2.7 per cent of the population. But the London bombings of 7 July 2005 and subsequent attempted attacks precipitated concern about the loyalty of young Muslims. Some people argue that multiculturalism has failed to provide a unifying national identity. Government policies shifted to emphasize 'social cohesion'. Citizenship tests for immigrants were introduced, based on ideas of 'Britishness' and 'core values'. However, critics point to the contrast between the formal equality enjoyed by ethnic minorities and their everyday experience of unemployment, inequality and social exclusion. The UK experience shows that citizenship is not necessarily a protection against social disadvantage and racism.

Sources: OECD (2007); ONS (2003; 2004a, b); Solomos (2003); Benyon (1986); Layton-Henry (2004); Schierup et al. (2006: Chapter 5).

introduced education and training measures for foreign workers and youth. Today, the great majority of workers have long-term residence permits, which give them virtual equality of labour market rights with nationals. Recent discussions on 'circular migration' sometimes suggest limitation of the rights of migrant workers (see Chapter 3), which could mean a return to forms of labour market incorporation that lead to long-term disadvantage.

Residential segregation, community formation and the global city

Some degree of residential segregation is to be found in many immigration countries, though nowhere is it as extreme as in the USA, where in certain areas there is almost complete separation between blacks and whites, and sometimes Asians and Hispanics too. In other countries there are city neighbourhoods where immigrant groups are highly concentrated, though they rarely form the majority of the population. Residential segregation arises partly from immigrants' situation as newcomers, lacking social networks and local knowledge. Equally important is their low social status and income. Another factor is discrimination by landlords: some refuse to rent to immigrants, while others make a business of charging high rents for poor accommodation.

Institutional practices may also encourage residential segregation. Many migrant workers were initially housed by employers or public authorities. There were migrant hostels and camps in Australia, barracks provided by employers in Germany and Switzerland, and hostels managed by the government *Fonds d'Action Sociale* (FAS, or Social Action Fund) in France. These generally provided better conditions than private rented accommodation, but led to control and isolation. Hostels also encouraged clustering: when workers left their initial accommodation they tended to seek housing in the vicinity.

In countries where racism is relatively weak, immigrants often move out of inner-city areas to better suburbs as their economic position improves. However, where racism and social exclusion are strong, concentration persists or may even increase. Segregation increases when members of the majority population move out of inner-city areas to the suburbs. The departure of better-off immigrants can lead to increased concentration by social class as well as ethnicity. In the Netherlands, it was reported that 70 per cent of Turks and 60 per cent of Moroccans associated mainly with members of their own ethnic groups, while two-thirds of the native Dutch population had little or no contact with immigrants (EUMAP, 2007).

Residential segregation is a contradictory phenomenon. In terms of the theory of ethnic minority formation (see Chapter 2), it contains elements of both other-definition and self-definition. Immigrants cluster together for economic and social reasons, and are often kept out of certain areas by racism. But they also frequently want to be together, in order to provide

Box 11.4 Minorities in France

The 4.9 million foreign-born persons in France made up 8.1 per cent of the total population in 2005 (see Table 11.1). The most recent data for foreign residents are for 1999, when 3.3 million foreign residents made up 5.6 per cent of France's total population. Over a million former immigrants have become naturalized. In addition there are about half a million French citizens of African, Caribbean and Pacific Island origin from overseas departments and territories. France's immigrant population has changed from one of Southern European origins in the 1970s to one of mainly North and West African background today.

France's 'republican model' is based on principle of civic citizenship and equal individual rights for all. Recognition of cultural difference or ethnic communities is unacceptable. The idea is that immigrants should become citizens, and will then enjoy equal opportunities. The reality is very different. People of non-European birth or parentage (whether citizens or not) face social exclusion and discrimination. Minorities have become concentrated in inner-city areas and in large high-rise estates on the periphery of the cities (*les banlieues*). The work situation of ethnic minorities is marked by low-status, insecure jobs and high unemployment rates, especially for youth. Racist discrimination and violence are widespread. However, from the 1980s a new middle class of ethnic professionals and business people emerged, popularly known as the *beurgeoisie* (from the term *beurs*, slang for people of Arab origins).

The position of ethnic minorities in French society has become highly politicized. In the 1970s, police raids, identity checks and deportations of immigrants convicted of even minor offences were common. Immigrants took an active role in major strikes, for instance in the car industry. In the 1980s, the Socialist government improved residence rights, granted an amnesty to illegals and allowed greater political participation. A series of special programmes attempted to improve housing and education, and combat youth unemployment. At the same time, the extreme-right anti-immigrant *Front National* (FN) became a major political force.

Youth protests against unemployment and police discrimination led to riots in Lyons, Paris and other cities. Campaigns by *beurs*, organized in movements such as *SOS-Racisme* and *France-Plus*, demanded genuine inclusion in French society, and called for a new type of 'citizenship by participation', based on residence rather than nationality or descent. But by the mid-1990s,

→

mutual support, to develop family and neighbourhood networks and to maintain their languages and cultures. Ethnic neighbourhoods allow the establishment of small businesses and agencies which cater for immigrants' needs, as well as the formation of associations of all kinds.

Interestingly, the countries where community formation has taken place most easily have been those with open and flexible housing markets, based mainly on owner occupation, such as Australia, the UK and the USA.

these secular movements were losing support, as Islam grew in importance. This aroused fears about fundamentalism, especially when violence in Algeria spilled over into bomb attacks on the Paris Métro in 1995. The centre-right government tightened up immigration and nationality rules, undermining the republican principle of *ius soli* (citizenship through birth in France), and there were mass deportations of *sans papiers* – immigrants who had lost their legal status through the new laws.

The Socialist government of 1997–2002 reinstated *ius soli* for descendants of immigrants and liberalized rules on entry and residence. However, claims that society was threatened by immigrant criminality and that French identity was being undermined remained powerful rallying points for the extreme right. Le Pen, leader of the FN, shocked Europe by gaining one-fifth of the votes in the first round of the 2002 presidential election.

The Centre-Right government elected in 2002 pledged to cut immigration and strengthen law and order. Minister of the Interior Nicolas Sarkozy brought in restrictive immigration rules. A law of 2004 forbade the wearing of Islamic headscarves and other 'conspicuous religious symbols' in public places such as schools. However, Sarkozy's public attacks on minorities and policies of tougher policing in the *banlieues* exacerbated youth discontent. In autumn 2005, France experienced severe rioting, with nightly battles between police and youths, attacks on public building, hundreds of cars burnt out and many people injured. The official response was not to question the existing policy approach to minorities, but to call for even tougher law and order measures.

The result was the Immigration and Integration Law of 2006 – known as the *Loi Sarkozy*. This had three main elements: a new immigration policy, based on selection according to economic criteria (*immigration choisie*), mandatory 'integration contracts' (*contrat d'accueil et d'intégration*) for long-term residents, and policies of 'co-development' to link migration, return and development of countries of origin. This law was popular with French voters, and appears to have helped Sarkozy to become President of France in 2007. One of his first actions as President was to establish a Ministry of Immigration and National Identity. However, new riots in late 2007 showed that deep problems remain.

Sources: Body-Gendrot and Wihtol de Wenden (2007); Wihtol de Wenden (1988, 1995); Wihtol de Wenden and Leveau (2001); Weil (1991b); Bertossi (2007); Chou and Baygert (2007); Hargreaves (2007); OECD (2006, 2007); Hollifield (2004b).

The continental European pattern of apartment blocks owned by private landlords has not been conducive to community formation, while large publicly owned housing developments have frequently led to isolation and social problems, which are the breeding-ground for racism.

Immigration and ethnic minority formation are transforming postindustrial cities in contradictory ways. Sassen (1988) has shown how new forms of global organization of finance, production and distribution lead to 'global cities'. These attract influxes of immigrants, both for highly specialized activities and for low-skilled service jobs which service the luxurious lifestyles of the elites. In turn, this leads to a spatial restructuring of the city, in which interacting factors of socioeconomic status and ethnic background lead to rapidly changing forms of differentiation between neighbourhoods.

Many immigrants are forced by powerful social and economic factors into isolated and disadvantaged urban areas, which they share with other marginalized social groups (Dubet and Lapeyronnie, 1992). Some local people perceive residential segregation as a deliberate and threatening attempt to form 'ethnic enclaves' or 'ghettos'. The extreme right has mobilized around fears of ghettos in Western European countries since the 1970s. Ethnic minority neighbourhoods can also be the site of confrontations with the state and its agencies of social control, particularly the police (see Chapter 12).

Ethnic clustering and community formation may be seen as necessary products of migration to the global cities. They may lead to conflicts, but they can also lead to renewal and enrichment of urban life and culture. Specific ethnic groups can never be completely isolated or self-sufficient in modern cities. Cultural and political interaction is negotiated around complex processes of inclusion and exclusion, and of cultural transference. Much of the energy and innovative capacity within the cities lies in the cultural syncretism of the multiethnic populations, as Davis (1990) has shown in the case of Los Angeles. Just as there can be no return to monoethnic populations (always a myth in any case), so there is no way back to static or homogeneous cultures. The global city with its multicultural population is a powerful laboratory for change.

Social policy

As migrants moved into the inner cities and industrial towns, they were blamed for rising housing costs, declining housing quality and deteriorating social amenities. In response, a whole set of social policies were developed. Sometimes policies designed to reduce ethnic concentrations and ease social tensions achieved the opposite.

Nowhere were the problems more severe than in France. After 1968, measures were taken to eliminate *bidonvilles* (shantytowns) and make public housing more accessible to immigrants. The concept of the *seuil de tolérance* (threshold of tolerance) was introduced, according to which the immigrant presence should be limited to a maximum of 10 or 15 per cent of residents in a housing estate or 25 per cent of students in a class (Verbunt, 1985: 147–155; MacMaster, 1991: 14–28). The implication was that immigrant concentrations presented a problem, and that dispersal was the precondition for assimilation. Subsidies to public housing societies (*habitations à loyer modéré*, or HLMs) were coupled to quotas for immigrants. To minimize conflicts with the French, immigrant

Table 11.1 *Foreign-born population in France, the Netherlands and Sweden (2005) by selected countries of origin (thousands)*

Country of origin	France	Netherlands	Sweden
Germany	–	117	42
Italy	342	–	–
United Kingdom	–	47	17
Spain	280	–	–
Portugal	565	–	–
Poland	–	–	46
Finland	–	–	184
Norway	–	–	45
Denmark	–	–	43
Former Yugoslavia	–	54	74
Bosnia and Herzogovina	–	–	55
Former Soviet Union	–	35	–
Algeria	677	–	–
Morocco	619	169	–
Tunisia	220	–	–
Cambodia	163	–	–
Turkey	225	196	36
Iraq	–	35	73
Iran	–	24	55
Surinam	–	189	–
Indonesia	–	153	0
Other countries	1,835	1,016	456
Total	4,926	1,735	1,126
Per cent of total population	8.1	10.6	12.4

Notes: – indicates that a certain country of origin is not among the main sources of immigrants for a given receiving country. Smaller groups are aggregated under 'others'.
Source: (OECD, 2007: Table B.1.4).

families were concentrated in specific estates. The HLMs could claim that they had adhered to the quotas – on an average of all their dwellings – while in fact creating new ghettos (Weil, 1991b: 249–258). This was the genesis of the ethnically concentrated *banlieues* (the urban periphery), which were to become one of France's main dilemmas in the early twenty-first century (Hargreaves, 2007; Body-Gendrot and Wihtol de Wenden, 2007).

By the 1980s, the *banlieues* were rapidly turning into areas of persistent unemployment, social problems and ethnic conflicts. Social policies focused on urban youth, and the Socialist government developed a range of programmes to improve housing and social conditions, boost educational outcomes and combat youth unemployment. According to one French scholar, these social policy measures were designed to achieve integration into French society, but in fact they 'linked all the problems of these towns and neighbourhoods to immigration'. Thus social policy encouraged

Box 11.5 Minorities in Germany

Until the late 1990s, politicians declared that Germany was 'not a country of immigration'. Yet, with over 20 million newcomers since 1945, it has in fact had more immigration than any other European country. Soon after World War II, over 8 million German 'expellees' (*Heimatvertriebene*) arrived from the regions annexed by the Soviet Union and Poland. In the 1960s and 1970s, millions of 'guestworkers' were recruited from Southern Europe and Turkey, and many stayed on with their families (see Box 5.1). With the end of the Cold War, there were new inflows of 'ethnic Germans' (*Spätaussiedler*) from Russia and Romania, as well as asylum seekers and economic migrants from all over the world.

By 2003, Germany had 10.6 million foreign-born persons – 12.9 per cent of its total population of 82.5 million. However, no breakdown of the foreign-born by origin is available, so it is necessary to use data on the foreign resident population. This grew from 0.7 million in 1961 (1.2 per cent of total population) to 4.6 million in 1981 (7.5 per cent) and 7.3 million in 2001 (8.9 per cent). The 2005 figure of 6.8 million (8.2 per cent) probably does not represent a real reduction, but rather the revision of population registers to take account of departures.

In 2005, 68 per cent of the foreign population came from outside the EU, while 25 per cent came from the older EU states and 7 per cent from the 10 states that joined the EU in 2004. Children born in Germany with foreign parents still do not automatically obtain German citizenship. One in five foreigners (1.4 million persons) was actually born in Germany.

Most of the 'guestworkers' were initially employed as manual workers in manufacturing industries, leading to residential concentration in industrial areas and city central districts. Later economic restructuring eliminated many of the jobs held by immigrants, leading to unemployment rates of 20 per cent or more – nearly twice the national average. Many foreigners left the workforce, or set up marginal small businesses. Lack of school programmes to address the problems faced by children of immigrants meant that they too tended to have poor labour market chances.

Following reunification in 1990, there was a wave of racist violence against immigrants and asylum seekers. The reality of permanent settlement and the dangers of creating an underclass became obvious. Attention focused on the Turkish minority, with its mainly Islamic background. Municipal authorities set up special offices to ensure appropriate service provision for minorities – in Frankfurt this was called the Office for Multicultural Affairs. But at the national level multiculturalism was rejected as threatening to national unity.

The Citizenship Law of 1999 marked a major change. It was designed to make it easier for immigrants and their children to become Germans, but it stopped short of recognizing dual citizenship – a key demand of Turkish immigrants. In 2001, a report commissioned by the Federal Interior Minister

$\longrightarrow$

concentration of minorities, slowed integration and strengthened group religious and cultural affiliations (Weil, 1991b: 176–179). This interpretation fits into the French republican tradition, which rejects any recognition of ethnic communities. In fact, the extent to which the state should provide

→

Foreign resident population in Germany by main nationalities (1995 and 2005)

Nationality	1995 thousands	2005 thousands	2005 per cent of foreign population	2005 per cent of total population
Turkey	2,014	1,764	26.1	2.1
Italy	586	541	8.0	0.7
Serbia and Montenegro	798	494	7.3	0.6
Poland	277	327	4.8	0.4
Greece	360	310	4.6	0.4
Croatia	185	229	3.4	0.3
Russian Federation	–	186	2.8	0.2
Austria	185	175	2.6	0.2
Bosnia & Herzogovina	316	157	2.3	0.2
Ukraine	–	131	1.9	0.2
Other	2,413	2,442	36.2	3.0
Total	7,134	6,756	100	8.2

recommended a fundamental shift and Germany's first Immigration Law was passed in 2004. This was designed to establish a modern system of migration management. It also paved the way for integration courses providing German language teaching as well as an introduction to the country's laws, history and culture. Such courses are compulsory for certain categories of new entrants and existing foreign residents.

At the same time, as a result of economic stagnation, a remarkable shift is taking place: Germans are beginning to emigrate for the first time in many years. The government is even providing courses to prepare unemployed skilled workers for jobs in Switzerland, Norway, Austria and the UK.

Germany is an important example of the unforeseen effects of migration. Labour recruitment was designed to bring in temporary workers who would not stay, but in the long run it led to permanent settlement and the emergence of a multiethnic society. Official denial made things worse, because it exacerbated the exclusion of migrants from society. In the long run public attitudes and policy approaches had to change. This is now happening, but it is a difficult and lengthy process.

Sources: BAMF (2006a, b); OECD (2006, 2007); Green (2004); Schierup et al. (2006: Chapter 6); Süssmuth (2001).

special social policies to facilitate immigrant integration is controversial in most immigration countries.

On the one hand, special policies for immigrants can reinforce tendencies to segregation. Up to the 1980s, German education authorities pursued a 'dual strategy', designed to provide skills needed for life in Germany while at the same time maintaining homeland cultures to facilitate return. This led to special classes for foreign children, causing social isolation and poor educational performance (Castles et al., 1984: Chapter 6). Housing policies in the UK were intended to be nondiscriminatory, yet they sometimes led to the emergence of 'black' and 'white' housing estates. Sweden's special public housing schemes for immigrants led to a high degree of ethnic concentration and separation from the Swedish population.

On the other hand, multicultural social policies are based on the idea that immigrants need services that address their special needs with regard to education, language and housing. The absence of such measures can put immigrants and their children at a disadvantage, and deny them opportunities for upward mobility. The key assumption of multiculturalism is that specific policies do not lead to separatism but, on the contrary, are the precondition for successful integration. This is because the situation of ethnic minorities is the result both of cultural and social difference, and of barriers to participation caused by discrimination.

It is possible to suggest a rough classification of social policy responses. From the 1970s, Australia, Canada, the UK, Sweden and the Netherlands pursued active social policies targeting immigrants and minorities. In the first three, the label 'multicultural' was used. Britain also spoke of 'race relations policy', while Sweden used the term 'immigrant policy' and the Netherlands 'minorities policy'. In all these countries, social policies that specifically target immigrants and minorities have been heavily criticized in recent years. As a result, multicultural policies have in some cases been replaced by an emphasis on 'integration', 'social cohesion' and 'shared citizenship values'. However, many of the social policies have been maintained under new labels.

A second group of countries rejects special social policies for immigrants. US authorities regard special policies for immigrants as unnecessary government intervention. Nonetheless, the equal opportunities, antidiscrimination and affirmative action measures introduced after the Civil Rights Movement of the 1960s benefited immigrants, and special social and educational measures are to be found at the local level. However, access to social benefits and education by noncitizens (especially irregular immigrants) has been under attack since the 1980s. French governments have rejected special social policies on the principle that immigrants should become citizens, and that any special treatment would hinder this. Yet despite this there have been programmes, such as Educational Priority Zones or, more generally, *la politique de la ville* (urban policy), which target areas of disadvantage, without special mention of immigrants.

The third group of countries is the former 'guestworker' recruiters. Germany has pursued rather contradictory policies. In the 1960s, the government commissioned charitable organizations (linked to the churches and the labour movement) to provide special social services for foreign workers. Foreign workers also had equal rights to work-related social benefits, but could be deported in the event of long-term unemployment or disability. After recruitment stopped in 1973, migrants (supported by labour unions and NGOs) won landmark court cases on welfare rights and family reunion. As settlement became more permanent, welfare, health and education agencies began to take account of the needs of immigrants – despite the official claim that 'Germany was not a country of immigration'. The experience in Austria was similar: while the Federal Government rejected long-term integration, city authorities recognized the real diversity of urban populations by providing special services for minorities. Switzerland, by contrast, leaves social provision to individual initiative and the private sector.

In the early twenty-first century there has been some convergence in social policy, fuelled by concerns about social exclusion or what a report into the 2001 riots in Northern England referred to as 'parallel lives' (Cantle, 2001). Political leaders have questioned multicultural approaches, and have introduced such measures as citizenship tests and integration contracts. Nonetheless, special programmes to combat the social disadvantages faced by immigrants and their descendants can also be found almost everywhere, despite differences in rhetoric.

Another general trend concerns policies to combat racism and discrimination. In 2000, the Council of the EU unanimously adopted a Racial Equality Directive. This required all EU member states to implement the principles of equal treatment of all people irrespective of racial or ethnic origin in employment and training, education, social security, healthcare and access to goods and services. Member states had to enact these principles in domestic law by 2003, and to set up national organizations to promote equal treatment and to assist victims of racial discrimination (CEC, 2007a). Although implementation of this Directive remains uneven, it represents an important change for many countries.

Racism and minorities

Three patterns may be distinguished in immigration countries. First, some settlers have merged into the general population and *do not constitute separate ethnic groups*. These are generally people who are culturally and socioeconomically similar to the majority of the receiving population: for instance British settlers in Australia or Austrians in Germany.

Second, some settlers form *ethnic communities*: they tend to cluster in certain neighbourhoods and to maintain their original languages and cultures, but they are not excluded from citizenship, political participation and opportunities for economic and social mobility. The ethnic community may have developed partly due to initial discrimination, but the principal reasons for its persistence are cultural and psychological. Examples are

Italians in Australia, Canada or the USA; the Irish in the UK; and people of Southern European background in France or the Netherlands. Such communities are likely to decline in saliency over time, as later generations intermarry with other groups, and move out of initial areas of concentration.

Third, some settlers form *ethnic minorities*. Like the ethnic communities, they tend to live in certain neighbourhoods and to maintain their languages and cultures. But, in addition, they may have a disadvantaged socioeconomic position and be partially excluded from the wider society by one or more of such factors as weak legal status, refusal of citizenship, denial of political and social rights, ethnic or racial discrimination, and racist violence and harassment. Examples are some Asian immigrants in Australia, Canada or the USA; Hispanics in the USA; Afro-Caribbeans and Asians in the UK; North Africans and Turks in most Western European countries; and asylum seekers of non-European background just about everywhere.

All the countries examined have settlers from all three categories, but our concern here is with the second and third categories. It is important to examine why some immigrants take on the character of ethnic communities, while others become ethnic minorities. A further important question is why more immigrants take on minority status in some countries than in others. Two groups of factors appear relevant: those connected with the characteristics of the settlers themselves, and those connected with the social structures, cultural practices and ideologies of the receiving societies.

Looking at the settlers, it is clear that phenotypical difference (skin colour, racial appearance) is the main marker for minority status. This applies even more to nonimmigrant minorities, such as aboriginal peoples in the USA, Canada and Australia, or African–Americans in the USA. They, together with non-European immigrants, make up the most marginalized groups in all the countries. There are four possible explanations for this: phenotypical difference may coincide with recent arrival, with cultural distance or with socioeconomic position, or, finally, it may serve as a target for racism.

The first explanation is partly correct: in many cases, black, Asian or Hispanic settlers are among the more recently arrived groups. Historical studies reveal examples of racism and discrimination against white immigrants quite as virulent as against nonwhites today (see Chapter 4). Recent arrival may make a group appear more threatening, and new groups tend to compete more with local low-income groups for jobs and housing. But recent arrival cannot explain why aboriginal populations are victims of exclusionary practices, nor why African–Americans and other long-standing minorities are discriminated against. Neither can it explain why racism against white immigrant groups tends to disappear in time, while that against nonwhites continues over generations.

What about cultural distance? Some non-European settlers come from rural areas with preindustrial cultures, and may find it hard to adapt to industrial or postindustrial cultures. But many Asian settlers in

North America and Australia are of urban background and highly edu-cated. This does not protect them from racism and discrimination. Many people perceive culture mainly in terms of language, religion and values, and see non-European migrants as very different. This applies particularly to Muslims. Fear of Islam has a tradition going back to the medieval crusades. In recent years, concerns about terrorism have led to widespread Islamophobia (hostility to Islam and Muslims), even though only a very small minority of Muslims actually support fundamentalist ideologies.

As for the third explanation, phenotypical difference does frequently coincide with socioeconomic status. Some immigrants from less developed countries lack the education and vocational training necessary for upward mobility in industrial economies. But even highly skilled immigrants may encounter discrimination. Many immigrants discover that they can only enter the labour market at the bottom, and that it is hard to move up the ladder later. Thus low socioeconomic status is as much a result of processes of marginalization as it is a cause of minority status.

We therefore conclude that the most significant explanation of minority formation lies in practices of exclusion by the majority populations and the states of the immigration countries. We refer to these practices as racism and to their results as the racialization of minorities (see Chapter 2). Traditions and cultures of racism are strong in all European countries and former European settler colonies (Goldberg, 1993). The increased sali-ency of racism and racist violence since the late 1970s can be linked to growing insecurity for many people resulting from rapid economic and social change.

Racist violence

In the mid-1980s, the European Parliament's Committee of Inquiry into Fascism and Racism in Europe found that 'immigrant communi-ties ... are daily subject to displays of distrust and hostility, to continuous discrimination ... and in many cases, to racial violence, including mur-der' (European Parliament, 1985). German reunification in 1990 was fol-lowed by outbursts of racist violence. Neo-Nazi groups attacked refugee hostels and foreigners on the streets, sometimes to the applause of bystand-ers. At first the violence was worst in the area of the former GDR, but in 1992 and 1993 several Turkish immigrants were killed in arson attacks in West Germany. All over Europe, such aggression had become common. According to one study: 'By the early 1990s, many groups of people have had to face racist violence and harassment as a threatening part of every-day life' (Björgo and Witte, 1993: 1).

The USA has a long history of white violence against African–Americans. Despite the antiracist laws secured by the Civil Rights Movement, the Ku Klux Klan and related groups remain a threat. Asians, Arabs and other minorities are also frequent targets. Police violence against minorities is

Box 11.6 Minorities in Italy

Italy has experienced a dramatic migration transition. From 1945 to 1975, 7 million Italians emigrated to escape economic stagnation and poverty. Large Italian communities remain in the USA, Argentina, Brazil, Australia, Germany and Switzerland. But, since the 1970s, rapid economic growth and declining fertility have reversed former patterns. In the early twenty-first century, Italy (together with Spain) had the largest migrant inflows in Europe.

Italy's legally resident foreign population rose from just 0.4 million in 1985 to 0.7 million in 1995, and then grew rapidly to 2.7 million in 2005. The main mode of entry has been undocumented labour migration, often followed later by legalization (see Chapter 8). Some of the apparent growth is therefore the result of change of status, and an unknown number of undocumented migrants remain. Legal foreign residents make up 4.6 per cent of Italy's population of 59 million. The table shows the diversity of the immigrant population, with substantial groups from Eastern Europe, North Africa, Asia and Latin America.

Immigrants are important in sustaining agriculture and industry, at a time when few young Italians are available. Undocumented workers are concentrated in the 'underground economy', which is responsible for about a quarter of Italy's economic activity. Legal immigrants are important as workers – both skilled and unskilled – in the industries of Northern Italy and also in services throughout the country. Several indicators show the trend to permanent settlement: increased family reunion (58 per cent of entrants in 2005), a higher female share (49 per cent of foreign residents in 2006), more births to foreign women (11 per cent of all births in 2004) and increasing numbers of children entering Italian schools.

The proportion of immigrants in Italy's population is still lower than that of older European immigration countries, but the rapid growth and the great diversity make immigration a challenge for society. The right-wing Northern League and National Alliance campaign against immigration as a threat to law and order, and there has been considerable violence, especially against non-Europeans. Trade unions, left-wing parties, church organizations and advocacy groups support migrant rights and call for multiculturalism, while employers' associations campaign for increased labour migration.

Italy had no immigration law until 1986, and it was not until 1998 that the Centre-Left Government tried to create a broadly based regulatory system, including a long-term residence permit (*carta di soggiorno*). This government also introduced integration measures. However, implementation proved slow and difficult. At the municipal level, right-wing authorities were reluctant to hand out residence permits, and bureaucratic delays led to long waiting periods. Left-wing local authorities were no more efficient,

→

common. The Los Angeles riots of May 1992 were provoked by police brutality towards a black motorist, which went unpunished by the courts. Even countries that pride themselves on their tolerance, like Canada, Sweden and the Netherlands, report a high incidence of racist attacks.

→

Italy: legal foreign residents by main nationalities 1995 and 2005

Nationality	1995 thousands	2005 thousands	2005 per cent of foreign population	2005 per cent of total population
Albania	30	349	13.1	0.6
Morocco	81	320	13.0	0.5
Romania	14	298	11.1	0.5
China	16	128	4.8	0.2
Ukraine	1	107	4.0	0.2
Philippines	36	90	3.4	0.2
Tunisia	31	84	3.1	0.1
Serbia and Montenegro	34	64	2.4	0.1
Ecuador	2	62	2.3	0.1
India	12	62	2.3	0.1
Other countries	472	1,107	41.5	1.9
Total	729	2,671	100.0	4.6

and their policies to recognize diversity and to improve services were often more rhetoric than reality. It remains extremely difficult for immigrants to become citizens.

In 2001 the Centre-Right Berlusconi coalition won national elections partly by portraying immigrants as a threat to the country. A year later it passed the Bossi-Fini Law, which repealed many of the 1998 measures. It favoured recruitment of seasonal workers and introduced tough measures against illegal immigration, including detention and increased deportations. But the Berlusconi government also introduced a legalization campaign, which led – probably unintentionally – to a big increase in the legal foreign population.

The Centre-Left Prodi government, elected in May 2006, promised a new approach. Two bills on citizenship and immigration reform were designed to create a comprehensive system of rights for immigrants, including secure residence status, integration measures and eventual access to citizenship. However, these planned reforms were not implemented. In early 2008, a new Centre-Right government was elected, following a campaign marked by anti-immigrant slogans, particularly from Berlusconi's coalition partners of the Northern League and other extreme-right parties. Racist attacks on immigrants soon ensued, including the burning down of migrant shacks by mobs in Naples.

Sources: Calavita (2004); Einaudi (2007); ISTAT (2007); King et al. (2000); Pastore (2006, 2007); Reyneri (2003); OECD (2006, 2007).

In its 2006 Report, 'the EU's European Monitoring Centre on Racism and Xenophobia (EUMC) pointed out that it was difficult to compare racist violence in EU member states due to differing laws and criminal justice practices. Only the UK and Finland had 'comprehensive data collection mechanisms', while five countries – Cyprus, Greece, Italy, Malta and Spain – had no official data at all (EUMC, 2006: 96). The UK recorded 57,902 'racist incidents' in 2004–2005, compared with 974 'racist, xenophobic and anti-Semitic acts' in France, and 15,914 'politically motivated – right wing' crimes in Germany in 2005. There is no reason to think that racism was actually greater in the UK: these figures simply reflect differing definitions and policy practices. EUMC identified trends in racist violence over the period 2000–2005. Of the 11 EU states for which data was available, eight (Denmark, Germany, France, Ireland, Poland, Slovakia, Finland and the UK) showed an upward trend. Three (the Czech Republic, Austria and Sweden) showed a downward trend (EUMC, 2006: 99–100). Key targets for racism included Europe's 8 million Roma, as well as Muslims and Jews. The Report also identified high levels of discrimination in employment, housing and education.

Clearly, racist violence and discrimination remain major problems. In 2001, the European Commission presented proposals for combating racism and xenophobia. In early 2007, the EU member states' justice and interior ministers finally agreed on a set of rules. However, these were considerably weaker than the Commission proposals. They set only minimum standards and allowed member states to opt out if they wished. Antiracist groups said these rules would do little to boost existing national laws (Brand, 2007).

The escalation of racist violence has not gone unchallenged. Antiracist movements have developed in most immigration countries, often based on coalitions between minority organizations, trade unions, left-wing parties, churches and welfare organizations. Antiracist organizations have helped to bring about equal opportunities and antidiscrimination legislation, as well as policies and agencies designed to curb violence.

However, as long as politicians are eager to make electoral capital out of anti-immigrant or anti-Muslim sentiments, racism will continue to be a problem. Racist campaigns, harassment and violence are important factors in the process of ethnic minority formation. By isolating minorities and forcing them into defensive strategies, racism may lead to self-organization and separatism, and even encourage religious fundamentalism. Conversely, antiracist action may help overcome the isolation of minorities, and facilitate their social and political incorporation into mainstream society.

Minorities and citizenship

Becoming a citizen is a crucial part of the incorporation process. *Citizenship* is a formal legal status (often referred to as *nationality*), designating membership of a nation-state. But it is also important to consider the contents of citizenship. These are usually defined in terms of civil, political and social rights, but linguistic and cultural rights are also very important for immigrants. Citizenship is not an either/or question: with increasing length of residence, immigrants sometime acquire forms of 'denizenship' or 'quasi-citizenship', which confer some, but not all, rights of citizenship.

Historically, laws on citizenship or nationality derive from two competing principles: *ius sanguinis* (literally: law of the blood), which is based on descent from a national of the country concerned, and *ius soli* (law of the soil), which is based on birth in the territory of the country. *Ius sanguinis* is often linked to an ethnic or folk model of the nation-state (typical of Germany and Austria), while *ius soli* generally relates to a nation-state built through incorporation of diverse groups on a single territory (such as France and the UK), or through immigration (the USA, Canada, Australia, Latin American countries). In practice, all modern states have citizenship rules based on a combination of *ius sanguinis* and *ius soli,* although one or the other may be predominant.

Acquisition of nationality by immigrants

Table 11.2 shows trends in acquisition of nationality. Acquisition includes naturalizations and other procedures, such as declarations on the part of descendants of foreign immigrant parents or conferral of nationality through marriage. The absolute number of acquisitions was high in the *ius soli* countries Australia, Canada and the USA, but it is not possible to calculate acquisition rates due to lack of data on the foreign population. But acquisition rates are no doubt high, as these 'classical immigration countries' see citizenship for newcomers as essential for national identity. In 2005 alone, the USA plus Canada granted citizenship to 800,000 immigrants, compared with 687,000 for all 25 EU countries.

Between 1988 and 1995 there was an upward trend in acquisitions in several European countries. Sweden and the Netherlands had the greatest increases, due to conscious efforts to encourage immigrants to become citizens. This trend continued from 1995 to 2005 for Sweden, but not for the Netherlands, where polices became more restrictive. Belgium and Switzerland also recorded increases in both periods, albeit from low bases. Germany moved away from its traditionally restrictive approach to citizenship for immigrants in the late 1990s, so acquisitions increased. Southern European countries have been very restrictive in the past, but Spain has become more open. Japan has maintained its very restrictive regime, while the Czech Republic is included to show the low naturalization rates typical of Central and Eastern Europe.

The rules for becoming a citizen in various countries are complex and have undergone considerable change in recent years (see Aleinikoff and Klusmeyer, 2000, 2001) In Europe, the distinction between *ius soli* and *ius sanguinis* countries was eroded by a trend towards more liberal rules in the 1990s (Bauböck et al., 2006a, b). However, a countertrend emerged in the early twenty-first century. Rules on naturalization of the immigrant

Table 11.2   *Acquisition of nationality in selected OECD countries (1988, 1995 and 2005)*

Country	Acquisition of nationality 1988		Acquisition of nationality 1995		Acquisition of nationality 2005	
	Thousands	Rate per cent	Thousands	Rate per cent	Thousands	Rate per cent
Australia	81	n.a.	115	n.a.	93	n.a.
Belgium	8	1.0	26	2.8	32	3.5
Canada	59	n.a.	228	n.a.	196	n.a.
Czech Rep.	n.a.	n.a.	n.a.	n.a.	3	0.9
France	46	1.3	n.a.	n.a.	155	4.8*
Germany	17	0.4	72	1.0	117	1.6
Italy	12	1.2	7	1.1	12**	0.5**
Japan	6	0.6	14	1.0	15	0.8
Netherlands	9	1.4	71	9.4	28	4.1
Spain	n.a.	n.a.	7	1.5	43	2.2
Sweden	18	4.3	32	6.0	40	8.2
Switzerland	11	1.1	17	1.3	38	2.6
UK	65	3.5	41	2.0	162	5.7
USA	242	n.a.	488	n.a.	604	n.a.
EU25	n.a.	n.a.	n.a.	n.a.	687	n.a.

Notes: Statistics cover all means of acquiring the nationality of a country.
The acquisition rate gives the number of persons acquiring the nationality of a country as a percentage of the stock of the foreign population at the beginning of the year.
n.a., data is not available.
* The 2005 rate for France is a rough estimate based on the 1999 foreign population figure.
** 2004 figures for Italy.

Sources: For 1988: own calculations based on OECD (1997). For 1995 and 2005: OECD (2006: Table A.1.6; 2007: Table A.1.6.).

generation and on birthright citizenship for the second generation became more restrictive, especially in Denmark, France, Greece, the Netherlands, the UK and Austria. Developments were more positive in Belgium, Finland, Germany, Luxembourg and Sweden (Bauböck et al., 2006b: 23). Compulsory integration programmes, language tests and citizenship tests (see boxes) all act as deterrents to naturalization.

It is important to look not only at the formal conditions, but also at the extent to which public policies welcome or deter new citizens (Bauböck et al., 2006b: 25). Legal requirements for naturalization (such as 'good character', regular employment, language proficiency, evidence of integration) are quite similar in various countries, but actual practices vary sharply. Switzerland, Austria and (until recently) Germany impose long waiting periods and complex bureaucratic practices, and treat naturalization as an act of grace by the state. Conversely, classical immigration countries encourage newcomers to become citizens. The act of becoming American (or Australian or Canadian) is seen as an occasion for celebration of the national myth. The recent introduction of citizenship ceremonies in some European countries is motivated by the desire to pass on 'national values', yet it could have positive effects by providing a symbolic welcome into the nation.

Status of the second generation

The transmission of citizenship to the second generation (the children of immigrants) and subsequent generations is the key issue for the future. National variations parallel those found with regard to naturalization. In principle, *ius soli* countries confer *birthright citizenship* on all children born in their territory. *Ius sanguinis* countries confer citizenship only on children of existing citizens. However, most countries actually apply models based on a mixture of the two principles. Increasingly, entitlement to citizenship grows out of long-term residence in the country: the *ius domicili*.

Ius soli is applied most consistently in Australia, Canada, New Zealand, the USA, the UK and Ireland. A child born to immigrant parents in the USA or Canada becomes a citizen, even if the parents are visitors or illegal residents. In Australia, New Zealand and the UK, the child obtains citizenship if at least one of the parents is a citizen or a legal permanent resident. Such countries only use the *ius sanguinis* principle to confer citizenship on children born to their citizens while abroad (Çinar, 1994: 58–60; Guimezanes, 1995: 159). However, birthright citizenship has led to accusations of 'citizenship tourism': pregnant women travelling to a country to obtain citizenship for a child. Ireland followed the US approach until 2004; then 79 per cent of voters supported a referendum to restrict conferral of Irish citizenship to children with at least one parent resident for at least three years (BBC News, 2004).

A combination of *ius soli* and *ius domicili* emerged in France, Italy, Belgium and the Netherlands in the 1990s. Children born to foreign parents in the territory obtained citizenship, providing they had been resident for a certain period and fulfilled other conditions. Since 2000, Germany, Finland and Spain have adopted similar arrangements. France, Belgium, the Netherlands and Spain also apply the so-called double *ius soli*. Children born to foreign parents, at least one of whom was also born in the country, acquire citizenship at birth. This means that members of the 'third generation' automatically become citizens, unless they specifically renounce this right upon reaching the age of majority (Çinar, 1994: 61; Bauböck et al., 2006a).

Where *ius sanguinis* is still applied strictly (Austria, Switzerland, Japan), children who have been born and grown up in a country may be denied not only security of residence, but also a clear national identity. They are formally citizens of a country they may never have seen, and can even be deported there in certain circumstances. Other *ius sanguinis* countries (notably Germany) have taken cautious steps towards *ius domicili*. This means giving an option of facilitated naturalization to young people of immigrant origin. In predominantly *ius soli* countries the second generation still generally have multiple cultural identities, but they have a secure legal basis on which to make decisions about their life perspectives.

Overall, the distinctions between *ius sanguinis* and *ius soli* countries have become weaker through policy changes since about 1990: in an early period there was a convergence towards more liberal policies, but, due to the increasingly hostile climate towards immigration and multiculturalism since about 2000, the main trend has been towards more restrictive approaches for both immigrants and their children (Bauböck et al., 2006a, b).

Dual citizenship

Trends are rather different with regard to dual or multiple citizenship (acquiring the nationality of a host country without renouncing the nationality of the country of origin). This is a way of recognizing the multiple identities of migrants and their descendants. Dual citizenship can be seen as a form of 'internal globalization' through which 'nation-state regulations implicitly or explicitly respond to ties of citizens across states' (Faist, 2007: 3). It represents a major shift, since the idea of singular national loyalties has been historically central to state sovereignty. One reason for change is the trend towards gender equality. In the past, nationality in binational marriages used only to be transmitted through the father. Nationality rules in European countries were changed in the 1970s and 1980s. Once mothers obtained the same right to transmit their nationality as fathers, binational marriages automatically led to dual citizenship.

Australia, Canada and the USA have long permitted or tolerated dual citizenship for immigrants. By contrast, most European countries signed the 1963 Strasbourg Convention on the Reduction of Cases of Multiple Nationality. However, attitudes and laws have changed: by 2004 only five of the EU15 states required renunciation of the previous nationality (Bauböck et al., 2006b: 24). The Netherlands introduced the right to dual citizenship in 1991, but withdrew it again in 1997 (Entzinger, 2003). Germany introduced measures to facilitate acquisition of nationality for immigrants and their children in 2000, but maintained its ban on dual citizenship. In both countries, however, there are important exceptions and many people do hold dual citizenship. In addition, many emigration countries have changed their nationality rules to allow emigrants to hold dual citizenship, as a way of maintaining links with their diasporas (see Chapter 3).

Linguistic and cultural rights

Many of the associations set up in the process of ethnic community formation are concerned with language and culture: they teach the mother tongue to the second generation, organize festivals and carry out rituals. Language and culture not only serve as means of communication, but take on a symbolic meaning which is central to ethnic group cohesion. In most cases, language maintenance applies in the first two to three generations, after which there is a rapid decline. The significance of cultural symbols and rituals may last much longer.

Many members of the majority see cultural difference as a threat to a supposed cultural homogeneity and to national identity. Migrant languages, religions and cultures become symbols of otherness and markers for discrimination, as shown particularly by the growth in hostility to Islam and its visible symbols – such as women's clothing. Renouncing such practices is seen as essential for success in the country of immigration. Failure to do so is regarded as indicative of a desire for separatism. Hostility to different languages and cultures is rationalized with the assertion that the official language is essential for economic success, and that migrant cultures are inadequate for a modern secular society. The alternative view is that migrant communities need their own languages and cultures to develop identity and self-esteem. Cultural maintenance helps create a secure basis which assists group integration into the wider society, while bilingualism brings benefits in learning and intellectual development.

Policies and attitudes on cultural and linguistic maintenance vary considerably. Some countries have histories of multilingualism. Canada's policy of bilingualism is based on two 'official languages', English and French. Multicultural policies have led to limited recognition of – and support for – immigrant languages, but they have hardly penetrated into mainstream contexts, such as broadcasting. Switzerland has a multilingual policy for its founding languages, but does not recognize immigrant languages. Australia and Sweden both accept the principle of linguistic and cultural maintenance, and have multicultural education policies. They provide language services (interpreting, translating, mother-tongue classes), funding for ethnic media and support for ethnic community cultural organizations. However, such measures have been reduced in recent years.

In the USA, language has become a contentious issue. The tradition of monolingualism is being eroded by the growth of the Hispanic community: in major cities like Los Angeles and Miami, the number of Spanish speakers is overtaking that of English speakers. This led to a backlash in the 1980s, in the form of 'the English-only movement', which called for a constitutional amendment to declare English the official language. Most states passed legislation to introduce this measure, but it proved extremely hard to implement, and public agencies and private companies continued to provide multilingual material and services. Monolingualism is the basic principle in France, the UK, Germany and the Netherlands. Nonetheless, all these countries have been forced to introduce language services to take account of migrant needs in communicating with courts, bureaucracies and health services. The multilingual character of inner-city school classes has also led to special measures for immigrant children, and to a gradual shift towards multicultural education policies.

Conclusions: the integration challenge

The reality in each country is much more complex and contradictory than our brief accounts can show. Nonetheless, comparison of these experiences provides some useful conclusions. The first is that temporary migrant labour recruitment almost always leads to permanent settlement of at least a proportion of migrants. The second is that the character of future ethnic groups will be partly determined by what the state does in the early stages of migration. Policies which deny the reality of immigration lead to social marginalization, minority formation and racism. Third, in order to cope with the difficult experience of settlement in a new society, immigrants and their descendants need their own associations and social networks, as well as their own languages and cultures. Fourth, the best way to prevent marginalization and social conflicts is to grant permanent immigrants full rights in all social spheres. This means making citizenship easily available, even if this leads to dual citizenship.

The approaches of states and the public in host countries towards the incorporation of immigrants have varied considerably. Starting in the 1990s, but especially from the early 2000s, policies on incorporation of immigrants and minorities have been questioned and revised, to the point where the older models discussed at the beginning of this chapter lack explanatory power. The inescapable reality of permanent settlement has led to the abandonment of the differential exclusionary approach in Germany. Immigration and citizenship laws have been reformed. While multiculturalism is rejected at the national level, local provision of special social and educational services for minorities is widespread. However, there are limits to change: Germany still rejects dual citizenship and has introduced compulsory integration measures. Austria and Switzerland still cling to exclusionary policies, although these are modified by local integration efforts. Of course, differential exclusion remains the dominant approach to foreign workers in many of the new industrial countries of Asia and the Gulf.

By the early 1990s, assimilation seemed to be on the way out everywhere, except in France. Democratic civil societies were thought to have an inherent trend towards multiculturalism (Bauböck, 1996). That is no longer the case: there has been a widespread backlash against multiculturalism. Canada has maintained its multicultural principles, but watered down their implementation, and Australia has gone even further in this direction. Sweden, the Netherlands and the UK have all relabelled policies with much greater emphasis on 'integration', 'social cohesion' and 'core national values'. The Netherlands has had perhaps the most dramatic turnaround and seems to be on the way to a new assimilationism (Vasta, 2007). Several scholars have sought to explain and theorize this return to an assimilation rhetoric (Alba and Nee, 1997; Brubaker, 2003; Joppke, 2004). Others have pointed out that assimilation is not a unitary process, but one linked to complex patterns of differentiation on the basis of race and class (Zhou, 1997; Portes and Rumbaut, 2006: 60–63, 271–280).

The backlash against multiculturalism has a number of causes. One is the growing awareness of the enduring social disadvantage and marginalization of many immigrant groups – especially those of non-European origin. The dominant approach is to claim that ethnic minorities are to blame by clustering together and refusing to integrate. Another factor is the growing fear of Islam and terrorism. Events like the bombings in Madrid and London, and the murder of Theo Van Gogh in the Netherlands, are seen as evidence of the incompatibility of Muslim values with modern European societies.

In this interpretation, recognition of cultural diversity has had the perverse effect of encouraging ethnic separatism and the development of 'parallel lives'. This is summed up in French academic Kepel's caricature of 'Londonistan' as a haven for Islamic ideologists (Kepel, 2005). A model of individual integration – based if necessary on compulsory integration contracts and citizenship tests – is thus seen as a way of achieving greater equality for immigrants and their children. The problem for such views, however, is that the one country that has maintained its model of individual assimilation is also experiencing dramatic problems. The minority youth riots of 2005 and 2007 in France showed that the republican model of individual integration has inadequately overcome inequality and racism.

All the different approaches to incorporation of immigrants thus seem problematic: differential exclusion is useless once settlement takes place; multiculturalism appears to lead to persistent separatism, and assimilation can perpetuate marginalization and conflict. In our view, this situation actually reflects the unwillingness of host societies to deal with two issues. The first is the deep-seated cultures of racism that are a legacy of colonialism and imperialism. In times of stress, such as economic restructuring or international conflict, racism can lead to social exclusion, discrimination and violence against minorities. The second issue is the trend to greater inequality resulting from globalization and economic restructuring. Increased international competition puts pressure on employment, working conditions and welfare systems. At the same time neoliberal economic policies encourage greater pay differences and reduce the capacity of states to redistribute income to reduce poverty and social disadvantage.

Taken together, these factors have led to a racialization of ethnic difference. Minorities may have poor employment situations, low incomes and high rates of impoverishment. This in turn leads to concentration in low-income neighbourhoods and growing residential segregation. The existence of separate and marginal communities is then taken as evidence of failure to integrate, and this in turn is perceived as a threat to the host society. The result, as Schierup et al. (2006) argue for Europe, is a 'dual crisis' of national identity and the welfare state. The attempt to resolve the crisis through racialization of minorities does not provide a solution. Rather, it threatens the fundamental values upon which democratic societies are based. Moreover, as analysed in Chapter 9, it threatens the security of democratic societies.

Guide to further reading

In earlier editions of *The Age of Migration*, we provided a detailed comparison of two very different immigration countries, Australia and Germany. For reasons of space, this chapter could not be included in the fourth edition, but it is available as item 11.1 on *The Age of Migration* website: www.the-age-of-migration.com. The website also includes short accounts of the situation of migrants and minorities in Canada (11.2), Netherlands (11.3) and Sweden (11.4).

It would take up too much space to give further reading for individual countries here – instead we refer readers to the sources used for the country boxes. The OECD *International Migration Outlook* provides up-to-date statistics and policy information for many countries, while the Migration Information Source contains data and good short country studies: http://www.migrationinformation.org/

Useful comparative studies include Reitz (1998), which covers Canada, the USA and Australia. Koopmans and Statham (2000) examine the politics of immigrant incorporation in Europe. Favell (1998) compares French and British approaches. King et al. (2000) provide studies of Southern European immigration countries. Good comparative studies on citizenship include: Aleinikoff and Klusmeyer (2000, 2001) and Bauböck et al. (2006a, b).

Chapter 12

Migrants and Politics

The most lasting significance of international migration may well be its effects upon politics. This is not inevitably the case. Much depends on how immigrants are treated by governments, and on the origins, timing, nature and context of a particular migratory flow. It makes a difference whether migrants were legally admitted and permitted to naturalize, or whether their entry (legal or illegal) was seen as merely temporary but they then stayed on permanently. On the one hand, immigrants can quickly become citizens without a discernible political effect, save for the addition of more potential voters. On the other hand, international migration may lead to an accretion of politically disenfranchised persons whose political marginality is compounded by various socioeconomic problems. Migrants have a major stake in the nature of public policies affecting them, particularly immigration policies. Unsurprisingly, migrant activism often focuses on influencing the future of immigration policies.

The universe of possible political effects of international migration is wide and characteristically intertwines the political systems of at least two states (the homeland and the receiving society) and sometimes one or more transit states as well. The political significance of international migration can be active or passive. Immigrants can become political actors in their own right or manifest apoliticism, which itself can be important to maintenance of the status quo. On the other hand, immigrants often become the object of politics: allies for some and foes for others. Chapter 11 has already dealt with one key political issue: the extent to which immigrants and their descendants can become citizens with full rights of political participation. Naturalization in democratic settings usually creates a 'feedback loop' enabling new citizens to vote and sometimes to decisively affect electoral outcomes and immigration policy content (Zolberg, 2006: 92, 96–98).

Chapter 9 focused on migration and security, so this chapter will analyse migration-related political phenomena bearing less directly upon security. The following themes are considered: homelands and expatriates, extraparliamentary forms of migrant participation and representation, noncitizen voting, migrant and ethnic voting blocs, anti-immigrant parties and movements, as well as the politics of immigration policy-making.

Homelands and expatriates

Mercantilist European states in the seventeenth and eighteenth centuries sought to discourage or bar emigration, as the loss of subjects was thought to detract from state economic and military power (Green and Weil, 2007). After the French Revolution and its proclamation of a human right to emigrate, the ability of European states to deter emigration began to erode. Concurrently, factors like decreasing economic barriers to transatlantic travel and, in some instances, state assistance to emigration resulted in massive emigration by Europeans between 1820 and 1920. Many of the patterns of interaction between states and emigrants witnessed in the nineteenth century persist into the twenty-first, although scholars differ over whether factors like transnationalism (see Chapter 2) constitute qualitatively new phenomena.

Whilst few states in the twenty-first century subscribe to mercantilism, a category of states did persist in endeavouring to prevent most emigration: Communist states like North Korea employed draconian means to stop citizens leaving. Nevertheless, tens of thousands of North Koreans succeeded in escaping northward to the People's Republic of China. Many such migrants sought to reach Bangkok, Thailand and from there points elsewhere, including the Republic of Korea.

In many other cases, especially in less developed countries after World War II, emigrants were not viewed positively by homeland governments, despite such governments often signing bilateral accords authorizing recruitment of their subjects or citizens for employment abroad. Such homeland governments often proclaimed that emigration would be temporary and that migrants would return home. Such blandishments often masked de facto policies of neglect of expatriate populations abroad. However, some homeland governments – such as that of Italy – did take active steps to support their citizens' rights in destination countries as early as the 1960s. In the twenty-first century, most states have significant populations of citizens or subjects living abroad. For many, if not most, expatriates, the country of origin and its politics remain the foremost concern (Ögelman, 2003). Likewise, governments of migrant-sending societies now increasingly nurture a relationship with citizens or subjects abroad. Such policies often are driven by economic concerns such as facilitating the sending of remittances.

The world's states, of course, vary widely in their political institutions. Migration taking place between two authoritarian or nondemocratic states differs from that taking place between two states that possess democratic institutions. Often, emigrants arrive in democratic settings from states with authoritarian governments. There are also myriad institutional arrangements in migrant homelands, and these too bear upon the theme of this chapter. Such variations importantly affect discernible patterns of migration participation and representation.

Migrants to nondemocratic settings are unlikely to participate much in political life in receiving states. The millions of largely South Asian and Arab-origin migrants in the Persian Gulf-area monarchies are largely politically quiescent, although their protests and strikes in 2006 and 2007 did achieve some reforms (DeParle, 2007; Surk and Abbot, 2008). In such cases, diplomatic representation in support of migrants' interests by homeland governments takes on particular significance. But the track record of homeland governments in defending the interests of expatriate compatriots is, at best, uneven.

For instance, both the Philippines and India tried to mandate minimum wages for their expatriates working in the Gulf states in 2007 and 2008 respectively. Bahraini companies resisted paying higher wages, thereby sparking strikes by Indian workers. The Bahraini Minister of Labour held that India had no authority to enforce the measure in the Gulf. The Filipino effort to secure a minimum wage for expatriate maids resulted in a drop in employer demand for them. The steps taken by India and the Philippines to better the lives of their expatriates were undercut by the ability of employers in the Gulf states to find similar labour elsewhere (Surk and Abbot, 2008).

International migration often takes place in bilateral relationships characterized by domination and subordination, with the homelands occupying the latter role. This disadvantage can adversely affect the ability of homeland governments to protect migrant interests through diplomatic means. Moreover, homeland governments sometimes collude with the governments of receiving states in maintenance of status quos unfavourable to, if not oppressive of, migrants. Such would appear to be the case of at least some of the governments of the many millions of migrants in the Persian Gulf monarchies. The acquiescence of homeland governments is linked to views that emigration relieves unemployment and underemployment, generates remittances that improve the lives of disfavoured populations and promotes development (see Chapter 3). But the costs paid by migrants are often very high in terms of work accidents, exploitative employment conditions and highly regimented, segregated housing arrangements, usually devoid of family life. The realities of the lives of millions of migrants are frequently overlooked in giddy global governance-style discussions of the merits of well planned temporary foreign worker policies.

The governments of Algeria, Turkey and Mexico, as seen in Chapter 7, similarly strove to defend the interests of expatriate populations abroad. Many homelands have developed extensive consular services to this end. A corollary to this involves another highly significant dimension of the politics of migration, the efforts of homeland governments to maintain the political loyalties and allegiance of expatriate populations (Smith, 2003). This is particularly significant in bilateral contexts involving migration from authoritarian homelands to democratic settings, such as the movements of Algerians to France.

More recently, Mexico, under the leadership of President Fox, sought to bolster the Mexican government's relationship with the large

Mexican-background population in the USA. Even prior to Fox's arrival in power in 2000, activist Mexican consular officials played an open and important role in leading opposition to Proposition 187 in California, which aimed to deny government services to non-US citizens, such as schooling for illegally resident children. President Fox's visit to the US shortly before 11 September 2001 had all the trappings of an election campaign and featured impassioned calls for legalization and increased legal admissions of Mexican workers (see Box 1.1 in Chapter 1). He made a similar trip before leaving office in 2006.

One factor influencing homeland government efforts to improve conditions for expatriates obtains only in cases where expatriates can vote in homeland elections. The modalities for expatriate voting vary considerably. Some homelands, like Turkey and Mexico, require emigrants to return home in order to vote. Other states, like Algeria, Italy and Israel, permit consular voting. Still others permit absentee voting, as in the USA. Indeed, absentee balloting by Floridians abroad played a key role in the contested outcome of the 2000 US presidential election. Electoral campaigning increasingly reflects the weight of voters abroad. Ecuadorian and Dominican Republic presidential candidates campaign for votes in New York City, just as Italian and Portuguese parties campaign for votes in Paris (Miller, 1978, 1981; Lee, Ramakrishnan and Ramirez, 2006). Nevertheless, the potential for emigrants to influence electoral outcomes at home does not necessarily translate into effective representation of their interests by homeland governments.

Extraparliamentary forms of migrant participation and representation

The act of emigration usually results in disenfranchisement of emigrants in their new setting, whether democratic or authoritarian. Larger-scale migration, thus, can create huge populations which are not entitled to vote in the democratic states in which they have taken up residency. Naturalization rates, which result in political enfranchisement of aliens, vary greatly. Hence, a major political consequence of international migration can be political passivity, but such is not necessarily the outcome, as exemplified by the emergence of migrants as political actors in Western Europe by the 1970s.

The inadequacy of diplomatic representation of foreign residents constituted one reason for the emergence of distinctive channels of alien political participation and representation in Europe. Indeed, there is reason to believe that nascent immigrant participation in Western European politics contributed to the decisions to curb foreign worker recruitment circa 1973. By the early 1970s, supposedly politically quiescent aliens had become involved in a number of significant industrial strikes and protest movements. In some instances, extreme leftist groups succeeded in mobilizing foreigners. Largely foreign worker strikes in French and German car plants demonstrated the disruptive potential of foreign labour and constrained trade unions to do more to represent foreign workers. Generally speaking, foreigners were poorly incorporated into unions in 1970. By 1980, significant strides had been made. This was reflected in growing unionization rates among foreign workers and the election of foreign workers to works councils and union leadership positions.

Since the 1970s, immigrants have increasingly articulated political concerns, participated in politics and sought representation. Immigrant protest movements became part of the tapestry of Western European politics and frequently affected policies. Persistent hunger strikes by undocumented immigrants and their supporters, for example, brought pressure to bear on French and Dutch authorities to liberalize rules regarding legalization (see Chapter 8). There was great variation in patterns of alien political participation and representation from country to country, with some countries, like Sweden, succeeding in institutionalizing much of it.

The protracted rioting in France in 2005 and 2007 (see Box 12.2) was foreshadowed by events in the 1970s and 1980s. Indeed, the first direct harbingers of the 2005 events were the riots in the Lyon suburb, La Grapinnière, in 1979 and in other suburbs of Lyon in 1981. Clashes with the police became almost routinized, scripted events throughout the 1980s and 1990s up to 2005. Other types of protests were also important. A largely peaceful rent strike in the SONACOTRA housing for migrant workers began in 1975 and was sustained for years, despite the deportation of some strike leaders. Tens of thousands of migrants and their French allies repeatedly rallied and marched (Miller, 1978). In the late 1970s and early 1980s, repeated strikes by mainly migrant and migrant-background workers disrupted the French automobile industry, where foreigners comprised one-quarter of employees (Miller, 1984).

Also during the 1980s, a countrywide movement of *beur* activists emerged. *Beur* means Arab in the *verlan* slang used especially by migrant and migrant-background youths in urban areas. The *beur* movement started in the French presidential and legislative elections of 1981. Migrant youths mobilized in support of the Socialist Party and overwhelmingly supported its presidential candidate Francois Mitterrand. However, the activists were disillusioned by the results of the legalization of 1981–1982 and by the new immigration law adopted in October 1981 (Bouamama, 1994: 44). Hence, they soon charted an autonomous course. *Beur* activists repeatedly organized mass rallies and participated in marches to protest at socioeconomic conditions and police–community relations as well as to affirm their identity and place in French society (Jazouli, 1986; Bouamama, 1994). The marches and rallies of 1983 and 1984 involved tens of thousands of mainly migrant youths. Many of the heavily migrant neighbourhoods that were the focus of *beur* activists in the 1980s would be rocked by riots in 2005.

Box 12.1 The unrest in France in 2005 and 2007

The riots of October/November 2005 resulted in the destruction of approximately 9,200 vehicles, one accidental death, 2,888 arrests and a cost of more than 200 million Euros. The unrest revealed the scope of the social malaise inherent in France's inability to incorporate its disaffected youths of migrant background. Erroneously interpreted in the German and American media as the '*intifada* of the French *banlieues*', the roots of the unrest were not to be found in Islam but in the interrelated phenomena of socioeconomic and ethnic exclusion. One must distinguish the long-term causes of the riots from the proximate causes, which precipitated the events.

The long-term factors included the pervasive feelings of anguish and hopelessness of many youths in the *banlieues* concerning their lives and their uncertain futures. French youths of migrant background, primarily North African/Maghrebi and Turkish, were confronted with endemic forms of discrimination in the job market, with unemployment rates in the HLM *cités* (see Chapter 11) reaching 40 per cent, nearly four times the national average. Police conducting routine identification verification regularly used racial profiling, while owners of clubs and bars denied entrance to their establishments to non-whites. Such practices reinforced the feeling of prejudice against '*beurs*' and '*blacks*'. Moreover, episodes of police violence tended to aggravate the strained relationship between migrant youths and the police, which resulted in further alienation from the institutions of the Republic.

Following a process of ghettoization, the *cités* became zones of exclusion in which poverty, high unemployment, and an absence of upward social mobility coexisted with petty crime and delinquency. Isolated from the inner cities due to the high cost and relative lack of public transportation, such environments fostered the development of a distinct male-dominated urban culture characterized by unique and creative forms of artistic and musical expression including graffiti and rap music. Furthermore, this seclusion led to a sense of territorial appropriation by rival bands of youngsters who felt a need to defend their territory against outsiders. Gangs provided many youths with a sense of belonging, giving meaning to their lives. Group dynamics of emulation and competition among members and between rival groups appeared to have played a crucial role in the incendiary attacks on cars. Additionally, the presence of the media helped to foster a kind of destructive competition between various youth gangs.

$\longrightarrow$

The twilight years of the twentieth century and the early years of the twenty-first century in the USA witnessed growing activism of migrants and migrant-background populations on US immigration policy issues. Largely Mayan Indian-background Guatemalan citizens working in poultry-processing plants in Delaware and Maryland regularly descended upon Washington, DC by the thousands to march in support of legalization

⟶

The immediate causes of the unrest consisted of several incidents, which occurred in a relatively short period of time, sparking angry outbursts in the *cités*. First, the fatal fire at the Hotel Paris-Opera in April 2005 resulted in the deaths of 25 persons: most were immigrants who were paying relatively high rent, and had been waiting for years to benefit from more social housing. This incident exposed the precarious and bleak living conditions of many immigrant families. Various associations, whose membership largely consisted of persons of African descent, the same as the fire victims, organized demonstrations.

Secondly, the French government cancelled several social programmes and subsidies that had been in place since the 1990s, including the *police de proximité*, a neighbourhood policing programme which had helped to maintain a relationship of trust between youths and law enforcement officers. Immediately prior to the riots, then Interior Minister Nicolas Sarkozy vowed to 'clean up the *banlieues*', starting with La Courneuve (where a boy of 11 years had been tragically gunned down during the Spring of 2005), and harshly rebuked the youth of Argenteuil, another Parisian suburb, following an incident on 25 October, referring to them as scum (*'racailles'*). Two days later, the deaths of two teenagers, electrocuted in a power substation while trying to hide from the police, triggered the riots.

As mentioned, the riots had no religious connotation. While many, but not all, participants were of Muslim background, no religious demands were made and the rioters ignored appeals by officials of Muslim organizations such as the *Union des Organisations Islamiques de France* (Union of French Islamic Organizations) or the *Tabligh Association*, a fundamentalist faction, to end the rioting. The majority of the participants were not delinquents, but were normal youths angered by their situation and constant harassment. Indeed, most were not known to the police prior to the riots. Those dangerous individuals known to police only became involved in the rioting later, during the week of 8–15 November. The riots were a spontaneous and genuine movement of disaffected youths aimed at showing their frustration with the French government and a society which, they felt, had forsaken them. Ironically, the violent protests of the largely immigrant-background youths constituted classically French political participation and mainly involved French citizens.

In 2007, little had changed in the suburbs and a further spate of rioting ensued. In 2008, newly elected President Sarkozy announced another plan to improve life in heavily immigrant suburbs, the sixteenth in 31 years.

policies. Mexican migrants organized relays of runners carrying the statue of Our Lady of Guadaloupe in the hope of securing divine intervention in the form of legalization policy. The spring of 2006 witnessed massive rallies and marches around the USA in opposition to a restrictive House of Representatives bill and in support of a Senate bill that, if adopted, would have authorized a legalization.

Box 12.2 The 10 April 2006 march in Madison, Wisconsin

Madison is the capital city of Wisconsin and the home of the University of Wisconsin. It is an historic centre of political activism in the USA and was an epicentre of violent protests against the Vietnam War in the 1960s. Madison has a population of over 200,000 which is changing rapidly in composition. This change is most marked in the growing diversity of Madison's public school population, almost half of which now consists of minority students as opposed to only a fraction as little as two decades ago. The Hispanic population of Madison has increased rapidly over the last decade with the arrival of many migrants from Mexico, most of whom are presumed to be undocumented.

An estimated 10,000 persons participated in the march and rally, which were part of a nationwide day of protests. The bulk of protestors were Hispanic, including many youths from local high schools. There were non-Hispanic protestors as well, including some student contingents from the university. A number of city and state officials, including Madison's mayor as well as the Roman Catholic bishop, expressed their support for the protestors. The chief sponsor of the restrictive House bill was Congressman James Sensenbrenner, who represents a nearby district north of Milwaukee, and who is a graduate of the University of Wisconsin law school.

The demonstration was one of the largest such events since the Vietnam War period. It was publicized and much commented upon in the area press. It brought into sharp relief the chasm separating those US citizens who favoured the Senate bill from those who favoured the House approach. Some viewed the march as brazen, while others viewed it sympathetically as an echo of the civil rights-era marches and anti-Vietnam War rallies that had so galvanized Madison in the 1960s and early 1970s. The march also testified to the emergence of a new force in state and national politics, the highly emotive power of a generation of young Hispanic citizens and noncitizens demonstrating for social justice and inclusion. Their chant *si se puede* (yes we can) would later become a theme for Senator Barack Obama's presidential bid in 2008. Obama went on to win the Democratic primary elections in Wisconsin in 2008 (Source: Wisconsin State Journal).

The single largest demonstration is thought to have taken place in Los Angeles, where an estimated 1 million protestors took to the streets, many waving Mexican and American flags. Huge protests also were staged in Chicago and Washington, DC. At the latter, US Senator Ted Kennedy of Massachusetts, a principal architect of US immigration law and policy since the 1980s, gave an impassioned speech in support of legalization. However, the most striking aspects of the protests involved their national scope, affecting virtually every area of the country, even areas only recently significantly affected by the massive immigration to the USA since the 1970s.

The extraparliamentary forms of migrant participation and representation in such diverse settings as France, the USA and the Gulf states were not unrelated. They all testified to the global challenge posed by migration to international norms concerning human rights and social justice.

Noncitizen voting rights: a global issue

The anomaly of foreign noncitizens living in democratic societies without political rights has long been viewed as problematic. Naturalization rules and practices vary from state to state, and in some places immigrants have little chance of becoming citizens. Consequently, many democratic states have authorized noncitizens to vote in local and, less frequently, in national elections. Some authoritarian states also permit aliens to vote in elections, although the outcomes of these elections have been predetermined. The perceived legitimacy or illegitimacy of noncitizen exclusion or enfranchisement in elections can spark conflict.

Overall, 65 of the world's nearly 200 states permit some form of noncitizen voting, and in 36 of these the voting is available to all aliens regardless of origin (Andrès, 2007: 80). 35 of the states are non-European. In many respects, the USA established a precedent for electoral enfranchisement of noncitizens. Between 1776 and 1926, at least 40 US federal states and territories authorized some form of noncitizen voting, including voting in statewide and US national elections. Indeed, the 1928 national elections marked the first time that aliens did not vote (Andrès, 2007: 68).

In Western Europe, the question of noncitizen voting rights emerged as an important issue in the 1970s. Immigrants often sought participation and representation in local government. In several countries, advisory councils were instituted to give immigrants a voice in local government. Experiences with these advisory councils varied and some were discontinued. Some people contested them as efforts to coopt aliens, while others saw them as illegitimate participation by aliens in the politics of the host society. In certain countries, aliens were accorded a right to vote in local and regional elections.

Sweden was the pacesetter in this regard; voting rights in local and regional elections for resident noncitizens were introduced in 1975, but alien participation declined over time. The Netherlands was the second country to accord qualified aliens voting rights, in 1985. However, the results of alien voting there also were somewhat disappointing (Rath, 1988: 25–35). Proposals to grant local voting rights to legally resident aliens became important domestic political and constitutional issues, particularly in France and Germany. By 2001, Belgium had the most extensive network of local government consultative structures for resident aliens. Luxemburg and Switzerland were also noteworthy for the variety and extent of consultation of foreign populations at the local level (Oriol, 2001: 20). However, the pattern of weak migrant participation in local elections persisted even as more and more European states authorized such voting (Oriol and Vianna, 2007: 40–44).

By the 1980s, the stakes involved in the granting of voting rights were quite high in many Western democracies. Aliens were often spatially concentrated in major cities and certain neighbourhoods. Enfranchising them would dramatically affect political outcomes in many local elections. Supporters of the granting of municipal voting rights generally regarded it as a way to foster incorporation and as a counterweight to the growing influence of parties like the FN in France. However, many immigrants were already politically enfranchised, particularly in the UK. This did not prevent the eruption of riots involving immigrants and their British-born children in the early 1980s. The granting of local voting rights was thus not in itself a panacea for the severe problems facing immigrants in Western Europe.

In 1992, the Council of Europe, an organization now comprising 47 states, approved a treaty on the participation of foreigners in public affairs at the local level. Member states that signed the treaty would undertake to authorize voting in local elections by aliens who had resided for five years in the state. As of 2007, only eight member states had signed and ratified the treaty and four others had signed it (Oriol, 2007: 84).

The Treaty on European Union was signed in 1992 as well (see Chapters 5 and 8). Under this treaty, citizens of EU member states became eligible to vote or to be elected to office in European and municipal elections if they resided anywhere within the European space. Aliens from other EU states became eligible to vote in and stand for election as of 1994 and subsequently in the 1999 and 2004 European elections. They became eligible to vote and to run in French municipal elections by 2001. France was the last of the then 15 EU member states to implement the TEU in this respect. Participation by non-French voters in European elections in France has been weak, starting with 4 per cent of such aliens voting in 1994, but doubling in each subsequent European election (Oriol, 2007: 41). Broadly similar weak or modest patterns of participation by non-national EU citizens could be discerned in European elections in Finland, Luxemburg and Belgium (Dervin and Wiberg, 2007; Dubajic, 2007; Zibouh, 2007).

Since 1992, there has been a growing movement in support of granting Third Country Nationals voting rights within member states of the EU and at the level of EU institutions. The European Parliament has voted several times in favour of extending European citizenship to all persons who have resided in a stable manner and for a long period within a member state (Oriol, 2007: 95). A 2001 European Parliament resolution called for the enfranchisement of all non-EU residents who had resided legally within an EU member state for three years. However, opposition within the European Council, which represents the interests of member states in the complex EU governance procedures, has thwarted such initiatives. Some

EU member states hold that the granting of voting rights to Third Country Nationals would devalue the importance of naturalization.

As of 2007, five groups of EU states could be differentiated with regard to their policies towards Third Country Nationals. Seven states gave them the right to vote and eligibility to stand in elections. Five accorded them the right to vote but not eligibility. Four states would accord voting rights and eligibility on the basis of reciprocity, that is, only if their nationals were extended the same voting rights in the homelands. Ten EU member states, including France and Germany, only accorded voting rights and electability to non-national EU citizens residing in their territory (Oriol, 2007: 84–88).

Elsewhere, half of the 23 states comprising the Caribbean and Central and North America authorize some form of noncitizen voting and/or electability. Most South American countries permit foreign residents to vote in municipal elections. Only Surinam and Ecuador reserve voting exclusively for nationals. Brazil allows Portuguese residents to vote on the basis of a bilateral treaty. Eight out of 53 African states allow noncitizens to vote, often on the basis of British Commonwealth ties or reciprocity agreements.

Several Asian states also allow noncitizen voting, including the Republic of Korea, which now permits foreign residents after three years of residency to vote in municipal elections. About 7000 non-Koreans voted in the 2006 elections, virtually all of whom were of Taiwanese background. One motivation for the Korean measure may be to increase pressure on Japan to extend voting rights to the sizeable Korean population in Japan. Australia used to grant voting rights to British and Irish citizens, but this was changed in 1984, although those who registered before that date can still vote. Three of the eight Australian states allow resident aliens to vote in local elections. New Zealand allows all permanent resident aliens to vote in all elections, but not to stand for office (Andrès, 2007).

The new wave of democratization since 1990, which some view as a global phenomenon, has only served to heighten the saliency of noncitizen voting issues around the world. One of the paradoxes of the period is the growing number of politically disenfranchised persons living in the same democratic societies that are held up for emulation elsewhere.

Migrants and ethnic voting blocs

The politics of the state of Israel, created in 1948, remain heavily influenced by Jewish immigration, although, from a Zionist perspective, such migration constitutes 'return' (Bartram, 2008: 303–304). As a result of the inflow of Oriental or Sephardic Jews primarily from largely Muslim societies during the 1950s and 1960s, the Sephardic-origin Jewish population surpassed that of European-origin Ashkenazi Jews in the mid-1970s. This demographic shift benefited the right-wing Likud bloc led by Menachem Begin, who was elected prime minister in 1977 with the support of Sephardic-origin Jews. In 1990, a new wave of Soviet Jewish immigration began, again affecting the balance between Ashkenazi and Sephardic Jews as well as the Arabs. Nearly one million Soviet Jews arrived in Israel between 1990 and 2002.

Now comprising about 15 per cent of the Israeli electorate, the Soviet Jewish or 'Russian' (see Chapter 7) vote importantly affected the outcomes of general elections beginning in 1992. By the 1996 election, an immigrant party led by the former Soviet dissident Natan Sharansky won seven seats in the Knesset (parliament) and joined the coalition government dominated by the Likud. In the 2001 Israeli election, there were several predominately Soviet Jewish parties competing for votes, with Sharansky's again receiving the most. A number of Soviet Jewish political leaders called for mass expulsion of Israeli Arabs and Palestinians from the West Bank and Gaza. In 2002, the government of Jordan sought reassurance that an attack on Iraq would not lead to mass deportation of Palestinians. Polls revealed growing support for 'transfer', the Israeli euphemism for ethnic cleansing of Palestinian Arabs. By 2007, the leader of a political party espousing transfer had become a minister in the beleaguered government of Prime Minister Ehud Olmert.

The Israeli case illustrates in the extreme the potential impact of an immigrant voting bloc upon electoral outcomes. Immigrants generally are not such an important factor as in Israel and immigrants do not necessarily vote in ethnic blocs. Yet immigration is clearly affecting electoral politics across Western democracies as growing numbers of aliens naturalize, and as immigrant-origin populations are mobilized to vote. In the 1996 referendum over the future of Quebec and the Canadian Federation, Quebec's immigrant voters overwhelmingly voted against the referendum and for maintenance of the status quo. They decisively affected the outcome, prompting angry anti-immigration remarks by Quebecois leaders. In the close 2002 German elections, the 350,000 Germans of Turkish background emerged as a potentially decisive voting bloc whose backing may have enabled the Social Democratic–Green coalition to scrape through to victory. Although only one per cent of the electorate in 2002, the Turkish-German voting bloc was expected to double in size by 2006 (Johnson and Gugath, 2002). Naturalized German citizens from Eastern Europe, on the other hand, strongly favour conservative parties, which prevailed in the 2006 elections that brought Angela Merkel to the Chancellorship (Wüst, 2000, 2002).

The growing mass of immigrant voters has made many political parties and their leaders more sensitive to migration-related concerns and issues. In some instances, immigration policy debates have been influenced by electoral calculations. In general, political parties on the left side of the political spectrum appear to take the lead in appealing to immigrant voters and are rewarded for their efforts (Messina, 2007). Conservative parties often benefit electorally from an anti-immigrant backlash. A number of conservative parties have begun to compete in earnest for the immigrant-origin electorate, particularly in Great Britain and the USA. Following the 1996 US elections, some Republicans felt that President Clinton and the Democrats had outmanoeuvred the Republicans by encouraging a naturalization campaign while several Republican presidential candidates embraced anti-immigrant positions. Subsequently, George W. Bush ran a campaign in 2000 that courted Hispanic voters, and electoral concerns drove his immigration initiative towards Mexico in 2001 (see Box 1.1).

Bush's narrow and much contested victory in the 2000 election reflected the heightened appeal of Bush and the Republican Party to Latino voters, who had generally voted Democratic in the past. The strongly Republican preferences of Cuban–Americans in Florida may have been critical to the outcome. The stronger showing by Bush and Republican candidates led to speculation about possible Latino realignment away from the Democrats. But the results of the 2006 mid-term elections strongly suggested that such realignment had not happened and was unlikely to happen in the foreseeable future.

Many naturalized immigrants do not register to vote or exercise their voting rights. This appears to constitute a pattern across democracies (Messina, 2007). DeSipio's review of studies of naturalized American participation in the 1996 election led him to conclude that the naturalized participate less than other Americans, even with controls for socioeconomic differences in place. Naturalized US citizens are more likely than the population as a whole to have sociodemographic characteristics associated with political marginalization. Moreover, he argues that immigrant political adaptation to the US is not a group process but a highly individual one. Participation of immigrants is shaped by class and education factors that shape participation in US politics in general (DeSipio, 2001).

More recently, DiSipio has analysed the impact of transnational political engagement on immigrant participation in US politics. He estimates that 20 per cent of Latino immigrants and a few in the second generation engage in the civic and political life of the sending country after emigration. But he found that such transnational engagement has little effect on US politics. Latino immigrants who belong to homeland-oriented associations tend to become more active than most immigrants in US politics. But this reflects political socialization rather than transnationalism. Individuals who are organizationally active are likely to be active in many areas (DiSipio, 2006). Relatedly, in a study of the implications of dual nationality for political participation, US citizens born abroad in countries that allow dual nationality are less likely to vote in the USA than are US citizens born abroad in countries that proscribe dual nationality. Also, US citizens with dual nationality are less likely to register and vote than are US citizens who come from the same homelands but do not claim dual nationality (Cain and Doherty, 2006).

The immigration trends of the last several decades have significantly affected electoral politics in many Western democracies. The ability of legal immigrants to naturalize, and eventually to vote, constitutes a

Box 12.3 Ireland's first black mayor

Rotimi Adebari (43) was elected Mayor of Port Laoise, a small town in the middle of Ireland, in June 2007. He was Ireland's first black mayor, and had arrived in the country as an asylum seeker from Nigeria just seven years earlier. A Christian from the Southwestern state of Ogun, he had fled with his wife and two children because of religious persecution. Mr Adebari's election as first citizen for a year in this ancient town is symbolic of the dramatic changes taking place in the age of migration.

Ireland has long been a land of emigration: from the 1830s, millions of people sought refugee from English colonialism and grinding poverty by going overseas. Irish migrants helped build the USA and Australia, and were important in shaping the culture of these settler nations. There are more people who identify themselves as Irish outside the country than within it. All that changed over the last 20 years, through an economic boom, which has transformed Ireland into the 'Celtic Tiger': one of the richest and fastest-growing economies of the EU.

Now immigrants are flooding in from many countries as workers, asylum seekers and family members – entries have doubled in the last 10 years.

→

major concern for any democracy. That immigrant political participation is viewed as legitimate and as an anticipated outcome demarcates the US, Australian and Canadian experiences from those of many Western European nations.

The UK constitutes an exception to the Western European pattern in that most post-1945 immigrants – those from the Commonwealth up to 1971, and the Irish – entered with citizenship and voting rights. Immigration became increasingly politicized in the mid-1970s. The extreme-right National Front played a key role in provoking immigration-related violence. The frequently violent clashes, which were regarded as uncharacteristic of normally civil British politics, combined with the mounting numbers of immigrants to make immigration a key issue in the 1979 general election. Margaret Thatcher adroitly capitalized on the immigration backlash to deflate support for the National Front and to score a victory over the Labour Party, which was supported by most immigrant voters (Layton-Henry, 1981).

In subsequent elections, black and Asian participation became more conspicuous. In 1987, four black Britons were elected to Parliament. But growing black and Asian participation and representation in British politics generally did not result in greater attention being paid to immigrant issues and grievances (Studlar and Layton-Henry, 1990: 288). However formation of an alternative immigrants' party is not a viable option. Hence, even in a Western European country where most immigrants are enfranchised, their participation and representation remain problematic. Immigrant-origin

⟶

Ireland was one of the few countries that opened its doors to workers from the 10 mainly Eastern and Central European states that joined the EU in 2004. Foreign-born people made up 11 per cent of the population in 2005. After centuries of emigration, Ireland is rapidly becoming a multicultural society.

Mr Adebari experienced joblessness and prejudice when he arrived, but he helped set up an unemployment support group in County Laois, and studied for a master's degree in intercultural studies at Dublin City University. He now works for the county council on an integration project for new immigrants. When the Adebaris arrived, their two children were the only foreign pupils in the local school. Now there are more than 30 nationalities.

Mr Adebari was elected as independent with the support of councillors from other parties. He says that Ireland is 'a country of a hundred, thousand welcomes and a land of opportunities'. He saw it as unique in embracing multiculturalism in a very short period, and as a model for Europe and the rest of the world.

(Sources: http://Ireland.com/newspaper/ 28 June 2007; *The Guardian*, 30 June 2007; OECD, 2007: 254–255).

voters can significantly affect electoral outcomes in 30–60 of Great Britain's 650 parliamentary constituencies. These are located in cities.

In Australia until the 1990s, most observers argued that the effects of migration on politics had been very limited (Jupp, York and McRobbie, 1989: 51). A prominent political scientist stated that post-war immigration 'has not resulted in any discernible change in the overall pattern of voting behaviour. Despite large-scale immigration, social class, not birthplace, has remained the basis for divisions between the political parties' (McAllister, 1988: 919). However, the endorsement of multiculturalism by the conservative coalition which was in power from 1975 to 1992 seemed to be connected with concern about the 'ethnic vote' (Castles et al., 1992). More recently, the Irish Republic has gone through a migration transition. Immigration issues have begun to affect Irish politics and immigrant voters have had some impact, as Box 12.3 attests.

Anti-immigrant movements and parties

The rise of anti-immigrant parties and movements in Europe since the 1970s has been thoroughly scrutinized (Betz, 1994; Schain et al., 2002; Givens, 2005; Norris, 2005). As seen in Chapter 7, anti-immigrant politics has figured importantly in a number of African states, including Ivory Coast and the Republic of South Africa. In the Middle East and North Africa, anti-immigrant politics has been manifested in Lebanon, pre-1990 Iraq,

Iran, Egypt, Libya, Kuwait and Saudi Arabia. In Latin America and the Caribbean, anti-immigrant politics figures importantly in the Dominican Republic and to a lesser extent in Costa Rica. In Asia and the Pacific, immigration issues have become highly politicized in Malaysia, Singapore, Korea, Taiwan and Japan, and anti-immigrant politics contributes to the instability in Fiji and in certain areas of India, most notably Assam.

Anti-immigrant politics in the transatlantic area is scarcely without historical precedent, as seen in Chapter 4. Nevertheless, with a few exceptions, anti-immigrant politics remained marginal until the 1980s. In both the UK and Switzerland, politicization of immigration issues by the late 1950s and the mid-1960s respectively led to curtailment of migrant worker admissions. In the following years, immigration became a major political issue and remains so today.

In France, politicization of immigration issues occurred in the 1970s, especially after extreme-right students began to demonstrate against *immigration sauvage*, or illegal immigration. After several clashes, the major protagonists were outlawed. Some elements of the neofascist New Order movement decided to continue the anti-immigrant campaign at the grassroots level and resurfaced later as part of the *Front National* (FN). Certainly support for anti-immigrant parties involved an element of protest voting. While 15 per cent of the electorate voted for the FN in France and one-third of all voters sympathized with FN positions on immigration (Weil, 1991a: 82), it was also clear that the FN was picking up part of the protest vote traditionally received by the French Communist Party. The FN did particularly well in areas with concentrations of *Pieds-Noirs*, Europeans repatriated from Algeria in 1962 and their offspring. FN opposition to the European institutions was also a major point of attraction to some of its electorate (Marcus, 1995).

By 1997, the FN dominated municipal governments in four southern cities, including Toulon, and was supported by about 15 per cent of the national electorate. Nearly 4 million French citizens voted for FN candidates in the first round of the 1997 legislative elections. Hence, the second-place finish of FN candidate Le Pen in the first round of the presidential elections of 2002 did not reflect a major, sudden increase in support for the FN. Support for the FN decreased in the 2007 presidential and parliamentary elections. The defection of former FN stalwart Bruno Mégret and his supporters played a role in the decline. Former Minister of Interior Sarkozy campaigned for election as President with a law and order line, which included strong measures against illegal migration (see Chapter 11). Once elected, President Sarkozy surprised many observers with the inclusion of leftists in his government, including Fadela Amara, a feminist and immigration activist.

Belgium became the scene of urban unrest in 1991, when youths who were largely of Moroccan origin clashed with police following a rumour that the *Vlaams Blok* (Flemish Bloc), traditionally a party seeking independence for Flanders, would stage a rally in a heavily immigrant-populated area.

By 1990, the Flemish Bloc had become both a regionalist party and an anti-immigrant party, a combination seen in several other European states, especially in Northern Italy. A core plank of the party's platform called for repatriation of immigrants. The Flemish Bloc won 12 seats in the National Assembly in the 1991 general elections as compared with two in the previous elections. It improved upon the 1991 results in the 1999 and 2003 elections, winning over 11 per cent of the vote in 2003. However, due to a Belgium Supreme Court ruling in 2004 that the party was racist, it dissolved itself and became the Flemish Interest (Messina, 2007: 63).

Similarly, in the 1991 Austrian municipal and regional elections, the anti-immigrant Freedom Party scored an important breakthrough by increasing its share of the vote to almost one-quarter. Eventually, the Freedom Party achieved a rough parity with the Austrian Socialist Party and the People's Party and formed a government with the latter. This precipitated a crisis in EU–Austria relations, as other EU member states regarded the Freedom Party's positions on immigration as unacceptable. In reality, Freedom Party preferences for migration were not that different from those of the EU mainstream. The Freedom Party's leader, Jörg Haider, resigned as chairman in 2000. After the Freedom Party's share of the vote slumped to 10 per cent in the 2002 national elections as compared with nearly 22 per cent in the 1995 elections, Haider left the party to form the Union for the Future of Austria. Most Freedom Party parliamentarians followed him in joining the new party (Messina, 2007: 61).

In Italy, a backlash against immigration has become a major political force. In the 1990s, the regionalist Northern League, *Forza Italia* (led by entrepreneur Silvio Berlusconi) and the neofascist National Alliance attacked immigration. Meanwhile, the politically influential Catholic clergy and the Pope himself voiced support for humanitarian initiatives such as legalization. Many Italian voters supported right-wing parties and protested against the deeply embedded corruption of the Christian Democrats and the Socialists. Protest voting against a discredited *partitocrazia* party machine was far more prevalent than anti-immigrant voting. But the second Berlusconi government announced a crackdown on illegal immigration by 2002. In the general elections of 1996 the Northern League gained 10 per cent of the vote, but its support declined to less than 5 per cent in 2006, when Berlusconi's centre-right coalition was forced out of government (Messina, 2007: 62–63). However, Berlusconi was back with an increased majority in early 2008. His election campaign relied heavily on stirring up anti-immigrant resentment, and the Northern League's posters exhorted voters: 'Defend your future: oust illegal immigrants'.

By 2007, anti-immigrant political movements had developed virtually across Europe, even in formerly Communist states like the Czech Republic and Bulgaria, where the Attack Party won 9 per cent of the legislative seats in the 2005 elections. Many of these movements had historical precedents. Part of the hardcore support for the French FN, for example, came from quarters traditionally identified with the anti-republican right.

These political forces had been discredited by World War II, and their programmes and policies were generally viewed as illegitimate until the anti-immigrant reaction of the 1980s and 1990s. Immigration issues have served as an entrée for extreme right-wing parties into mainstream politics across Europe, even in Scandinavia. However, the Bulgarian Attack Party principally targeted Gypsies and ethnic Turks with its slogan 'Let us give back Bulgaria to the Bulgarians' (Stefanova, 2007).

It would be a mistake to dismiss the upsurge in voting for anti-immigrant parties as simply an expression of racism and intolerance. As pointed out in Chapter 2, support for extreme-right groups is often the result of bewilderment in the face of rapid economic and social change. The erosion in strength of labour organizations due to changes in occupational structures is also important. Extreme-right parties also attract support as a result of public dissatisfaction with certain policies, such as those concerning asylum seekers and illegal immigration. Other extremist parties have fared less well. The National Front in the UK, for example, appeared to be gaining strength in the mid-1970s before the Conservative Party, under the leadership of Margaret Thatcher, pre-empted it by adopting key parts of its programme (Layton-Henry and Rich, 1986: 74–75). Britain's two-party system and its 'first past the post' electoral law make it very difficult for any new party to win seats in the House of Commons. However, following the riots of 2001 in some Northern British cities (see Chapter 11), the extremist British National Party gained in following and had some electoral successes in municipal elections.

Similarly, constitutional and institutional barriers made it difficult for extremist, anti-immigrant political parties to progress in Germany (Norris, 2005). The Basic Law empowers the German government to ban political parties that threaten the German republic. However, following German reunification, fringe extreme-right parties like the National Democratic Party (NPD) gained many supporters, including violent skinheads, who carried out a series of attacks on asylum seekers and migrants. With the decline of Germany's old three-party system since the 1990s, the extreme right has been able to gain some representation in city councils and regional parliaments.

Some scholars have suggested that the emergence of right-wing parties has had anti-immigrant effects across the political spectrum, especially in Europe. In the USA, by contrast, a two-party system and a single-member district winner-take-all electoral law make it very difficult for any third party to compete, but strongly right-wing opinions can be found within the mainstream parties. In Canada, aside from previously noted complaints about immigrant voting results in Quebec, political opposition to immigration per se is virtually nonexistent.

In Australia the situation is rather different. In the 1996 Federal Election, immigration became a major concern in mainstream politics. A new One Nation Party, led by Pauline Hanson, campaigned against special services for migrants and Aborigines. Hanson was elected as a member of parliament, and the new conservative Coalition Government led by Prime Minister John Howard took on much of her anti-immigrant rhetoric. The 2001 election was strongly influenced by Howard's anti-asylum seeker politics (Castles and Vasta, 2004). The election of an Australian Labor Party Government in 2007 seemed to herald a new softer approach, yet immigration remained an important political topic.

The politics of immigration policy-making

Ultimately, the political dimension of international migration matters the most because the modern world has been structured by a nation-state system that renders international migration inherently problematic or aberrant (Zolberg, 1981). In this sense, international migration is intrinsically political. A major debate surrounding formulation of immigration policies, particularly in the most developed, democratic states, arises from disagreements over the autonomy of national states and continuities and discontinuities in the nature of the nation-state system in an era of globalization. This debate has influenced scholarship that seeks to elucidate why states adopt immigration policies and why certain migration policy outcomes occur.

Freeman has argued that a gap in immigration policy preferences between the political elite and the general public prevailed in Western democracies (1995, 2002). Political elites favoured expansive immigration policies generally opposed by the mass of the public. He hypothesized that immigration produced concentrated benefits, especially to employers and investors, and diffuse costs borne by the general public, especially over the medium and long term. The insulation of pro-immigration political elites from electorates generally less supportive of liberal immigration policies led to a general pattern of expansive immigration policies in Western democracies. However, he observed significant variations between traditional immigration lands like the USA, Canada and Australia, Northern European states and Southern European states. Freeman's views ran decidedly counter to those analysts who viewed OECD-area immigration policies as draconian and restrictive.

For Hollifield, liberal democracies face embedded constraints, which limit their prerogatives in formulation of immigration policies (1992). International migrants are human beings with rights, and immigration policies are thereby constrained. The classic illustration of this came in France in 1977, when a Council of State ruling invalidated the government's effort to prevent family reunification. The French government declared a zero immigration policy, but could not translate that declaration into policy because France had a bilateral treaty with Portugal that granted legally admitted Portuguese workers a right to family reunification. Hence, the expansive nature of immigration policies in many Western democracies reflects underlying, diffuse liberal values, such as notions of elementary human rights, but this should not be construed as an erosion of the sovereign state.

Soysal viewed the emergence of an embryonic international regime concerning migrant rights as effectively constraining the immigration policy-making of European democracies (1994). Multilateral and bilateral treaties and the influence of international organizations such as the ILO and the Council of Europe empowered international migrants and shaped immigration policy-making. Joppke disagreed, viewing such constraints as largely self-imposed by national legal systems or as resulting from past policies (1998, 1999). In his view, states need to regulate immigration, but by making commitments, such as signing the Geneva Convention on refugees, they impose limitations on what they can do. Joppke does not view these limitations as external constraints.

Other important perspectives include the globalization thesis, which views democratic states as increasingly unable to control migration between countries due to underlying socioeconomic and political transformations that are eroding governmental capacity to regulate international migration. This thesis is explicitly rejected by scholars who affirm that, over the medium to long term, immigration policies reflect state interests (Messina, 2007: 239–245). The path dependency perspective views immigration policy outcomes as due to entrenched institutional arrangements that delimit policy options and shape decision-making (Messina, 2007: 102–105). Hence, the French propensity for recourse to legalization in the 1970s and 1980s had much to do with decisions taken in the 1930s and 1940s to legalize aliens (Miller, 2002). Recent scholarship about the EU and immigration policy-making suggests that member states are pooling sovereign prerogatives in order to better achieve immigration policy goals that can be achieved more readily at the regional level (Geddes, 2003; Lahav, 2004).

Concerning the USA, Zolberg contends that immigration policy has always been central to the development of the American state and society. It is a 'nation by design' (2006). He views US immigration policy history as composed of expansive and restrictionist eras in which a policy status quo, once achieved, is difficult to alter, due in part to the institutional nature of the American state, characterized by a division of powers between the judicial, legislative and executive branches of government. Tichenor (2002: 294) identified four interlocking processes affecting US immigration law-making: 1) changing institutional opportunities and constraints, 2) the shifting views of immigration experts, 3) perceived international threats and the lack thereof and 4) the changing nature of interest group coalitions. Together these processes determine US immigration law and policy outcomes.

Conclusions

International migration has played a major role in fostering multicultural politics. Migration can dramatically affect electorates, as witnessed in the

Israeli case, and immigrants can influence politics through nonelectoral means as well. Immigrants have fostered transnational politics linking homeland and host society political systems in fundamental ways. Migrants and minorities are both subjects and objects of politics. An anti-immigrant backlash has strengthened the appeal of right-wing parties in Western Europe. One way in which migration has fundamentally altered the Western European political landscape is through the constitution of increasingly vocal Islamic organizations, which present a dilemma for democratic political systems: refusal to accept their role would violate democratic principles, yet many people see their aims and methods as intrinsically antidemocratic. International migration has fostered new constituencies, new parties and new issues. Many of Western Europe's newer political parties, such as the FN in France, feature anti-immigrant themes. Violence against immigrants is also a factor in ethnic minority formation and political mobilization.

In the USA, Canada and Australia immigrant political participation and representation is less of an issue, partly because of the preponderance of family-based legal immigration. However, disenfranchisement of legally resident aliens and illegally resident aliens in major US cities increasingly troubles authorities. Much of New York's population cannot vote, either because they are not naturalized or because they are illegally resident.

Virtually everywhere, international migration renders politics more complex. Ethnic mobilization and the ethnic vote are becoming important issues in many countries. Another new issue may be seen in the politics of naturalization. One or two decades ago, virtually no one knew naturalization law or considered it important. The changing nature of international migration and its politicization have changed that. Most democracies now face a long-term problem stemming from growing populations of resident aliens who are unable or unwilling to naturalize; the status of illegal immigrants is particularly problematic (Rubio-Marin, 2000).

Immigrant politics are in a continual state of flux because of the rapid changes in migratory flows as well as the broader transformations in political patterns, which are taking place in many Western societies. As migratory movements mature – moving through the stages of immigration, settlement and minority formation – the character of political mobilization and participation changes. There is a shift from concern with homeland politics to mobilization around the interests of ethnic groups in the immigration country. If political participation is denied through refusal of citizenship and failure to provide channels of representation, immigrant politics is likely to take on militant forms. This applies particularly to the descendants of immigrants born in the countries of immigration. If they are excluded from political life through noncitizenship, social marginalization or racism, they are likely to present a major challenge to existing political structures in the future.

Guide to further reading

The Age of Migration website www.age-of-migration includes a brief account of the 1964 revision of the Italo-Swiss bilateral labour accord (12.1), as an example of influence by a migrant homeland on immigration policy in a neighbouring state. The website also contains (12.2) an analysis of the Algerian governmental efforts to retain the loyalty of Algerians in France (the *Amicale des Algeriéns en Europe* 1962–1992), and (12.3) material based on a book by Fadela Amara (who was appointed Junior Minister for Urban Affairs in 2007) on the movement to improve immigrant women's lives in France. *The Age of Migration website* material includes an account of strike movements by immigrant workers in France (10.3). A useful further source (to be found on commercial video websites) is the French language film *La Haine* (Hate), which depicts the routine violence between French police and migrant background youths circa 2000.

The Age of Migration website material on the USA includes a summary of the 'lost story' (Motomura, 2006) about noncitizen voting in US history (12.4), information on Latino voters in the 2006 US mid-term elections (12.5), and an account of the contested politics of immigration reform (12.6).

Classic contributions on migrants and politics include Castles and Kosack (1973); Miller (1981); Baldwin-Edwards and Schain (1994); Freeman (1979, 1986, 1995); Hammar (1990); Hollifield (1992); Layton-Henry (1990); Ireland (1994); and Soysal (1994). Cohen and Layton-Henry (1997) provide a valuable collection of contributions to the study of the politics of migration prior to 1995.

Important more recent scholarship includes Brochman and Hammar (1999); Cornelius et al. (2004); Castles and Davidson (2000); Feldblum (1999); Freeman (1998); Geddes (2000, 2003); Guiraudon and Joppke (2001); Joppke (1998, 1999); Koslowski (2000); Koopmans and Statham (2000); and Lahav (2004). Important work on citizenship and diversity includes: Aleinikoff and Klusmeyer (2000, 2001); Bauböck (1994b); Bauböck et al. (2006a, b); Bauböck et al. (1996); Bauböck and Rundell (1998); Faist (2007); Money (1994); and Togman (2002). Zolberg (2006) and Tichenor (2002) are invaluable for the USA, while Messina (2007) makes a seminal contribution to understanding of migration and politics in Europe.

Chapter 13

Conclusion: Migration and Mobility in the Twenty-First Century

This book has argued that international migration is a constant, not an aberration, in human history. Population movements have always accompanied demographic growth, technological change, political conflict and warfare. Over the last five centuries, mass migrations have played a major role in colonialism, industrialization, nation-state formation and the development of the capitalist world market. However, international migration has never been as pervasive, or as socioeconomically and politically significant, as it is today. Never before have political leaders accorded such priority to migration concerns. Never before has international migration seemed so pertinent to national security and so connected to conflict and disorder on a global scale.

The hallmark of the age of migration is the global character of international migration: the way it affects more and more countries and regions, and its linkages with complex processes affecting the entire world. This book has endeavoured to elucidate the principal causes, processes and effects of international migration. Contemporary patterns, as discussed in Chapters 5, 6 and 7, are rooted in historical relationships and shaped by a multitude of political, demographic, socioeconomic, geographical and cultural factors. These flows result in greater ethnic diversity within countries and deepening transnational linkages between states and societies. International migrations are greatly affected by governmental policies and may, in fact, be precipitated by decisions to recruit foreign workers or to admit refugees.

Yet, international migrations may also possess a relative autonomy and be impervious to governmental policies. Official policies often fail to achieve their objectives, or even bring about the opposite of what is intended. People as well as governments shape international migration. Decisions made by individuals, families and communities – often with imperfect information and constrained options – play a vital role in determining migration and settlement. The social networks which arise through the migratory process help shape long-term outcomes. The agents and brokers who make up the burgeoning 'migration industry' have their own interests and aims. Despite the growth in migratory movements, and the strength of the factors that cause them, resistance to migration is also of growing importance. Large sections of the populations of receiving countries may oppose immigration. As seen in Chapter 8, governments sometimes react by adopting strategies of denial, hoping that the problems will go away if they are ignored. In other instances, mass deportations and repatriations have been carried out. Governments vary greatly in their capacities to regulate international migration and in the credibility of their efforts to regulate unauthorized migration.

In Chapter 2, we provided some theoretical perspectives on the reasons why international migrations take place and discussed how they often lead to permanent settlement and the formation of distinct ethnic groups in the receiving societies. We suggested that the migratory process needs to be understood in its totality as a complex system of social interactions with a wide range of institutional structures and informal networks in sending, transit and receiving countries, and at the international level. In a democratic setting, legal admission of migrants will almost always result in some settlement, even when migrants are admitted temporarily.

Acceptance of the seeming inevitability of permanent settlement and formation of ethnic groups is the necessary starting point for any meaningful consideration of desirable public policies. The key to adaptive policy-making in this realm (as in others) is understanding of the causes and dynamics of international migration. Policies based on misunderstanding or mere wishful thinking are virtually condemned to fail. Hence, if governments decide to admit foreign workers, they should from the outset make provision for the legal settlement of that proportion of the entrants that is almost sure to remain permanently: a consideration that needs to be taken to heart by the governments of countries as diverse as Japan, Malaysia, the Republic of Korea, Spain, Italy and Greece at present.

Today governments and peoples have to face up to some very serious dilemmas. The answers they choose will help shape the future of their societies, as well as the relations between the rich countries of the North and the developing countries of the South. Central issues include:

- future perspectives for global migration and mobility
- improving international cooperation and governance in the migration arena
- policies to cope with irregular migration
- regulating legal immigration and integrating settlers
- the role of ethnic diversity in social and cultural change, and the consequences for the nation-state.

Future perspectives for global migration and mobility

When the first edition of *The Age of Migration* was published in 1993, its central concern was with immigration and its effects on advanced industrial economies. We showed how the labour migrations of the post-1945 period had led to (often unexpected) settlement and minority formation processes, which were challenging ideas on national identity and citizenship. We also showed how migration within and from Africa, the Middle East, Latin America and Asia was growing in volume and significance. Since 1993, the globalization of migration has advanced rapidly. Its patterns and its consequences for societies of origin, transit and destination are changing constantly. This fourth edition has tried to reflect these trends, but inevitably can only cover a fraction of the massive shifts occurring.

A first key shift concerns the growing connectivity between processes of globalization, social transformation and migration. Chapter 3 explored these links, showing that processes of economic, political and cultural change also transform social relationships in both rich and poor countries, creating the conditions for much greater human mobility. The combination of increased North–South inequality, improved transport and communication technologies, and rising transnational consciousness all lead to more movement and to greater diversity in patterns and outcomes. One result has been increasing international concern with the nexus between migration and development, as we will discuss below.

A second, closely connected shift has been the rapid demographic transition to low mortality and fertility and greater longevity in developed countries. Declining cohorts of young labour market entrants and increasing age-dependency ratios make future labour demand at all skill levels seem certain. As noted in Chapter 1, virtually all of the expected 3 billion additional human beings in the coming decades will be born in the developing world. Like it or not, Europeans and North Americans are likely to have to rely increasingly on newcomers from Africa, Asia and Latin America. Yet by 2050, or earlier, the global population is forecast to stabilize and then to begin to decline (Chamie, 2007). Industrializing Asian countries like Korea are undergoing amazingly fast demographic transitions, and China appears fated to undergo the same process. Some areas that constituted important zones of emigration in the twentieth century, like North Africa and Mexico, may soon become zones of immigration. By the middle of the twenty-first century, prosperous countries may be competing not just for highly skilled personnel – as they already do today – but also for low-skilled workers to build their houses, run their services and look after the elderly.

A third important shift relates to labour force dynamics. We touched on this theme for developing regions in Chapters 6 and 7, and explored it in more detail for advanced economies in Chapter 10. Migration has played a crucial role in labour force growth in the OECD countries. Migrant labour market positions and outcomes have become more diverse than in the past, yet many migrant workers still experience disadvantage. This is linked to a new political economy of labour, in which much of manufacturing employment has been outsourced to low-wage economies. Paradoxically, today's advanced economies are characterized by the resurgence of exploitative and poorly regulated work in agriculture, services and manufacturing sweatshops. Complicated patterns of labour market segmentation by gender, ethnicity, race, origins and legal status force many migrants into precarious forms of employment, characterized by subcontracting, spurious self-employment, temporary and casual work, and informalization.

A fourth major shift results from the emergence of a multipolar world of regions, characterized by disparate and distinctive regionalization patterns. At the same time, the growing political and economic influence of emerging powers like China, India, Korea, South Africa, Brazil and Mexico will increasingly mark and change the global landscape of migration.

A fifth closely connected shift is the emergence of more flexible types of international mobility: changes in transportation, technology and culture are making it normal for people to think beyond national borders and to cross them frequently for all types of reasons. Mobility for study, tourism, marriage and retirement is assuming greater significance and affecting ideas on migration. Mobility implies an opening of borders for at least some kinds of movement. For instance, the agreement between the EU and the USA to create a single transatlantic space for air travel by 2008 will facilitate greater transatlantic mobility in spite of persistent fears about possibly adverse security implications. Mobility implies more flexible types of movement, for a variety of purposes, which do not necessarily lead to long-term stay. For the foreseeable future, the world will experience both migrations in the traditional sense and new types of mobility.

Improving international cooperation and governance

These trends are likely to increase the economic importance of international migration for many countries, thus reinforcing its potential to bring about cultural and social change. That in turn may further increase the political saliency of migration. This raises the question of whether this might give rise to improved international cooperation and governance, as has happened with finance (IMF and World Bank), trade (WTO) and many other forms of global connectivity (Held et al., 1999). International migration constitutes the most important facet of the international political economy not covered by a global regime for cooperation and governance.

What is needed became clearer in the aftermath of 11 September 2001, when UN Secretary General Annan called for a global response to the violence of that day through lessening of global socioeconomic disparities. However, achievement of real change through international cooperation remains elusive despite three important developments since 2001: the creation of the Global Commission on International Migration and publication of its influential report (GCIM, 2005), the convening of a High Level Dialogue on Migration and Development at the UN in 2006, and its follow-up through an annual Global Forum on Migration and Development starting in 2007.

For all their merits, these consultative démarches have not resulted in concrete measures towards a regime for international cooperation on migration. The unwillingness of states to move forward in this area is seen in the very poor ratification record of the 1990 *International Convention on the Protection of the Rights of All Migrant Workers and Members of their Families*, passed by the UN General Assembly on 18 December 1990. As mentioned in Chapter 1, only 34 states (out of 192 UN member states) had ratified it by 2006. These were virtually only countries of emigration; immigration countries have not been willing to support measures designed to protect migrants.

There are at least four reasons not to expect a global migration regime to emerge anytime soon. First, at least for several additional decades, there will remain an abundant supply of foreign labour at the global level. This creates a disincentive to multilateral cooperation, as individual states can sign bilateral agreements to recruit foreign labour or tolerate illegal entry of foreign labour. However, this situation may change with the predicted coming stabilization and decline of global population.

Second, there is no inherent reciprocity of interests between workers in more socioeconomically advanced states and those in less developed states. The rich countries perceive little benefit in reciprocity. Their workers generally will not benefit from facilitated entry to less developed states. Labour movements would be largely unidirectional, from less developed areas to the more developed areas. Why would the most developed states cede sovereign prerogatives to regulate international migration to establish an international regime?

Third, as Koslowski has argued, leadership is vital to regime formation (2008). US leadership since 1945 has helped forge liberal international trade regimes in many areas. Neither the USA nor any of the other most powerful states have evidenced much leadership in forging a global regime concerning international migration. To the contrary, the USA has been very sceptical about international fora on international migration, something clearly evident already in 1986 when the OECD convened the first major multilateral conference on international migration since World War II (Miller and Gabriel, 2008). Similarly, the record of the Bush Administration has made much of the rest of the world sceptical about the idea of US leadership.

Fourth, political leaders and public debates in immigration countries still generally treat migration as something fundamentally abnormal and problematic. The overwhelming concern seems to be to stop or reduce migration, as if it were inherently bad. This is very clear in debates on migration and development (Chapter 3). Even well meaning initiatives, like attempts to address the 'root causes' of emigration from poor countries through efforts to achieve 'durable solutions' to impoverishment and violence, are driven by the idea that migration should be reduced. Political leaders still seem to believe that development will curtail migration from poorer countries.

Yet, as we have shown in this book, migration has taken place throughout history and is stimulated by economic change and growth. One sign of this is the growth of highly skilled mobility between advanced economies. Another is the realization that rich countries like the USA, UK and Australia have large diasporas, which make important contributions to both sending and receiving countries. Rather than reducing migration, we suggest, the aim should be to work for greater economic and social equality between North and South, so that migration will take place under better conditions and will enrich the experiences and capabilities of migrants and communities. Thus reducing 'unwanted migration' is a valid aim only if it is coupled with the understanding that this may well mean greater mobility overall – but mobility of a different and more positive kind. This would require measures that go well beyond the usual range of migration-related policies.

Reform of trade policies, for instance, could encourage economic growth in less developed countries. A key issue is the level of prices for primary commodities as compared with industrial products. This is linked to constraints on world trade through tariffs and subsidies. Reforms could bring important benefits for less developed countries. But trade policies generally operate within tight political constraints: few politicians are willing to confront their own farmers, workers or industrialists, particularly in times of economic recession. Reforms favourable to the economies of the less developed countries will only come gradually, if at all (Castles and Delgado Wise, 2008).

Development assistance is a second strategy which might help to reduce 'unwanted' migration over the long term. Some states have good records in this respect, but international assistance generally has not been at a level sufficient to make a real impression on problems of underdevelopment. Indeed, the balance of nearly six decades of development policies is not a positive one. Although some countries have managed to achieve substantial growth, in general the gap between poor and rich countries has grown. Income distribution in the South has also become more inequitable, increasing the gulf between the wealthy elites and the impoverished masses. The problems of rapid demographic growth, economic stagnation, ecological degradation, weak states and abuse of human rights still affect many countries of Africa, Asia and Latin America. Moreover, control of world finance by bodies like the IMF and the World Bank has led to credit policies that have increased the dependency and instability of many countries of the South.

Regional integration – the creation of free-trade areas and regional political communities – is sometimes seen as a way of diminishing 'unwanted' migration by reducing trade barriers and spurring economic growth, as well as by legalizing international movement of labour. But successful regional integration usually takes place between states that share political and cultural values and which resemble one another economically. Consequently, as seen in Chapters 5 and 8, the world's most successful regional integration unit, the EU, has witnessed relatively low labour mobility between member states. The fact that EU disparities between old and new member states closely match the socioeconomic gap between the USA and Mexico in the NAFTA context makes the results of the EU enlargements of 2004 and 2007 a subject for serious reflection by the NAFTA partners (Bruecker, 2007). Thus far, however, the absence of a commitment to narrowing socioeconomic disparities between partner states through redistributional measures has sharply demarcated NAFTA from the EU.

Thus the 'migration and development mantra' (as we called it in Chapter 3) will not bring about substantial reductions in international migration. The initial effect of development and integration into the world market is to increase migration from less developed countries. This is because the early stages of development lead to rural–urban migration, and to acquisition by many people of the financial and cultural resources needed for international migration. The 'migration transition' – through which emigration declines, and is eventually replaced by a more balanced relationship between in- and out-migration – requires specific demographic and economic conditions, which may take generations to develop. Neither restrictive measures nor development strategies can stop international migration, because there are such powerful forces stimulating population movement. These include the increasing pervasiveness of a global culture and the growth of cross-border movements of ideas, capital and commodities. The world community will have to learn to live with mass population movements for the foreseeable future.

Coping with irregular immigration

A major trend since the 1980s has been the emergence of a new generation of temporary foreign worker policies often touted as a way to better manage and substitute for irregular migration. The principal recommendation of the GCIM appears to endorse this trend, using the more positive label of 'circular migration'. As analysed in Chapters 3, 5 and 8, there are many reasons to doubt that such policies will succeed.

In European countries such as Germany some observers have suggested a need for increased immigration to compensate for low birth rates and an ageing population: foreign workers might provide the labour for age-care and other services as well as the construction industry. But immigration cannot effectively counteract the demographic ageing of Western societies unless it is substantially increased. Political constraints will not permit this. Public opinion may accept entry programmes for highly skilled labour, family reunification and refugees, but not a resumption of massive recruitment of foreign labour for low-level jobs. Most industrial democracies have to struggle to provide adequate employment for existing populations of low-skilled citizen and resident alien workers.

One of the most pressing challenges for many countries today, therefore, is to find ways of coping with irregular or 'unwanted' migratory flows. 'Unwanted immigration' is a somewhat vague blanket term, which embraces:

- illegal border-crossers
- legal entrants who overstay their entry visas or who work without permission
- family members of migrant workers, prevented from entering legally by restrictions on family reunion
- asylum seekers not regarded as genuine refugees.

Most such migrants come from poor countries and seek employment, but generally lack work qualifications. They may compete with lower-qualified local people for unskilled jobs, and for housing and social amenities. Many regions throughout the world have had an enormous increase in such immigration in the last 30 years or so. Of course, the migration is not always as 'unwanted' as is made out: employers often benefit from cheap workers who lack rights, and some governments (especially those of the USA and Southern European countries) tacitly permit such movements. Often there is a significant contradiction between government policy statements and actual implementation on the ground. Yet 'unwanted immigration' is often seen as being at the root of public fears of mass influxes. It is therefore a catalyst for racism and is at the centre of extreme-right agitation.

Appearing to crack down on 'unwanted immigration' is increasingly regarded by governments as essential for safeguarding social peace. In Western Europe, the result has been a series of agreements designed to secure international cooperation in stopping illegal entries, and to speed up the processing of applications for asylum (see Chapters 5, 8 and 9). In the USA, Canada and Australia, measures have also been taken to improve border control and to speed up refugee determination. Several African and Asian countries have carried out quite draconian measures, such as mass expulsions of foreign workers (for example, Nigeria, Libya, Malaysia), building fences and walls along borders (South Africa), severe punishments for illegal entrants (corporal punishment in Singapore) and sanctions against employers (South Africa, Japan and other countries). In addition, nonofficial punishments such as beatings by police are routinely meted out in some countries. The effectiveness of these measures is hard to assess; however, unauthorized migration clearly remains a concern almost everywhere.

The difficulty in achieving effective control is not hard to understand. Barriers to mobility contradict the powerful forces of globalization which are leading towards greater economic and cultural interchange. In an increasingly international economy, it is difficult to open borders for movements of information, commodities and capital and yet close them to people. Global circulation of investment and know-how always means movements of people too. Moreover, flows of highly skilled personnel tend to encourage flows of less-skilled workers. The instruments of border surveillance cannot be sufficiently fine-tuned to let through all those whose presence is wanted, but to stop all those who are not. Nevertheless, there should be no mistaking that measures like enforcement of employer sanctions have a deterrent effect where there exists the political will to punish unauthorized employment of undocumented foreign workers.

The matter is further complicated by a number of factors: the eagerness of employers to hire foreign workers (whether documented or not) for menial jobs, when nationals are unwilling to take such positions; the difficulty of adjudicating asylum claims and of distinguishing economically motivated migrants from those deserving of refugee status; and the inadequacies or insufficiencies of immigration law. The weakening of organized labour and declining trade union membership in many Western democracies has also tended to increase unauthorized foreign employment. Similarly, policies aimed at reducing labour market rigidities and enhancing competitiveness may result in expanded employer hiring of unauthorized foreign workers (see Chapter 10). Social welfare policies may also have unintended consequences, making employment of unauthorized alien workers more propitious.

Thus, despite the claimed desire of governments to stop illegal migration, many of the causes are to be found in the political and social structures of the immigration countries, and their relations with less developed areas. Yet in the current political climate there is no doubt that receiving countries will continue to regulate migration and attempt to curb illegal immigration. Enforcement of immigration laws will probably be accorded higher priority in the future (requiring more investment in personnel and resources), if only because of growing apprehension over the possible political consequences of continuing illegal migration and implications for security. How successful such measures can be remains to be seen.

Legal migration and integration

Virtually all democratic states and many not so democratic states have growing foreign populations. As shown in Chapters 5, 6 and 7, the presence of these immigrants is generally due to conscious labour recruitment or immigration policies, or to the existence of various linkages between sending and receiving countries. In some cases, policies of large-scale immigration still exist. Invariably they are selective: economic migrants, family members and refugees are admitted according to certain quotas which are politically determined.

There is considerable evidence that planned and controlled entries are conducive to acceptable social conditions for migrants as well as to relative social peace between migrants and local people. Countries with immigration quota systems generally decide on them through political processes which permit public discussion and the balancing of the interests of different social groups. Participation in decision-making increases the acceptability of immigration programmes. At the same time this approach facilitates the introduction of measures to prevent discrimination and exploitation of immigrants, and to provide social services to support successful settlement. There is therefore a strong case for advocating that all countries that continue to have immigration should move towards planned immigration policies.

As Chapters 8 and 12 showed, governmental obligations towards immigrant populations are shaped by the nature of the political system in the host society, as well as the mode of entry of the newcomers. Governments possess an internationally recognized right to regulate entry of aliens, a right that may be voluntarily limited through governmental signature of bilateral or multilateral agreements (for example, in the case of refugees). Clearly it makes a difference whether or not an alien has arrived on a territory through legal means of entry. In principle, the proper course for action with regard to legally admitted foreign residents in a democracy is straightforward. They should be rapidly afforded equality of socioeconomic rights and a large measure of political freedom, for their status would otherwise diminish the quality of democratic life in the society. However, this principle is frequently ignored in practice. As analysed in Chapters 8 and 10, unauthorized immigration and employment make immigrants especially vulnerable to exploitation. The perceived illegitimacy of their presence can foster conflict and anti-immigrant violence.

'Guestworker'-style restrictions on the employment and residential mobility of legally admitted aliens appear difficult to reconcile with prevailing market principles, to say nothing of democratic norms. The same goes for restrictions on political rights. Freedom of speech, association and assembly should be unquestionable. The only restriction on the rights of legally admitted aliens which seems compatible with democratic principles is the reservation of the right to vote and to stand for public office to citizens. This is only justifiable if resident aliens are given the opportunity of naturalization, without daunting procedures or high fees. But, even then, some foreign residents are likely to decide not to become citizens for various reasons. A democratic system needs to secure their political participation too. This can mean setting up special representative bodies for resident noncitizens, or extending voting rights to noncitizens who fulfil certain criteria of length of stay (as in Sweden, the Netherlands and, in the nineteenth century, much of the USA).

The global character of international migration results in the intermingling and cohabitation of people from increasingly different physical and cultural settings. Older immigration countries have developed approaches to incorporate newcomers into their societies, with a view to making them into citizens in the long run. Some newer immigration countries, for instance in the Middle East (see Chapter 7), and East and Southeast Asia (see Chapter 6), reject the idea of permanent settlement, and treat migrants as temporary sojourners, however long they stay.

Chapter 11 analysed incorporation models in Europe, North America and Oceania, showing that there are important variations, ranging from 'exclusionary' approaches that keep migrants as a separate (and usually disadvantaged) part of the population, through 'assimilationist' approaches that offer full membership but at the price of abandoning migrants' original languages and cultures, to 'multicultural' approaches that offer both full membership and recognition of cultural difference. We argued that a trend away from exclusionary and assimilationist models and towards multicultural approaches could be discerned from the 1970s to the 1990s. Changes in citizenship laws to offer easier naturalization for migrants and birthright citizenship for their children were an important sign of change.

However, this trend has been questioned in recent years. Critics of multiculturalism argue that it is detrimental to the economic integration and success of minorities, and that it can lead to permanent cultural and political divisions. The increased security concerns since 9/11 have led to a new emphasis on 'national values' and loyalty. The result is a call to replace multicultural policies with measures to strengthen 'social cohesion'. Symptomatic of this trend has been the tightening up of naturalization rules, restrictions on dual citizenship in some places, and the introduction of citizenship tests in Australia and several European countries. Yet, at the same time, many countries have maintained the multilingual services and antidiscrimination rules typical of multicultural societies. In some places the rhetoric on multiculturalism seems to have changed more than the reality. At the time of writing, the picture is confused, indicating the persistence of important struggles in the public arena.

Ethnic diversity, social change and the nation-state

The age of migration has already changed the world and many of its societies. Most highly developed countries and many less developed ones have become far more diverse than they were even a generation ago. In fact, few modern nations have ever been ethnically homogeneous. However, the nationalism of the last two centuries strove to create myths of homogeneity. In its extreme forms, nationalism even tried to bring about such homogeneity through expulsion of minorities, ethnic cleansing and genocide. But the reality for most countries today is that they have to contend with a new type of pluralism, and that – even if migration were to stop tomorrow – this will affect their societies for generations.

One reason why immigration and the emergence of new ethnic groups have had such an impact is that these trends have coincided with the crisis of modernity and the transition to postindustrial societies. The labour migration of the pre-1973 period appeared at the time to be reinforcing the economic dominance of the old industrial nations. Today we can interpret it as part of a process of capital accumulation which preceded a seminal change in the world economy. Growing international mobility of capital, the electronic revolution, the decline of old industrial areas and the rise of new ones are all factors which have led to rapid change in advanced economies. The erosion of the old blue-collar working class and the increased polarization of the labour force have led to a social crisis in which immigrants find themselves doubly at risk: many of them suffer unemployment and social marginalization, yet at the same time they are often portrayed as the cause of the problems. That is why the emergence of the 'two-thirds society', in which the top strata are affluent while the bottom third is impoverished, is often accompanied by ghettoization of the disadvantaged and the rise of racism.

Nowhere is this more evident than in today's global cities: Los Angeles, Toronto, Paris, London, Tokyo, Bangkok and Sydney – to name just a few – are crucibles of social change, political conflict and cultural innovation. They are marked by great gulfs: between the corporate elite and the informal sector workers who service them, between rich, well guarded suburbs and decaying and crime-ridden inner cities, between citizens of democratic states and illegal noncitizens, between dominant cultures and minority cultures. The gulf may be summed up as that between inclusion and exclusion. The included are those who fit into the self-image of a prosperous, technologically innovative and democratic society. The excluded are the shadow side: those who are needed to do the menial jobs in industry and the services, but who do not fit into the ideology of the model.

Both groups include nationals and immigrants, though the immigrants are more likely to belong to the excluded. But the groups are more closely bound together than they might like to think: the corporate elite need the illegal immigrants, the prosperous suburbanites need the slum-dwellers they find so threatening. It is out of this contradictory and multilayered character of the global city that its enormous energy, its cultural dynamism and its innovative capability emerge. But these coexist with potential for social breakdown, conflict, repression and violence.

The new ethnic diversity affects societies in many ways. Amongst the most important are issues of political participation, cultural pluralism and national identity. As Chapter 12 showed, immigration and formation of ethnic groups have already had major effects on politics in most developed countries. These effects are potentially destabilizing. The only resolution appears to lie in broadening political participation to embrace immigrant groups, which in turn may mean rethinking the form and content of citizenship, and decoupling it from ideas of ethnic homogeneity or cultural assimilation.

This leads on to the issue of cultural pluralism. Processes of marginalization and isolation of ethnic groups have gone so far in many countries that culture has become a marker for exclusion on the part of some sections of the majority population, and a mechanism of resistance by the minorities. Even if serious attempts were made to end all forms of discrimination and racism, cultural and linguistic difference would persist for generations, especially if new immigration took place. That means that majority populations will have to learn to live with cultural pluralism, even if it means modifying their own expectations of acceptable standards of behaviour and social conformity.

If ideas of belonging to a nation have been based on myths of ethnic purity or of cultural superiority, then they are threatened by the growth of ethnic diversity. Whether the community of the nation has been based on belonging to an ethnic group (as in Germany) or on a unitary culture (as in France), ethnic diversity inevitably requires major political and psychological adjustments. The shift is smaller for countries that have seen themselves as nations of immigrants, for their political structures and models of citizenship are geared to incorporating newcomers. However, these countries too have historical traditions of racial exclusion and cultural homogenization which still need to be worked through.

Countries of immigration may have to re-examine their understanding of what it means to belong to their societies. Monocultural and assimilationist models of national identity are no longer adequate for the new situation. Immigrants may be able to make a special contribution to the development of new forms of identity. It is part of the migrant condition to develop multiple identities, which are linked to the cultures both of the homeland and of the country of origin. Such personal identities possess complex new transcultural elements, manifest in growing transnationalism and expanding diasporic populations around the world.

Immigrants are not unique in this; multiple identities are becoming a widespread characteristic of contemporary societies. But it is above all migrants who are compelled by their situation to have multilayered sociocultural identities, which are constantly in a state of transition and renegotiation. Moreover, migrants frequently develop a consciousness of their transcultural position, which is reflected not only in their artistic and cultural work, but also in social and political action. Despite current conflicts about the effects of ethnic diversity on national cultures and identity, immigration does offer perspectives for change. New principles of identity may emerge, which may be neither exclusionary nor discriminatory, and may provide the basis for better intergroup cooperation.

Inevitably transcultural identities will affect fundamental political structures. The democratic nation-state is a fairly young political form, which came into being with the American and French revolutions and achieved global dominance in the nineteenth century. It is characterized by principles defining the relationship between people and government which are mediated through the institution of citizenship. The nation-state was an innovative and progressive force at its birth, because it was inclusive and defined the citizens as free political subjects, linked together through democratic structures. But the nationalism of the nineteenth and twentieth centuries turned citizenship on its head by equating it with membership of a dominant ethnic group, defined on biological, religious or cultural lines. In many cases the nation-state became an instrument of exclusion and repression.

National states, for better or worse, are likely to endure. But global economic and cultural integration and the establishment of regional agreements on economic and political cooperation are undermining the exclusiveness of national loyalties. The age of migration could be marked by the erosion of nationalism and the weakening of divisions between peoples. Admittedly there are countervailing tendencies, such as racism, or the resurgence of nationalism in certain areas. Coming transformations are likely to be uneven, and setbacks are possible, especially in the event of economic or political crises. But the inescapable central trends are the increasing ethnic and cultural diversity of most countries, the emergence of transnational networks which link the societies of emigration and immigration countries and the growth of cultural interchange. The age of migration may yet be a period of greater unity in tackling the pressing problems that beset our small planet.

Bibliography

Abadan-Unat, N. (1988) 'The socio-economic aspects of return migration to Turkey', *Revue Européenne des Migrations Internationales,* 3, 29–59.

Abella, M. (1994) 'Introduction to special issue on turning points in international labour migration', *Asian and Pacific Migration Journal,* 3:1, 1–6.

Abella, M.I. (1995) 'Asian migrant and contract workers in the Middle East', in Cohen, R. (ed.) *The Cambridge Survey of World Migration* (Cambridge: Cambridge University Press).

Abella, M.I. (2002) *Complexity and Diversity of Asian Migration* (Geneva: unpublished manuscript).

ABS (2007a) *2006 Census Quickstats: Australia* (Canberra: Australian Bureau of Statistics). http://www.censusdata.abs.gov.au/, accessed 7 August 2007.

ABS (2007b) *Year Book Australia 2006* (Canberra: Australian Bureau of Statistics). http://www.abs.gov.au/, accessed 7 August 2007.

Adams, R. (2006) *Migration, Remittances and Development: the Critical Nexus in the Middle East and North Africa.* United Nations Expert Group Meeting on International Migration and Development in the Arab Region (Beirut: 15–17 May 2006, Population Division, Department of Economic and Social Affairs, United Nations Secretariat). http://www.un.org/esa/population/meetings/EGM_ Ittmig_Arab/P01_Adams.pdf

Adamson, F.B. (2004) 'Displacement, Diaspora Mobilization and Transnational Cycles of Political Violence' in Tirman, J. (ed.) *The Maze of Fear* (New York/ London: The New Press).

Adamson, F.B. (2006) 'Crossing borders: International Migration and National Security', *International Security,* 31:1, 165–199.

Adepoju, A. (2001) 'Regional integration, continuity and changing patterns of intra-regional migration in Sub-Saharan Africa', in Siddique, M.A.B. (ed.) *International Migration into the 21st Century* (Cheltenham/Northampton, MA: Edward Elgar).

Adepoju, A. (2006) 'Leading issues in international migration in sub-Saharan Africa', in Cross, C., Gelderblom, D., Roux, N. and Mafukidze, J. (eds) *Views on Migration in Sub-Saharan Africa* (Cape Town: HSRC Press) 25–47.

'African Immigrants in the United States are the Nation's Most Highly Educated Group' (1999–2000). *The Journal of Blacks in Higher Education,* 26, 60–61.

Aggoun, L. and Rivoire, J.-B. (2004) *Francalgerie, Crimes et Mensonges d'Etats* (Paris: La Decouverte).

Agunias, D. (2007) *Linking temporary worker schemes with development.* (Washington DC: Migration Information Source). http://www.migrationinformation. org/Feature/display.cfm?id=576, accessed 6 February 2007.

Akokpari, J.K. (2000) 'Globalisation and migration in Africa', *African Sociological Review,* 4:2, 72–92.

Alba, R. and Nee, V. (1997) 'Rethinking assimilation theory for a new era of immigration', *International Migration Review,* 31:4, 826–874.

Aleinikoff, T.A. and Klusmeyer, D. (eds) (2000) *From Migrant to Citizens: Membership in a Changing World* (Washington, DC: Carnegie Endowment for International Peace).

Aleinikoff, T.A. and Klusmeyer, D. (eds) (2001) *Citizenship Today: Global Perspectives and Practices* (Washington, DC: Carnegie Endowment for International Peace).

Alexseev, M. (2005) *Immigration Phobia and the Security Dilemma* (Cambridge: Cambridge University Press).

Alkire, S. and Chen, L. (2006) "Medical exceptionalism' in international migration: should doctors and nurses be treated differently?', in Tamas, K. and Palme, J. (eds) *Globalizing Migration Regimes* (Aldershot: Ashgate), 100–117.

Amin, S. (1974) *Accumulation on a World Scale* (New York: Monthly Review Press).

Andall, J. (2003) *Gender and Ethnicity in Contemporary Europe* (Oxford: Berg).

Anderson, B. (1983) *Imagined Communities* (London: Verso).

Anderson, B. (2000) *Doing the Dirty Work: The Global Politics of Domestic Labour* (London: Zed Books).

Andreas, P. (2001) 'The transformation of migrant smuggling across the US-Mexico border', in Kyle, D. and Koslowski, R. (eds) *Global Human Smuggling* (Baltimore, MD: The Johns Hopkins Press).

Andrès, H. (2007) 'Le droit de vote des étrangers: Une utopie déjà réalisée sur cinq continents'. *Migrations Société,* 19:114, 65–81.

Anthias, F. and Yuval-Davis, N. (1989) 'Introduction', in Yuval-Davis, N. and Anthias, F. (eds) *Woman-Nation-State* (London: Macmillan) 1–15.

Appenzeller, G. et al. (2001) 'Kardinal Sterzinsky in Gespraech: Die Union fragt nur, was tut uns Deutschen gut' (*Tagesspiegel,* 19 May 2001).

Appleyard, R. T. (1991) *International Migration: Challenge for the Nineties* (Geneva: International Organization for Migration).

Appleyard, R. T. (ed.) (1998) *Emigration Dynamics in Developing Countries,* Vol. II: *South Asia* (Aldershot: Ashgate).

Archdeacon, T. (1983) *Becoming American: An Ethnic History* (New York: The Free Press).

Argun, B.E. (2003) *Turkey in Germany* (London: Routledge).

Arnold, F., Minocha, U. and Fawcett, J.T. (1987) 'The changing face of Asian immigration to the United States', in Fawcett, J.T. and Cariño, B.V. (eds) *Pacific Bridges: The New Immigration from Asia and the Pacific Islands* (New York: Center for Migration Studies).

Aronson, G. (1990) *Israel, Palestinians and the Intifada: Creating Facts on the West Bank* (Washington, DC: Institute for Palestine Studies).

Asis, M.M.B. (2005) 'Recent Trends in International Migration in Asia and the Pacific', *Asia-Pacific Population Journal,* 20:3, 15–38.

Asis, M.M.B. (2008) 'How international migration can support development: a challenge for the Philippines', in Castles, S. and Delgado Wise, R. (eds) *Migration and Development: Perspectives from the South,* (Geneva: International Organization for Migration) 175–201.

Avci, G. and Kirişci, K. (2008) 'Turkey's immigration and emigration dilemmas at the gates of the European Union', in Castles, S. and Delgado Wise, R. (eds) *Migration and Development: Perspectives from the South* (Geneva: International Organization for Migration) 203–252.

Ayres, R. and Barber, T. (2006) *Statistical Analysis of Female Migration and Labour Market Integration in the EU* Integration of Female Immigrants in Labour Market and Society Working Paper 3. (Oxford: Oxford Brookes University).

Bade, K. (2003) *Migration in European History* (Oxford: Blackwells).

Baeck, L. (1993) *Post-War Development Theories and Practice* (Paris: UNESCO and the International Social Science Council).

Baganha, M. (ed.) (1997) *Immigration in Southern Europe* (Oeiras: Celta Editora).

Bakewell, O. (2007) *Keeping them in their place: the ambivalent relationship between development and migration in Africa.* IMI Working Paper 8 (Oxford: International Migration Institute).

Bakewell, O. and de Haas, H. (2007) 'African migrations: continuities, discontinuities and recent transformations', in Chabal, P., Engel, U. and de Haan, L. (eds) *African Alternatives* (Leiden: Brill) 95–117.

Balci, B. (2003) 'La communauté ouzbèke d'Arabie Saoudite: entre assimilation et renouveau identitaire', *Revue Européenne des Migrations Internationales,* 19:3, 205–226.

Baldwin-Edwards, M. (2005) 'Migration in the Middle East and Mediterranean'. *A Regional Study prepared for the Global Commission on International Migration* (Geneva: Global Commission on International Migration). http://mmo.gr/pdf/news/Migration_in_the_Middle_East_and_Mediterranean.pdf,accessed 7 July 2007.

Baldwin-Edwards, M. and Schain, M.A. (eds) (1994) *The Politics of Immigration in Western Europe* (Portland: Frank Cass).

Baldwin-Edwards, M. and Schain, M.A. (1994) 'The politics of immigration: introduction', in Baldwin-Edwards, M. and Schain, M.A. (eds) *The Politics of Immigration in Western Europe* (Ilford, Essex: Frank Cass) 1–16.

Balibar, E. (1991) 'Racism and nationalism', in E. Balibar and I. Wallerstein (eds) *Race, Nation, Class: Ambiguous Identities* (London: Verso) 37–67.

Balibar, E. and Wallerstein, I. (eds) (1991) *Race, Nation, Class: Ambiguous Identities* (London: Verso).

BAMF (2006a) *Ausländerzahlen* (Nurenberg: Bundesanstalt für Migration und Flüchtlinge). http://www.bamf.de/, accessed 23 March 2008.

BAMF (2006b) *Integration* (Nurenberg: Bundesanstalt für Migration und Flüchtlinge)

Barlán, J. (1988) *A System Approach for Understanding International Population Movement: The Role of Policies and Migrant Community in the Southern Cone* (IUSSP Seminar, Genting Highlands, Malaysia) September 1988.

Barnett, T.P. (2004) *The Pentagon's New Map: War and Peace in the Twenty-first Century* (New York: G.P. Putnam's Sons).

Bartram, D. (1999) *Foreign Labor and Political Economy in Israel and Japan* (Madison: Dissertation, Department of Sociology, University of Wisconsin).

Bartram, D. (2005) *International labor migration: foreign workers and public policy* (New York: Palgrave Macmillan).

Bartram, D (2008) 'Immigrants and natives in Tel Aviv: What's the difference?' in M. Price and L. Benton-Short (eds) *Migrants to the Metropolis* (Syracuse: Syracuse University Press).

Basch, L., Glick-Schiller, N. and Blanc, C.S. (1994) *Nations Unbound: Transnational Projects, Post-Colonial Predicaments and Deterritorialized Nation-States* (New York: Gordon and Breach).

Batalova, J. (2005) *College-Educated Foreign Born in the US Labor Force* (Washington DC: Migration Information Source). http://www.migrationinformation.org/USfocus/print.cfm?ID=285, accessed 23 July 2007.

Batata, A.S. (2005) 'International nurse recruitment and NHS vacancies: a cross-sectional analysis'. *Global Health,* 1:7.

Bauböck, R. (1991) 'Migration and citizenship', *New Community,* 18:1.

Bauböck, R. (1994a) *Transnational Citizenship: Membership and Rights in International Migration* (Aldershot: Edward Elgar).

Bauböck, R. (ed.) (1994b) *From Aliens to Citizens: Redefining the Status of Immigrants in Europe* (Aldershot: Avebury).

Bauböck, R. (1996) 'Social and cultural integration in a civil society', in Bauböck, R., Heller, A. and Zolberg, A.R. (eds) *The Challenge of Diversity: Integration and Pluralism in Societies of Immigration* (Aldershot: Avebury) 67–131.

Bauböck, R. and Rundell, J. (eds) (1998) *Blurred Boundaries: Migration, Ethnicity, Citizenship* (Aldershot: Ashgate).

Bauböck, R., Ershøll, E., Groenendijk, K. and Waldrauch, H. (eds) (2006a) *Acquisition and Loss of Nationality: Policies and Trends in 15 European States, Volume I: Comparative Analyses,* IMISCOE Research (Amsterdam: Amsterdam University Press).

Bauböck, R., Ershøll, E., Groenendijk, K. and Waldrauch, H. (eds) (2006b) *Acquisition and Loss of Nationality: Policies and Trends in 15 European States, Volume II: Country Analyses,* IMISCOE Research (Amsterdam: Amsterdam University Press).

Bauman, Z. (1998) *Globalization: the Human Consequences* (Cambridge: Polity).

Bawer, B. (2006) *While Europe Slept: How Radical Islam is Destroying the West from Within* (New York: Doubleday).

BBC Mundo.com (17 April 2006) *Argentina legaliza inmigrantes* (London: BBC). http://news.bbc.co.uk/hi/spanish/latin_america/newsid_4917000/4917232.stm, accessed 17 April 2006.

BBC News (2003) *Asylum Claims will be Halved - Blair* (London: BBC). http://news.bbc.co.uk/1/low/uk_politics/2736101.stm, accessed 3 May 2007.

BBC News (2004) *Ireland votes to end birth right* (London: BBC). http://news.bbc.co.uk/1/hi/world/europe/3801839.stm, accessed 28 February 2007.

BBC News (24 May 2007) *Profile: Mercosur – Common Market of the South* (London: BBC). http://news.bbc.co.uk/1/hi/world/americas/5195834.stm, 15 July 2007.

Bedzir, B. (2001) 'Migration from Ukraine to Central and Eastern Europe', in Wallace, C. and Stola, D. (eds) *Patterns of Migration in Central Europe* (Basingstoke: Palgrave).

Beggs, J. and Pollock, J. (2006) *Non-National Workers in the Irish Economy* (Dublin: AIB Global Treasury Economic Research). http://www.aibeconomicresearch.com, accessed 15 June 2007.

Bell, D. (1975) 'Ethnicity and social change', in Glazer, N. and Moynihan, D.P. (eds) *Ethnicity - Theory and Experience* (Cambridge, MA: Harvard University Press).

Bello, W. (2006) 'The capitalist conjuncture: over-accumulation, financial crises, and the retreat from globalisation'. *Third World Quarterly,* 27:8, 1345–1367.

Bello, W. and Malig, M. (2004) 'The crisis of the globalist project and the new economics of George W. Bush' in Freeman, A. and Kagarlitsky, B. (eds) *The Politics of Empire: Globalisation in Crisis* (London, Ann Arbor, MI: Pluto Press) 84–96.

Benjamin, D. and Simon, S. (2005) *The Next Attack* (New York: Times Books/H. Holt).

Benyon, J. (1986) 'Spiral of decline: race and policing', in Layton-Henry Z. and Rich, P.B. (eds) *Race, Government and Politics in Britain* (London: Macmillan).

Berlinski, C. (2007) *Menace in Europe: Why the Continent's Crisis is America's Too* (New York: Crown Forum Books).

Bertossi, C. (2007) *French and British models of integration: public philosophies, policies and state institutions.* Working Paper 46 (Oxford: Centre on Migration, Policy and Society). http://www.compas.ox.ac.uk/, accessed 25 November 2007.

Betz, H.-G. (1994) *Radical right-wing populism in Europe* (New York: St. Martin's).

Binur, Y. (1990) *My Enemy, Myself* (New York: Penguin).

Björgo, T. and Witte, R. (eds) (1993) *Racist Violence in Europe* (London: Macmillan).

Black, R. (1998) *Refugees, Environment and Development* (London: Longman).

Blackburn, R. (1988) *The Overthrow of Colonial Slavery 1776–1848* (London and New York: Verso).

Böhning, W.R. (1984) *Studies in International Labour Migration* (London: Macmillan; New York: St Martin's Press).

Body-Gendrot, S. and Wihtol de Wenden, C. (2007) *Sortir des banlieues: pour en finir avec la tyrannie des territories* (Paris: Autrement).

Borjas, G.J. (1989) 'Economic theory and international migration', *International Migration Review,* Special Silver Anniversary Issue, 23:3, 457–485.

Borjas, G.J. (1990) *Friends or Strangers: The Impact of Immigration on the US Economy* (New York: Basic Books).

Borjas, G.J. (2001) *Heaven's door: immigration policy and the American economy* (Princeton, N.J. and Oxford: Princeton University Press).

Bouamama, S. (1994) *Dix ans de marche des Bears* (Paris: Desclée de Brouwer).

Boudahrain, A. (1985) *Nouvel Ordre Social International et Migrations* (Paris: L'Harmattan/CIEMI).

Boulanger, P. (2000) 'Un regard français sur l'immigration Kurde en Europe', *Migrations Société,* 12:72, 19–29.

Bourdieu, P. and Wacquant, L. (1992) *An Invitation to Reflexive Sociology* (Chicago: University of Chicago Press).

Boyd, M. (1989) 'Family and personal networks in migration', *International Migration Review,* Special Silver Anniversary Issue, 23:3, 638–670.

Boyle, P., Halfacree, K. and Robinson, V. (1998) *Exploring Contemporary Migration* (Harlow, Essex: Longman).

Brand, C. (2007) *EU agrees on weakened anti-racism rules* (New York: ABC News). http://abcnews.go.com/International/wireStory?id=3056841, accessed 14 August 2007.

Branigan, T. (2007) 'Crackdown pledged on sex with trafficked women' (*The Guardian* (London), 18 July 2007).

Breton, R., Isajiw, W.W., Kalbach, W.E. and Reitz, J.G. (1990) *Ethnic Identity and Equality* (Toronto: University of Toronto Press).

Brettell, C.B. and Hollifield, J.F. (eds) (2007) *Migration Theory: Talking Across Disciplines*, 2nd edn (New York and London: Routledge).

Briggs, V.M., Jr (1984) *Immigration Policy and the American Labor Force* (Baltimore, MD, and London: Johns Hopkins University Press).

Brochman, G. and Hammar, T. (eds) (1999) *Mechanisms of Immigration Control: A Comparative Analysis of European Regulation Policies* (Oxford: Berg).

Browne, I. and Misra, J. (2003) 'The intersection of gender and race in the labor market', *Annual Review of Sociology,* 29, 487–513.

Brownell, P. (2005) 'The Declining Enforcement of Employer Sanctions', *Migration Information Source* (Washington DC: Migration Policy Institute).

Brubaker, R. (1992) *Citizenship and Nationhood in France and Germany* (Cambridge, Mass.: Harvard University Press).

Brubaker, R. (2003) 'The return of assimilation? Changing perspectives on immigration and its sequels in France, Germany and the United States', in Joppke, C. and Morawaska, E. (eds) *Towards Assimilation and Citizenship: Immigration in Liberal Nation-States* (Basingstoke: Palgrave-Macmillan).

Bruecker, H. (2007) 'Labor Mobility After the European Union's Eastern Enlargement: Who wins, Who loses?' Paper presented at the Joint Seminar on Labour Mobility in a Transnational Perspective, Dublin European Foundation for the Improvement of Living and Working Conditions and the German Marshall Fund of the United States, 30–31 October.

Buzan, B., Waever, O. and de Wilde, J. (1998) *Security: A New Framework for Analysis* (Boulder: Lynne Rienner).

Cahill, D. (1990) *Intermarriages in International Contexts* (Quezon City: Scalabrini Migration Center).

Cain, B. and B. Doherty (2006) 'The Impact of Dual Nationality on Political Participation', in Lee, T., Ramakrishnan, S. K. and Ramirez, R. (eds) *Transforming Politics, Transforming America: The Political and Civic Incorporation of Immigrants in the United States* (Charlottesville: University of Virginia Press).

Calavita, K. (2004) 'Italy: immigration, economic flexibility, and policy responses', in Cornelius, W., Martin, P.L. and Hollifield, J.F. (eds) *Controlling Immigration: A Global Perspective* (Stanford, CA: Stanford University Press).

Cantle, T. (2001) *Community Cohesion: A Report of the Independent Review Team* (London: Home Office).

Card, D. (2005) 'Is the new immigration really so bad?' *The Economic Journal,* 115:507, 300–323.

Castells, M. (1996) *The Rise of the Network Society* (Oxford: Blackwells).

Castells, M. (1997) *The Power of Identity* (Oxford: Blackwells).

Castells, M. (1998) *End of Millennium* (Oxford: Blackwells).

Castles, S. (1995) 'How nation-states respond to immigration and ethnic diversity', *New Community,* 21:3, 298–308.

Castles, S. (2002) *Environmental Change and Forced Migration: Making Sense of the Debate.* New Issues in Refugee Research, Working Paper No. 70 (Geneva: UNHCR).

Castles, S. (2004a) 'The factors that make and unmake migration policy', *International Migration Review,* 38:3, 852–884.

Castles, S. (2004b) 'The myth of the controllability of difference: labour migration, transnational communities and state strategies in the Asia-Pacific region', in Yeoh, B.S.A. and Willis, K. (eds) *State/Nation/Transnation: Perspectives on Transnationalism in the Asia-Pacific* (London and New York: Routledge) 3–26.

Castles, S. (2005) 'Nation and empire: hierarchies of citizenship in the new global order', *International Politics,* 42:2, 203–224.

Castles, S. (2006a) *Back to the Future? Can Europe meet its Labour Needs through Temporary Migration?* International Migration Institute IMI Working Papers 1 (Oxford: IMI Oxford University).

Castles, S. (2006b) 'Guestworkers in Europe: A Resurrection?' *International Migration Review,* 40:4, 741–766.

Castles, S. and Davidson, A. (2000) *Citizenship and Migration: Globalisation and the Politics of Belonging* (London: Macmillan).

Castles, S. and Delgado Wise, R. (eds) (2008) *Migration and Development: Perspectives from the South* (Geneva: International Organization for Migration).

Castles, S. and Kosack, G. (1973) *Immigrant Workers and Class Structure in Western Europe* (Oxford: Oxford University Press).

Castles, S. and Van Hear, N. (2005) *Developing DFID's Policy Approach to Refugees and Internally Displaced Persons.* Report to the Conflict and Humanitarian Affairs Department (Oxford: Refuge Studies Centre).

Castles, S. and Vasta, E. (2004) 'Australia: new conflicts around old dilemmas', in Cornelius, W., Tsuda, T., Martin, P.L. and Hollifield, J.F. (eds) *Controlling Immigration: A Global Perspective.* 2nd edn (Stanford CA: Stanford University Press) 141–173.

Castles, S., Foster, W., Iredale, R. and Withers, G. (1998) *Immigration and Australia: Myths and Realities* (Sydney: Allen & Unwin).

Castles, S., Loughna, S. and Crawley, H. (2003) *States of Conflict: Causes and Patterns of Forced Migration to the EU and Policy Responses* (London: Institute of Public Policy Research).

Castles, S., Rando, G. and Vasta, E. (1992) 'Italo-Australians and politics', in Castles, S., Alcorso, C., Rando, G. and Vasta, E. (eds) *Australia's Italians - Culture and Community in a Changing society* (Sydney: Allen & Unwin) 125–139.

Castles, S., with Booth, H. and Wallace, T. (1984) *Here for Good: Western Europe's New Ethnic Minorities* (London: Pluto Press).

CCCS (Centre for Contemporary Cultural Studies) (1982) *The Empire Strikes Back* (London: Hutchinson).

CEC (2005a) *Communication from the Commission: Policy Plan on Legal Migration* COM(2005)669 final (Brussels: Commission of the European Communities).

CEC (2005b) *Green Paper on an EU Approach to Managing Economic Migration* COM(2004)811 final (Brussels: Commission of the European Communities).

CEC (2005c) *The Hague Programme – Ten Priorities for the Next Five Years* (Brussels: Commission of the European Communities: Justice and Home Affairs). http://ec.europa.eu/justice_home/news/information_dossiers/the_hague_priorities/, accessed 27 April 2007.

CEC (2007a) *For diversity, against discrimination: an initiative of the European Union* (Brussels: Commission of the European Union) http://www.stop-discrimination.info/index.php?id=43, accessed 15 August 2007.

CEC (2007b) 'Proposal for a Directive of the European Parliament and of the Council providing for sanctions against employers of illegally staying third-country nationals' (Brussels: Commission of the European Union) 21.

Cernea, M.M. and McDowell, C. (eds) (2000) *Risks and Reconstruction: Experiences of Resettlers and Refugees* (Washington, DC: World Bank).

Cesari, J. (2004) *When Islam and Democracy Meet* (New York: Palgrave Macmillan).

Chamie, J. (2007) *Populations Trends: Humanity in Transition* (New York: International Peace Academy).

Chiffoleau, S. (2003) 'Un champ à explorer: le rôle des pèlerinages dans les mobilités nationales, régionales et internationales du Moyen-Orient', *Revue Européenne des Migrations Internationales,* 19:3, 285–289.

Chimni, B.S. (1998) 'The geo-politics of refugee studies: a view from the South', *Journal of Refugee Studies,* 11:4, 350–374.

Chin, K. (1999) *Smuggled Chinese: Clandestine Immigration to the United States* (Philadelphia: Temple University Press).

Chishti, M. (2007) *The Rise in Remittances to India: a Closer Look* (Washington, DC: Migration Information Source). http://www.migrationinformation.org/ Feature/display.cfm?ID=577 accessed 6 February 2007.

Chiswick, B.R. (2000) 'Are immigrants favorably self-selected? An economic analysis', in Brettell, C B. and Hollifield, J. F. (eds) *Migration Theory: Talking Across Disciplines* (New York and London: Routledge) 61–76.

Chou, M.-H. and Baygert, N. (2007) *The 2006 French Immigration and Integration Law.* Working Paper 45 (Oxford: Centre on Migration, Policy and Society) http://www.compas.ox.ac.uk/, accessed 12 March 2008.

CIA (2007) 'Malawi - People', *The World Factbook,* 17 April 2007.

CIC (2006) *Facts and Figures: Immgration Overview – Permanent and Temporary Residents* (Ottawa: Citizenship and Immigration Canada) http://www.cic. gc.ca/english/pdf/pub/facts2006.pdf, accessed 15 June 2007.

Cinanni, P. (1968) *Emigrazione e Imperialismo* (Rome: Riuniti).

Çinar, D. (1994) 'From aliens to citizens: a comparative analysis of rules of transition', in Bauböck, R. (ed.) *From Aliens to Citizens* (Aldershot: Avebury) 49–72.

Clarke, R.A. (2004) *Against all enemies* (New York: Free Press).

Clearfield, E. and Batalova, J. (2007) *Foreign-born health-care workers in the United States* (Washington, DC: Migration Information Source). www.migrationinformation.org/USFocus/, accessed 6 February 2007.

Cohen, P. and Bains, H.S. (eds) (1988) *Multi-Racist Britain* (London: Macmillan).

Cohen, R. (1987) *The New Helots: Migrants in the International Division of Labour* (Aldershot: Avebury).

Cohen, R. (1991) 'East-West and European migration in a global context', *New Community,* 18:1.

Cohen, R. (1995) 'Asian indentured and colonial migration', in Cohen, R. (ed.) *The Cambridge Survey of World Migration* (Cambridge: Cambridge University Press).

Cohen, R. (1997) *Global Diasporas: An Introduction* (London: UCL Press).

Cohen, R. and Deng, F.M. (1998) *Masses in Flight: The Global Crisis of Internal Displacement* (Washington, DC: Brookings Institution Press).

Cohen, R. and Kennedy, P. (2000) *Global Sociology* (Basingstoke: Palgrave).

Cohen, R. and Layton-Henry, Z. (eds) (1997) *The Politics of Migration* (Cheltenham/ Northampton, MA: Edward Elgar).

Collins, J. (2006) 'The changing political economy of Australian immigration', *Tijdschrift voor Economische en Sociale Geografie,* 97:1, 7–16.

Collins, J. (1991) *Migrant Hands in a Distant Land: Australia's Post-War Immigration,* 2nd edn (Sydney: Pluto Press).

Collins, J., Gibson, K., Alcorso, C., Castles, S. and Tait, D. (1995) *A Shop Full of Dreams: Ethnic Small Business in Australia* (Sydney: Pluto Press).

Collins, J., Noble, G., Poynting, S. and Tabar, P. (2001) *Kebabs, Kids, Cops and Crime: Youth, Ethnicity and Crime* (Sydney: Pluto Press Australia).

Comunidad Andina (2006) *Quienes Somos.* http://www.comunidadandina.org/quienes.htm, accessed 20 July 2007.

Cooper, R. (2003) *The Breaking of Nations* (New York: Grove Press).

Cordeiro, A. (2006) 'Portugal and the Immigration Challenge' in Majtczak, O. (ed.) *The Fifth International Migration Conference* (Warsaw: Independent University of Business and Government).

Cornelius, W.A. (2001) 'Death at the border: efficacy and unintended consequences of US immigration control policy', *Population and Development Review,* 27:4, 661–685.

Cornelius, W., Tsuda, T., Martin, P. and Hollifield, J. (eds) (2004) *Controlling Immigration: A Global Perspective*, 2nd edn (Stanford: Stanford University Press).

Cox, R. (2000) 'Exploring the growth of paid domestic labour: A case study of London', *Geography,* 85, 241–251.

Crock, M. and Saul, B. (2002) *Future Seekers: Refugees and the Law in Australia* (Sydney: Federation Press).

Cross, C., Gelderblom, D., Roux, N. and Mafukidze, J. (eds) (2006) *Views on Migration in Sub-Saharan Africa* (Cape Town: HSRC Press).

Cross, G.S. (1983) *Immigrant Workers in Industrial France: The Making of a New Laboring Class* (Philadelphia: Temple University Press).

Crossette, B. (2000) 'UN warns that trafficking in human beings is growing' (*New York Times,* 25 June 2000).

Crush, J. (2003) *South Africa: New Nation, New Migration Policy?* (Washington, DC: Migration Information Source). http://www.migrationinformation.org/, accessed 25 January 2008.

CSIS (2006) *Currents and Crosscurrents of Radical Islam* (Washington, DC: CSIS).

CSIS (2007) *Commission on Smart Power* (Washington, DC: CSIS).

Curtin, P.D. (1997) 'Africa and Global Patterns of Migration', in Gungwu, W. (ed.) *Global History and Migrations* (Boulder, CO: Westview) 63–94.

Daniels, R. (2004) *Guarding the Golden Door* (New York: Hill and Wang).

Danis, D.A. and Pérouse, J.-F. (2005) 'La Politique Migratoire Turque: vers une Normalisation?' *Migrations et Société,* 17:98, 93–106.

Dávila, R. (1998) *The Case of Venezuela* (The Hague: UN Technical Symposium on International Migration and Development paper).

Davis, M. (1990) *City of Quartz: Excavating the Future in Los Angeles* (London: Verso).

De Bel-Air, F. (2003) 'Migrations internationales et politique en Jordanie'. *Revue Européenne des Migrations Internationales,* 19:3, 9–39.

De Bruycker, P. (ed.) (2000) *Regularisations of Illegal Immigrants in the European Union* (Belgium: Bruylant).

de Haas, H. (2006a) 'Migration, remittance and regional development in Southern Morocco'. *Geoforum,* 37565–80.

de Haas, H. (2006b) *Engaging Diasporas* (Oxford: International Migration Institute for Oxfam Novib).

de Haas, H. (2006c) *Turning the Tide? Why 'Development Instead of Migration' Policies are Bound to Fail.* IMI Working Paper 2. (Oxford: International Migration Institute).

de Haas, H. (2006d) *Trans-Saharan migration to North Africa and the EU: historical roots and current trends* (Washington, DC: Migration Information Source). www.migrationinformation.org/, accessed 3 November 2006.

de Lattes, A. and de Lattes, Z. (1991) 'International migration in Latin America: Patterns, implications and policies', Informal Expert Group Meeting on International Migration (Geneva: UN Economic Commission for Europe/ UNPF paper).

de Lepervanche, M. (1975) 'Australian immigrants 1788–1940', in Wheelwright, E.L. and Buckley, K. (eds) *Essays in the Political Economy of Australian Capitalism,* Vol. 1 (Sydney: ANZ Books).

Decloîtres, R. (1967) *The Foreign Worker* (Paris: OECD).

Delgado Wise, R. and Guarnizo, L.E. (2007) *Migration and Development: Lessons from the Mexican Experience* (Washington DC: Migration Information Source). http://www.migrationinformation.org/Feature/display.cfm?id=581, accessed 6 February 2007.

Delrue, T. (2006) 'Burundi: Sliding off the Humanitarian Radar Screen?' *Forced Migration Review,* 26, 62–63.

DeParle, J. (2007) 'Fearful of Restive Foreign Labor, Dubai Eyes Reforms' (*New York Times*, 6 August 2007).

Derderian, R.L. (2004) *North Africans in Contemporary France* (Houndsmills: Palgrave).

Derisbourg, J.P. (2002) 'L'Amérique latine entre Etats-Unis et Union européenne', *Politique Etrangère,* 67:2, 415–434.

Dervin, F. and Wiberg, M. (2007) 'Présence absente des électeurs étrangers en Finlande', *Migrations Societe,* 19:114, 99–113.

DeSipio, L. (2001) 'Building America, one person at a time: Naturalization and political behavior of the naturalized in contemporary American politics', in Gerstle, G. and Mollenkopf, J. (eds) *E Pluribus Unum?* (New York: Russell Sage Foundation).

DeWind, J., Hirschman, C. and Kasinitz, P. (eds) (1997) *Immigrant Adaptation and Native-born Responses in the Making of Americans, International Migration Review* (Special Issue) Vol. 31 (New York: Center for Migration Studies).

DFID (1997) *Eliminating World Poverty: A Challenge for the 21st Century* (London: Department for International Development). http://www.dfid.gov.uk/ pubs/files/whitepaper1997.pdf, accessed 9 July 2007.

DFID (2007) *Moving Out of Poverty - Making Migration Work Better for Poor People* (London: Department for International Development).

DHS (2006a) *2004 Yearbook of Immigration Statistics* (Washington, DC: US Department of Homeland Security, Office of Immigration Statistics) http://www. dhs.gov/ximgtn/statistics/publications/yearbook.shtm, accessed 29 June 2007.

DHS (2006b) *2005 Yearbook of Immigration Statistics* (Washington, DC: US Department of Homeland Security, Office of Immigration Statistics) http://www. dhs.gov/ximgtn/statistics/publications/yearbook.shtm, accessed 29 June 2007.

DIAC (2007a) *Fact Sheet 2: Key Facts in Immigration* (Canberra: Department of Immigration and Citizenship) http://www.immi.gov.au/media/fact-sheets/, accessed 30 April 2007.

DIAC (2007b) *Fact Sheet 60: Australia's Refugee and Humanitarian Programme* (Canberra: Department of Immigration and Citizenship) http://www.immi.gov. au/media/fact-sheets, accessed 30 April 2007.

DIAC (2007c) *Migration Program Statistics* (Canberra: Department of

Immigration and Citizenship) http://www.immi.gov.au/media/statistics/, accessed 30 April 2007.

DiSipio, L. (2006) 'Transnational Politics and Civic Engagement: Do Home-Country Political Ties Limit Immigrant Pursuit of U.S. Civic Engagement and Citizenship?', in Lee,T., Ramakrishnan, S.K. and Ramirez, R. (eds) *Transforming Politics, Transforming America: The Political and Civic Incorporation of Immigrants in the United States* (Charlottesville: University of Virginia Press).

Dohse, K. (1981) *Ausländische Arbeiter and bürgerliche Staat* (Konistein/Taunus: Hain).

DRC Sussex (2005) *GATS Mode 4: How Trade in Services Can Help Developing Countries* Briefing (Brighton: Development Research Centre on Migration Globalisation and Poverty) http://www.migrationdrc.org/publications/briefing_papers/BP4.pdf, accessed 19 Feburary 2008.

Dubajic, N. (2007) 'Le vote des étrangers au Luxembourg: Evolution de 1999 à 2005'. *Migrations Société,* 19:114, 129–140.

Dubet, F. and Lapeyronnie, D. (1992) *Les Quartiers d'Exil* (Paris: Seuil).

Duffield, M. (2001) *Global Governance and the New Wars: The Merging of Development and Security* (London and New York: Zed Books).

Dustmann, C. and Fabbri, F. (2005) 'Immigrants in the British labour market', *Fiscal Studies,* 26:4, 423–470.

Dustmann, C. and Glitz, A.C.E. (2005) *Immigration, Jobs and Wages: Evidence and Opinion* (London: Centre for Economic Policy Research, Centre for Research and Analysis of Migration).

Düvell, F. (ed.) (2005) *Illegal Immigration in Europe: Beyond Control* (Basingstoke: Palgrave/Macmillan).

ECLAC (Economic Commission for Latin America and the Caribbean) (2006) *Social Panorama of Latin America 2006* (Santiago, Chile: United Nations Publications) http://www.eclac.cl/id.asp?id=27484, accessed 23 July 2007.

Economist Intelligence Unit (2006) 'Latin American Economy: Reaping the benefits of remittances'. http://www.viewswire.com/article1770253762.html?pubtypeId=930000293&text=latin%20america%20economy%20remittances, accessed 20 July 2007.

ECOSOC (2006) 'UN Commission on Population and Development to meet at Headquarters, 3–7 April, with Focus on International Migration, Development', *Economic and Social Council* (New York: United Nations Economic and Social Council).

Einaudi, L. (2007) *Le Politiche dell'Immigrazione in Italia dall'Unità a oggi* (Rome: Editori Laterza).

Ellerman, D. (2003) *Policy Research on Migration and Development* Policy Research Working Paper 3117 (Washington, DC: World Bank).

Emmott, R. (2007) 'More migrants die as U.S. tightens border security' (*Reuters News Service,* 12 July).

Engels, F. (1962) 'The condition of the working class in England' in *Marx, Engels on Britain* (Moscow: Foreign Languages Publishing House). (First published in German in 1845.)

Entzinger, H. (2003) 'The rise and fall of multiculturalism: the case of the Netherlands' in Joppke, C. and Morawaska, E. (eds) *Towards Assimilation and Citizenship: Immigration in Liberal Nation-States* (Basingstoke: Palgrave-Macmillan).

Esposito, J. and Mogahed, D. (2007) *Who Speaks for Islam? What a Billion Muslims Really Think* (New York: Gallup Press).

Essed, P. (1991) *Understanding Everyday Racism* (London and Newbury Park, New Delhi: Sage).

EUMAP (2007) *The Netherlands: Executive Summary* (Vienna: EU Monitoring and Advocacy Program). http://www.eumap.org/, accessed 11 November 2007.

EUMC (2006) *The Annual Report on the Situation regarding Racism and Xenophobia in the Member States of the EU* (Vienna: European Monitoring Centre on Racism and Xenophobia). http://eumc.europa.eu/eumc/material/pub/ar06/AR06-P2-EN.pdf, accessed 11 November 2007.

European Parliament (1985) *Committee of Inquiry into the Rise of Fascism and Racism in Europe: Report on the Findings of the Inquiry* (Strasbourg: European Parliament).

Faist, T. (2000) *The Volume and Dynamics of International Migration and Transnational Social Spaces* (Oxford: Oxford University Press).

Faist, T. (ed.) (2007) *Dual Citizenship in Europe* (Aldershot: Ashgate).

Faist, T. and Ette, A. (eds) (2007) *The Europeanization of National Policies and Politics of Immigration: Between Autonomy and the European Union* (New York: Palgrave Macmillan).

Faist, T., Gerdes, J. and Rieple, B. (2004) 'Dual citizenship as a path-dependent process', *International Migration Review*, 38:3, 913–944.

Fakiolas, R. (2002) 'Greek migration and foreign immigration in Greece', in Rotte, R. and Stein, P. (eds) *Migration Policy and the Economy: International Experiences* (Munich: Hans Seidel Stiftung).

Fargues, P. (2006) 'Afrique du Nord et Moyen-Orient: des migrations en quête d'une politique', *Politique Etrangère*, 4, 1017–1029.

Fargues, P. (ed.) (2007) *Mediterranean Migration: 2006–2007 report* (San Domenico di Fiesole (FI), Italy: European University Institute, RSCAS).

Farrag, M. (1999) 'Emigration dynamics in Egypt', in Appleyard, R. (ed.) *Emigration Dynamics in Developing Countries*, Vol. IV: *The Arab Region* (Aldershot: Ashgate).

Favell, A. (1998) *Philosophies of Integration: Immigration and the Idea of Citizenship in France and Britain* (London: Macmillan).

Fawcett, J.T. and Arnold, F. (1987) 'Explaining diversity: Asian and Pacific immigration systems', in Fawcett, J.T. and Cariño, B.V. (eds) *Pacific Bridges: The New Immigration from Asia and the Pacific islands* (New York: Center for Migration Studies).

Fawcett, J.T. and Cariño, B.V. (eds) (1987) *Pacific Bridges: The New Immigration from Asia and the Pacific Islands* (New York: Center for Migration Studies).

Feagin, J.R. (1989) *Racial and Ethnic Relations* (Englewood Cliffs, NJ: Prentice-Hall).

Feldblum, M. (1999) *Reconstructing Citizenship* (Albany, NY: State University of New York Press).

Findlay, A.M. (2002) *From brain exchange to brain gain: policy implications for the UK of recent trends in skilled migration from developing countries* (Geneva: International Labour Office).

Fishman, J.A. (1985) *The Rise and Fall of the Ethnic Revival: Perspectives on Language and Ethnicity* (Berlin, New York and Amsterdam: Mouton).

Fix, M. and Passel, J.S. (1994) *Immigration and Immigrants: Setting the Record Straight* (Washington, DC: The Urban Institute).

Fleming, L. (2006) 'Gambia – new front in migrant trade' (*BBC News Online*, 10 October).

Foot, P. (1965) *Immigration and Race in British Politics* (Harmondsworth: Penguin).

Foster, W. (1996) *Immigration and the Australian Economy* (Canberra: DIMA).

Fox-Genovese, E. and Genovese, E.D. (1983) *Fruits of Merchant Capital: Slavery and Bourgeois Property in the Rise and Expansion of Capitalism* (New York and Oxford: Oxford University Press).

Frank, A.G. (1969) *Capitalism and Underdevelopment in Latin America* (New York: Monthly Review Press).

Freedman, J. (2004) *Immigration and Insecurity in France* (Aldershot: Ashgate).

Freeman, A. (2004) 'The inequality of nations' in Freeman, A. and Kagarlitsky, B. (eds) *The Politics of Empire: Globalisation in Crisis* (London and Ann Arbor MI: Pluto Press) 46–83.

Freeman, A. and Kagarlitsky, B. (eds) (2004) *The Politics of Empire: Globalisation in Crisis* (London and Ann Arbor MI: Pluto Press).

Freeman, G. (1979) *Immigrant Labor and Racial Conflict in Industrial Societies: the French and British Experience, 1945–1975* (Princeton: Princeton University Press).

Freeman, G.P. (1998) 'Reform and retreat in United States immigration policy', *People and place,* 6:4, 1–11.

Freeman, G. (2002) 'Winners and Losers: Politics and the Costs and Benefits of Migration', in Messina, A. (ed.) *West European Immigration and Immigration Policy in the New Century* (Westport, CT: Praeger).

Freeman, G.P. (1986) 'Migration and the political economy of the welfare state', *Annals AAPSS*: 485, 51–63.

Freeman, G. P. (1995) 'Modes of Immigration Politics in Liberal Democratic States', *International Migration Review,* 29:4, 881–902.

Fregosi, R. (2002) 'Au-delà de la crise financière et institutionnelle, l'Argentine en quête d'un véritable projet', *Politique Etrangère,* 67:2, 435–454.

Froebel, F., Heinrichs, J. and Kreye, O. (1980) *The New International Division of Labour* (Cambridge: Cambridge University Press).

Gallagher, A. (2002) 'Trafficking, smuggling and human rights: tricks and treaties', *Forced Migration Review,* 12, 25–28.

Gallagher, D. and Diller, J.M. (1990) *At the Crossroads between Uprooted People and Development in Central America.* Working Paper No. 27 (Washington, DC: Commission for the Study of International Migration and Cooperative Economic Development).

Gamburd, M.R. (2005) ''Lentils there, lentils here!' Sri Lankan domestic workers in the Middle East', in Huang, S., Yeoh, B.S.A. and Abdul Rahman, N. (eds) *Asian Women as Transnational Domestic Workers* (Singapore: Marshall Cavendish Academic) 92–114.

GAO (2000) *Alien Smuggling* (Washington, DC: US General Accounting Office).

GAO (2006) *Foreign Workers – Information on Selected Countries Experiences* (Washington, DC: US Governmental Accountability Office).

Garrard, J.A. (1971) *The English and Immigration: A Comparative Study of the Jewish Influx 1880–1910* (Oxford: Oxford University Press).

GCIM (2005) *Migration in an Interconnected World: New Directions for Action: Report of the Global Commission on International Migration* (Geneva: Global

Commission on International Migration). http://www.gcim.org/en/finalreport. html, accessed 11 July 2007.

Geddes, A. (2000) *Immigration and European Integration: Towards Fortress Europe?* (Manchester and NY: Manchester University Press).

Geddes, A. (2003) *The Politics of Migration and Immigration in Europe* (London: Sage).

Geertz, C. (1963) *Old Societies and New States – The Quest for Modernity in Asia and Africa* (Glencoe, IL: Free Press).

Gellner, E. (1983) *Nations and Nationalism* (Oxford: Blackwell).

Gerges, F. (2005) *The Far Enemy: Why Jihad went global* (New York: Cambridge University Press).

Ghosh, B. (2006) *Migrants' Remittances and Development: Myths, Rhetoric and Realities* (Geneva: International Organization for Migration).

Gibney, M J. (2000) *Outside the Protection of the Law: The Situation of Irregular Migrants in Europe* (Oxford: Refugee Studies Centre).

Giddens, A. (2002) *Runaway World: how Globalisation is Reshaping our Lives*, 2nd edn (London: Profile).

Givens, T. (2005) *Voting Radical Right in Western Europe* (New York: Cambridge University Press).

Glazer, N. and Moynihan, D.P. (1975) 'Introduction', in Glazer, N. and Moynihan, D.P. (eds) *Ethnicity: Theory and Experience* (Cambridge, MA: Harvard University Press).

Glick-Schiller, N. (1999) 'Citizens in transnational nation-states: the Asian experience', in Olds, K., Dicken, P., Kelly, P. F., Kong, L., and Yeung, H.W.-C. (eds) *Globalisation and the Asia-Pacific: Contested Territories* (London: Routledge) 202–218.

Glover, S., Gott, C., Loizillon, A., Portes, J., Price, R., Spencer, S., Srinivasan, V. and Willis, C. (2001) *Migration: an Economic and Social Analysis.* RDS Occasional Paper 67 (London: Home Office).

Go, S.P. (2002) 'Detailed case study of the Philippines', in Iredale, R., Hawksley, C. and Lyon, K. (eds) *Migration Research and Policy Landscape: Case Studies of Australia, the Philippines and Thailand* (Wollongong: Asia-Pacific Migration Research Network) 61–89.

Goldberg, D. (1993) *Racist Culture: Philosophy and the Politics of Meaning* (Oxford: Blackwell).

Goldberg, D.T. and Solomos, J. (eds) (2002) *A Companion to Racial and Ethnic Studies* (Malden, MA and Oxford: Blackwell).

Goldberg, D.T. (2005) 'Racial Americanization' in Murji, K. and Solomos, J. (eds) *Racialization: Studies in Theory and Practice* (Oxford: Oxford University Press) 87–102.

Graham, D. and Poku, N. (eds) (2000) *Migration, Globalization and Human Security* (London: Routledge).

Green, N. and Weil, P. (2007) *Citizenship and Those Who Leave* (Urbana: University of Illinois Press).

Green, S. (2004) *The Politics of Exclusion: Institutions and Immigration Policy in Contemporary Germany* (Manchester: Manchester University Press).

Guarnizo, L.E., Portes, A. and Haller, W. (2003) 'Assimilation and transnationalism: determinants of transnational political action among contemporary migrants', *American Journal of Sociology,* 108:6, 1211–1248.

Guild, E. and van Selm, J. (2005) *International Migration and Security: Opportunities and Challenges* (New York: Routledge).

Guimezanes, N. (1995) 'Acquisition of nationality in OECD countries', in *Trends in International Migration: Annual Report* (Paris: OECD) 157–179.

Guiraudon, V. and Joppke, C. (2001) *Controlling a New Migration World* (London: Routledge).

Gutmann, A. (ed.) (1994) *Multiculturalism: Examining the Politics of Recognition* (Princeton, NJ: Princeton University Press).

Habermas, J. and Pensky, M. (2001) *The Postnational Constellation: Political Essays* (Cambridge: Polity in association with Blackwell Publishers).

Haddad, Y. (ed.) (2002) *Muslims in the West* (Oxford: Oxford University Press).

Hage, G. (1998) *White Nation: Fantasies of White Supremacy in a Multicultural Society* (Sydney and New York: Pluto Press and Routledge).

Halliday, F. (1985) 'Migrations de main d'oeuvre dans le monde arabe: l'envers du nouvel ordre économique', *Revue Tiers Monde,* 26: 103, 665–679.

Hamilton, K. and Yau, J. (2004) 'The global tug-of-war for health care workers', *Migration Information Source* (Washington DC: Migration Policy Institute). http://www.migrationinformation.org/Feature/display.cfm?ID=271, accessed 9 July 2007.

Hammar, T. (ed.) (1985) *European Immigration Policy: A Comparative Study* (Cambridge: Cambridge University Press).

Hammar, T. (1990) *Democracy and the Nation-State: Aliens, Denizens and Citizens in a World of international Migration* (Aldershot: Avebury).

Hanafi, S. (2003) 'L'impact du capital social sur le processus de rapatriement des réfugiés palestiniens', *Revue Européenne des Migrations Internationales,* 19:3, 43–70.

Hardt, M. and Negri, A. (2000) *Empire* (Cambridge, MA: Harvard University Press).

Hargreaves, A.C. (2007) *Multi-Ethnic France: Immigration, Politics, Culture and Society* (New York and London: Routledge).

Harris, N. (1996) *The New Untouchables: Immigration and the New World Worker* (Harmondsworth: Penguin).

Hatton, T.J. and Williamson, J.G. (1998) *The Age of Mass Migration: Causes and Economic Effects* (Oxford and New York: Oxford University Press).

Hatton, T.J. and Williamson, J.G. (2005) *Global Migration and the World Economy* (Boston: MIT Press).

Heckmann, F. and Wunderlich, T. (eds) (2005) *Amnesty for All Migrants?* (Bamberg, Germany: European Forum for Migration Studies).

Held, D. and Kaya, A. (eds) (2007) *Global Inequality: Patterns and Explanations,* (Cambridge and Malden, MA.: Polity).

Held, D., McGrew, A., Goldblatt, D. and Perraton, J. (1999) *Global Transformations: Politics, Economics and Culture* (Cambridge, MA: Polity).

Hiemenz, U. and Schatz, K.W. (1979) *Trade in Place of Migration* (Geneva: International Labour Organization).

Hirst, P. and Thompson, G. (1996) *Globalization in Question* (Cambridge, MA: Polity).

HKCSD (2007) *2006 Population By-Census – Summary Results* (Hong Kong: Hong Kong Census and Statistics Department).

HKG (2006) *Entry of Foreign Domestic Helpers* (Hong Kong: Hong Kong Government).

Hollifield, J. (1992) *Immigrants, Markets and States: The Political Economy of Postwar Europe* (Cambridge, MA: Harvard University Press).

Hollifield, J. F. (2000) 'The politics of international migration: how can we "bring the state back in"?', in Brettell, C.B. and Hollifield, J.F. (eds) *Migration Theory: Talking Across Disciplines* (New York and London: Routledge) 137–185.

Hollifield, J. (2004a) 'The emerging migration state', *International Migration Review*, 38:3, 885–912.

Hollifield, J.F. (2004b) 'France: Republicanism and the limits of immigration control', in Cornelius, W., Martin, P.L. and Hollifield, J.F. (eds) *Controlling Immigration: A Global Perspective*, 2nd edn (Stanford, CA: Stanford University Press) 183–214.

Holzmann, R. and Münz, R. (2006) 'Challenges and opportunties of international migration for Europe and its neighbourhood' in Tamas, K. and Palme, J. (eds) *Globalizing Migration Regimes* (Aldershot: Ashgate) 233–257.

Home Office (2006) *Accession Monitoring Report May 2004–June 2006* (London: Home Office, Department for Work and Pensions, HM Revenue and Customs, and Office of the Deputy Prime Minister).

Homze, E.L. (1967) *Foreign Labor in Nazi Germany* (Englewood Cliffs, NJ: Princeton University Press).

Hönekopp, E. (1999) *Central and East Europeans in the Member Countries of the European Union since 1990: Development and Structure of Migration, Population and Employment* (Munich: Institute for Employment Research).

Horowitz, D. and Noiriel, G. (1992) *Immigrants in Two Democracies: French and American Experience* (New York: New York University Press).

Huang, S., Yeoh, B. and Rahman, N.A. (2005) *Asian Women as Transnational Domestic Workers* (Singapore: Marshall Cavendish Academic).

Hufbauer, G., Clyde, G. and Chott, J. (2005) *NAFTA Revisited-Achievements and Challenges* (Washington, DC: Institute for International Economics).

Hugo, G. (2005) *Migration in the Asia-Pacific Region* (Geneva: Global Commission on International Migration). http://www.gcim.org/en/ir_experts.html, accessed 5 September 2007.

Hunger, U. and Thränhardt, D. (2001) 'Die Berliner Integrationspolitik im Vergleich der Bundesländer', in Gesemann, F. (ed.) *Migration und Integration in Berlin* (Opladen: Leske und Budrich) 109–125.

Huntington, S.P. (2004) *Who Are We?* (New York: Simon and Schuster).

Içduygu, A. (2000) 'The Politics of International Migratory Regimes', *International Social Science Journal*, 165:357–366.

Içduygu, A. (2004) 'Transborder crime between Turkey and Greece: Human Smuggling and its Regional Consequences', *Southeast European and Black Seas Studies*, 4:2, 294–311.

IDC (2004) *Migration and Development: How to Make Migration work for Poverty Reduction* HC 79-II. (London: House of Commons International Development Committee).

IDMC (2006) *Internally displaced persons (IDPs) in Somalia* (Geneva: Internal Displacement Monitoring Centre).

IDMC (2007) *Internal Displacement: Global Overview of Trends and Developments in 2006* (Geneva: Internal Displacement Monitoring Centre and Norwegian Refugee Council). http://www.internal-displacement.org/, accessed 23 January 2007.

Ignatieff, M. (1994) *Blood and Belonging: Journeys into the New Nationalism* (New York: Vintage).

ILO (2006) *Realizing Decent Work in Asia: Fourteenth Asian Regional Meeting: Report of the Director-General* (Geneva: International Labour Office).

ILO (2007) *Labour and Social Trends in ASEAN 2007* (Bangkok: International Labour Office Regional Office for Asia and the Pacific).

INS (2002) *Statistical Yearbook of the Immigration and Naturalization Service, 1999* (Washington, DC: US Government Printing Office) http://www.dhs.gov/xlibrary/assets/statistics/yearbook/1999/FY99Yearbook.pdf, accessed 27 July 2007.

Institute for Employment Studies (Dench, S., Hurstfield, J., Hill, D. and Akroyd, K.) (2006) *Employers' Use of Migrant Labour: Summary Report.* Online Report (London: Home Office) http://www.employment-studies.co.uk/pubs/summary.php?id=rdsolr0406, accessed 23 June 2007.

International Migration Review (1989) Special Silver Anniversary Issue, 23:3.

IOM (1999) *Trafficking in Migrants* (Geneva: IOM Policy and Responses).

IOM (2000a) *Migrant Trafficking and Human Smuggling in Europe* (Geneva: International Organization for Migration).

IOM (2000b) *World Migration Report 2000* (Geneva: International Organization for Migration).

IOM (2003) *World Migration 2003: Managing Migration - Challenges and Responses for People on the Move* (Geneva: International Organization for Migration).

IOM (2005) *World Migration 2005: Costs and Benefits of International Migration* (Geneva: International Organization for Migration).

Ireland, P. (1994) *The Policy Challenge of Ethnic Diversity* (Cambridge, MA: Harvard University Press).

ISTAT (2007) *Demografia in cifre* (Rome: Istituto Nazionale di Statistica). http://demo.istat.it/, accessed 16 August 2007.

Jaber, H. (2005) 'Introduction: Migrants et migrations au Moyen-Orient, entre contraintes et opportunites' in Jaber, H. and France, M. (eds) *Mondes en mouvements: Migrants et migrations au Moyen-Orient au tournant du XXIe siècle* (Beyrouth: Institut Français du Proche-Orient).

Jachomiowicz, M. (2006) *Argentina: A new era of Migration and Migration Policy* (Washington DC: Migration Information Source). http://www.migrationinformation.org/Profiles/display.cfm?ID=374, accessed 23 July 2007.

Jackson, J.A. (1963) *The Irish in Britain* (London: Routledge and Kegan Paul).

Jazouli, A. (1986) *L'action collective des jeunes maghrébins en France* (Paris: Editions Harmattan).

Johnson, I. and Gugath, B. (2002) 'Turkish voters are transforming political landscape in Germany' (*The Wall Street Journal,* 29 September 2002).

Joppke, C. (1998) *The Challenge to the Nation-State: Immigration in Western Europe and the United States* (New York: Oxford University Press).

Joppke, C. (1999) *Immigration and the Nation-State: The United States, Germany and Great Britain* (Oxford: Oxford University Press).

Joppke, C. (2004) 'The retreat of multiculturalism in the liberal state: theory and policy', *British Journal of Sociology,* 55:2, 237–257.

Jordan, B. and Düvell, F. (2002) *Irregular Migration: The Dilemmas of Transnational Mobility* (Cheltenham and Northampton, MA: Edward Elgar).

Jupp, J. (ed.) (2001) *The Australian People: An Encyclopedia of the Nation, its People and their Origins,* 2nd edn (Cambridge: Cambridge University Press).

Jupp, J. (2002) *From White Australia to Woomera: The History of Australian Immigration* (Melbourne: Cambridge University Press).

Jupp, J., York, B. and McRobbie, A. (1989) *The Political Participation of Ethnic Minorities in Australia* (Canberra: Australian Government Publishing Service).

Jureidini, R. (2003) 'L'échec de la protection de l'État: les domestiques étrangers au Liban'. *Revue Européenne des Migrations Internationales,* 19:3, 95–125.

Kaba, A.J. (2006) 'Kenya-U.S. Relations: The Urgent Need to Manage Kenya's Migrant and HIV-AIDS Brain Drain'. *Journal of Pan-African Studies,* 1:6, 79–86.

Kaldor, M. (1999) *New and Old Wars: Organized Violence in a Global Era* (Cambridge: Polity).

Kapur, D. (2004) *Remittances: the New Development Mantra?* Discussion Paper (Washington DC: World Bank).

Kay, D. and Miles, R. (1992) *Refugees or Migrant Workers? European Volunteer Workers in Britain 1946–1951* (London: Routledge).

Keely, C.B. (2001) 'The international refugee regime(s): the end of the Cold War matters', *International Migration Review,* 35:1, 303–314.

Keohane, R. and Nye, J. (1977) *Power and Interdependence* (Boston: Little, Brown).

Kepel, G. (2002) *Jihad: the trail of political Islam* (Cambridge, MA: Belknap Press of Harvard University).

Kepel, G. (2004) *The war for Muslim minds: Islam and the West* (Cambridge, MA: Belknap Press of Harvard University).

Kepel, G. (2005) *Europe's answer to Londonistan* (London: Open Democracy). http://www.opendemocracy.net/conflict-terrorism/londonistan_2775.jsp, accessed 5 September 2007 and 25 February 2008.

Khadria, B. (2008) 'India; skilled migration to developed countries, labour migration to the Gulf', in Castles, S. and Delgado Wise, R. (eds) *Migration and Development: Perspectives from the South* (Geneva: International Organization for Migration) 79–112.

Kindleberger, C.P. (1967) *Europe's Postwar Growth: The Role of Labor Supply* (Cambridge, MA: Harvard University Press).

King, R. (2000) 'Southern Europe in the changing global map of migration', in R. King, G. Lazaridis and C. Tsardanidis (eds) *Eldorado or Fortress? Migration in Southern Europe* (London: Macmillan) 3–26.

King, R. (ed.) (2001) *The Mediterranean Passage: Migration and New Cultural Encounters in Southern Europe* (Liverpool: Liverpool University Press).

King, R. (2002) 'Towards a new map of European migration', *International Journal of Population Geography* 8:2, 89–106.

King, R., Lazaridis, G. and Tsardanidis, C. (eds) (2000) *Eldorado or Fortress? Migration in Southern Europe* (London: Macmillan).

King, R., Thomson, M., Fielding, T. and Warnes, T. (2006) 'Time, generations and gender in migration and settlement' in Penninx, R., Berger, M. and Kraal, K. (eds) *The Dynamics of International Migration and Settlement in Europe* (Amsterdam: Amsterdam University Press) 233–267.

Kirişci, K. (2006) 'National identity, asylum and immigration: the EU as a vehicle of post-national transformation in Turkey', in Kieser, H.-L. (ed.) *Turkey Beyond Nationalism: Toward Post-Nationalist Identities* (London: IB Tauris).

Kiser, G. and Kiser, M. (eds) (1979) *Mexican Workers in the United States* (Albuquerque: University of New Mexico Press).

Klausen, J. (2005) *The Islamic Challenge* (Oxford: Oxford University Press).

Kleinschmidt, H. (ed.) (2006) *Migration, Regional Integration and Human Security* (Aldershot: Ashgate).

Klekowski Von Koppenfels, A. (2001) *The Role of Regional Consultative Processes in Managing International Migration* (Geneva: International Organization for Migration).

Kloosterman, R. and Rath, J. (2003) *Immigrant Entrepreneurs: Venturing Abroad in the Age of Globalization* (Oxford: Berg).

Klug, F. (1989) ' "Oh to be in England": the British case study', in Yuval-Davis, N. and Anthias, F. (eds) *Woman-Nation-State* (London: Macmillan).

Komai, H. (1995) *Migrant Workers in Japan* (London: Kegan Paul International).

Koopmans, R. and Statham, P. (eds.) (2000) *Challenging Immigration and Ethnic Relations Politics* (Oxford: Oxford University Press).

Kop, Y. and Litan, R.E. (2002) *Sticking Together: The Israeli Experiment in Pluralism* (Washington, DC: The Brookings Institute).

Koslowski, R. (2000) *Migrants and Citizens* (Ithaca, NY: Cornell University Press).

Koslowski, R (2008) 'Global Mobility and the Quest for an International Migration Regime' Paper presented at the Conference on International Migration and Development: Continuing the Dialogue-Legal and Policy Perspectives CMS and IOM: New York. New York, 17–18 January.

Kramer, R. (1999) *Developments in International Migration to the United States* (Washington, DC: Department of Labor).

Kratochwil, H.K. (1995) 'Cross-border population movements and regional economic integration in Latin America', *IOM Latin America Migration Journal*, 13:2, 3–11.

Kreienbrink, A. (2006) 'Refugees Labour Force-Illegal Migrant Challenges for Migration Policy in Europe', in Majtczak, O. (ed.) *The Fifth International Migration Conference* (Warsaw: Independent University of Business and Government).

Kress, B. (2006) 'Burkina Faso: Testing the Tradition of Circular Migration', *Migration Information Source* (Washington DC: Migration Policy Institute).

Kritz, M.M., Lin, L.L. and Zlotnik, H. (eds) (1992) *International Migration Systems: A Global Approach* (Oxford: Clarendon Press).

Kubat, D. (1987) 'Asian immigrants to Canada', in Fawcett, J.T. and Cariño, B.V. (eds) *Pacific Bridges: The New Immigration from Asia and the Pacific Islands* (New York: Center for Migration Studies).

Kupchan, C.A. (1998) *Atlantic Survey: Contending Visions* (New York: Council on Foreign Relations).

Kyle, D. and Koslowski, R. (2001) *Global Human Smuggling* (Baltimore and London: Johns Hopkins University Press).

Kyle, D. and Liang, Z. (2001) *Migration Merchants: Human Smuggling from Ecuador and China*. Working Paper 43 (San Diego: The Center for Comparative Immigration Studies).

Kymlicka, W. (1995) *Multicultural Citizenship* (Oxford: Clarendon Press).

Laacher, S. (2002) 'Comment les "papiers" peuvent changer la vie', in *Le Monde Diplomatique, Histoires d'Immigration*, 64–66.

Laczko, F. and Gozdziak, E. (eds) (2005) *Data and Research on Human Trafficking: A Global Survey* (Geneva: International Organization for Migration).

Lahav, G. (2004) *Immigration and Politics in the New Europe: Reinventing Borders* (New York: Cambridge University Press).

Lapper, R. (30 October 2006) *Call for caution over migrants' cash* (London: Financial Times). http://www.ft.com/home/uk, accessed 3 November 2006.

Laqueur, W. (2003) *No End to War* (London/New York: Continuum).

Laurence, J. and Vaisse, J. (2006) *Integrating Islam: Political and Religious Challenges in Contemporary France* (Washington, DC: Brookings Institution Press).

Laurens, H. (2005) 'Les migrations au Proche-Orient de l'Empire ottoman aux Etats-nations. Une perspective historique', in Jaber, H. and France, M. (eds) *Mondes en mouvements: Migrants et migrations au Moyen-Orient au tournant du XXIe siècle* (Beyrouth: Institut Français du Proche-Orient).

Lavenex, S. and Uçarer, E. (eds) (2002) *Migration and Externalities of European Integration* (Lanham, MD: Lexington Books).

Lavergne, M. (2003) 'Golfe arabo-persique: un système migratoire de plus en plus tourné vers l'Asie', *Revue Européenne des Migrations Internationales,* 19:3, 229–241.

Layton-Henry, Z. (1981) *A Report on British Immigration Policy since 1945* (Coventry: University of Warwick).

Layton-Henry, Z. (2004) 'Britain: from immigration control to migration management', in Cornelius, W., Martin, P.L. and Hollifield, J.F. (eds), *Controlling Immigration: A Global Perspective,* 2nd edn (Stanford, CA: Stanford University Press) 294–333.

Layton-Henry, Z. (ed.) (1990) *The Political Rights of Migrant Workers in Western Europe* (London: Sage).

Layton-Henry, Z. and Rich, P.B. (eds) (1986) *Race, Government and Politics in Britain* (London: Macmillan).

Lee, J.S. and Wang, S.-W. (1996) 'Recruiting and managing of foreign workers in Taiwan', *Asian and Pacific Migration Journal,* 5: 2–3.

Lee, T., Ramakrishnan, S.K. and Ramirez, R. (eds) (2006) *Transforming Politics, Transforming America: The Political and Civic Incorporation of Immigrants in the United States* (Charlottesville: University of Virginia Press).

Leikcn, R. (2005) 'Europe's Angry Muslims', *Foreign Affairs,* July/August.

Lever-Tracy, C. and Quinlan, M. (1988) *A Divided Working Class* (London: Routledge).

Levinson, A. (2005) *The Regularisation of Unauthorized Migrants: Literature Survey and Case Studies* (Oxford: Centre on Migration, Policy and Society).

Levitt, P. (1998) 'Social remittances: migration driven local-level forms of cultural diffusion', *International Migration Review,* 32:4, 926–948.

Levitt, P. and Glick Schiller, N. (2004) 'Conceptualising simultaneity: a transnational social field perspective on society', *International Migration Review,* 38:3, 1002–1039.

Levy, D. (1999) 'Coming home? Ethnic Germans and the transformation of national identity in the Federal Republic of Germany' in Geddes, A. and Favell, A. (eds) *The Politics of Belonging: Migrants and Minorities in Contemporary Europe* (Aldershot: Ashgate).

Lidgard, J.M. (1996) 'East Asian migration to Aotearoa/New Zealand: Perspectives of some new arrivals', *Population Studies Centre Discussion Papers: 12* (Hamilton: University of Waikato).

Light, I. and Bonacich, E. (1988) *Immigrant Entrepreneurs* (Berkeley, CA: University of California Press).

Light, I.H. and Gold, S.J. (1999) *Ethnic Economies* (San Diego, CA; London: Academic).

Lindberg, T. (2005) *Beyond Paradise and Power* (New York: Routledge).

Lindley, A. (2007) *The early morning phonecall: remittances from a refugee diaspora perspective* Working Paper 07–47. (Oxford: COMPAS).

Lluch, V. (2002) 'Apartheid sous plastique à El Ejido', *Le Monde Diplomatique, Histoires d'Immigration*, 85–89.

Loescher, G. (2001) *The UNHCR and World Politics: A Perilous Path* (Oxford: Oxford University Press).

Lohrmann, R. (1987) 'Irregular migration: A rising issue in developing countries', *International Migration*, 25: 3.

Lomonoco, C. (2006) 'U.S.-Mexico Border: The Season of Death', *Frontline World Dispatches* (PBS), 27 June.

Lopez-Garcia, B. (2001) 'La régularisation des Maghrébins sans papiers en Maroc', in Leveau, R., Wihtol de Wenden, C. and Mohsen-Finan, K. (eds), *Nouvelles cityoyennetés: Réfugiés et sans-papiers dans l'espace européen* (Paris: IFRI).

Lowell, B.L., Findlay, A.M. and International Labour Office. International Migration Branch. (2002) *Migration of Highly Skilled Persons from Developing Countries: Impact and Policy Responses: Synthesis Report International Migration Papers, 44* (Geneva: ILO).

Lucassen, J. (1995) 'Emigration to the Dutch colonies and the USA', in Cohen, R. (ed.) *The Cambridge Survey of World Migration* (Cambridge: Cambridge University Press).

Lucassen, L. (2005) *The Immigrant Threat: the Integration of Old and New Migrants in Western Europe since 1890* (Urbana and Chicago: University of Illinois Press).

Lucassen, L., Feldman, D. and Oltmer, J. (2006) 'Immigrant integration in Western Europe, then and now' in Lucassen, L., Feldman, D. and Oltmer, J. (eds) *Paths of Integration: Migrants in Western Europe (1880–2004)* (Amsterdam: Amsterdam University Press) 7–23.

Luso-American Development Foundation (1999) *Metropolis International Workshop Proceedings* (Lisbon: Luso-America Development Foundation).

Lutz, H., Phoenix, A. and Yuval-Davis, N. (eds) (1995) *Crossfires: Nationalism, Racism and Gender in Europe,* (London: Pluto Press).

Lyman, R. (2006) 'Census shows growth of immigrants' (*New York Times*, New York). http://www.nytimes.com/2006/08/15/us/15census.html, accessed 23 March 2007.

Lyon, A. and Ucarer, E. (2001) 'Mobilizing ethnic conflict: Kurdish separatism in Germany and the PKK', *Ethnic and Racial Studies*, 26:6, 925–948.

McAllister, I. (1988) 'Political attitudes and electoral behaviour', in Jupp, J. (ed.) *The Australian People: An Encyclopedia of the Nation, its People and their Origins* (Sydney: Angus & Robertson).

McCarthy, J. (1995) *Death and Exile: The Ethnic Cleansing of Ottoman Muslims 1821–1922* (Princeton: Darwin Press).

McKinnon, M. (1996) *Immigrants and Citizens: New Zealanders and Asian Immigration in Historical Context* (Wellington: Institute of Policy Studies).

MacMaster, N. (1991) 'The "seuil de tolérance": the uses of a "scientific" racist concept', in Silverman, M. (ed.) *Race, Discourse and Power in France* (Aldershot: Avebury).

Mafukidze, J. (2006) 'A discussion of migration and migration patterns and flows in Africa', in Cross, C., Gelderblom, D., Roux, N. and Mafukidze, J. (eds) *Views on Migration in Sub-Saharan Africa* (Cape Town: HSRC Press) 103–129.

Manuh, T. (ed.) (2005) *At Home in the World? International Migration and Development in Contemporary Ghana and West Africa* (Accra: Sub-Saharan Publishers).

Marcus, J. (1995) *The National Front and French Politics: The Resistible Rise of Jean-Marie Le Pen* (New York: New York University Press).

Marosi, R. (2005) 'Border Crossing Deaths Set a 12-Month Record' (*Los Angeles Times*, 1 October).

Marshall, T.H. (1964) 'Citizenship and social class', in *Class, Citizenship and Social Development: Essays by T.H. Marshall* (New York: Anchor Books).

Martin, D. (2005a) *The US Refugee Program in Transition*. (Washington, DC: Migration Information Source). http://www.migrationinformation.org/Feature/display.cfm?id=305, accessed 1 August 2007.

Martin, H.-P. and Schumann, H. (1997) *The Global Trap: Globalization and the Assault on Prosperity and Democracy* (London and New York, and Sydney: Zed Books and Pluto Press Australia).

Martin, P.L. (1991) *The Unfinished Story. Turkish Labour Migration to Western Europe* (Geneva: International Labour Office).

Martin, P.L. (1993) *Trade and Migration: NAFTA and Agriculture* (Washington, DC: Institute for International Economics).

Martin, P.L. (1996) 'Labor contractors: a conceptual overview', *Asian and Pacific Migration Journal*, 5:2–3.

Martin, P.L. (2004) 'Germany: managing migration in the twenty-first century', in Cornelius, W., Tsuda, T., Martin, P.L. and Hollifield, J.F. (eds) *Controlling Migration: a Global Perspective*, 2nd edn (Stanford, California: Stanford University Press) 221–253.

Martin, P.L. (2005) *Migrants in the global labour market* in GCIM (ed.) (Geneva: GCIM). http://www.gcim.org/attachements/TP1.pdf, accessed 1 February 2006.

Martin, P.L. and Miller, M.J. (2000a) 'Smuggling and trafficking: A conference report'. *International Migration Review*, 34:3, 969–975.

Martin, P.L. and Miller, M.J. (2000b) *Employer Sanctions: French, German and US Experiences* (Geneva: ILO).

Martin, P.L. and Taylor, J.E. (2001) 'Managing migration: the role of economic policies', in Zolberg, A.R. and Benda, P.M. (eds) *Global Migrants, Global Refugees: Problems and Solution* (New York and Oxford: Berghahn) 95–120.

Martin, P.L., Abello, M. and Kuptsch, C. (2006) *Managing Labor Migration in the Twenty-First Century* (New Haven: Yale University Press).

Martin, P.L., Mason, A. and Nagayama, T. (1996) 'Introduction to special issue on the dynamics of labor migration in Asia'. *Asian and Pacific Migration Journal*, 5:2–3, 163–173.

Martin, P.L. and Widgren, J. (1996) 'International migration: a global challenge', *Population Bulletin*, 51:1, 2–48.

Martiniello, M. (1994) 'Citizenship of the European Union: a critical view', in Bauböck, R. (ed.) *From Aliens to Citizens* (Aldershot: Avebury) 29–48.

Marx, K. (1976) *Capital* I (Harmondsworth: Penguin). (First published in German in 1867.)

Massey, D.S., Alarcón, R., Durand, J. and Gonzalez, H. (1987) *Return to Aztlan – The Social Process of International Migration from Western Mexico* (Berkeley, CA: University of California Press).

Massey, D.S., Arango, J., Hugo, G. and Taylor, J.E. (1993) 'Theories of international migration: a review and appraisal', *Population and Development Review,* 19, 431–466.

Massey, D.S., Arango, J., Hugo, G. and Taylor, J.E. (1994) 'An evaluation of international migration theory: the North American case', *Population and Development Review,* 20, 699–751.

Massey, D.S., Arango, J., Hugo, G., Kouaouci, A., Pellegrino, A. and Taylor, J.E. (1998) *Worlds in Motion: Understanding International Migration at the End of the Millennium* (Oxford: Clarendon Press).

Meissner, D., Papademetriou, D. and North, D. (1987) *Legalization of Undocumented Aliens: Lessons from Other Countries* (Washington, DC: Carnegie Endowment for International Peace).

Messina, A. (ed.) (2002) *West European Immigration and Immigrant Policy in the New Century* (Westport, CT, and London: Praeger).

Messina, A.M. (2007) *The Logics and Politics of Post-World War II Migration to Western Europe* (Cambridge: Cambridge University Press).

Migration Information Source (2007a) *Australia* (Washington, DC: Migration Information Source). http://www.migrationinformation.org/Resources/australia. cfm, accessed 16 July 2007.

Migration Information Source (2007b) *Canada* (Washington, DC: Migration Information Source). http://www.migrationinformation.org/Resources/canada. cfm, accessed 16 July 2007.

Migration News (2006) *Latin America* (Davis, C.A.: Migration News). http:// www.migration.ucdavis.edu/mn, accessed 24 July 2007.

Milanovic, B. (2007) 'Globalization and inequality', in Held, D. and Kaya, A. (eds) *Global Inequality: Patterns and Explanations* (Cambridge and Malden, MA.: Polity).

Miles, R. (1989) *Racism* (London: Routledge).

Miller, M.J. (1978) *The Problem of Foreign Worker Participation and Representation in France, Switzerland and the Federal Republic of Germany* (Madison, WI: University of Wisconsin).

Miller, M.J. (1981) *Foreign Workers in Western Europe: An Emerging Political Force* (New York: Praeger).

Miller, M.J. (1984) 'Industrial policy and the rights of labor: the case of foreign workers in the French automobile assembly industry'. *Michigan Yearbook of International Legal Studies,* vi.

Miller, M.J. (1986) 'Policy ad-hocracy: the paucity of coordinated perspectives and policies'. *The Annals,* 485, 65–75.

Miller, M.J. (1989) 'Continuities and Discontinuities in Immigration Reform in Industrial Democracies', in H. Entzinger and J. Carter (eds), *International Review of Comparative Public Policy,* Vol. 1 (Greenwich, CT and London: JAI Press).

Miller, M.J. (1999) 'Prevention of unauthorized migration', in A. Bernstein and M. Weiner (eds) *Migration and Refugee Policies: An Overview* (London and New York: Pinter).

Miller, M.J. (2000) 'A durable international migration and security nexus: the problem of the Islamic periphery in transatlantic ties', in Graham, D.

and Poku, N. (eds) *Migration, Globalization and Human Security* (London: Routledge).

Miller, M.J. (2002) 'Continuity and change in postwar French legalization policy', in A. Messina (ed.) *West European Immigration and Immigrant Policy in the New Century* (Westport, CT and London: Praeger).

Miller, M.J. (2007) 'Disquiet on the Western Front: Sleeper Cells, Transatlantic Rift and the War in Iraq' in Miller, M.J. and Stefanova, B. (eds) *The War on Terror in Comparative Perspective* (Houndmills: Palgrave Macmillan).

Miller, M.J. and Gabriel, C. (2008) 'The US-Mexico Honeymoon of 2001: A Retrospective' in Gabriel, C. and Pellerin, H. (eds) *Governing International Labour Migration: Current issues, challenges and dilemmas* (New York: Routledge), 147–162.

Miller, M.J. and Stefanova, B. (2006) 'NAFTA and the European Referent: Labor Mobility in European and North American Regional Integration', in Messina, A. and Lahav, G. (eds) *The Migration Reader: Exploring Politics and Policies* (Boulder: Lynne Reinner).

Ministry of Social Development (2006) *Social Report* (Wellington: New Zealand Government). http://www.socialreport.msd.govt.nz/people/ethnic-composition-population.html, accessed 16 July 2007.

Mitchell, C. (1989) 'International migration, international relations and foreign policy', *International Migration Review,* Special Silver Anniversary Issue, 23:3, 681–708.

Mitchell, C. (1992) *Western Hemisphere Immigration and United States Foreign Policy* (University Park, PA: The Penn State University Press).

Mitter, S. (1986) 'Industrial Restructuring and Manufacturing Homework: Immigrant Women in the UK Clothing Industry', *Capital and Class,* 27: winter, 37–80.

Moch, L.P. (1992) *Moving Europeans: Migration in Western Europe since 1650* (Bloomington: Indiana University Press).

Moch, L.P. (1995) 'Moving Europeans: historical migration practices in Western Europe', in Cohen, R. (ed.) *The Cambridge Survey of World Migration* (Cambridge: Cambridge University Press).

MOJ (2006) *Basic Plan for Immigration Control (3rd edn): Salient Points* (Tokyo: Ministry of Justice) http://www.moj.go.jp/ENGLISH/information/bpic3rd-02.html, accessed 4 May 2007.

Money, J. (1994) *Fences and Neighbors: the Political Geography of Immigration Control* (Ithaca, NY: Cornell University Press).

MONUC (2007) *United Nations Organization Mission in the Democratic Republic of the Congo: Facts and Figures.* United Nations Organization Mission in the Democratic Republic of the Congo (New York: United Nations).

Mori, H. (1997) *Immigration Policy and Foreign Workers in Japan* (London: Macmillan).

Morokvasic, M. (1984) 'Birds of passage are also women'. *International Migration Review,* 18:4, 886–907.

Morrison, J. (1998) *The Cost of Survival: The Trafficking of Refugees to the UK* (London: British Refugee Council).

Mosse, G.C. (1985) *Towards the Final Solution* (Madison: University of Wisconsin Press).

Motomura, H. (2006) *Americans in Waiting* (Oxford: Oxford University Press).

Münz, R. (1996) 'A continent of migration: European mass migration in the twentieth century', *New Community,* 22:2, 201–226.

Münz, R., Straubhaar, T., Vadean, F. and Vadean, N. (2007) *What are the Migrants' Contributions to Employment and Growth? A European Approach* HWWI Policy Papers 3–3 (Hamburg: Hamburg Institute of International Economics).

Murji, K. and Solomos, J. (eds) (2005) *Racialization: Studies in Theory and Practice* (Oxford: Oxford University Press).

Mutluer, M. (2003) 'Les migrations irrégulières en Turquie', *Revue Européenne des Migrations Internationales,* 19:3, 151–172.

Mwakugu, N. (2007) *Money transfer service wows Kenya.* BBC News Online, April 3 2007.

Myers, N. (1997) 'Environmental refugees', *Population and Environment,* 19:2, 167–182.

Myers, N. and Kent, J. (1995) *Environmental Exodus: an Emergent Crisis in the Global Arena* (Washington, DC: Climate Institute).

National Commission on Terrorist Attacks Upon the United States (2004) *The 9/11 Commission Report* (New York: W.W. Norton).

Nayar, D. (1994) 'International labour movements, trade flows and migration transitions: a theoretical perspective', *Asian and Pacific Migration Journal,* 3:1, 31–47.

Ness, I. (2005) *Immigrants, Unions and the New U.S. Labor Market* (Philadelphia, PA: Temple University Press).

New Internationalist (2006) 'Urban explosion – the facts', *New Internationalist:* 386, 18–19.

Newland, K. (2003) *Migration as a factor in development and poverty reduction* (Washington, DC: Migration Information Source) http://www.migrationinformation.org/Feature/display.cfm?ID=136, accessed 2 February 2007.

Newland, K. (2007)*A new surge of interest in migration and development*(Washington, DC: Migration Information Source). http://www.migrationinformation.org, accessed 6 February 2007.

Noiriel, G. (1988) *Le creuset français: Histoire de l'immigration XIXe-XXe siècles* (Paris: Seuil).

Noiriel, G. (2007) *Immigration, antisémitisme et racisme en France (XIXe-XXe siècle)* (Paris: Fayard).

Norris, P. (2005) *Radical Right* (Cambridge: Cambridge University Press).

Nyberg-Sørensen, N., Van Hear, N. and Engberg-Pedersen, P. (2002) *The Migration-Development Nexus: Evidence and Policy Options* (Copenhagen: Centre for Development Research).

Nye, J.P. (2004) *Soft Power: the means to success in world politics* (New York: Public Affairs).

O'Neil, K., Hamilton, K. and Papademetriou, D. (2005) 'Migration in the Americas', *Global Commission on International Migration.* http://http://www.gcim.org/attachements/RS1.pdf, accessed 27 September 2007.

OECD (1987) *The Future of Migration* (Paris: Organisation for Economic Cooperation and Development).

OECD (1992) *Trends in International Migration: Annual Report 1991* (Paris: Organisation for Economic Cooperation and Development).

OECD (1994) *Trends in International Migration: Annual Report 1993* (Paris: Organisation for Economic Cooperation and Development).

OECD (1995) *Trends in International Migration: Annual Report 1994* (Paris: Organisation for Economic Cooperation and Development).

OECD (1997) *Trends in International Migration: Annual Report 1996* (Paris: Organisation for Economic Cooperation and Development).

OECD (1998) *Migration, Free Trade and Regional Integration in North America* (Paris: Organisation for Economic Cooperation and Development).

OECD (2000) *Combating the Illegal Employment of Foreign Workers* (Paris: Organisation for Economic Cooperation and Development).

OECD (2001) *Trends in International Migration: Annual Report 2000* (Paris: Organisation for Economic Cooperation and Development).

OECD (2004) *Trends in International Migration: Annual Report 2003* (Paris: Organisation for Economic Cooperation and Development).

OECD (2005) *Trends in International Migration: Annual Report 2004* (Paris: Organisation for Economic Cooperation and Development).

OECD (2006) *International Migration Outlook: Annual Report 2006* (Paris: Organisation for Economic Cooperation and Development).

OECD (2007) *International Migration Outlook: Annual Report 2007* (Paris: Organisation for Economic Cooperation and Development).

Ögelman, N. (2003) 'Documenting and Explaining the Persistence of Homeland Politics among Germany's Turks'. *International Migration Review*, 37:1, 163–193.

Ohmae, K. (1995) *The End of the Nation-State: The Rise of Regional Economies* (New York: Harper Collins).

Okólski, M. (2001) 'Incomplete migration: a new form of mobility in Central and Eastern Europe. The Case of Polish and Ukrainian Migrants', in Wallace, C. and Stola, D. (eds) *Patterns of Migration in Central Europe* (Basingstoke: Palgrave).

ONS (2002) *Social Focus in Brief: Ethnicity 2002* (London: Office for National Statistics).

ONS (2003) *Religion in Britain* (London: Office for National Statistics). http://www.statistics.gov.uk, accessed 15 August 2007.

ONS (2004a) *Ethnicity and Identity: Population Size: 7.9% from a non-White Ethnic Group* (London: Office for National Statistics). http://www.statistics.gov.uk/cci/nugget.asp?id=455, accessed 15 August 2007.

ONS (2004b) *Religion: 7 in 10 identify as White Christian* (London: Office for National Statistics). http://www.statistics.gov.uk/CCI/nugget.asp?ID=1086&Pos=2&ColRank=1&Rank=326, accessed 6 August 2007.

Oriol, P. (2001) 'Des commissions consultatives au droit de vote', *Migrations Société*, 13:73, 19–22.

Oriol, P. (2007) 'Le droit de vote des résidents étrangers dans l'Union européenne', *Migrations Société*, 19:114, 83–97.

Oriol, P. and Vianna, P. (2007) 'Résidents étrangers et droit de vote', *Migrations Société*, 19:114, 37–46.

Orozco, M. and Rouse, R. (2007) *Migrant Hometown Associations and Opportunities for Development: a Global Perspective* (Washington, DC: Migration Information Source) http://www.migrationinformation.org/Feature/display.cfm?ID=579, accessed 6 February 2007.

Ostegaard-Nielsen, E. (2003) *Transnational Politics: Turks and Kurds in Germany* (London: Routledge).

Oucho, J.O. (2006) 'Migration and refugees in Eastern Africa: a challenge for the East Africa Community' in Cross, C., Gelderblom, D., Roux, N. and Mafukidze, J. (eds) *Views on Migration in Sub-Saharan Africa* (Cape Town: HSRC Press) 130–147.

Oxfam (2002) *Rigged Rules and Double Standards: Trade, Globalisation, and the Fight against Poverty* (Oxford: Oxfam).

Padilla, B. and Peixoto, J. (2007) *Latin American Immigration to Southern Europe* (Washington, DC: Migration Information Source). http://www.migrationinformation.org/feature/display.cfm?id=609, accessed 28 June 2007.

Paice, E. (2006) *Tip & Run: the Untold Tragedy of the Great War in Africa* (London: Weidenfeld and Nicolson).

Paine, S. (1974) *Exporting Workers: The Turkish Case* (Cambridge: Cambridge University Press).

Pankevych, I. (2006) 'Migrant Integration in Ukraine: Legislation, Political and Social Aspects', in Majtczak, O. (ed.) *The Fifth International Migration Conference* (Warsaw: Independent University of Business and Government).

Parisot, T. (1998) 'Quand l'immigration tourne à l'esclavage' (*Le Monde Diplomatique,* 20–21 June 1998).

Passel, J.S. (2006) *Size and Characteristics of the Unauthorized Migrant Population in the U.S. Pew Hispanic Center Report* (Washington, DC: Pew Hispanic Center). http://pewhispanic.org/reports, accessed 20 March 2006.

Pastore, F. (2006) 'Italian modes of migration regulation' (Istanbul: 10–12 March 2006, IMISCOE Cluster A1 Workshop).

Pastore, F. (2007) *La politica migratoria italiana a una svolta* (Rome: Centro Studi di Politica Internazionale). http://www.cespi.it/, accessed 17 June 2007.

Pellegrino, A. (2004) 'Migration from Latin America to Europe: Trends and Policy Challenges', IOM Migration Research Series, 16 (Geneva: International Organization for Migration). http://www.oas.org/atip/Migration/IOM%20 Report%20Migration%20LAC%20to%20EU.pdf, accessed 27 January 2008.

Penninx, R. (2006) 'Dutch Immigrant Policies Before and After the Van Gogh Murder', *Journal of International Migration,* 7:2, 242–254.

Pe-Pua, R., Mitchell, C., Iredale, R. and Castles, S. (1996) *Astronaut Families and Parachute Children: The Cycle of Migration from Hong Kong* (Canberra: AGPS).

Perry, J. and Power, S. (2007) 'Shortage of Skilled Labor Pinches Eastern Europe' (*Wall Street Journal,* New York, 10 July 2007).

Pessar, P. and Mahler, S. (2003) 'Transnational migration: bringing gender in', *International Migration Review,* 37:3, 812–846.

Petras, J. and Veltmayer, H. (2000) 'Globalisation or imperialism?' *Cambridge Review of International Affairs,* 14:1, 1–15.

Pfahlmann, H. (1968) *Fremdarbeiter and Kriegsgefangene in der deutschen Kriegswirtschaft 1939–45* (Darmstadt: Wehr and Wissen).

Philips, M. (2006) *Londonistan* (New York: Encounter Books).

Phizacklea, A. (ed.) (1983) *One Way Ticket? Migration and Female Labour* (London: Routledge and Kegan Paul).

Phizacklea, A. (1990) *Unpacking the Fashion Industry: Gender, Racism and Class in Production* (London: Routledge).

Phizacklea, A. (1998) 'Migration and globalisation: a feminist perspective' in Koser, K. and Lutz, H. (eds) *The New Migration in Europe* (London: Macmillan) 21–38.

Picquet, M., Pellegrino, A. and Papil, J. (1986) 'L'immigration au Venezuela', *Revue Européenne des Migrations Internationales,* 2:2, 25–47.

Piore, M. J. (1979) *Birds of Passage: Migrant Labor and Industrial Societies* (Cambridge: Cambridge University Press).

Plewa, P. (2006) 'How Have Regularization Programs Affected Spanish Governmental Efforts to Integrate Migrant Populations', in Majtczak, O. (ed.) *The Fifth International Migration Conference* (Warsaw: Independent University of Business and Government).

Plewa, P. (2007) 'The Rise and Fall of Temporary Foreign Worker Policies: Lessons from Poland', *International Migration*, 45:2, 3–36.

Plewa, P. and Miller, M.J. (2005) 'Postwar and post-Cold War generations of European temporary foreign worker policies: implications from Spain', *Migraciones Internacionales*, 3:2, 58–83.

Poku, N. and Graham, D. (eds) (1998) *Redefining Security* (Westport, CT: Praeger).

Polanyi, K. (1944) *The Great Transformation: The Political and Economic Origins of Our Time* (New York: Farrar and Rinehart).

Portes, A. (1997) 'Neoliberalism and sociology of development: emerging trends and unanticipated facts', *Population and Development Review*, 23:2, 229–259.

Portes, A. (1999) 'Conclusion: towards a new world: the origins and effects of transnational activities', *Ethnic and Racial Studies*, 22: 2, 463–477.

Portes, A. and Bach, R.L. (1985) *Latin Journey: Cuban and Mexican Immigrants in the United States* (Berkeley, CA: University of California Press).

Portes, A. and Böröcz, J. (1989) 'Contemporary immigration: theoretical perspectives on its determinants and modes of incorporation', *International Migration Review*, 23:3, 606–630.

Portes, A. and DeWind, J. (eds) (2004) Conceptual and Methodological Developments in the Study of International Migration. *International Migration Review* Special Issue 38:3 (New York: Center for Migration Studies) 828–1255.

Portes, A. and Rumbaut, R.G. (2006) *Immigrant America: a Portrait*, 3rd edn (Berkeley, CA: University of California Press).

Portes, A., Escobar, C. and Radford, A.W. (2007) 'Immigrant transnational organizations and development: a comparative study', *International Migration Review*, 41:1, 242–282.

Portes, A., Guarnizo, L.E. and Landolt, P. (1999) 'The study of transnationalism: pitfalls and promise of an emergent research field', *Ethnic and Racial Studies*, 22:2, 217–237.

Potts, L. (1990) *The World Labour Market: A History of Migration* (London: Zed Books).

Preston, J. (2007) 'U.S. set for a crackdown on illegal hiring' (*New York Times*, 8 August 2007).

Price, C. (1963) *Southern Europeans in Australia* (Melbourne: Oxford University Press).

Prost, A. (1966) 'L'immigration en France depuis cent ans', *Esprit*, 34:348.

Rath, J. (1988) 'La participation des immigrés aux élections locales aux Pays-Bas', *Revue Européenne des Migrations Internationales*, 4: 3, 23–36.

Rath, J. (2002) *Unravelling the Rag Trade: Immigrant Entrepreneurship in Seven World Cities* (Oxford: Berg).

Ratha, D. and Shaw, W. (2007) *South-South Migration and Remittances* (Washington, DC: Development Prospects Group, World Bank). http://siteresources. worldbank.org/INTPROSPECTS/Resources/South-SouthmigrationJan192006. pdf, accessed 7 March 2008.

Ratha, D. and Zhimei, X. (2008) *Migration and Remittances Factbook* (Washington, DC: World Bank Development Prospect Group). www.worldbank.org/prospects/migrationandremittances, accessed 19 June 2008.

Ravenstein, E.G. (1885) 'The laws of migration', *Journal of the Statistical Society,* 48, 167–235.

Ravenstein, E.G. (1889) 'The laws of migration', *Journal of the Statistical Society,* 52, 241–305.

Rawls, J. (1985) 'Justice as fairness: political not metaphysical', *Philosophy and Public Affairs,* 14:3, 223–251.

Reitz, J.G. (1998) *Warmth of the Welcome: The Social Causes of Economic Success for Immigrants in Different Nations and Cities* (Boulder, CO: Westview Press).

Reitz, J.G. (2007a) 'Immigrant Employment Success in Canada, Part I: Individual and Contextual Causes', *Journal of International Migration and Integration,* 8:1, 11–36.

Reitz, J.G. (2007b) 'Employment Success in Canada, Part II: Understanding the Decline', *Journal of International Migration and Integration,* 8:1, 37–62.

Rex, J. and Mason, D. (eds) (1986) *Theories of Race and Ethnic Relations* (Cambridge: Cambridge University Press).

Rex, J. (1986) *Race and Ethnicity* (Milton Keynes: Open University Press).

Reyneri, E. (2001) *Migrants' Involvement in Irregular Employment in the Mediterranean Countries of the European Union* (Geneva: International Labour Organization).

Reyneri, E. (2003) 'Immigration and the underground economy in new receiving South European countries: manifold negative effects, manifold deep-rooted causes', *International Review of Sociology,* 13:1, 117–143.

Ricca, S. (1990) *Migrations internationales en Afrique* (Paris: L'Harmattan).

Richards, A.O. (1999) *International Trafficking in Women to the United States: A Contemporary Manifestation of Slavery and Organized Crime* (Washington, DC: Center for the Study of Intelligence).

Ricks, T.E. (2007) *Fiasco* (New York: Penguin Books).

Romero, F. (1993) 'Migration as an issue in European interdependence and integration: the case of Italy', in Milward, A., Lynch, F., Ranieri, R., Romero, F. and Sorensen V. (eds) *The Frontier of National Sovereignty* (London: Routledge).

Rosenau, J.N. (1997) *Along the Domestic Foreign Frontier* (Cambridge: Cambridge University Press).

Rosenberg, C.D. (2006) *Policing Paris: the Origins of Modern Immigration Control Between the Wars* (Ithaca, NY; London: Cornell University Press).

Rostow, W.W. (1960) *The Stages of Economic Growth: a Non-Communist Manifesto* (Cambridge: Cambridge University Press).

Roussel, C. (2003) 'Désenclavement et mondialisation: les réseaux migratoires familiaux des druzes du sud syrien', *Revue Européenne des Migrations Internationales,* 19:3, 263–283.

Rowthorn, R. (2004) *The Economic Impact of Immigration: Evidence to the House of Lords Select Committee on Economic Affairs* Civitas On-line Report (London: Civitas). http://www.parliament.uk/documents/upload/EA246%20RowthornFINAL10102007.doc, accessed 21 May 2008.

Roy, O. (1994) *The Failure of Political Islam* (Cambridge: Harvard University Press).

Roy, O. (2003) 'Euroislam: The Jihad Within?' *The National Interest,* Spring, 63–73.

Roy, O. (2004) *Globalized Islam: the search for a new Ummah* (New York: Columbia University Press).

Rubio-Marin, R. (2000) *Immigration as a Democratic Challenge* (Cambridge: Cambridge University Press).

Rudolph, H. (1996) 'The new *Gastarbeiter* system in Germany', *New Community,* 22:2, 287–300.

Ruhs, M. (2005) *The potential of temporary migration programmes in future international migration policy,* in Global Commission on International Migration (GCIM) (ed.) *GCIM Working Papers* (Geneva: GCIM). http://www. gcim.org/attachements/TP3.pdf, accessed 1 February 2006.

Rycs, J.F. (2005) 'Le "Sponsorship"peut-il encore canaliser les flux migratoires dan les pays du Golfe? Le cas des Emirats arabes unis', in Jaber, H. and France, M. (eds) *Mondes en mouvements: Migrants et migrations au Moyen-Orient au tournant du XXIe siècle* (Beyrouth: Institut Francais du Proche-Orient).

Safir, N. (1999) 'Emigration Dynamics in the Maghreb', in R. Appleyard (ed.) *Emigration Dynamics in Developing Countries,* Vol. IV: *The Arab Region* (Aldershot: Ashgate).

Sassen, S. (1988) *The Mobility of Labour and Capital* (Cambridge: Cambridge University Press).

Sassen, S. (1991) *The Global City: New York, London, Tokyo* (Princeton, NJ: Princeton University Press).

Saul, J.R. (2006) *The Collapse of Globalism and the Reinvention of the World* (London: Atlantic Books).

Schain, M., Zolberg, A. and Hossay, P. (2002) *Shadows over Europe* (New York: Palgrave).

Schama, S. (2006) *Rough Crossings: Britain, the Slaves and the American Revolution* (London: BBC Books).

Scheuer, M. (2004) *Imperial Hubris* (Washington, DC: Brassey's).

Scheuer, M. (2008) *Marching Toward Hell* (New York: Free Press).

Schierup, C.-U. and Ålund, A. (1987) *Will they still be Dancing? Integration and Ethnic Transformation among Yugoslav Immigrants in Scandinavia* (Stockholm: Almquist & Wiksell International).

Schierup, C.-U., Hansen, P. and Castles, S. (2006) *Migration, Citizenship and the European Welfare State: A European Dilemma* (Oxford: Oxford University Press).

Schnapper, D. (1991) 'A host country of immigrants that does not know itself', *Diaspora,* 1:3, 353–364.

Schnapper, D. (1994) *La Communauté des Citoyens* (Paris: Gallimard).

Schrank, P. (2007) 'The European Union needs to hold a proper debate on migration' (*The Economist,* 31 May).

Schrover, M., Van der Leun, J. and Quispel, C. (2007) 'Niches, Labour Market Segregation, Ethnicity and Gender'. *Journal of Ethnic and Migration Studies,* 33:4, 529–540.

Scoliano, E., Burnett, V. and Schmitt, E. (2008) 'In Spanish Case, Officials See Terror Threat Rising from Pakistan' (*The New York Times,* New York, 10 February 2008).

Seccombe, I.J. (1986) 'Immigrant workers in an emigrant economy', *International Migration* 24:2, 377–396.

SCIRP (1981) *Staff Report* (Washington, DC: Select Commission on Immigration and Refugee Policy).

Semyonov, M. and Lewin-Epstein, N. (1987) *Hewers of Wood and Drawers of Water* (Ithaca, NY: ILR Press).

Seton-Watson, H. (1977) *Nations and States* (London: Methuen).

Shanker, T. and Kulish, N. (2008) 'U.S. Ties Europe's Safety to Afghanistan' (*The New York Times,* New York, 11 February 2008).

Shaw, M. (2000) *Theory of the Global State: Globality as Unfinished Revolution* (Cambridge: Cambridge University Press).

Shenon, P. (2008) *The Commission* (New York: Hachette Book Group USA).

Shimpo, M. (1995) 'Indentured migrants from Japan', in Cohen, R. (ed.), *The Cambridge Survey of World Migration* (Cambridge: Cambridge University Press).

Silverstein, P. (2004) *Algeria in France* (Bloomington: Indiana University Press).

Sinn, E. (ed.) (1998) *The Last Half Century of Chinese Overseas* (Hong Kong: Hong Kong University Press).

Skeldon, R. (1992) 'International migration within and from the East and South-east Asian region: a review essay', *Asian and Pacific Migration Journal,* 1: 1.

Skeldon, R. (1997) *Migration and Development: A Global Perspective* (Harlow, Essex: Addison Wesley Longman).

Skeldon, R. (ed.) (1994) *Reluctant Exiles? Migration from Hong Kong and the New Overseas Chinese* (Hong Kong: Hong Kong University Press).

Skeldon, R. (2002) 'Migration and Poverty', *Asia-Pacific Population Journal,* 17:4, 67–82.

Skeldon, R. (2006a) 'Interlinkages between internal and international migration and development in the Asian region', *Population, Space and Place*: 12, 15–30.

Skeldon, R. (2006b) 'Recent trends in migration in East and Southeast Asia', *Asian and Pacific Migration Journal,* 15:2, 277–293.

Skerry, P. and Rockwell, S.J. (1998) 'The Cost of a Tighter Border: People-Smuggling Networks' (*Los Angeles Times* 3 May).

Smith, A.D. (1986) *The Ethnic Origins of Nations* (Oxford: Blackwell).

Smith, A.D. (1991) *National Identity* (Harmondsworth: Penguin).

Smith, J.P. and Edmonston, B. (eds) (1997) *The New Americans: Economic, Demographic and Fiscal Effects of Immigration* (Washington, DC: National Academy Press).

Smith, R. (2003) 'Migrant Membership as an Instituted Process: Transnationalization, the State and Extra-Territorial Conduct of Mexican Politics', *International Migration Review,* 37:2, 297–343.

Solomos, J. (2003) *Race and Racism in Britain*, 3rd edn (Basingstoke: Palgrave-Macmillan).

SAMP (2005) 'South Africa' *News* (Cape Town: Southern African Migration Project), July 2005.

Soysal, Y.N. (1994) *Limits of Citizenship: Migrants and Postnational Membership in Europe* (Chicago and London: University of Chicago Press).

Stahl, C. (1993) 'Explaining international migration', in Stahl, C., Ball, R., Inglis, C. and Gutman, P. (eds), *Global Population Movements and their Implications for Australia* (Canberra: Australian Government Publishing Service).

Stalker, P. (2000) *Workers without Frontiers: The Impact of Globalization on International Migration* (Geneva, London and Boulder, Co: International Labour Office and Lynne Rienner Publishers).

Stark, O. (1991) *The Migration of Labour* (Oxford: Blackwell).

Stasiulis, D.K. and Yuval-Davis, N. (eds) (1995) *Unsettling Settler Societies* (London: Sage).

Statistics Canada (2007) *Immigration and Citizenship: Highlight Tables, 2001 Census* (Ottawa: Statistics Canada). http://www.census2006.ca/english/census01/, accessed 3 August 2007.

Stefanova, B. (2007) 'Voting a la carte: Electoral Support for the Radical Right in the 2005 Bulgarian Elections', *Politics in Central Europe*, 2:2, 38–70.

Steinberg, S. (1981) *The Ethnic Myth: Race, Ethnicity and Class in America* (Boston, MA: Beacon Press).

Stiglitz, J.E. (2002) *Globalization and its Discontents* (London: Penguin).

Stirn, H. (1964) *Ausländische Arbeiter im Betrieb* (Frechen/Cologne: Bartmann).

Stola, D. (2001) 'Poland', in C. Wallace and D. Stola (eds) *Patterns of Migration in Central Europe* (Basingstoke: Palgrave).

Straubhaar, T. (2006) 'Labor market relevant migration policy', *Zeitschrift für Arbeitsmarktforschung,* 39:1, 149–157.

Straubhaar, T. and Zimmermann, K. (1992) *Towards a European Migration Policy* (London: Centre for Economic Policy Research).

Strozza, S. and Venturini, A. (2002) 'Italy is no longer a country of emigration. Foreigners in Italy: how many, where they come from', in R. Rotte and P. Stein (eds) *Migration Policy and the Economy: International Experiences* (Munich: Hans Seidel Stiftung).

Studlar, D T. and Layton-Henry, Z. (1990) 'Non-white minority access to the political agenda in Britain', *Policy Studies Review*, 9:2 (Winter).

Suhrke, A. and Klink, F. (1987) 'Contrasting patterns of Asian refugee movements: the Vietnamese and Afghan syndromes', in Fawcett, J. T. and Cariño, B. V. (eds), *Pacific Bridges: The New Immigration from Asia and the Pacific Islands* (New York: Center for Migration Studies).

Surk, B. and Abbot, S. (2008) 'India wants oil-rich Emirates to pay workers better wages', *Sunday News Journal* (Wilmington, DE).

Süssmuth, R. (2001) *Zuwanderung gestalten, Integration fördern: Bericht der unabhängigen Kommission 'Zuwanderung'* German Government Report (Berlin: Bundesminister des Innern).

Swift, R. (2007) 'Death by cotton', *New Internationalist*: 399, 7–9.

Sze, L.-S. (2007) *New Immigrant Labour from Mainland China in Hong Kong* (Hong Kong: Asian Labour Update). http://www.amrc.org.hk/alu_article/discrimination_at_work/new_immigrant_labour_from_mainland_china_in_hong_kong, accessed 23 March 2007.

Tapinos, G. (1975) *L'Immigration Etrangère en France* (Paris: Presses Universitaires de France).

Tapinos, G. (1984) 'Seasonal workers in French agriculture', in Martin, P. (ed.) *Migrant Labor in Agriculture* (Davis: Gianni Foundation of Agricultural Economics).

Tapinos, G.P. (1990) *Development Assistance Strategies and Emigration Pressure in Europe and Africa* (Washington, DC: Commission for the Study of International Migration and Co-operative Economic Development).

Taylor, J.E. (1987) 'Undocumented Mexico-US migration and the returns to households in rural Mexico', *American Journal of Agricultural Economics*, 69, 626–638.

Taylor, J.E. (1999) 'The new economics of labour migration and the role of remittances in the migration process', *International Migration*, 37:1, 63–88.

Tekeli, I. (1994) 'Involuntary displacement and the problem of resettlement in Turkey from the Ottoman Empire to the present', in Shami, S. (ed.) *Population Displacement and Resettlement: Development and Conflict in the Middle East* (New York: Center for Migration Studies).

Thränhardt, D. (1996) 'European migration from East to West: present patterns and future directions', *New Community*, 22:2, 227–242.

Tichenor, D.J. (2002) *Dividing Lines* (Princeton: Princeton University Press).

Tirman, J. (2004) *The maze of fear: Security and Migration after 9/11* (New York/London: The New Press).

Tirtosudarmo, R. (2001) 'Demography and security: transmigration policy in Indonesia', in Weiner, M. and Russell, S.S. (eds) *Demography and National Security* (New York and Oxford: Berghahn Books) 199–227.

Togman, J. (2002) *The Ramparts of Nations* (Westport and London: Praeger).

Tomas, K. and Münz, R. (2006) *Labour Migrants Unbound? EU Enlargement, Transitional Measures and Labour Market Effects* (Stockholm: Institute for Futures Study).

Tribalat, M. (1995) *Faire France: Une Enquête sur les Immigrés et leurs Enfants* (Paris: La Découverte).

Trlin, A.D. (1987) 'New Zealand's admission of Asians and Pacific Islanders', in Fawcett, J.T. and Cariño, B.V. (eds) *Pacific Bridges: The New Immigration from Asia and the Pacific Islands* (New York: Center for Migration Studies).

TUC (2007) *The Economics of Migration: Managing the Impacts* (London: Trades Union Congress). http://www.tuc.org.uk, accessed 11 May 2008.

Turton, D. (2006) *Ethnic Federalism: the Ethiopian Experience in Comparative Perspective* (Oxford: James Currey).

UN (2000) *Replacement Migration: is it a Solution to Declining and Ageing Populations?* (New York: United Nations Population Division).

UN (2004) 'Rwandans returning home as UN prepares to observe 10th anniversary of genocide', *United Nations News Centre* (5 April 2004).

UNDESA (2004) *World Economic and Social Survey 2004: International Migration* (New York: United Nations Department of Economic and Social Affairs).

UNDESA (2005) *Trends in Total Migrant Stock: the 2005 Revision* (New York: United Nations Department of Economic and Social Affairs).

UNDESA (2006a) *International Migration 2006* (New York: United Nations Department of Economic and Social Affairs).

UNDESA (2006b) *International Migration and Development: Analysis Prepared by UN Department of Economic and Social Affairs* (New York: UN Department of Public Information).

UNDP (2006) *Human Development Report 2006-Beyond Scarcity: Power, Poverty, and the Global Water Crisis* (New York: United Nations Development Programme).

UNFPA (2006) *State of World Population 2006* (New York: United Nations Population Fund).

UN-HABITAT (2007) 'Urbanization: A Turning Point in History' *United Nations Human Settlements Programme*.

UNHCR (1995) *The State of the World's Refugees: In Search of Solutions* (Oxford: Oxford University Press).

UNHCR (2000a) *Global Report 2000: Achievements and Impact* (Geneva: United Nations High Commissioner for Refugees).

UNHCR (2000b) *The State of the World's Refugees: Fifty Years of Humanitarian Action* (Oxford: Oxford University Press).

UNHCR (2002) *Afghan Humanitarian Update,* 63 (Geneva: United Nations High Commissioner for Refugees).

UNHCR (2004) *Protracted Refugee Situations* (Geneva: UNHCR Executive Committee of the High Commissioner's Programme).

UNHCR (2006a) *Global Report 2006* (Geneva: United Nations High Commissioner for Refugees). http://www.unhcr.org/publ.html, . accessed 23 August 2007.

UNHCR (2006b) *Refugees by Numbers 2006 Edition* (Geneva: United Nations High Commissioner for Refugees). http://www.unhcr.org/basics/BASICS/3b028097c.html#Numbers, accessed 31 July 2007.

UNHCR (2006c) *UNHCR Statistical Yearbook 2006* (Geneva: United Nations High Commissioner for Refugees).http://www.unhcr.org/statistics/STATISTICS/478cda572.html, accessed 23 August 2007.

UNHCR (2007a) *2006 Global Trends: Refugees, Asylum-Seekers, Internally Displaced and Stateless Persons* (Geneva: United Nations High Commission for Refugees: Division of Operational Services). http://www.unhcr.org/statistics/STATISTICS/4676a71d4.pdf, accessed 23 August 2007.

UNHCR (2007b) *Asylum Levels and Trends in Industrialized Countries, 2006* (Geneva: UNHCR).

UNHCR (2007c) *Statistics on Displaced Iraqis around the World* (Geneva: United Nations High Commissioner for Refugees) URL http://www.unhcr.org/statistics.html, accessed 23 August 2007.

UNODC (2006) *Trafficking in Persons: Global Patterns* (Vienna: United Nations Office on Drugs and Crime).

US Census Bureau (2005) *2005 American Community Survey.* (Washington, DC: US Census Bureau). http://factfinder.census.gov/home/saff/main.html?_lang=en, accessed 3 August 2007.

US Department of Labor (1989) *The Effects of Immigration on the US Economy and Labor Market* US Government Document (Washington, DC: US Department of Labor).

USCR (US Committee for Refugees) (1996) *World Refugee Survey 1996* (Washington, DC: Immigration and Refugee Services of America).

USCR (US Committee for Refugees) (2001) *World Refugee Survey 2001* (Washington, DC: USCR, Immigration and Refugee Services of America).

USCR (US Committee for Refugees) (2004) *World Refugee Survey 2004* (Washington, DC: US Committee for Refugees).

USCRI (2006) *World Refugee Survey 2006* Country Reports (Washington, DC: US Committee for Refugees and Immigrants).

USCRI (2007a) *Country Report: Australia* (Washington, DC: US Committee on Refugees). http://www.refugees.org/countryreports.aspx?id=1569, accessed 1 August 2007.

USCRI (2007b) *Country Report: Canada* (Washington, DC: US Committee on Refugees and Immigrants). http://www.refugees.org/countryreports.aspx?__VI EWSTATE=dDwtOTMxNDcwOTk7O2w8Q291bnRyeUREOkdvQnV0dG9uO z4%2BUwqzZxIYLI0SfZCZue2XtA0UFEQ%3D&cid=1986&subm=&ssm=&

map=&searchtext=&CountryDD%3ALocationList=, accessed 1 August 2007.

USCRI (2007c) *Country Report: USA* (Washington, DC: US Committee for Refugees and Migrants). http://www.refugees.org/countryreports.aspx?subm=&ssm=&cid=1607, accessed 27 April 2007.

USDS (2006) *Sierra Leone: Country Reports on Human Rights Practices-2006* (Washington, DC: US Department of State).

USDS (2007) '2007 Trafficking in Persons Report' (Washington, DC: US Department of State).

Van Hear, N. (1998) *New Diasporas: the Mass Exodus, Dispersal and Regrouping of Migrant Communities* (London: UCL Press).

Van Hear, N., Pieke, F. and Vertovec, S. (2004) *The Contribution of UK-Based Diasporas to Development and Policy Reduction* (Oxford: Centre for Migration, Policy and Society (COMPAS) for the Department for International Development (DFID)).

Vasta, E. (1990) 'Gender, class and ethnic relations: the domestic and work experiences of Italian migrant women in Australia', *Migration,* 7.

Vasta, E. (1992) 'The second generation', in Castles, S., Alcorso, C., Rando, G. and Vasta, E. (eds) *Australia's Italians: Culture and Community in a Changing Society* (Sydney: Allen & Unwin) 155–168.

Vasta, E. (1993) 'Immigrant women and the politics of resistance', *Australian Feminist Studies,* 18: 5–23.

Vasta, E. (2007) 'From ethnic minorities to ethnic majority policy: multiculturalism and the shift to assimilationism in the Netherlands', *Ethnic and Racial Studies,* 30:5, 713–740.

Vasta, E. and Castles, S. (eds) (1996) *The Teeth are Smiling: The Persistence of Racism in Multicultural Australia* (Sydney: Allen & Unwin).

Veiga, U.M. (1999) 'Immigrants in the Spanish labour market' in Baldwin-Edwards and Arango, J. (eds) *Immigrants and the Informal Economy in Southern Europe* (London and Portland: Frank Cass) 105–129.

Verbunt, G. (1985) 'France', in Hammar, T. (ed.) *European Immigration Policy: A Comparative Study* (Cambridge: Cambridge University Press).

Vertovec, S. (1999) 'Conceiving and researching transnationalism', *Ethnic and Racial Studies,* 22:2, 445–462.

Vertovec, S. (2004) 'Migrant transnationalism and modes of transformation', *International Migration Review,* 38:3, 970–1001.

Waever, O., Buzan, B., Kelstrup, M. and Lemaitre, P. (1993) *Identity, Migration and the New Security Agenda in Europe* (New York: St. Martin's Press).

Waldinger, R., Aldrich, H. and Ward, R. (1990) *Ethnic Entrepreneurs: Immigrant Business in Industrial Societies* (Newbury Park, CA, London, New Delhi: Sage Publications).

Waldinger, R.D. (1996) *Still the Promised City?: African-Americans and New Immigrants in Postindustrial New York* (Cambridge, MA: Harvard University Press).

Waldinger, R.D. and Lichter, M.I. (2003) *How the Other Half Works: Immigration and the Social Organization of Labor* (Berkeley, CA; London: University of California Press).

Wallace, C. and Stola, D. (eds) (2001) *Patterns of Migration in Central Europe* (Basingstoke/New York: Palgrave).

Wallerstein, I. (1984) *The Politics of the World Economy: The States, the Movements, and the Civilisations* (Cambridge: Cambridge University Press).

Wallman, S. (1986) 'Ethnicity and boundary processes', in Rex, J. and Mason, D. (eds) *Theories of Race and Ethnic Relations* (Cambridge: Cambridge University Press).

Wasem, R.E. (2007) *Immigration Reform: Brief Synthesis of Issue* (Washington, DC: Congressional Research Service).

Weber, M. (1968) *Economy and Society: An Outline of Interpretive Sociology,* Roth, G. and Wittich, C. (eds) (New York: Bedminster Press).

Weil, P. (1991a) 'Immigration and the rise of racism in France: the contradictions of Mitterrand's policies', *French Society and Politics,* 9: 3–4.

Weil, P. (1991b) *La France et ses Étrangers* (Paris: Calmann-Levy).

Weiner, M. (ed.) (1993) *International Migration and Security* (Boulder, CO: Westview Press).

Weiner, M. and Hanami, T. (eds) (1998) *Temporary Workers or Future Citizens? Japanese and US Migration Policies* (New York: New York University Press).

Weiner, M. and Russell, S. (2001) *Demography and National Security* (New York and Oxford: Berghahn Books).

Weiss, L. (1997) 'Globalization and the myth of the powerless state', *New Left Review:* 225, 3–27.

Werner, H. (1973) *Freizügigkeit der Arbeitskräfte und die Wanderungsbewegungen in den Ländern der Europäischen Gemeinschaft* (Nuremburg: Institut für Arbeitsmarkt-und Berufsforschung).

Wieviorka, M. (1991) *L'Espace du Racisme* (Paris: Seuil).

Wieviorka, M. (1992) *La France Raciste* (Paris: Seuil).

Wieviorka, M. (1995) *The Arena of Racism* (London: Sage).

Wihtol de Wenden, C. (1988) *Les Immigrés et la Politique: cent-cinquante ans d'évolution* (Paris: Presses de la Fondation Nationale des Sciences Politiques).

Wihtol de Wenden, C. (1995) 'Generational change and political participation in French suburbs', *New Community,* 21:1, 69–78.

Wihtol de Wenden, C. and Leveau, R. (2001) *La Beurgeoisie: les trois ages de la vie associative issue de l'immigration* (Paris: CNRS Editions).

Wilpert, C. and Laacher, S. (1999) 'New forms of migration and the informal labour market in old receiving countries: France and Germany' in Reyneri, E. (ed.) *Migrant Insertion in the Informal Economy, Deviant Behaviour and the Impact on Receiving Societies* (Brussels: European Commission) 39–56.

Wong, D. (1996) 'Foreign domestic workers in Singapore', *Asian and Pacific Migration Journal,* 5:1, 117–138.

Wooden, M. (1994) 'The economic impact of immigration' in Wooden, M., Holton, R., Hugo, G. and Sloan, J. (eds) *Australian Immigration: A Survey of the Issues.* 2nd edn (Canberra: AGPS).

World Bank (2006) *Global Economic Prospects 2006: Economic Implications of Remittances and Migration* (Washington, DC: World Bank).

World Bank (2007) *Remittance Trends 2006* (Washington, DC: Migration and Remittances Team, Development Prospects Group, World Bank).

Wüst, A. (2000) 'New Citizens – New Voters? Political Preferences and Voting Intentions of Naturalized Germans: A Case Study in Progress', *International Migration Review,* 34:2, 560–567.

Wüst, A. (2002) *Wie Wählen Neubürger?* (Opladen: Leske & Budrich).

Yeoh, B.S.A. (2007) *Singapore: Hungry for Foreign Workers at All Skill Levels* (Washington DC: Migration Information Source). http://www.migrationinformation.org/Profiles/display.cfm?id=570, accessed 19 July 2007.

Ye'or, B. (2005) *Eurabia: The Euro-Arab Crisis* (Madison, NJ: Dickenson University Press).

Zaiotti, R. (2005) 'From Engagement to Deadlock: A Regional Analysis of Refugee Policies in the Middle East Between the Two 'Gulf Crises' (1990–2003)', in Jaber, H. and France, M. (eds) *Mondes en mouvements: Migrants et migrations au Moyen-Orient au tournant du XXIe siècle* (Beyrouth: Institut Français du Proche-Orient).

Zelinsky, W. (1971) 'The hypothesis of the mobility transition', *Geographical Review,* 61:2, 219–249.

Zhao, G. (2007) 'The rise of Chindia and its impact on world system', *Emerging Powers in Global Governance* (Paris: 6–7 July, Institut du développement durable et des relations internationales (IDDRI)).

Zhou, M. (1997) 'Segmented assimilation: issues, controversies, and recent research on the new second generation', *International Migration Review,* 31:4, 975–1008.

Zibouh, F. (2007) 'Le droit de vote des étrangers aux elections municipales de 2006 en Belgique', *Migrations Societe,* 19:4, 141–168.

Zlotnik, H. (1999) 'Trends of international migration since 1965: what existing data reveal', *International Migration,* 37:1, 21–62.

Zlotnik, H. (2004) *International Migration in Africa: an Analysis based on Estimates of the Migrant Stock* (Washington, DC: Migration Information source), accessed 29 August 2006.

Zolberg, A. (1981) 'International Migration in Political Perspective' in Kritz, M., Keely, C. and Tomasi, S. (eds) *Global Trends in Migration: Theory and Research on International Population Movements* (New York: Center for Migration Studies).

Zolberg, A. (2006) *A Nation by Design* (Cambridge, MA and New York: Harvard University Press and Russell Sage Foundation).

Zolberg, A.R. and Benda, P. M. (eds) (2001) *Global Migrants, Global Refugees: Problems and Solutions* (New York and Oxford: Berghahn Books).

Zolberg, A.R., Suhrke, A. and Aguao, S. (1989) *Escape from Violence* (New York: Oxford University Press).

Name Index

Subject Index

357